WAR IN IRAQ:
Is there an exit?

WAR IN IRAQ:
Is there an exit?

George W. Gipe

iUniverse, Inc.
New York Lincoln Shanghai

WAR IN IRAQ: Is there an exit?

iUniverse, Inc.

For information address:
iUniverse, Inc.
2021 Pine Lake Road, Suite 100
Lincoln, NE 68512
www.iuniverse.com

ISBN: 0-595-32390-1

Printed in the United States of America

Contents

PART I
WHY IRAQ?

1

The Methodology

This book was inspired by the march to the Iraq war, which spilled into public discourse shortly after the Sept. 11 terrorist attacks. Vice President Dick Cheney's eagerness to promote a connection between Saddam Hussein and the tragic events of that day was somewhat suspicious. When no weapons of mass destruction were found, finding the truth about the driving force behind the unprovoked invasion of Iraq became a quest. The replacement justifications for the war, which were provided after the fact, may have satisfied some parties, but there was a credibility problem that just didn't go away.

Was this an intelligence failure, or merely a presentation failure with the real reasons for launching a war not disclosed?

It's interesting to consider what would have happened if stockpiles of the dreaded weapons were in fact found in Iraq. Few would have doubted the Bush administration's claim that it "knew" illicit weapons were there—when the President would only have been lucky, and there wouldn't have been a search for any possible hidden agenda.

Another reason for this book was to compare and contrast the Iraq war with the long and tragic American experience in Vietnam. Are there more similarities than differences? Are the differences of a nature that would prevent the nation from entering another protracted quagmire with no politically acceptable exit?

While the primary objective was seeking out the most compelling motivation(s) for the invasion of Iraq and the prospects for success in the war, the events relating to the Sept. 11 attacks could hardly be ignored:

- Was there a link between Iraq and the attacks on U.S. soil?

- Did the terrorist strike trigger the motivation for war with Iraq?

- Was the fixation on Iraq a distraction from the terror warnings?

- Did Sept. 11 interrogation tactics impact Iraq detainees?
- Was regime change in Iraq a positive step in the war on terror?

The threats leading up to and the impact of the Sept. 11 attacks, the war on terror, the Iraq war, and the prisoner abuse scandal are far from separate and distinct defining features of the Bush administration; and each one has roots and warnings that begin sooner than the casual observer might suspect.

The plan was to present the sequence of events that would provide insight on the motivations and relationships that have impacted both the decision-making and the outcome of each of these troubling situations.

The search for answers was predicated on the premise that actions and events speak louder than words. However, the intention was to give U.S. administrations the benefit of the doubt, and accept their policy statements—even if they appear to be a glossy spin—unless there is at least one telling event that indicates otherwise.

All the relevant facts were gleaned from news sources deemed sufficiently credible, from newspaper clippings, web sources, declassified government documents, and news databases. Due to the nature of this project, an extremely large number of facts and events were needed, and hence, many sources to back them up. Footnotes referencing citations are abundant, with the author's comments following in some cases.

Due to the nature of unfolding news, most articles contain many facts, sometimes referencing more than one time period, but the intent was to lay out the events in chronological order to paint the clearest possible picture of the conflicts and situations as they develop.

The methodology entailed selecting almost 500 sources of news, stripping them down to the several thousand facts and events, and splitting them up into separate information from different time periods when applicable. This process resulted in over 750 citations, which were sorted in chronological order for proper placement into the sequence of events. This procedure frequently resulted in the same source being referenced multiple times because each group of facts needed to retain its citation.

As an example, the August 6, 2001 Presidential Daily Brief that was declassified and released in April 2004. Other facts related to this event were all placed in August 2001 in order to provide the reader with everything that was eventually learned about this event in the actual time frame that the event occurred. Since the release of this 2001 brief shed light on the credibility of certain parties in

2004, the same event is also placed in 2004 with comments appropriate in that time frame.

In order to collect the needed pieces of the puzzle, facts were gathered from the Vietnam Era, some early history of Iraq, many of the pre-2001 terrorist strikes around the world, the Sept. 11 events including the numerous threat warnings, the march into the 2003 invasion of Iraq, and the crisis with the detainees.

Even though all facts, statements, and activities covered in this book have already occurred, the reader is placed into the timeline with the present tense. Every entry in the sequence of events has a date or time period as a point of reference. The description of the event refers to activity within this time period in the present tense, to activity prior to this time period in past tense, and to activity following this time period in the future tense.

The end result is a march through time providing a comprehensive portrait of both the early formation and the relationships between the September 11 attacks, the war on terror, the march to the war with Iraq, and the prisoner abuse scandal.

The citations for the chapters in *Part Two: Sequence of Events* are included in the notes at the end of each chapter. The chapters in the other two parts of the book are supported by the sequence of events and refer back to them by date.

The Bush administration loathes investigations, and made no secret about it, preferring instead to follow the "Imperial Presidency" model, which allows a head of state the maximum latitude without the pesky interference of public investigations and the two other branches of government. But due to the sequence of events following the 2001 terror strikes, there were investigations aplenty.

The congressional inquiry into the failure to protect America from the Sept. 11 attacks didn't quite go far enough, so four women, the "Jersey Girls," pressed for an independent commission, which eventually conducted over 1,000 interviews, reviewed thousands of materials, and led to the declassification of many documents.

Whether these investigations were witch hunts seeking to assign blame, typical partisan bickering, or a conscientious effort to better prepare for the future, they brought a considerable amount of otherwise hidden details into the public domain—providing a rich set of facts with which to draw conclusions. After all, you can't construct a solution unless you understand the problem.

Before selecting an item for inclusion, the credibility of the news source was considered. If the source or any circumstance was in doubt, corroborating and/or refuting evidence was sought and weighed to minimize the possibility of drawing a conclusion on facts that weren't valid. For an example of this process, a quote taken out of context that could have been improperly included to draw a conclusion is provided.

On June 4, 2003, the following quote was picked up from U.S. Deputy Defense Secretary Paul Wolfowitz, "Let's look at it simply. The most important difference between North Korea and Iraq is that economically, we just had no choice in Iraq. The country swims on a sea of oil." Then several Web sites claimed that Wolfowitz finally admitted that the U.S. went to war in Iraq primarily for its oil.

The quote was misinterpreted and quickly debunked. Dr. Wolfowitz was speaking to delegates at an Asian Security Summit in Singapore. He was answering a question regarding why the U.S. thought using economic pressure would work with respect to North Korea and not with regard to Iraq. His point was that the availability of oil revenue to the Iraqi regime would frustrate attempts to use economic pressure on Saddam Hussein.

Even though every attempt was made to select news sources with credibility and to avoid picking up false alarms or misleading quotes, to the extent that any factually inaccurate information from other sources did get included in this book, the author will take full responsibility.

2

Persons, Groups, and Companies of Interest

Persons of Interest

<u>Richard L. Armitage</u>: Mr. Armitage graduated in 1967 from the U.S. Naval Academy, where he was commissioned an Ensign in the U.S. Navy.

In May 1975, Mr. Armitage came to Washington as a Pentagon consultant and was posted in Tehran, Iran until November 1976.

From 1981 until June 1983, Mr. Armitage was Deputy Assistant Secretary of Defense for East Asia and Pacific Affairs in the Office of the Secretary of Defense. In the Pentagon from June 1983 to May 1989, he served as Assistant Secretary of Defense for International Security Affairs.

From 1989 through 1992, Mr. Armitage filled key diplomatic positions as Presidential Special Negotiator for the Philippines Military Bases Agreement and Special Mediator for Water in the Middle East. President Bush sent him as a Special Emissary to Jordan's King Hussein during the 1991 Gulf War.

From 1993 to 2000, Mr. Armitage was President of Armitage Associates L.C.

In March 2001, Mr. Armitage started his tenure as Deputy Secretary of State.[1]

Mr. Armitage is a neoconservative, a charter member of the Project for a New American Century, and a strong proponent of regime change in Iraq.

<u>Osama bin Laden</u>: Born in Saudi Arabia to a Yemeni family, bin Laden left Saudi Arabia in 1979 to fight against the Soviet invasion of Afghanistan. The Afghan jihad was backed with American dollars and had the blessing of the governments of Saudi Arabia and Pakistan. He received security training from the CIA itself, according to Middle Eastern analyst Hazhir Teimourian.

After the Soviet withdrawal, bin Laden's faction was dubbed al Qaeda, meaning "the base," and they turned their fire against the U.S. and its allies in the Middle East.

Bin Laden returned to Saudi Arabia to work in the family construction business, but was expelled in 1991 because of his anti-government activities there. He spent the next five years in Sudan until U.S. pressure prompted the Sudanese Government to expel him, whereupon bin Laden returned to Afghanistan.

His power is founded on a personal fortune earned by his family's construction business in Saudi Arabia, and terrorism experts say bin Laden has been using his millions to fund attacks against the U.S.

According to the U.S., bin Laden was involved in at least three major attacks prior to the Sept. 11 attacks that were executed by his al Qaeda group: the 1993 World Trade Center bombing, the 1996 killing of 19 U.S. soldiers in Saudi Arabia, and the 1998 bombings in Kenya and Tanzania.[2]

There are complicated financial connections between the bin Laden and Bush families.

George H. W. Bush: On his 18th birthday, President Bush enlisted in the armed forces. On one of his 58 combat missions over the Pacific as a torpedo bomber pilot, he was shot down by Japanese antiaircraft fire and was rescued from the water by a U. S. submarine. He was awarded the Distinguished Flying Cross for bravery in action.

He served two terms as a Representative to Congress from Texas. Twice he ran unsuccessfully for the Senate. Then he was appointed to a series of high-level positions: Ambassador to the United Nations, Chairman of the Republican National Committee, Chief of the U. S. Liaison Office in the People's Republic of China, and Director of the Central Intelligence Agency.

In 1980, President Bush ran as Ronald Reagan's Vice President and spent eight years in this role. In 1988, he was elected to be the 41st President.[3]

The first President Bush's approval rating went over 80% during the first Gulf War when the U.S. successfully expelled Iraqi troops from Kuwait and declined to attempt a regime change in Iraq. However, in less than 12 months, the massive deficit spending of the Reagan years brought the U.S. economy to its knees, and a well-funded third-party challenge from Ross Perot created the opening for Bill Clinton. Bush generally followed a multinational approach to foreign policy, and his years in the CIA supported his understanding of the world's trouble spots.

Unfortunately, his stellar military service, skills as commander in chief, interest in diplomacy, and foreign policy savvy did not automatically pass down to the next generation.

George W. Bush: President Bush received a bachelor's degree from Yale University in 1968 and an MBA from Harvard Business School in 1975. Then, he moved back to Midland, Texas for a career in the energy business.

He became the first Governor in Texas history to be elected to consecutive four-year terms when he was re-elected on November 3, 1998, with 68.6 percent of the vote.

George W. Bush was sworn into office January 20, 2001 as the 43rd President of the United States.[4]

He chose to serve as an F-102 fighter pilot in the Texas Air National Guard in lieu of Vietnam service and missed a physical that resulted in the loss of his flying status.

Although he didn't receive the most votes in the 2000 election, he entered the White House claiming to have a strong mandate, and quickly proceeded with his agenda. Domestically, he reduced taxes on dividends, capital gains, and inheritances, much to the delight of his well-heeled constituency.

Ahmed Chalabi: Ahmed Chalabi is the head of the Iraqi National Congress (INC) and a leading member of the Iraqi Governing Council. He is a Shiite Muslim who was born to a wealthy banking family in Iraq. At the age of 12, his family left Iraq and Chalabi has since spent most of his life in the West.

In 1992, after his Petra Bank folded under questionable circumstances, Chalabi was sentenced in absentia by a Jordanian court for bank fraud. Chalabi has repeatedly insisted that he is innocent and claims the bank's failure was orchestrated by former Iraqi President Saddam Hussein.

In the mid-1990s, his INC tried to organize an uprising in Kurdish areas of Iraq. When that effort failed and hundreds of his supporters were killed, Chalabi and many of his INC cohorts fled the country.

Individuals promoting Chalabi include Richard Perle, Donald Rumsfeld, Paul Wolfowitz, Douglas Feith, and Vice President Dick Cheney. Groups promoting Chalabi include the Project for a New American Century (PNAC), the Washington Institute for Near East Policy (WINEP) and the Jewish Institute for National Security Affairs (JINSA).[5]

Richard B. Cheney: Mr. Cheney won a scholarship to the prestigious Yale University, but due to his poor academic performance, was asked to leave. He returned to Wyoming, where he earned his Bachelors and Masters Degrees in Political Science.

Several years later Mr. Cheney was Chief of Staff under Gerald Ford and was nicknamed "backseat" for his behind the scenes style. In 1978, Cheney ran successfully for Wyoming's lone seat in the U.S. House of Representatives. Later, Cheney served as Secretary of Defense for President George H.W. Bush,.

He served as CEO of Halliburton Corporation, the world's largest oilfield services and products company, and used his government connections to win over $3.5 billion in federal contracts and taxpayer-insured loans for Halliburton.

Mr. Cheney was selected as George W. Bush's vice presidential running mate in 2000.[6]

The quintessential neoconservative, Mr. Cheney was a strong proponent of regime change in Iraq, even before taking office in 2001.

Richard A. Clarke: Mr. Clarke is a graduate of the Boston Latin School, the University of Pennsylvania, and the Massachusetts Institute of Technology.

He was a career member of the Senior Executive Service, having begun his federal service in 1973 in the Office of the Secretary of Defense.

In the Reagan administration, Mr. Clarke was the Deputy Assistant Secretary of State for Intelligence.

In the George H.W. Bush administration, he was the Assistant Secretary of State for Politico-Military Affairs. In that capacity, he coordinated State Department support of Desert Storm and lead efforts to create post-war security architecture. In 1992, General Scowcroft appointed Mr. Clarke to the National Security Council staff.

Mr. Clarke continued as a member of the NSC staff throughout the Clinton administration.

He has served in several senior national security posts. Most recently he served as National Coordinator for Security, Infrastructure Protection, and Counter-terrorism on the National Security Council. As National Coordinator, he led the U.S. government's efforts on counter-terrorism, cyber security, continuity of government operations, domestic preparedness for weapons of mass destruction, and international organized crime.

National security advisor Condoleezza Rice and Director of Homeland Security Governor Ridge announced the appointment of Richard A. Clarke as Special Advisor to the President for Cyberspace Security on October 9, 2001.[7]

Mr. Clarke retired early in 2003 after 30 years in government service and wrote the book, *Against All Enemies*, which questioned the Bush administration's commitment in the fight against terror.

<u>Douglas J. Feith</u>: Mr. Feith holds a J.D. (magna cum laude) from the George-town University Law Center and an A.B. (magna cum laude) from Harvard College.

Mr. Feith served as Special Counsel to Assistant Secretary of Defense Richard Perle. From March 1984 until September 1986, he served as Deputy Assistant Secretary of Defense for Negotiations Policy in the Reagan administration.

Mr. Feith was an attorney in Washington D.C. for 15 years until July 2001 when he was appointed the Under Secretary of Defense for Policy reporting to Defense Secretary Donald Rumsfeld.[8]

He is a neoconservative, an ardent supporter of Israel, and has been a strong proponent of regime change in Iraq.

<u>Saddam Hussein</u>: In the early 1960's, Saddam was pushing for a position of influence with Iraq's ruling Baath party, but when it was overthrown, he was sent to prison. In 1968, the Baath party returned to power in a coup, and he was released from prison and gained a position on the ruling Revolutionary Command Council.

For years Saddam was the power behind the president, Ahmed Hassan Bakr, and in 1979, he achieved his ambition of becoming the head of state. He immediately put to death dozens of his rivals and continued torturing and killing any who challenged his rule.

Although Saddam was criticized for his cruelty, none of his opponents could even nominate an alternate who could keep Iraq's diverse factions: the Sunnis, Shiites, and Kurdish together with any stability. Saddam remained in power for 24 years—an extremely long time by Iraqi standards—before the U.S. invasion deposed him in April 2003.[9]

<u>Richard N. Perle</u>: A long time Washington insider dubbed the "prince of darkness," Richard Perle was Assistant Secretary of Defense during the Reagan administration. He served as foreign policy advisor to the George W. Bush presidential campaign. In 2001, he was appointed chairman of the defense policy board, an advisory panel to the Pentagon until March 2003, and remained on the board until a controversy triggered his resignation in February 2004. Mr. Perle is a former Likud policy adviser, media manager, international investor, editorial writer, the quintessential neoconservative, and a fervent supporter of the Iraq war. He is prominent in the American Enterprise Institute and the Project for a New American Century, both of which have been influential behind-the-scenes architects of the Bush administration's foreign policy, including the push for war

with Iraq since 1997. Mr. Perle is a strong supporter of Israel and is on the Advisory Board of the Jewish Institute for National Security Affairs (JINSA). He is a close associate of Defense Secretary Donald Rumsfeld and his assistant Paul Wolfowitz.[10]

Colin L, Powell: Secretary Powell graduated from the City College of New York (CCNY) where he earned a bachelor's degree in geology. He received a commission as an Army second lieutenant upon graduation in June 1958. Secretary Powell also earned a Master of Business Administration degree from George Washington University.

Secretary Powell was a professional soldier for 35 years, during which time he held myriad command and staff positions and rose to the rank of four-star General. He was Assistant to the President for National Security Affairs from December 1987 to January 1989. His last assignment, from October 1, 1989 to September 30, 1993, was as the 12th Chairman of the Joint Chiefs of Staff, the highest military position in the Department of Defense. During this time, he oversaw 28 crises, including Operation Desert Storm in the victorious 1991 Persian Gulf War.

Secretary Powell was sworn in as the 65th Secretary of State on January 20, 2001.[11]

Secretary Powell brings a commanding reputation and a keen understanding of foreign affairs to the Bush administration, but as the lone member of the Bush foreign policy team who is not a neoconservative, he frequently finds himself isolated and frustrated.

Ronald W. Reagan: The 40th American President graduated from Eureka College to become a radio sports announcer.

A screen test in 1937 won him a contract in Hollywood. During the next two decades he appeared in 53 films.

As president of the Screen Actors Guild, Reagan became embroiled in disputes over the issue of Communism in the film industry; his political views shifted from liberal to conservative.

In 1966 he was elected Governor of California and he was re-elected in 1970.

Ronald Reagan was elected president in 1980 and was reelected in 1984. During his two terms, defense spending increased 35 percent.[12]

Reagan was the first modern neoconservative, although merely referred to as a conservative at the time. He was a strong supporter of Saddam Hussein during the Iran-Iraq war, and his defense spending created the largest federal deficit in the history of the nation—that is until the second President Bush was elected.

Condoleezza Rice: Dr. Rice earned her Bachelor's Degree in Political Science, cum laude and Phi Beta Kappa, from the University of Denver in 1974; her Master's from the University of Notre Dame in 1975; and her Ph.D. from the Graduate School of International Studies at the University of Denver in 1981.

As a professor of political science, Dr. Rice has been on the Stanford faculty since 1981.

From 1989 through March 1991, Dr. Rice served in the first Bush administration as Director, and then Senior Director, of Soviet and East European Affairs in the National Security Council, and a Special Assistant to the President for National Security Affairs. In 1986, she served as Special Assistant to the Director of the Joint Chiefs of Staff.

In June 1999, Dr. Rice completed a six-year tenure as Stanford University's Provost.

Dr. Rice has been a member of the boards of directors for Chevron, Hewlett Packard, the Charles Schwab Corporation, National Council for Soviet and East European Studies, and several other corporations and foundations.

Dr. Rice became the Assistant to the President for National Security Affairs, commonly referred to as the national security advisor, on January 22, 2001.[13]

Dr. Rice, dubbed "Warrior Princess" by her staff, has been close to the Bush family for many years. She has a strong background in Soviet and European international security issues but had virtually no experience with counterterrorism prior to January 2001.

Dr. Rice has a much longer and more impressive resume than presented above, and is very intelligent, articulate, and persuasive. Unlike Colin Powell, she willingly adopted Dick Cheney's neoconservative ideology, and has frequently been used in a role more often reserved for a Secretary of State with her public footprint akin to a cabinet officer.

Donald H. Rumsfeld: After attending Princeton University (A.B., 1954), Secretary Rumsfeld served in the U.S. Navy (1954-57) as an aviator and flight instructor. He was elected to the U.S. House of Representatives from Illinois in 1962, at the age of 30, and was re-elected in 1964, 1966, and 1968.

Secretary Rumsfeld resigned from Congress in 1969 during his fourth term to join President Nixon's Cabinet. From 1969 to 1970, he served as Director of the Office of Economic Opportunity and Assistant to the President. From 1971 to

1972, he was Counselor to the President and Director of the Economic Stabilization Program. In 1973, he left Washington, DC, to serve as U.S. Ambassador to the North Atlantic Treaty Organization (NATO) in Brussels, Belgium (1973-1974).

In August 1974, he was called back to Washington, DC to serve as chairman of the transition to the presidency of Gerald R. Ford. He then became Chief of Staff of the White House and a member of the President's Cabinet (1974-1975). He served as the 13th U.S. Secretary of Defense, the youngest in the country's history (1975-1977).

From 1977 to 1985 he served as Chief Executive Officer, President, and then Chairman of G.D. Searle & Co., a worldwide pharmaceutical company. From December 1983 through 1984 he served as a special envoy for President Ronald Reagan in order to improve relations with and supply arms to Saddam Hussein. From 1985 to 1990 he was in private business. Secretary Rumsfeld served as Chairman and Chief Executive Officer of General Instrument Corporation from 1990 to 1993.

Before returning for his second tour as Secretary of Defense in 2001, Secretary Rumsfeld chaired the bipartisan U.S. Ballistic Missile Threat Commission, in 1998, and the U.S. Commission to Assess National Security Space Management and Organization, in 2000.[14]

Secretary Rumsfeld is a neoconservative who strongly promoted the invasion of Iraq.

George P. Shultz: Dr. Shultz received his B.A. in Economics at Princeton University in 1942, served in the Marine Corps from 1945 to 1949, and earned a Ph.D. from MIT in Industrial Economics.

Dr. Shultz taught at MIT from 1948 until 1957 when he joined the faculty at the University of Chicago.

Dr. Shultz served as Secretary of Labor from 1969 to 1970, then as director of the Office of Management and Budget. He served as Secretary of the Treasury from May 1972 to May 1974.

In 1974, Dr. Shultz left government service to become president and director of Bechtel Group.

On July 16, 1982, Dr. Shultz was appointed by President Ronald Reagan to serve as the 60th Secretary of State.

Dr. Shultz left government in 1989 and has been a director of Bechtel ever since.[15]

Dr. Shultz didn't accept all of the neoconservative doctrine, but was an avid proponent of one of their objectives: getting U.S. corporations, especially his Bechtel, as much business as possible in the Middle East.

<u>George J. Tenet</u>: Mr. Tenet holds a B.S.F.S. from the Georgetown University School of Foreign Service and an M.I.A. from the School of International Affairs at Columbia University.

Mr. Tenet came to the Senate Select Committee on Intelligence in August of 1985, as designee to the Vice Chairman, Senator Patrick Leahy, and directed the Committee's oversight of all arms control negotiations between the Soviet Union and the United States. He also served as Staff Director of the Committee for over four years under the chairmanship of Senator David Boren.

Mr. Tenet served as Special Assistant to the President and Senior Director for Intelligence Programs at the National Security Council. He served as the Deputy Director of Central Intelligence, having been confirmed in that position in July 1995. Following the departure of John Deutch in December 1996, he served as Acting Director.

George Tenet was sworn in as Director of Central Intelligence on July 11, 1997.[16]

<u>Paul D. Wolfowitz</u>: Dr. Wolfowitz taught at Yale (1970–73) and Johns Hopkins (1981).

From 1973 to 1977 he served in the Arms Control and Disarmament Agency, and from 1977 to 1980 as Deputy Assistant Secretary of Defense for Regional Programs.

From 1981 to 1982 Dr. Wolfowitz served as head of the State Department's Policy Planning Staff, and later in the Reagan administration, served for three years as U.S. Ambassador to Indonesia.

From 1989 to 1993, he served as Under Secretary of Defense for Policy when Dick Cheney was the Secretary of Defense. In 1993, Dr. Wolfowitz was the George F. Kennan Professor of National Security Strategy at the National War College.

In March 2001, he started his tenure as Deputy Secretary of Defense reporting to Defense Secretary Donald Rumsfeld in the second Bush administration.[17]

Dr. Wolfowitz is a neoconservative and the intellectual architect of the pre-emptive invasion of Iraq. On paper, he appears to be fully qualified for that role.

Groups of Interest

American Enterprise Institute (AEI) for Public Policy Research: This think tank was formed in 1943 and is exercising increasing influence in Washington. Lynne Cheney, wife of Vice President Dick Cheney, is a senior staff member of the institute, which has recently taken a more aggressive and conservative public policy role, and is a favorite amongst the neoconservatives.[18]

The Committee for the Liberation of Iraq (CLI): was set up in late 2002 by Bruce Jackson, a director of the Project for a New American Century and former Lockheed Martin vice president. The group also has close links to The American Enterprise Institute (AEI).

In an interview with the *American Prospect's* John Judis, Jackson said that acquaintances in the Bush administration asked him if he could replicate the success he had had pushing for NATO expansion through his U.S. Committee for NATO. He was asked to create an organization aimed at supporting the administration's campaign to convince Congress and the public to go along with a war. He said, "People in the White House said, 'We need you to do for Iraq what you did for NATO.'"

Since the "official end of hostilities" in Iraq, the committee appears to have disbanded, and its web site has been taken down.[19]

Iraqi National Congress (INC): This organization was created at the behest of the U.S. government for the purpose of fomenting the overthrow of Iraqi dictator Saddam Hussein. Since 1992, the INC has received millions of dollars in U.S. aid., and together with the Rendon Group—which has also received millions of taxpayer dollars—worked with the CIA to gather information, distribute propaganda, and recruit dissidents. Ahmed Chalabi is the current leader of the group, which is strongly supported by Vice President Dick Cheney, Richard Perle, and Paul Wolfowitz.

Neoconservatives: As a general rule, this group believes that tyrants must be overthrown and that diplomacy, arms control, containment, etc. are worthless avenues to pursue. The U.S. must always take preemptive action. Some of the neocons were involved in the first Bush presidency, but they reject the 41st President's multilateral approach, favoring a unilateral approach where America can use its military power to bring progress and morality to the World's trouble spots.

Rogue states and terrorism have replaced communism for the second coming of the McCarthyism Era, and the Sept. 11 attacks provided an excellent pretext to further the neocons' goals. They possess a deeply held conviction of U.S. moral superiority and of America's responsibility to create a new world order. This would be done with allies if they're willing, but alone if not. For the most part, international organizations and alliances are considered misguided restraints that America must discard. The quintessential neocon interest group is the Project for a New American Century, and the icon of this club is Ronald Reagan.

Below is a chart of the neoconservative involvement in two postwar mini-eras. The listed persons were involved with both the Reagan/George H. W. Bush and the George W. Bush timeframes, creating a strong link between the periods. One exception is Ronald Reagan who retired after his presidency, but his influence lived on as the Project for a New American Century website reveals. The other exception is the first President Bush who also retired, but the two Bush presidents do create a strong link because they not only belong to the same political party, they are also from the same immediate family.

Neoconservative	Neocon I Era	Clinton Era	Neocon II Era
	1981–1992	1993–2000	2001–2004
Richard Armitage	DOD 80–88, Diplomat 89–91	consultant	State Dept.
George HW Bush	VP 81–88, President 89–92	retired	
George W Bush	Energy business	Governor	President
Dick Cheney	DOD 89–92	Halliburton	Vice President
Douglas Feith	DOD 84–86	attorney	DOD
Richard Pearl	DOD 81–87		DOD Adviser
Ronald Reagan	President 81–88	retired	
Donald Rumsfeld	DOD 75–76, envoy 83–84	GD Searle	DOD
George Shultz	State Dept. 82–88	Bechtel	Bechtel
Paul Wolfowitz	State 81-82, DOD 89–93	War college	DOD

It should be noted that the first President Bush didn't always toe the neocon hard line, but he did place three of the neocons—Richard Armitage, Dick Cheney, and Paul Wolfowitz—into high positions in his administration. The link between the two neocon eras is very important because it shines a bright light on the true motivations for the preemptive invasion of Iraq in 2003. The actions and positions of these parties will be noted throughout the sequence of events because of their significance.

Project for a New American Century (PNAC): A group of neoconservatives form the non-profit, "educational organization" in 1997 called the *Project for a New American Century* (PNAC). This group claims American foreign policy was adrift under former President Clinton's administration, wants to readopt former President Ronald Reagan's ideology and "moral clarity," supports significant increases in defense spending, and then recommends using it against hostile adversaries.

Noting that the United States stands as the world's preeminent power, the use of U.S. military power is urged to achieve global leadership and to shape a new century favorable to American principles and economic interests.

By early 1998, the group was aggressively promoting a war in Iraq to depose Saddam Hussein. The 25 inaugural members include: Jeb Bush, Dick Cheney, Steve Forbes, Dan Quayle, Donald Rumsfeld, and Paul Wolfowitz; Richard L. Armitage and Richard Perle joined soon thereafter to promote the war for regime change in Iraq.

Companies of Interest

Bechtel: Founded in 1898 and based in San Francisco, Bechtel is privately held and has been under the leadership of its founding family for four generations. It is one of the world's premier engineering, construction, and project management companies.

Bechtel has 42,000 employees and provides premier technical, management, and directly related services to develop, manage, engineer, build, and operate installations for its customers worldwide.

Bechtel claims to adhere to the highest standards of ethical business culture, and its reputation for adhering to these standards is one of its most valuable assets.[20]

Ethical business culture notwithstanding, Bechtel has been challenged by the "revolving door" syndrome. In 1974, George Shultz left government service to become president and director of Bechtel Group. On July 16, 1982, Shultz was appointed by President Ronald Reagan to serve as the sixtieth Secretary of State. Soon thereafter, Shultz, with the assistance of Donald Rumsfled, tried vigorously to get a major construction contract from Iraq for an oil pipeline to Aqaba. Shultz left government in 1989 and has been a director of Bechtel ever since.

<u>Halliburton</u>: Founded in 1919, Halliburton is one of the world's largest providers of products and services to the oil and gas industries. It provides and integrates products and services, starting with exploration and drilling, through production, operations, maintenance, refining, and finally abandonment.[21]

Halliburton has expanded through mergers over the years, has operations all over the world, and has won significant government contracts, sometimes with well-placed connections and the infamous "revolving door." Frequently, these contracts have been embroiled in over-billing controversies.

Its subsidiary, Brown & Root, won a defense contract in 1992 while Dick Cheney was the Secretary of Defense. Dick Cheney became Halliburton's CEO in 1995 with no previous corporate experience. Mr. Cheney left Halliburton in 2000 to be George W. Bush's running mate. Halliburton won a no-bid multi-billion dollar contract in Iraq in 2003.

NOTES TO CHAPTER 2

1 Secretary of State Web site: http://www.state.gov/r/pa/ei/biog/2991.htm.

2 "Who is Osama bin Laden," *BBC News*, September 18, 2001, http://news.bbc.co.uk/1/hi/world/south_asia/155236.stm.

3 White House Web site, http://www.whitehouse.gov/history/presidents/gb41.html.

4 White House Web site, http://www.whitehouse.gov/president/gwbbio.html.

5 Robert Dreyfuss, "Tinker, Banker, Neocon, Spy: Ahmed Chalabi's Long and Winding Road to (and from?) Baghdad," The American Prospect, November 18, 2002.

6 White House Web site: http://www.whitehouse.org/administration/dick.asp.

7 U.S. Dept. of State Web site: http://usinfo.org/USIA/usinfo.state.gov/topical/pol/nsc.htm#Clarke.

8 DOD Web site, http://www.defenselink.mil/policy/bio/feith.html.

9 "Saddam Hussein Profile," BBC News, January 4, 2001, http://news.bbc.co.uk/1/hi/world/middle_east/1100529.stm.

10 Disinfopedia, http://www.disinfopedia.org/wiki.phtml?title=Richard_N._Perle.

11 Secretary of State Web site: http://www.state.gov/r/pa/ei/biog/1349.htm.

12 http://www.whitehouse.gov/history/presidents/rr40.html.

13 White House Web site: http://www.whitehouse.gov/nsc/ricebio.html.

14 Department of Defense Web site: http://www.defenselink.mil/bios/rumsfeld.html.

15 Wikipedia, http://en.wikipedia.org/wiki/George_Shultz.

16 CIA Web site: http://www.cia.gov/cia/information/tenet.html.

17 Department of Defense Web site:
http://www.defenselink.mil/bios/wolfowitz.html.

18 "American Enterprise Institute for public policy research," Media Transparency, http://www.mediatransparency.org/recipients/aei.htm.

19 IRC, December 18, 2003, http://rightweb.irc-online.org/org/cli.php.

20 Bechtel Web site, http://www.bechtel.com/overview.htm.

21 Halliburton Web site, http://www.halliburton.com/about/index.jsp.

3

Possible Justifications for War

Saddam provides ample ammunition for promoting a regime change, but what was the primary driving force justifying the invasion of Iraq? Fourteen possible motivations/justifications for the Iraq war will be examined. Of these, the first nine were presented by the Bush administration, the next four by critics of the administration, and the last is one that hasn't yet received much attention.

[1] <u>The concern about the proliferation of weapons of mass destruction</u>

Nothing could more clearly represent a threat to world peace than nuclear, chemical, or biological weapons in the hands of a rogue nation. If a President wants to drum up support for a war, claiming a threat of weapons of mass destruction (WMD) is an excellent way to focus attention on a desired foe. And if the target is a ruthless dictator, who has previously used chemical weapons on multiple occasions, and even on a segment of his own population, this argument will possess significant clout.

There is little doubt that this issue could be a plausible justification for starting a war. But to what extent were WMD actually a motivation for the 2003 invasion of Iraq?

[2] <u>The link between Iraq, al Qaeda, and September 11, 2001 attacks</u>

The justification for invading Iraq that President Bush wanted above all others was that Saddam was involved with the Sept. 11 attacks. His pressing Richard Clarke for this connection on the very next day (events 9-12-2001) was anything but subtle. In one of Bush's speeches prior to the 2003 invasion, he mentioned Sept. 11 eight times. Going into the war, almost half of the nation believed that Saddam was somehow involved with the Sept. 11 attacks.

Was there a link? And whether there was a link or not, was this issue a significant motivation for the second Persian Gulf War?

[3] Saddam was a ruthless dictator

Saddam Hussein was a ruthless dictator who routinely tortured political prisoners. He had used poison gas on the rebelling Kurds who are Iraqi citizens. His behavior eventually became a primary justification offered by the Bush administration for the war, and few people stepped forward to proclaim that Saddam was such a nice guy that he should remain in power.

Unfortunately, the world has many ruthless dictators. How much of a role did Saddam's actions actually play in the motivation of the Bush administration to start a war?

[4] To provide freedom and democracy for Iraq and eventually throughout the Middle East

President Bush's position on promoting freedom and democracy for Iraq—and eventually the entire Middle East—was remarkably consistent. Both before and after the start of the war, he would repeat this vision. How much did this objective influence the push to war in Iraq?

[5] To support the War on Terror

President Bush and Condoleezza Rice consistently promoted the war on Iraq as part of the war on terror—both before and after the preemptive invasion. Saddam Hussein's support for Palestinian terrorism enabled them to claim that a connection between Iraq and terrorism did in fact exist.

Was the invasion of Iraq an appropriate action to take in order to counter terrorism? How much did this factor motivate the Bush administration to launch a preemptive strike at Iraq?

[6] Due to Iraqi U.N. resolution violations

From November 1990 to December 1999, Saddam Hussein repeatedly violated 16 United Nations Security Council Resolutions (UNSCR's) designed to ensure that Iraq did not pose a threat to international peace and security (events 1990-1999).

To what extent did these violations prompt the Bush administration in the march to war?

[7] The U.S. strategic interest in maintaining the flow of oil

The importance of oil in U.S.—Middle Eastern foreign policy is no secret. In 1956, President Eisenhower said publicly, "Middle Eastern oil is of importance mainly through its contribution to the Western European economy (events 1956)." President Bush mentioned that Iraq was a threat to U.S. security interests "in the region," which includes oil-producing countries such as Saudi Arabia and Kuwait that could be destabilized by Iraqi aggression, which would disrupt the flow of oil, and impact the U.S. economy.

With U.N. sanctions on Iraq, its oil production was far short of its potential considering its vast oil reserves. With Saddam Hussein gone, there would be no more need for sanctions and oil production in Iraq could be significantly increased.

How much of a threat was Saddam to the oil-producing countries in the region? How much was the concern to maintain the flow of oil a motivator to attack Iraq? How much interest was there in increasing Iraq's oil production?

[8] U.S. allies in the region

President Bush mentioned his concern for the many U.S. allies in the region, several of which are oil-producing nations. Saddam Hussein invaded Kuwait in late 1990, and he could possibly have been a threat to the smaller countries adjacent to Iraq. Even the U.S. didn't know how dramatically his military and weapons programs were marginalized due to the many years of U.N. sanctions.

But of all the Middle East countries, the special relationship that the U.S. has with Israel is second to none. The U.S. has vetoed over 40 U.N. resolutions critical of Israel since 1972, which confirms the close relationship that the United States has with Israel (events 3-8-2003).

And Saddam Hussein fired 39 Scud missiles at Israel during the 1991 Gulf War, which is a clue that the security of Israel was a potential concern of the U.S. (events 1-17-1991).

How important was the security of Israel as a driver for the 2003 Gulf War?

[9] <u>U.S. national security</u>

During the march to war, President Bush suggested that regime change in Iraq was necessary for U.S. national security. Even before Saddam's decline in the nineties, he never had any weapons with a range to threaten the North American continent. However, Bush's argument is that Saddam could provide terrorists with weapons of mass destruction, which could then be deployed against U.S. interests, possibly even on American soil.

How much did a threat to U.S. national security motivate the Bush administration in the march to war?

[10] <u>To avenge the assassination attempt on the first President Bush</u>

The Kuwaitis uncovered an assassination attempt by Saddam on the first President Bush and notified U.S. authorities (events 4-1993). Since he was no longer in office, the 41st President was unable to do anything about it himself. President Clinton responded by firing a missile into the intelligence headquarters in Baghdad (events 6-27-1993). After that, the issue received little public attention.

Did the son have a grudge against Saddam Hussein due to the attempt on his father's life?

[11] <u>Gain a better military foothold in the Middle East</u>

There is a need to rely less on military bases in Saudi Arabia, where the U.S. is very unpopular. Also, Turkey balked at the use of military bases that were desired by the U.S. for the 2003 invasion of Iraq. Would cooperation from Qatar and Kuwait be sufficient in order to provide the desired bases for future U.S. endeavors in the Persian Gulf?

How much motivation was there to force a regime change in Iraq in order to establish more military bases in the region?

[12] <u>For political gain—War for reelection</u>

The first President Bush pushed his approval rating well over 80% in the first Persian Gulf War, and George W. Bush maintained his elevated Sept. 11 approval rating throughout the Afghanistan war. Was the White House interested in chumming his approval rating prior to the 2004 election enough to promote a war for this purpose?

[13] <u>Control of oil and corporate profits in Iraq and Middle East</u>

Is oil at the heart of the crisis that leads towards a U.S. war against Iraq? Are the major international oil companies, headquartered in the United States and the United Kingdom, anxious to regain control over Iraq's oil? They were all kicked out when Saddam nationalized Iraq's oil industry in 1972. How high are the stakes for oil in Iraq?

For more than a hundred years, major powers have battled to control this enormous source of wealth and strategic power, and oil in Iraq is especially attractive to the big international oil companies for three reasons: huge reserves, high quality, and low production costs (events 12-2002).

The abundance of valuable oil itself doesn't prove that the 2003 Gulf War was motivated—in part or entirely—by Iraq's lucrative oil deposits. Hopefully, the sequence of events will provide some clues.

[14] <u>Place the United States on permanent war footing</u>

When President Bush was asked at his April 13, 2004 news conference if he felt any personal responsibility for September 11, given that Osama bin Laden was not a central focus of his administration in the months before September 11, Bush said that, "The country was not on a war footing, and yet the enemy was at war with us. And it didn't take me long to put us on a war footing." In the same briefing, he also noted with respect to the war on terror that, "We are in a long war."

Because the president has declared that we are in a war against terror, not just against Iraq and Afghanistan, that it will be a long war, and that no time frame for a return to peace has been provided, a question emerges: Has the country been placed into a permanent war?

PART II
SEQUENCE OF EVENTS

4

The Vietnam Era

France is growing weary of its military intervention in Vietnam so the U.S. gradually moves in to take its turn. President Eisenhower promotes the "domino theory," notes the importance of Middle Eastern oil, and recognizes the dangers of the "military industrial complex." The Gulf of Tonkin resolution is passed, which formally begins the war in Vietnam. The escalating troop counts, atrocities, and major offensives in Vietnam are tracked. The Baath Party takes permanent control of Iraq. President Nixon maintains Iran and Saudi Arabia as client states even though neither offers democracy or freedom. The U.S. experience in Vietnam comes to an end. Defense Secretary Donald Rumsfeld drops the investigation of the Tiger Force atrocities.

August 3, 1950: SAIGON—A U.S. Military Assistance Advisory Group (MAAG) of 35 men arrives in Saigon. By the end of the year, the U.S. is bearing half of the cost of France's war effort in Vietnam.[1]

1950's–1980's: In 2001, Dobson and Marsh note that in managing the postwar balance of power in the Indian Ocean and Persian Gulf, U.S. foreign policy-makers have toppled progressive governments, supported dictators, and even abandoned their closest allies due to the dependence of the Western world on Middle Eastern oil.[2]

August 1953: TEHRAN, Iran—The CIA manufactures a coup in Iran to topple the democratically elected Mohammed Mosadeq in favor, ultimately, of the autocratic Shah and his brutal police, Savak, around whom the U.S. build a client state.[3]

April 7, 1954: WASHINGTON—President Eisenhower at a news conference, "Finally, you have broader considerations that might follow what you would call the 'falling domino' principle. You have a row of dominoes set up, you knock over the first one, and what will happen to the last one is the certainty that it will go over very quickly. So you could have a beginning of a disintegration that would have the most profound influences."[4]

This is the origin of the infamous "domino theory" that was inspired by McCarthyism hysteria. It will become the dubious justification for the Vietnam War.

June 1954: SAIGON—The CIA establishes a military mission in Saigon.[5]

1954: TEHRAN, Iran—The Eisenhower administration is instrumental in obtaining, at Britain's expense, a major share of the Anglo-Iranian Oil Company's (AIOC) concession in Iran.[6]

July 20, 1954: GENEVA—The Geneva Conference on Indochina declares a demilitarised zone at the 17th parallel.[7]

October 24, 1954: WASHINGTON—President Eisenhower pledges support to Diem's government and military forces.[8]

1955: SAIGON—The U.S.-backed Ngo Dinh Diem organizes the Republic of Vietnam as an independent nation and declares himself president.[9]

1956: President Eisenhower says publicly, "Middle Eastern oil is of importance mainly through its contribution to the Western European economy."

What Eisenhower doesn't say when he discusses the importance of oil in U.S. Middle Eastern foreign policy, is that in 1954 his administration was instrumental in obtaining, at Britain's expense, a major share of the Anglo-Iranian Oil Company's (AIOC) concession in Iran. There is no disguising the fact that American economic interests are the primary beneficiaries of U.S. policy and yield enormous profits from oil operations.

However, American geostrategic planning for the Middle East is couched in terms of denying the Soviets oil resources and potential bases from which to launch an assault upon the Persian Gulf.[10]

January 1957: WASHINGTON—The Eisenhower Doctrine implies a firm commitment to the existing order in the Middle East—including the Shah of Iran.[11]

<u>April 4, 1959</u>: President Eisenhower makes his first public commitment to South Vietnam at Gettysburg College.[12]

<u>July 8, 1959</u>: SAIGON—The first American combat deaths in Vietnam occur when the Viet Cong attacks Bien Hoa billets; two American "advisors" are killed.[13]

<u>December 31, 1960</u>: SAIGON—The total American troop count is approximately 850.[14]

<u>January 17, 1961</u>: WASHINGTON—President Eisenhower's farewell speech, "We must guard against the acquisition of unwarranted influence, whether sought or unsought, by the military industrial complex."[15]

Could President Eisenhower have known how prescient this observation was?

<u>January 28, 1961</u>: WASHINGTON—President Kennedy tells Diem to reform his government and military.[16]

<u>July 1961</u>: WASHINGTON—President Kennedy orders the military to recruit 200,000 more men.[17]

<u>December 31, 1961</u>: SAIGON—The total American troop count is 3,200.[18]

<u>December 31, 1962</u>: SAIGON—The total American troop count is 11,300.[19]

<u>1963</u>: BAGHDAD—The Baath Party, representing minority Sunni Muslims, comes to power briefly in Iraq.[20]

<u>July 7, 1963</u>: SAIGON—Saigon police beat Buddhist demonstrators, 1400 are arrested after pagodas are raided.[21]

<u>September 1963</u>: WASHINGTON—President Kennedy downgrades American military help to "Support role."[22]

<u>October 1963</u>: SAIGON—CIA operative Lucien Conien gives Major General's Tran Van Don and Duong Van Minh the American nod for a coup attempt.[23]

November 1, 1963: SAIGON—Diem and brother ND Nhu are assassinated.[24]

November 22, 1963: DALLAS—President Kennedy is assassinated.

December 31, 1963: SAIGON—The total American troop count is 16,300.[25]

August 5, 1964: GULF OF TONKIN—The front page of *The New York Times* reports, "President Johnson has ordered retaliatory action against gunboats and 'certain supporting facilities in North Vietnam' after renewed attacks against American destroyers in the Gulf of Tonkin."[26]

August 7, 1964: WASHINGTON—Congress passes the Gulf of Tonkin Resolution, which results in a de-facto declaration of war against North Vietnam. Two courageous senators, Wayne Morse of Oregon and Ernest Gruening of Alaska, provide the only "no" votes. The resolution authorizes the president "to take all necessary measures to repel any armed attack against the forces of the United States and to prevent further aggression."

But there are no "renewed attacks against American destroyers" by North Vietnam, or gunboats attacking our destroyers. In 1965, Lyndon Johnson comments in reference to the "phantom" gunboats, "For all I know, our Navy was shooting at whales out there."[27]

This maneuver transforms the American involvement in Vietnam to a full-scale war.

February 7, 1965: SAIGON—The Viet Cong attack Americans at Pleiku, 8 Americans are killed.[28]

February 1965: SAIGON—The Air Force begins Operation Flaming Dart.[29]

February 8, 1965: North Vietnam—U.S. jets begin a massive retaliation against the North.[30]

February 12, 1965: North Vietnam—160 U.S. planes attack northern cities in another retaliation.[31]

February 28, 1965: North Vietnam—In fear of B-52 strikes, Hanoi evacuates all northern cities.[32]

<u>March 2, 1965</u>: North Vietnam—Operation "Rolling Thunder" air strikes on the North begin.[33]

<u>April 6, 1965</u>: SAIGON—President Johnson permits Americans to engage in ground offensive operations.[34]

<u>April 1965</u>: SAIGON—The U.S. Air Force begins Operation Steel Tiger in Laos.[35]

<u>April 7, 1965</u>: WASHINGTON—President Johnson offers $1 billion in aid to end war.[36]

In 1965, $1 billion is a lot of money, especially to a small country with a tiny economy. And with its cities severely bombed, North Vietnam could sure use the funds. Also, the peace proposal would mean no more war casualties and destructive bombing. This is a quintessential U.S. "carrot and stick" foreign policy maneuver. Surely this will do the trick.

<u>April 8, 1965</u>: HANOI—North Vietnam's Prime Minister says no to President Johnson's peace proposal.[37]

It doesn't take long for the peace proposal to be rejected. It would have given half of their country to a foreign power and its puppet government. Everything that they are fighting for, including the victory over the French in 1954 would be lost. Do Western nations ever underestimate the nationalism of smaller countries?

<u>April 13, 1965</u>: WASHINGTON—Students for a Democratic Society protest the Vietnam War in Washington, DC.[38]

<u>July 28, 1965</u>: WASHINGTON—President Johnson increases U.S. combat forces, doubles the draft.[39]

<u>August 18, 1965</u>: SAIGON—Marines begin Operation Starlight.[40]

<u>October 15, 1965</u>: A massive U.S. protest to the Vietnam War begins nationwide.[41]

<u>December 1965</u>: SAIGON—The U.S. Air Force begins Operation Tiger Hound on the border with Laos.[42]

December 25, 1965: WASHINGTON—President Johnson suspends Operation Rolling Thunder.[43]

December 31, 1965: SAIGON—The total American troop count is 185,300.[44]

January 10, 1966: WASHINGTON—Congress informs Johnson some of his domestic programs will have to take cuts if he wants to continue the war escalation.[45]

February 4, 1966: WASHINGTON—The U.S. Senate televises hearings on the Vietnam War.[46]

March 1, 1966: WASHINGTON—The U.S. Senate refuses to repeal the Gulf of Tonkin resolution.[47]

March 16, 1966: SAIGON—Buddhists lead a massive demonstration to restore a civilian to head government.[48]

April 1966: SAIGON—Operation Arc Light is extended to North Vietnam.[49]

May 10, 1966: SAIGON—Operations Paul Revere and Than Phone begin.[50]

June 2, 1966: SAIGON—Operations El Paso, Hawthorne, and Dan begin.[51]

July 4, 1966: SAIGON—Operation Macon begins.[52]

July 7, 1966: SAIGON—Operations Hastings and Deckhouse begin.[53]

August 1, 1966: SAIGON—Operation Paul Revere II begins.[54]

August 3, 1966: SAIGON—Operation Prairie begins.[55]

August 6, 1966: SAIGON—Operations Colorado and Lien Ket 52 begin.[56]

August 26, 1966: SAIGON—Operation Byrd begins.[57]

September 14, 1966: SAIGON—Operation Attleboro begins.[58]

October 1966: SAIGON—The Navy commences Operation Sea Dragon.[59]

October 2, 1966: SAIGON—Operation Irving commences.[60]

October 18, 1966: SAIGON—Operation Paul Revere IV begins.[61]

October 25, 1966: SAIGON—Operation Thayer II begins.[62]

October 26, 1966: SAIGON—President Johnson visits Vietnam, offers to with-draw troops in six months if Hanoi "abandons war."[63]

    No dice.

November 30, 1966: SAIGON—Operation Fairfax begins.[64]

May-November, 1967: CENTRAL HIGHLANDS, Vietnam—In the longest series of atrocities by a U.S. fighting unit in the Vietnam War, the Tiger Force platoon engages in brutal sweeps through 40 villages where civilians are tortured and killed.

    Though the Army will spend four and a half years investigating the special force starting in 1971—substantiating 20 war crimes against 18 soldiers—the case will never reach a military court and no one will ever be charged.[65]

1967: BAGHDAD—Following the 1967 Arab-Israeli War, Iraq breaks off for-mal diplomatic relations with the U.S.[66]

March 16, 1968: MY LAI, Vietnam—My Lai lies in the South Vietnamese dis-trict of Son My, a heavily mined area of Viet Cong entrenchment. Numerous members of Charlie Company were maimed or killed in the area during the pre-ceding weeks. The agitated troops, under the command of Lt. William Calley, enter the village poised for engagement with the elusive Viet Cong.

    "This is what you've been waiting for—search and destroy—and you've got it," say their superior officers. Lt. William Calley orders his men to enter the vil-lage firing, though there has been no report of opposing fire.

    As the "search and destroy" mission unfolds, it soon degenerates into the mas-sacre of over 300 apparently unarmed civilians including women, children, and the elderly. Eyewitnesses recount the gruesome details…[67]

Well-intentioned young soldiers are sent to Vietnam, but they are forced to endure guerilla warfare, where distinguishing friend from foe is especially difficult, and sometimes fatal. How long does it take in this kind of environment before the frustration and anger get out of control?

1968: BAGHDAD—The Baath Party gains permanent control of Iraq with a bloodless coup orchestrated primarily by Saddam Hussein. A new constitution for Iraq formalizes the Baath control of the country. The first Baath president, Ahmed Hasan al-Bakr, institutes socialist reforms and creates strong ties to the Soviet Union.[68]

Fall 1968: Richard M. Nixon wins the presidency with a promise of bringing "peace with honor" in Vietnam. However, despite his talk of peace, honor in Vietnam means the same to Nixon as it did to his White House predecessors—force an unwanted puppet government on the southern half of Vietnam.

How do American presidents prolong such a hopeless quagmire? In a war without any legitimate justification, some device must be used to silence the critics. The president can say, "If the mission is abandoned to achieve peace right away, too many lives would be lost in vain." This commitment to the fallen, the "Vietnam syndrome," extends the war for many years, adding horribly to the statistics and the tragedy.

Will this argument be used again in the future to extend an ill-advised war?

1969–1972: WASHINGTON—In President Nixon's first term, he develops a Twin Pillar approach where both Iran and Saudi Arabia would be client states that police the Persian Gulf. In 1974 alone, the U.S. supplied the ruthless Shah of Iran with $4 billion of weapons.[69]

September 1969: WASHINGTON—Lt. William Calley, the officer who ordered the My Lai Massacre, is charged with murder. Later he will be sentenced to life in prison, but he will be paroled in 1974.[70]

November 21, 1969: WASHINGTON—News has just broken of an unimaginable atrocity committed by U.S. soldiers, and Secretary of Defense Melvin Laird and National Security Adviser Henry Kissinger debate whether there is any way to stop newspapers and TV news programs from showing graphic photographs of the victims.

"They're pretty terrible," says Laird of the color photographs of the men, women, and children killed in the My Lai massacre in South Vietnam.

Kissinger responds that one of President Nixon's top aides has "heard that the Army is trying to impound the pictures—that can't be done."

In their conversation Nov. 21, 1969, about the My Lai massacre, Laird tells Kissinger that although he would like "to sweep it under the rug," the photos prevent it. "There are so many kids just laying there, these pictures are authentic," he says.

In other conversations, Nixon is too drunk to talk to the British prime minister, and on another, he jokes about dropping a nuclear bomb on Capital Hill during his impeachment proceedings.

On May 26, 2004, a transcript of many phone conversations occurring between 1969 and 1974 will be released by the National Security Archive—over the objections of Kissinger.[71]

November 1969: WASHINGTON—When news of the atrocities in the My Lai Massacre becomes public, it sends shockwaves through the U.S. political establishment, the military's chain of command, and an already divided American public.[72]

1969–1973: The killing of an American by another American tossing a fragmentation grenade during the Vietnam War is dubbed "fragging." This usually involves a frustrated draftee killing an American officer.

From 1969 through 1973, fragging reaches its peak. Terry Anderson, a history professor at Texas A &M University in College Station, Texas, says the military reported at least 600 murdered in fragging incidents, with another 1,400 dying under mysterious circumstances. In 1970 alone, 383 are believed killed by fragging.[73]

1970: WASHINGTON—After a series of violent hijackings around the world, the sky marshal program is created to stop hijackings to and from Cuba.[74]

1973: BAGHDAD—The Baath Party completes a takeover of foreign oil companies in Iraq. With the rising oil prices, Iraq enjoys enormous oil profits.[75]

April 30, 1975: SAIGON—After more than 10 years, eight million tons of bombs (three hundred tons for every man, woman, and child in Vietnam), 11 million gallons of Agent Orange, nearly 400,000 tons of napalm, more than

58,000 American deaths, and more than three million Vietnamese deaths, the Vietnam War comes to an end.[76]

Some parties argue that the U.S. should have fought harder and stayed longer in Vietnam.

However, the international outrage at what the U.S. was doing in Vietnam finally subsides after the attempt to install a puppet government in South Vietnam fails and the U.S. pulls out. No American President would come close to creating such worldwide ill-will until the fury from this war is eclipsed 29 years later.

November 20, 1975: WASHINGTON—Donald Rumsfeld becomes the 13th Secretary of Defense under President Gerald Ford.

December 1975: The original Army inquiry into the Tiger Force atrocities and war crimes is suddenly dropped in December 1975 with no charges filed. The Secretary of Defense at the time is Donald Rumsfeld.[77]

1970's: WASHINGTON—The number of sky marshals peaks during the 1970s, after which the program is scaled back as hijackings dropped off.[78]

NOTES TO CHAPTER 4

1 http://plumtree.net.nz/history_vietnam_1950_1966.htm.

2 Alan P. Dobson and Steve Marsh, *US Foreign Policy since 1945*, (New York: Routledge, 2001), p. 102.

3 Alan P. Dobson and Steve Marsh, *US Foreign Policy since 1945*, (New York: Routledge, 2001), p. 97.

4 "Domino Theory Principle, Dwight D. Eisenhower, 1954," Public Papers of the Presidents Dwight D. Eisenhower, 1954, p. 381-390, http://coursesa.matrix.msu.edu/~hst306/documents/domino.html.

5 http://plumtree.net.nz/history_vietnam_1950_1966.htm.

6 Alan P. Dobson and Steve Marsh, p. 95.

7 http://plumtree.net.nz/history_vietnam_1950_1966.htm.

8 Ibid.

9 Ibid.

10 Alan P. Dobson and Steve Marsh, p. 95.

11 Ibid, p. 97.

12 http://plumtree.net.nz/history_vietnam_1950_1966.htm.

13 Ibid.

14 Ibid.

15 Dwight D. Eisenhower, "'Military-Industrial Complex' speech," *CNN.com*, 1961, http://edition.cnn.com/SPECIALS/cold.war/episodes/12/documents/eisenhower.speech/.

16 http://plumtree.net.nz/history_vietnam_1950_1966.htm.

17 Ibid.

18 Ibid.

19 Ibid.

20 "HISTORY OF IRAQ", *The Mercury News*, March 21, 2003, p. 10AB.

21 http://plumtree.net.nz/history_vietnam_1950_1966.htm.

22 Ibid.

23 Ibid.

24 Ibid.

25 Ibid.

26 Tom Wells and Todd Gitlin, *The War within: America's Battle Over Vietnam*, (Berkeley: UC Press, 1994).

27 Ibid.

28 http://plumtree.net.nz/history_vietnam_1950_1966.htm.

29 Ibid.

30 Ibid.

31 Ibid.

32 Ibid.

33 Ibid.

34 Ibid.

35 Ibid.

36 Ibid.

37 Ibid.

38 Ibid.

39 Ibid.

40 Ibid.

41 Ibid.

42 Ibid.

43 Ibid.

44 Ibid.

45 Ibid.

46 Ibid.

47 Ibid.

48 Ibid.

49 Ibid.

50 Ibid.

51 Ibid.

52 Ibid.

53 Ibid.

54 Ibid.

55 Ibid.

56 Ibid.

57 Ibid.

58 Ibid.

59 Ibid.

60 Ibid.

61 Ibid.

62 Ibid.

63 Ibid.

64 Ibid.

65 Michael D. Sallah and Mitch Weiss, "Investigators will question ex-GIs about killing spree," Toledoblade.com, February 15, 2004, http://www.toledoblade.com/apps/pbcs.dll/article?AID=/20040215/SRTIGERFORCE/102150175.

66 Declassified confidential document AN: 0830735-0522, http://www.gwu.edu/~nsarchiv/NSAEBB/NSAEBB82/iraq28.pdf.

67 "My Lai Massacre," *Vietnam Online*, http://www.pbs.org/wgbh/amex/vietnam/trenches/mylai.html.

68 "HISTORY OF IRAQ",…

69 Alan P. Dobson and Steve Marsh, p. 99.

70 "My Lai Massacre,"…

71 Elizabeth Becker, "Nixon aides' views of My Lai incident echo Iraq scandal," *The Mercury News*, May 27, 2004, p. 3A.

72 "My Lai Massacre,"…

73 Jessica Wehrman, "Fragging Stirs Memories of Vietnam," *Scripps Howard News Service*, March 24, 2003 05:57.

74 Glen Johnson, "Some want to put marshals on flights or arm airline pilots," *The Boston Globe*, September 16, 2001.

75 HISTORY OF IRAQ",…

76 Tom Wells and Todd Gitlin, *The War within: America's Battle Over Vietnam*, (Berkeley: UC Press, 1994); http://www.spartacus.schoolnet.co.uk/VNchemical.htm, http://www.globalsecurity.org/military/systems/munitions/incendiary.htm.

77 Michael D. Sallah and Mitch Weiss, "Investigators will question ex-GIs…"

78 RICARDO ALONSO-ZALDIVAR, "Air Marshals' Future Full of Questions," *Los Angeles Times*, January 14, 2002, http://www.latimes.com/news/nationworld/nation/la-011402marshal,0,2997642.story.

5

Neocons I: Building Iraq's Arsenal

The Soviet Union invades Afghanistan. The U.S. counters this move by providing support and training for Osama bin Laden and his group. The U.S. loses Iran as a client state due to an Islamic revolution. There is an eight-year war between Iran and Iraq. President Reagan supports Iraq in the war. He moves aggressively to arm Saddam with WMD using Donald Rumsfeld as an envoy. Many U.S. firms participate in the arms bonanza.

Saddam Hussein uses chemical weapons against Iran on many occasions and several times against his own Kurdish population. Reagan takes Iraq off of the State Department's list of states supporting terror to expedite weapons sales to Saddam. Secretary of State George Shultz promotes business for Bechtel, his former company. The CIA assists Saddam with the calibration of his mustard gas used on Iran. Iraq uses U.S. helicopters in a chemical weapons attack against the Kurds. Bechtel is the lead contractor to build a chemical weapons plant in Iraq. Reagan and George H.W. Bush continue to arm Saddam even after his war against Iran is over. Donald Rumsfeld and Richard Armitage successfully argue against a U.N. resolution condemning Iraq's use of chemical weapons in 1989 while Dick Cheney is Secretary of Defense.

Osama bin Laden forms al Qaeda in Afghanistan.

1979: Afghanistan—The Soviet Union invades Afghanistan. President Carter invokes economic sanctions on the USSR and the CIA begins covert support of Afghan resistance fighters, which includes Osama bin Laden.[1]

1979–1989: Afghanistan—During the anti-Soviet jihad, bin Laden and his fighters receive American and Saudi Arabian funding. Some analysts say bin Laden himself receives security training from the CIA during the 1980s.[2]

<u>1979</u>: BAGHDAD—When the first Baath president, Ahmed Hasan al-Bakr, resigns, Saddam Hussein succeeds him and will remain in power until 2003.[3]

<u>November 3, 1979</u>: TEHRAN, Iran—An Islamic fundamentalist revolution against the U.S.-supported Shah of Iran is successful. Under the Shah, Iran was a client state of the United States, but after the revolution, the U.S.-Iranian economic and security ties dissolve. Due to the years of U.S. support for the Shah, Iran becomes a bastion of anti-Americanism. Militants who are angry about the U.S. support for the Shah hold 52 American embassy staff as their hostages in Tehran, Iran.[4]

<u>November 1979</u>: TEHRAN, Iran—Iran now supports the Kurds in Iraq and tries to foment a rebellion by the majority Shiite Muslims in Iraq.[5]

<u>November 1979</u>: WASHINGTON—President Carter is seriously considering a dramatic rescue of the hostages held in Tehran, Iran. Secretary of State Cyrus Vance argues strongly against it, and insists that he will resign if the President orders the mission.[6]

<u>April 25, 1980</u>: TEHRAN, Iran—President Carter orders a top-secret attempt by the United States to free the American hostages held in Iran's capital, Tehran. Three of the eight helicopters fail before they reach Tehran, and the doomed mission is aborted with the death of eight soldiers.[7]

<u>April 28, 1980</u>: WASHINGTON—The persistent disagreements between Cyrus Vance and President Carter reach a climax over the abortive hostage rescue attempt. Vance becomes only the second Secretary of State in U.S. history to quit over a clear policy issue—resigning in protest over the botched attempt to rescue American hostages in Iran.

"I knew I could not honorably remain as Secretary of State when I so strongly disagreed with a presidential decision that went against my judgment as to what was best for the country and for the hostages," according to Vance in "Hard Choices," his account of the Carter years.

"Even if the mission worked perfectly, and I did not believe it would, I would have to say afterwards that I opposed it, give my reasons for opposing it and publicly criticize the president," according to Vance.[8]

September 22, 1980: BAGHDAD—Iraq's response to Iran's attempt to stir up a rebellion by the Shiites is to invade Iran. The war will last eight years and destroy both Iraqi oil facilities and its economy.[9]

Late 1980: WASHINGTON—The U.S. Defense Intelligence Agency (DIA) asserts in a report that Iraq has been 'actively acquiring' Chemical Weapons [CW] capacities since the mid-1970s.[10]

January 21, 1981: TEHRAN, Iran—Tehran frees the 52 U.S. hostages after 444 days of captivity in Iran. The release occurs on the day that Ronald Reagan is inaugurated.[11]

January 1981: WASHINGTON—Fears of Iran's Shiite revolution cause President Reagan to support Iraq throughout its eight-year war with Iran.[12]

1982: WASHINGTON—President Reagan instructs his U.N. envoy to invoke U.S. veto power on a Security Council resolution that would have been a prohibition against the use of chemical and bacteriological weapons.[13]

Reagan supports Iraq in its war against Iran knowing that Saddam is using chemical weapons.

July 1982: BAGHDAD—Iraq starts the use of tear gas and skin irritants against invading Iranian forces.[14]

September 1982: WASHINGTON—Despite intelligence reports that Iraq still sponsors groups on the State Department's terrorist list, and "apparently without consulting Congress," the Reagan administration removes Iraq from the State terrorism sponsorship list.[15]

George Shultz is Secretary of State, Paul Wolfowitz is in the State Department, and Richard Armitage and Richard Pearl are in the Defense Department when President Reagan is supporting Saddam Hussein and his chemical warfare.

October 1982: MANDALI, Iraq—Iraq uses lethal chemical weapons in battles in the Mandali area.[16]

April 18, 1983: BEIRUT, Lebanon—A suicide bomber drives a truck loaded with high explosives into the U.S. embassy in Beirut. The blast kills 60 people, including 17 Americans. Hours later, an organization called Islamic Jihad claims responsibility.[17]

President Reagan does not retaliate, which encourages more terrorist acts against Americans.

<u>Early 1983</u>: WASHINGTON—Shortly after removing Iraq from the terrorism sponsorship list, the Reagan administration approves the sale of 60 Hughes helicopters to Iraq. Despite some objections from the National Security Council (NSC), the Secretaries of Commerce and State (George Baldridge and George Shultz) lobby the NSC advisor into agreeing to the sale to Iraq of 10 Bell helicopters, officially for crop spraying.

Analysts recognize that "civilian" helicopters can be weaponized in a matter of hours and selling a civilian kit is a way of giving military aid under the guise of civilian assistance. These U.S. Helicopters will be used in 1988 to spray the Kurds with chemical weapons.[18]

Paul Wolfowitz, Richard Armitage, and Richard Pearl are still in the Reagan administration while George Shultz is helping Reagan arm Saddam Hussein.

<u>July 1983</u>: BAGHDAD—Iraq uses lethal chemical weapons against invading Iranian forces.[19]

<u>Fall 1983</u>: BAGHDAD—Iraq uses lethal chemical weapons against Kurdish insurgents.[20]

<u>October 23, 1983</u>: BEIRUT, Lebanon—A suicide bomber from the Islamist group Hezbollah drives a truck full of explosives into U.S. Marine barracks near the Beirut airport killing 241 American soldiers.

Many experts and historians cite this incident as the beginning of America's war with Islamist terrorists.[21]

President Reagan does not retaliate.

<u>November 1, 1983</u>: WASHINGTON—The U.S., which follows developments in the Iran-Iraq war with extraordinary intensity, has intelligence confirming Iran's accusations, and describing Iraq's "almost daily" use of chemical weapons, concurrent with its policy review and decision to support Iraq in the war.

A declassified document notes that Western firms provided the chemical weapons, possibly through a U.S. foreign subsidiary.[22]

<u>Late 1983</u>: The Reagan administration secretly begins to allow Jordan, Saudi Arabia, Kuwait, and Egypt to transfer U.S. howitzers, helicopters, bombs, and other weapons to Iraq. Reagan personally asks Italy's Prime Minister Guilio Andreotti to channel arms to Iraq.[23]

<u>1983–1990</u>: BERLIN—On December 18, 2002, the Berlin daily, *die tageszeitung*, will state it has obtained a copy of part of the document handed by Baghdad to the U.N. on December 7, 2002 with details of its weapons programs. The extract includes a list of foreign companies supplying Iraq, of which more than half—80—are German.

The document identifies 27 German companies, including some of the best-known names in German industry such as Daimler-Benz (prior to its merger with Chrysler of the U.S.), MAN, and Siemens.

The document identifies 24 companies from the U.S., the second-highest tally, and lists the type of weapons program support (nuclear, biological, chemical, rocket, or conventional including building weapons plants) provided by each company. The American companies include Hewlett Packard (nuclear, rocket, and conventional), Honeywell (rocket and conventional), Rockwell (conventional), Bechtel (conventional), ICS (nuclear, rocket, and conventional) and Unisys (nuclear and conventional).

In addition to these 24 companies home-based in the U.S. are 50 subsidiaries of foreign enterprises, which conducted their arms business with Iraq from within the U.S. Also designated as suppliers for Iraq's arms programs (nuclear, biological, chemical and conventional) are the U.S. Departments of Defense, Energy, Trade and Agriculture as well as the Lawrence Livermore, Los Alamos and Sandia National Laboratories.

Great Britain is next in line with 17 companies, including its Ministry of Defense.

The English and German web sites footnoted have all the names of all of the companies—along with their types of weapon program assistance—for all of the countries except for Germany.[24]

The American companies are ramping up Iraq's WMD during the Reagan administration with George Shultz, Paul Wolfowitz, Richard Pearl, Richard Armitage, and Douglas Feith; and the first Bush administration with Dick Cheney, Paul Wolfowitz, and Richard Armitage .

<u>1983–1990</u>: A 1990 study lists 207 firms from 21 countries that contributed to Iraq's non-conventional weapons program during and after the Iran-Iraq war.

Some of the tallies are: West German (86); British (18); Austrian (17); French (16); Italian (12); Swiss (11); and American (18).[25]

This study doesn't exactly match Iraq's 2002 declarations listed above, but it is a similar picture of vast western arms support. One of the reasons why the U.S., Britain, Germany, and so many other industrialized nations thought that Iraq had weapons of mass destruction is they all had firms tripping over each other to make it happen back in the first neocon years.

November 8, 1983: TEHRAN, Iran—By the summer of 1983 Iran is reporting Iraqi use of using chemical weapons for some time according to a declassified State Department document. The Geneva protocol requires that the international community respond to chemical warfare, but a diplomatically isolated Iran receives only a muted response to its complaints. It intensified its accusations in October 1983, however, and in November asks for a U.N. Security Council investigation.[26]

November 21, 1983: WASHINGTON—The intelligence indicates that Iraq used chemical weapons against Iranian forces, and, according to a November 1983 memo, against "Kurdish insurgents" as well.

The declassified State Department document wonders if European nations should be informed that American firms are selling chemical weapon production related technology to Iraq.[27]

November 21, 1983: WASHINGTON—What is the Reagan administration's response? A declassified State Department account indicates that the administration decides to limit its "efforts against the Iraqi Chemical Weapons (CW) program to close monitoring because of our strict neutrality in the Gulf war, the sensitivity of sources, and the low probability of achieving desired results." But the department notes in late November 1983, "with the essential assistance of foreign firms, Iraq had become able to deploy and use CW and probably has built up large reserves of CW for further use. Given its desperation to end the war, Iraq may again use lethal or incapacitating CW, particularly if Iran threatens to break through Iraqi lines in a large-scale attack. Addressee should take no action on this issue until instructed separately."[28]

November 26, 1983: WASHINGTON—The State Department argues that the U.S. needs to respond in some way to maintain the credibility of its official opposition to chemical warfare, and recommends that the National Security Council discuss the issue.

Following further high-level policy review, Ronald Reagan issues National Security Decision Directive (NSDD) 114, dated November 26, 1983, concerning specifically U.S. policy toward the Iran-Iraq war. The directive reflects the administration's priorities: it calls for heightened regional military cooperation to defend oil facilities, and measures to improve U.S. military capabilities in the Persian Gulf, and directs the secretaries of state and defense and the chairman of the Joint Chiefs of Staff to take appropriate measures to respond to tensions in the area. It states, "Because of the real and psychological impact of a curtailment in the flow of oil from the Persian Gulf on the international economic system, we must assure our readiness to deal promptly with actions aimed at disrupting that traffic."

It does not mention chemical weapons.[29]

December 1983: WASHINGTON—After serving as Treasury Secretary in the Nixon administration, George Shultz was Bechtel's president for seven years before he left in 1981 to become Secretary of State in the Reagan administration. While Shultz was America's top diplomat, the U.S. government tried to convince Saddam Hussein to let Bechtel build a pipeline that would have transported Iraq's crude oil through Jordan to the Red Sea port of Aqaba.

Saddam Hussein will nix the proposed pipeline in 1986.

Shultz will return to Bechtel's board of directors in 1989.[30]

December 20, 1983: BAGHDAD—According to declassified confidential document AN: 0830735-0522, Donald Rumsfeld makes the first of two trips to Iraq as a special envoy for President Reagan in order to create close ties between the U.S. and Saddam Hussein. At the time, he is a private citizen, but he had been the Secretary of Defense for the Ford administration. He has a number of items on his agenda, including the conflict in Lebanon. However, one of his main objectives is to establish a direct contact between President Reagan and Iraqi President Saddam Hussein—he carries a letter from Reagan to Saddam to further this process.

His trips, and other overtures by the U.S., are necessary because the Reagan administration has decided to assist Iraq in its war against Iran in order to prevent an Iranian victory, which the administration sees as contrary to U.S. interests. But until the early 1980s, U.S.-Iraqi relations were very cool. Iraq broke off formal diplomatic relations in 1967. In order to enable the U.S. to provide Iraq with various forms of assistance, Iraq had to be removed from the State Department's list of countries supporting terrorism, which was already accomplished. Diplomatic relations needed to be re-established with Iraq, which will occur in November 1984.[31]

December 20, 1983: BAGHDAD—Rumsfeld meets with Saddam, and the two discuss regional issues of mutual interest and share enmity toward Iran and Syria. They also discuss U.S.'s efforts to find alternative routes to transport Iraq's oil since its facilities in the Persian Gulf had been shut down by Iran and Syria had cut off a pipeline that transported Iraqi oil through its territory.

Rumsfeld encourages an increase in oil exports from Iraq as well as the building of a new pipeline through Jordan to Aqaba (a pitch for George Shultz and Bechtel). Saddam considers Israel a threat to the security of such a pipeline.

Rumsfeld makes no attempt to discourage the use of chemical weapons, according to detailed notes on the meeting in the declassified State Department Secret document. It isn't even discussed.[32]

The Reagan administration's private policy toward Iraq's use of chemical weapons is in stark contrast to America's public position against chemical weapons.

March 1984: BAGHDAD—Donald Rumsfeld makes a second trip to Iraq in order to improve ties with Saddam. The declassified briefing notes indicate that President Reagan, Donald Rumsfeld, and George Shultz all three agree on the importance of meeting with and improving relations with Saddam Hussein.[33]

March 20, 1984: WASHINGTON—U.S. intelligence officials say they have "what they believe to be incontrovertible evidence that Iraq has used nerve gas in its war with Iran and has almost finished extensive sites for mass-producing the lethal chemical warfare agent".[34]

March 1984: TEHRAN, Iran—European-based doctors examine Iranian troops and confirm exposure to mustard gas.[35]

August 1984: BAGHDAD—According to the *Washington Post*, in 1984 the CIA secretly began to give Iraq intelligence that Iraq uses to "calibrate" its mustard gas attacks on Iranian troops. In August, the CIA establishes a direct Washington-Baghdad intelligence link, and for 18 months, starting in early 1985, the CIA will provide Iraq with "data from sensitive U.S. satellite reconnaissance photography…to assist Iraqi bombing raids." The *Post*'s source says that this data is essential to Iraq's war effort.[36]

November 26, 1984: WASHINGTON—Diplomatic relations between Iraq and the U.S. are re-established by President Reagan just over a year after Iraq's first well-publicized chemical weapons use and only eight months after the U.N. and U.S. reported that Iraq used chemical weapons on Iranian troops.[37]

1985: WASHINGTON—The U.S. House of Representatives passes a bill to put Iraq back on the State terrorism sponsorship list. After the bill's passage, Secretary of State George Shultz writes to the bill's sponsor, Representative Howard Berman, cites the U.S.' "diplomatic dialogue on this and other sensitive issues," claims that "Iraq has effectively distanced itself from international terrorism," and states that if the U.S. found that Iraq supports groups practicing terrorism "we would promptly return Iraq to the list." Representative Berman drops the bill and explicitly cites Shultz's assurances.[38]

June 1985: BEIRUT—Armed hijackers take control of TWA Flight 847 and divert it to Beirut, where they execute a U.S. Navy diver, Robert Stethem.

President Reagan responds by expanding the federal sky marshal program to include some international flights.[39]

November 1985: WASHINGTON—Iraq's Saad 16 General Establishment's director writes a letter to the Commerce Department detailing the activities in Saad's 70 laboratories. These activities have the trademarks of ballistic missile development.[40]

November 1985: WASHINGTON—The Defense Department's Under Secretary for Trade Security Policy, Stephen Bryen, informs the Commerce Department's Assistant Secretary for Trade Administration in November that intelligence links the Saad 16 research center with ballistic missile development.

Between 1985 and 1990, Commerce will approve many computer sales to Iraq that will go directly to Saad 16. Commerce will approve over $1 million worth of computer equipment for sale to Saad 16 after Commerce received the above-mentioned November letter from Defense.

As of 1991, Saad 16 reportedly will comprise up to 40 percent U.S.-origin equipment.[41]

<u>1985–1990</u>: BAGHDAD—It is Donald Rumsfeld's trips to Baghdad which open up the floodgates during 1985-90 for lucrative U.S. weapons exports—some $1.5 billion worth—including chemical/biological and nuclear weapons equipment and technology, along with critical components for missile delivery systems for all of the above. According to a 1994 GAO Letter Report (GAO/NSIAD-94-98) some 771 weapons export licenses for Iraq are approved during this six year period…not by our European allies, but by the U.S. Department of Commerce.

There are few if any reservations evident in the range of weapons which President Ronald Reagan and his successor George W. H. Bush are willing to sell Saddam Hussein. Under the Arms Export Control Act of 1976, the foreign sale of munitions and other defense equipment and technology could not be sold or diverted to Communist states, nor to those on the U.S. list of terrorist-supporting countries. But Reagan solved this problem when he took Iraq off that list in 1982.

It is through the purchase of $1.5 billion of American "dual-use items," having, sometimes arguably, both military and civilian functions, that Iraq obtains the bulk of its weapons of mass destruction in the late 80s. "Duel-use items" are controlled and licensed by the Department of Commerce under the Export Administration Act of 1979. This is where the real damage is done.[42]

<u>March 21, 1986</u>: NEW YORK—The Security Council could only condemn Iraq by name for using chemical weapons through non-binding presidential statements, over which permanent members of the Security Council do not have an individual veto.

The Security Council President, making a "declaration" and "speaking on behalf of the Security Council," states that the Council members are "profoundly concerned by the unanimous conclusion of the specialists that chemical weapons on many occasions have been used by Iraqi forces against Iranian troops…and the members of the Council strongly condemn this continued use of chemical weapons in clear violation of the Geneva Protocol of 1925 which prohibits the use in war of chemical weapons".

The U.S. [President Ronald Reagan and Secretary of State George Shultz] votes against the issuance of this statement, and the UK, Australia, France, and Denmark abstain. However, the concurring votes of the other 10 members of the Security Council ensure that this statement constitutes the first criticism of Iraq by the Security Council.[43]

<u>May 26, 1986</u>: On secret orders from President Reagan, former national security advisor Robert McFarlane and Marine Lt. Col. Oliver L. North arrive in Tehran to negotiate with Iranian moderates about giving Iran arms in exchange for the release of U.S. hostages.[44]

Publicly President Reagan vows never to deal with terrorists. Privately, he trades arms for hostages providing encouragement that future terrorist acts against Americans will be rewarded.

<u>1986</u>: ASHKELON—Mordechai Vanunu, a technician at Israel's Dimona nuclear power plant, reveals to a London newspaper Israel's secret nuclear weapons program.

Peter Hounam, the journalist who wrote the London *Times* story that quoted Vanunu in 1986, calls Vanunu "a living reminder that Israel is lying about its nuclear weapons…"

After the London *Times'* story breaks, Vanunu is lured to Rome by a woman working for Mossad, Israel's foreign intelligence agency. He says he was drugged and bound by Israeli agents, then hauled back to Israel for a closed-door trial.

He will be convicted on charges of revealing state secrets, sent to prison, and his parents will disown him.[45]

<u>1986</u>: BAGHDAD—Saddam Hussein nixes the proposed Aqaba pipeline pitched by Donald Rumsfeld on behalf of Bechtel while former Bechtel president, George Shultz, is Secretary of State.[46]

<u>November 6, 1986</u>: The secret administrative initiative to sell Iran arms for hostages is revealed. In late November, it becomes known that the Reagan administration diverted proceeds from the arms sales to fund the Nicaraguan Contras. Direct military aid to the Contras had been outlawed by Congress.[47]

Richard Armitage, Douglas Feith, and Richard Pearl are in the Department of Defense during this scandal.

<u>January 1988</u>: WASHINGTON—The Commerce Department approves exports in January and February to Iraq's SCUD missile program's procurement agency. These exports allow Iraq to extend its SCUD range far enough to hit allied soldiers in Saudi Arabia and Israeli civilians in Tel Aviv and Haifa.[48]

<u>February 1988</u>: Iraq—According to the Iraq Liberation Act of 1998, Iraq "forcibly relocated Kurdish civilians from their home villages in the Anfal campaign, killing an estimated 50,000 to 180,000 Kurds."[49]

<u>March 16, 1988</u>: HALABJAH, Iraq—The first bomb flattens the House of Charity mosque. It collapses the dome and topples the minaret, and within minutes hundreds of townspeople are twitching and blistering to death.

The terrible clouds of sarin, cyanide, and mustard gas kill 5,000, over half women and children, and impacts 15,000 other Halabjahans, unwiring their nervous systems or clouding their minds. This little Kurdish town will be inhabited with the slow, the blind, and the lame for years to come.

The chemical attack on Halabjah, which stands as one of the great horrors in modern warfare, will be cited the Bush administration as a principal reason to justify the 2003 war in Iraq.[50]

U.S. intelligence will report in 1991 that the American helicopters sold to Iraq in 1983 with President Reagan's approval were used in 1988 to spray the Kurds with chemicals.[51]

There is no attempt by the neocons during the Reagan and first Bush administrations to punish or even condemn Saddam for this action when prospects for doing business with Iraq appeared bright.

<u>Spring 1988</u>: BAGHDAD—Bechtel is the lead contractor for the PC2 petrochemical complex, producing chemicals with dual civil-military use including a precursor used in mustard gas. The deal is up and running after the Kurds are gassed at Halabjah in 1988.[52]

Bechtel is being paid to help Saddam produce his own mustard gas so that he won't have to depend upon outside sources. Secretary of State George Shultz worked for Bechtel both before and after his stint with the Reagan administration, and he took good care of his company.

<u>May 1988</u>: WASHINGTON—Two months after the Halabjah assault, Peter Burleigh, Assistant Secretary of State in charge of northern Gulf affairs, encourages U.S.-Iraqi corporate cooperation at a symposium hosted by the U.S.-Iraq Business Forum. The U.S.-Iraq Business Forum has strong (albeit unofficial) ties to the Iraqi government.[53]

<u>Summer 1988</u>: ISTANBUL, Turkey—The U.S. Senate Foreign Relations Committee sends a team to Turkey to speak to Iraqi Kurdish refugees and assess

reports that Iraq "was using chemical weapons on its Kurdish population." This report reaffirms that between 1984 and 1988 "Iraq repeatedly and effectively used poison gas on Iran" and that the chemical attack by Iraq on Halabjah left 4,000 to 5,000 people dead.[54]

August 1988: BAGHDAD—The war between Iran and Iraq ends, leaving Iraq's economy in ruins.[55]

August 1988: WASHINGTON—President Reagan is still supporting Saddam with loans, weapons, and high technology even after the conflict with Iran ends, continuing to make financial payments to him in spite of his use of chemical weapons, and his repression within Iraq.[56]

September 8, 1988: WASHINGTON—Following the Halabjah attack and Iraq's August chemical weapons offensive against Iraqi Kurds, the U.S. Senate unanimously passes the "Prevention of Genocide Act of 1988" the day after it is introduced.[57] The act cuts off Iraq from U.S. loans, military and non-military assistance, credits, credit guarantees, items subject to export controls, and U.S. imports of Iraqi oil.[58]

Immediately after the bill's passage, the Reagan administration announces its opposition to the bill[59], and State Department spokesman Charles Redman calls the bill "premature".[60] The administration works with House opponents on a House companion bill, and after numerous legislation compromises and end-of-session haggling, the Senate bill dies "on the last day of the legislative session".[61]

September-December 1988: WASHINGTON—Reagan administration records show that between September and December 1988, 65 licenses were granted for dual-use technology exports to Iraq. This averages out as an annual rate of 260 licenses, more than double the rate for January through August 1988.[62]

President Reagan accelerates the weapons of mass destruction buildup for Iraq, even after Saddam's widespread use of chemicals on civilians, and in spite of the fact that its war with Iran is over. George Shultz is the Secretary of State and Richard Armitage is in the Department of Defense during this process.

December 21, 1988: LOCKERBIE, Scotland—Pan Am Flight 103 explodes and pieces land in the Scottish town of Lockerbie, killing 259 people on the plane and 11 people on the ground.[63]

After learning that Libya is behind the terrorist act, President George H.W. Bush does not retaliate. He has no counterterrorism strategy.

<u>March 24, 1989</u>: WASHINGTON—Secretary of State James Baker receives a State Department memo stating that Iraq is diligently developing chemical and biological weapons, and new missiles, and that Baker is to "express our interest in broadening U.S.-Iraqi ties" to Iraqi Under-Secretary Hamdoon.[64]

<u>1989</u>: WASHINGTON—The State Department releases a report that details Iraq's violation of human rights, including Saddam Hussein use of chemical weapons and torture. President George W. Bush will refer to these atrocities in 2003 when pressing for the removal of Saddam Hussein.

But in spite of the report, the first Bush administration refuses to vote in favor of a U.N. resolution calling for an inquiry into Iraq's actions and possibly indicting Saddam for war crimes and human rights abuses. The two people most vocal about refusing to go along with the U.N. investigation in 1989 are Donald Rumsfeld and Richard Armitage.

The first Bush administration refuses to join the U.N. in publicly protesting the forced relocation of at least half a million ethnic Kurds and Syrians in the late 1980s, even though the act violated principles of the 1948 Genocide Convention. At this time, Dick Cheney is the Secretary of Defense and Paul Wolfowitz is his assistant.

However, in 2003, Vice President Dick Cheney, Defense Secretary Donald Rumsfeld, Deputy Defense Secretary Paul Wolfowitz, and Deputy Secretary of State Richard Armitage will all lobby for a U.N. resolution authorizing an invasion of Iraq, for the very same behavior, and will be highly critical of the countries that refuse to back a U.S. led coalition to use military force to remove Saddam from power.

Saddam Hussein "made it clear that Iraq was not interested in making mischief in the world," Rumsfeld says, who, as a Middle East envoy for the Reagan administration, reopened discussions with Saddam in 1983. "It struck us as useful to have a relationship with him."[65]

<u>1989</u>: Afghanistan—al Qaeda, meaning "the base", is created in 1989 as Soviet forces withdraw from Afghanistan and Osama bin Laden and his colleagues begin looking for new jihads. The organization grows out of the network of Arab volunteers who went to Afghanistan in the 1980s to fight under the banner of Islam against Soviet Communism.

During the anti-Soviet jihad, bin Laden and his fighters received American and Saudi Arabian funding. Some analysts believe bin Laden himself had security training from the CIA during the 1980s.

The "Arab Afghans", as they become known, are battle-hardened and highly motivated. In the early 1990s al Qaeda will operate in Sudan.[66]

1989: WASHINGTON—Although the CIA and the Bush administration know that Iraq's Ministry of Industry and Military Industrialization (MIMI) "controlled entities were involved in Iraq's clandestine nuclear, chemical, and biological weapons programs and missile programs…the Bush administration [approves] dozens of export licenses that [allow] United States and foreign firms to ship sophisticated U.S. dual-use equipment to MIMI-controlled weapons factories".[67]

October 1989: WASHINGTON—When all international banks had cut off loans to Iraq, President Bush signs National Security Directive 26 mandating closer links with Iraq and $1 billion in agricultural loan guarantees. These guarantees provide cash for Iraq to continue to buy and develop WMD, and will be suspended only on August 2, 1990, the same day that Iraq invades Kuwait. Richard Haass, then a National Security Council official, and Robert Kimmitt, Under Secretary of State for Political Affairs, tell the Commerce Department not to single Iraq out for dual-use technology restrictions.[68]

Late 1989: WASHINGTON—One American firm contacts the Commerce Department twice with concerns that their product could be used for nuclear weapons and ballistic missiles. Commerce simply requests Iraqi written guarantees about civilian use, says that a license and review is unnecessary, and convinces the company that the shipment is acceptable.[69]

1990: Richard Armitage admits that the Reagan and Bush administrations are well aware of Saddam's brutality, but still, the U.S. is more interested in maintaining a healthy relationship with Iraq because the country's vast oil reserves are beneficial to U.S. economic interests.

"We knew this wasn't the League of Women Voters," Armitage says, referring to Saddam's regime, according to the Daily News story.[70]

July 18, 1990: WASHINGTON—From July 18 to August 1 (Iraq invaded Kuwait on August 2) the Bush administration approves $4.8 million in advanced technology product sales to Iraq. End-buyers include MIMI and Saad 16. MIMI was identified in 1988 as a facility for chemical, biological, and nuclear weapons programs. In 1989 Saad was linked to chemical and nuclear weapons development.[71]

<u>August 1, 1990</u>: WASHINGTON—The Bush administration approves $695,000 worth of advanced data transmission devices the day before Iraq invades Kuwait.[72]

NOTES TO CHAPTER 5

1 Alan P. Dobson and Steve Marsh, *US Foreign Policy since 1945*, (New York: Routledge, 2001), p. 100.

2 BBC News, "al Qaeda's origins and links", last updated Friday, 16 May, 2003, http://news.bbc.co.uk/1/hi/world/1670089.stm.

3 "HISTORY OF IRAQ", *The Mercury News*, March 21, 2003, p. 10AB.

4 Alan P. Dobson and Steve Marsh, p. 97,100.

5 "HISTORY OF IRAQ",…

6 Reuters, January 12, 2002, http://slick.org/deathwatch/mailarchive/msg00633.html.

7 BBC, "1980: Tehran hostage attempt fails," http://news.bbc.co.uk/onthisday/hi/dates/stories/april/25/newsid_2503000/2503899.stm.

8 Reuters, January 12, 2002, http://slick.org/deathwatch/mailarchive/msg00633.html.

9 "HISTORY OF IRAQ",…; Steve LaRocque, "Congress First Voted to Back Regime Change in Iraq in 1998," U.S. Department of State, September 19, 2002, http://usinfo.state.gov/regional/nea/iraq/text/0919cngr.htm.

10 Nathaniel Hurd, "U.S. Diplomatic and Commercial Relationships with Iraq, 1980—2 August 1990," July 15, 2000, http://www.casi.org.uk/info/usdocs/usiraq80s90s.html#thirtythree, Hurd cites Mark Phythian, <u>Arming Iraq: How the U.S. and Britain Secretly Built Saddam's War Machine</u>, (Boston: Northeastern University Press, 1997), p. 73-74.

11 BBC, "1980: Tehran hostage attempt fails," http://news.bbc.co.uk/onthisday/hi/dates/stories/april/25/newsid_2503000/2503899.stm.

12 Alan P. Dobson and Steve Marsh, p. 116.

13 30 Years Of U.S. UN Vetoes," Information Clearinghouse, March 8, 2003, http://www.informationclearinghouse.info/article2000.htm.

14 Jonathon T. Howe and Richard W. Murphy, "Iraqi Use of Chemical Weapons," Declassified State Department document, November 21, 1983, http://www.gwu.edu/~nsarchiv/NSAEBB/NSAEBB82/iraq25.pdf.

15 Hurd, who cites Milt Freudenheim, Barbara Slavin and William C. Rhoden, "The World in Summary; Readjustments In the Mideast", *The New York Times*, 28 February 1982.

16 Jonathon T. Howe and Richard W. Murphy,…iraq25.pdf.

17 "1983–1991: Target America," *Frontline World*, http://www.pbs.org/frontlineworld/stories/lebanon/tl03.html.

18 Hurd, who cites Mark Phythian, <u>Arming Iraq: How the U.S. and Britain Secretly Built Saddam's War Machine</u>, (Boston: Northeastern University Press, 1997), p. 35-38.

19 Jonathon T. Howe and Richard W. Murphy,…

20 Ibid.

21 Drew Brown, "U.S. battle deaths in Iraq are worst since Vietnam War," *The Mercury News*, April 18, 2004, p. 21A.

22 Jonathon Howe and Richard W. Murphy,…iraq24.pdf.

23 Hurd, who cites Mark Phythian, <u>Arming Iraq: How the U.S. and Britain Secretly Built Saddam's War Machine</u>, (Boston: Northeastern University Press, 1997), p. 35-38.

24 John Hooper in Berlin and Suzanne Goldenberg in Washington, "Germany was 'key supplier' of Saddam supplier," *The Guardian*, December 18, 2002, http://www.guardian.co.uk/Iraq/Story/0,2763,861902,00.html, "The Corporations That Supplied Iraq's Weapons Program," *Die Tageszeitung*, No. 6934, 19 Dec 2002, page 3, http://www.thememoryhole.org/corp/iraq-suppliers.htm (English), http://www.taz.de/pt/2002/12/19/a0080.nf/textdruck (German).

25 Hurd, who cites Leonard A. Cole, <u>The Eleventh Plague: The Politics of Biological and Chemical Warfare</u>, (New York: W.H. Freeman, 1997), p. 243, *n36*. See Seymour M. Hersh, "U.S. Aides Say Iraqis Made Use of a Nerve Gas," *The New York Times* (March 30, 1984), p. 82. Cole cites Kenneth R. Timmerman,

The Poison Gas Connection, (Los Angeles: Simon Wiesenthal Center, 1990) p. 46.

26 Jonathon T. Howe and Richard W. Murphy,…iraq25.pdf.

27 Ibid.

28 Ibid.

29 Ronald Reagan, "U.S. Policy Toward the Iran-Iraq War," Declassified White House National Security Decision Directive, November 26, 1983, http://www.gwu.edu/~nsarchiv/NSAEBB/NSAEBB82/iraq26.pdf.

30 Michael Liedtke, "Bechtel's political clout helps land Iraq reconstruction bid," *The Wichita Eagle*, April 18, 2003, http://www.kansas.com/mld/kansas/business/5662973.htm.

31 Declassified confidential document AN: 0830735-0522, "Rumsfeld Visit to Iraq," http://www.gwu.edu/~nsarchiv/NSAEBB/NSAEBB82/iraq28.pdf.

32 "Rumsfeld Mission: December 20 Meeting with Iraq," Declassified State Department Secret document, December 20, 1983, http://www.gwu.edu/~nsarchiv/NSAEBB/NSAEBB82/iraq31.pdf.

33 Declassified secret document, "Briefing Notes for Rumsfeld Visit to Baghdad," March 1984, http://www.gwu.edu/~nsarchiv/NSAEBB/NSAEBB82/iraq48.pdf.

34 Hurd, who cites Leonard A. Cole,…p. 243, *n36*. See Seymour M. Hersh, "U.S. Aides Say Iraqis Made Use of a Nerve Gas," *The New York Times* (March 30, 1984). Quotation marks are for Hersh's words.

35 Hurd, who cites Bruce W. Jentleson, With Friends Like These: Reagan, Bush, and Saddam, 1982-1990, (New York: W.W. Norton, 1994), p. 78.

36 Hurd, who cites Bob Woodward, "CIA Aiding Iraq in Gulf War; Target Data From U.S. Satellites Supplied for Nearly 2 Years," *Washington Post*, 15 December 1986.

37 Declassified confidential document AN: 0830735-0522,…; and Hurd, who cites Bernard Gwertzman, "U.S. Restores Full Ties With Iraq But Cites Neutrality in Gulf War," *The New York Times*, 27 November 1984.

38 Hurd, who cites Bruce W. Jentleson,…p. 54. Jentleson quotes from Letter from Secretary of State George Shultz to Congressman Howard L. Berman, 20 June 1985.

39 Glen Johnson, "Some want to put marshals on flights or arm airline pilots," *The Boston Globe*, September 16, 2001, http://www.boston.com/news/packages/underattack/globe_stories/0916/Some_want_to_put_marshals_on_flights_or_arm_airline_pilots+.shtml

40 Hurd, who cites Prepared statement of Gary Milhollin, director, Wisconsin Project on Nuclear Arms Control, before the Subcommittee on Technology and National Security of the Joint Economic Committee of the U.S. Congress, 23 April 1991. Cited in Committee on Government Operations, House, "Strengthening the Export Licensing System," 2 July 1991, para.11.

41 Hurd, who cites Committee on Government Operations, House, "Strengthening the Export Licensing System," 2 July 1991, paragraphs 9 and10.

42 Stephen Green, "Rumsfeld Account Book: Who Armed Saddam?" *CounterPunch*, February 24, 2003, http://www.counterpunch.org/green02242003.html.

43 Hurd, who cites S/17911 and Add. 1, 21 March 1986. Note that this is a "decision" and not a resolution.

44 Diana Stickler, "Moments in a life," *The Mercury News*, June 6, 2004, p. 15S.

45 Michael Matza, "Israel frees 'atomic spy'," *The Mercury News*, April 22, 2004, p. 3A.

46 Michael Liedtke, "Bechtel's political clout helps land Iraq reconstruction bid,"…

47 Diana Stickler, "Moments in a life," *The Mercury News*, June 6, 2004, p. 15S.

48 Hurd, who cites Prepared statement of Gary Milhollin,…Cited in…"Strengthening the Export Licensing System," 2 July 1991, par. 25.

49 Steve LaRocque,...

50 Mark McDonald, "Lethal 'blue snow' maimed villagers," *The Mercury News*, June 20, 2004, p. 25A.

51 Hurd, who cites Henry Weinstein and William C. Rempel, "Big Help from U.S.; Technology was Sold with Approval—and Encouragement—from the Commerce Department but Often over Defense Officials' Objections," *The Los Angeles Times*, 13 February 1991.

52 Greg Dropkin, "Bechtel: skeletons in the Iraqi cupboard," April 19, 2003, http://www.labournet.net/world/0304/bechtel1.html.

53 Hurd, who cites Bruce W. Jentleson,...p. 84,85.

54 Hurd, who cites Peter W. Galbraith and Christopher van Hollen, Jr., staff report to the Committee on Foreign Relations, U.S. Senate, <u>Chemical Weapons Use in Kurdistan: Iraq's Final Offensive</u>, October 1988, p. v. and 30.

55 "HISTORY OF IRAQ",...

56 Alan P. Dobson and Steve Marsh, p. 116.

57 Hurd, who cites Bruce W. Jentleson,...p. 78.

58 Hurd, who cites U.S. Senate, "Prevention of Genocide Act of 1988," 100th Congress, 2nd session, 8 September 1988.

59 Hurd, who cites Bruce W. Jentleson,...p. 78.

60 Hurd, who cites Robert Pear,...

61 Hurd, who cites Bruce W. Jentleson,...p. 78.

62 Hurd, who cites Bruce W. Jentleson,...p. 88. Jentleson cites U.S. Department of Commerce, "Approved Licenses to Iraq, 1985-1990".

63 http://www.geocities.com/CapitolHill/5260/headpage.html.

64 Hurd, who cites Bruce W. Jentleson,...p. 107. Jentleson cites and quotes State Department memorandum, "Meeting with Iraqi Under Secretary Hamdoon," 24 March 1989.

65 Jason Leopold, "Rumsfeld, Bush Sr. Refused To Back 1989 UN Resolution To Investigate Iraq For Human Rights Abuses," Information Clearing House, March 13, 2003, http://www.informationclearinghouse.info/article2103.htm.

66 BBC News, "al Qaeda's origins and links",…

67 Hurd, who cites Statement by Rep. Henry Gonzalez (D-Tex), "Details on Iraq's Procurement Network," 102nd Congress, 2nd session, 10 August 1992.

68 Hurd, who cites Douglas Frantz and Murray Waas, "Bush Secret Effort Helped Iraq Build It's War Machine," *Los Angeles Times*, 23 February 1992.

69 Hurd, who cites Bruce W. Jentleson,…p. 110.

70 Jason Leopold, "Rumsfeld, Bush Sr. Refused To Back…"

71 Hurd, who cites Committee on Government Operations, House, "Strengthening the Export Licensing System".

72 Hurd, who cites Stuart Auerbach, "$1.5 Billion in U.S. Sales to Iraq", *Washington Post*, 11 March 1991.

6

The Persian Gulf War

Saddam Hussein's army invades Kuwait and fires 39 scud missiles at Israel. U.S. policy on Iraq turns 180 degrees and General Schwarzkopf drives Saddam's army out of Kuwait. President George H. W. Bush decides not to march on Baghdad to force a regime change. Iraq's WMD programs are starved for funds due to U.N. sanctions. Iraq is no longer purchasing arms from western firms and U.S. and Britain start bombing raids on existing Iraqi weapons facilities.

The lucrative relationship between Defense Secretary Dick Cheney and Halliburton begins with a contract for the firm. Osama bin Laden's al Qaeda terrorist group attacks the World Trade Center for the first time. Many war victims of Gulf War Syndrome sue several American companies for providing Iraq with chemical weapons technology. The French foil an attempt by Algerian hijackers to slam a plane into the Eiffel Tower. Halliburton awards Dick Cheney with the firm's CEO position.

Neoconservatives form the Project for a New American Century and press for a regime change in Iraq. Osama bin Laden declares war against the U.S. Paul Wolfowitz presses for a regime change in Iraq. The Clinton administration and CIA Director George Tenet shift the national security focus more toward counterterrorism. Al Qaeda attacks the USS *Cole,* killing 17 sailors. More terror warnings follow. The abuse of prisoners is common in the U.S.—especially Texas. Dick Cheney receives a golden handshake from Halliburton and runs for Vice President.

August 2, 1990: BAGHDAD—Saddam's army invades Kuwait.[1]

Saddam blames high Kuwaiti oil production on the falling price of oil, and also has disagreements with Kuwait on territory and money owed.

August 1990: WASHINGTON—U.S. foreign policy on Saddam Hussein changes 180 degrees. There will be no more weapons and loans for Iraq, Saddam is now considered a liability, and the U.S. favors a regime change in Iraq. The speed, nature, and intensity of the U.S. response cause great discussion. Is it motivated by concern for oil, human rights, non-proliferation of weapons of mass destruction, territorial integrity of Kuwait, or by revenge for Saddam Hussein's 'betrayal?'[2]

Late 1990: NEW YORK—U.N. Sanctions are placed on Iraq limiting the sale of oil and invoking import restrictions.[3]

This action severely frustrates Saddam's weapons programs.

1990–1999: From November 1990 to December 1999, Saddam Hussein repeatedly violates 16 United Nations Security Council Resolutions (UNSCRs) designed to ensure that Iraq does not pose a threat to international peace and security.[4]

January 12, 1991: BAGHDAD—The American Congress authorizes military force against Iraq due to the invasion of Kuwait.[5]

January 16, 1991: BAGHDAD—President Bush orders the air strikes for Operation Desert Storm to begin.[6]

January 17, 1991: TEL AVIV—Iraq launches its first Scud missile strikes on Tel Aviv and Haifa in Israel. Another Scud fired at U.S. forces in Saudi Arabia is shot down by a U.S. Patriot missile—the first of many mid-air interceptions.

Israel says it will not be drawn into retaliation, relying instead on batteries of U.S. Patriot missiles hastily stationed on its territory. In total, 39 Scud missiles are fired into Israel, causing damage but few casualties.[7]

February 1991: Kuwait—The Iraq army retreats from Kuwait and heads back to Iraq. General Schwarzkopf bombs the elite Iraqi Republican Guard units on their way home.

There is no plan to march on Baghdad or occupy Iraq, and no advocates for such a costly and reckless plan—until the mid-nineties when the neocons will call for regime change. However, if Schwarzkopf is allowed to destroy the Republican Guard, Saddam's regime might fall.

Schwarzkopf is ordered to stop the bombing.

With his Republican Guard units intact, Saddam orders the massacre of the Iraqi Shiites and Kurds who had rebelled against him. The Shiites will remember for years how Washington had called on them to rise up, but did nothing while they were slaughtered.[8]

April 3, 1991: NEW YORK—The U.N. passes Resolution 687, establishing a cease-fire in the Persian Gulf War and setting terms for gradual lifting of sanctions. The resolution says that Iraq will destroy its weapons of mass destruction and comply with weapons monitoring. Iraq accepts the terms on April 6.[9]

May 1991: President George H. W. Bush signs a presidential directive instructing the CIA to create the conditions for Saddam Hussein's removal.[10]

Due to this directive, the CIA started funding the Iraqi National Accord led by Iyad Allawi. During the 1990's, Allawi's group smuggled car bombs and other explosive devices into Iraq and used the weapons in terrorist acts to destabilize Saddam's regime. In late May 2004, Allawi will become the Prime Minister of Iraq and will threaten strong measures against the terrorists who use car bombs and other explosives to destabilize Iraq.[11]

June 9, 1991: BAGHDAD—The U.N. Special Commission (UNSCOM) begins weapons inspections in Iraq.[12]

June 28, 1991: BAGHDAD—Iraq denies access to U.N. weapons inspectors, the first of many blocked inspections.[13]

1992: WASHINGTON—Halliburton subsidiary Brown and Root is paid $9 million to prepare a classified report for the Pentagon under Defense Secretary Dick Cheney detailing how private companies (like itself, for example) could provide logistical support for American troops in potential war zones around the world. Shortly after this report, the Pentagon awards Brown and Root a five-year contract to provide logistics for the U.S. Army Corp of Engineers. The GAO estimates that through this contract, Brown and Root made $2.2 billion in the Balkans.[14]

1992–1994: In 1992 and again in 1994, hearings are conducted by the Senate Banking, Housing and Urban Affairs Committee, which has Senate oversight responsibility for the Export Administration Act. The purpose of the hearings is the Committee's concern that "tens of thousands" of Gulf War veterans are suffering from symptoms associated with the "Gulf War Syndrome", possibly due to their exposure to chemical and biological agents that had been exported from the

U.S. during that brief period of "normalization" of relations with Iraq in 1985-90.[15]

President Reagan and the neocons leave quite a legacy.

December 1992: SANAA, Yemen—Al Qaeda attacks a hotel in Yemen where U.S. military personnel are staying.[16]

February 26, 1993: NEW YORK—At approximately 12:18 p.m., an improvised explosive device explodes on the second level of the World Trade Center parking basement. The resulting blast produces a crater, approximately 150 feet in diameter and five floors deep, in the parking basement. The structure consists mainly of steel-reinforced concrete, 12 to 14 inches thick. The epicenter of the blast is approximately eight feet from the south wall of Trade Tower Number One, near the support column K31/8. The device had been placed in the rear cargo portion of a one-ton Ford F350 Econoline van, owned by the Ryder Rental Agency, Jersey City, New Jersey. Approximately 6,800 tons of material are displaced by the blast.

The attack is attributed to the terrorist group al Qaeda.[17]

This is the first time that al Qaeda attacked the World Trade Center. Should their selection of this target in 2001 come as a complete surprise?

April 1993: KUWAIT CITY—The Kuwaitis announce they have broken up an Iraqi plot to assassinate the first President Bush as he was visiting Kuwait.[18]

May 8, 1993: WASHINGTON—The Clinton administration concludes that there is credible evidence that the government of Iraq tried to assassinate former President George Bush.[19]

June 27, 1993: BAGHDAD—President Clinton orders U.S. forces to launch a missile attack on the Iraqi intelligence headquarters in Al-Mansur district, Baghdad, in retaliation for the attempted assassination of President Bush in Kuwait.[20]

In marked contrast to President Reagan who never retaliated, President Clinton takes action. Since then, Saddam hasn't committed any acts of violence against the United States.

September 1993: UNITED NATIONS—When President Clinton speaks to the U.N., he lists four criteria for future interventions: (1) clear mission objectives,

(2) palpable danger to international peace, (3) a clear exit strategy, and (4) calculable costs.[21]

<u>October 1993</u>: MOGADISHU, Somalia—Two helicopters are shot down, 18 American servicemen are killed, and angry mobs drag the bodies of American soldiers through the streets of Mogadishu. The battle inspires the movie *Black Hawk Down*.[22]

<u>November 26, 1993</u>: BAGHDAD—Iraq agrees to cooperate with U.N. Resolution 715, which mandates U.N. inspections to prevent Iraq from developing weapons of mass destruction.[23]

<u>April 6, 1994</u>: NKONGI, Rwanda—A plane crash kills Rwandan President Juvenal Habyarimana, a Hutu, and his Burundian counterpart, Cyprien Ntaryamira, who were attending a regional summit in Arusha, Tanzania.[24]

<u>April 7, 1994</u>: NKONGI, Rwanda—When it becomes clear the plane was shot down, Hutu extremists accuse Tutsis of assassinating the Rwandan president and begin attacking their longtime ethnic foes. The slaughter lasts about 100 days and claims the lives of an estimated 500,000 to 800,000 Tutsis and moderate Hutus.[25]

The U.N. and the U.S. take no action throughout the entire crisis. This is the low point of the Clinton administration.

<u>1994</u>: HOUSTON—A group of 26 veterans, suffering from what has come to be known as Gulf War Syndrome, file a billion-dollar lawsuit in Houston against Fisher, Rhone-Poulenc, Bechtel Group, and Lummus Crest, as well as American Type Culture Collection (ATCC) and six other firms, for helping Iraq to obtain or produce the compounds which the veterans blamed for their illnesses. By 1998, the number of plaintiffs will rise to more than 4,000 and the suit is still pending in Texas.[26]

<u>1994</u>: PARIS—French authorities foil an attempt by Algerian hijackers to slam a plane into the Eiffel Tower in Paris.[27]

<u>November 10, 1994</u>: BAGHDAD—The Iraqi National Assembly recognizes Kuwait's borders and its independence.[28]

January 1995: MANILA—Philippine police complete a report outlining three terrorist plots after they shut down a terrorist cell. According to the report, one of the plots details the use of hijacked airliners to hit targets, including the CIA headquarters in Langley, Virginia, the Pentagon, and the World Trade Center.

One member of the cell is Ramzi Yousef, the mastermind behind the 1993 World Trade Center bombing. Yousef was convicted in the United States for plotting to blow up U.S. airliners in Asia.[29]

Al Qaeda starts preparing a major attack against the U.S.

April 14, 1995: NEW YORK—UNSC Resolution 986 allows the partial resumption of Iraq's oil exports to buy food and medicine, the "oil for food" program. It will not be accepted by Iraq until May 1996, and it won't start until December 1996.[30]

April 19, 1995: OKLAHOMA CITY—A truck filled with a fertilizer bomb explodes in front of the Alfred P. Murrah federal building in Oklahoma City, Oklahoma killing 168 people in America's worst domestic terrorist attack.

1995: Former Congressman Paul Findley notes in his book, *Deliberate Deceptions: Facing the Facts About the US-Israeli Relationship*, that Israel was in violation of 68 U.N. Resolutions from 1955 to 1992.[31]

1995–2001: WASHINGTON—Vice President Dick Cheney's easy transition from Secretary of Defense to private industry and then to Vice President has earned him millions and Dallas-based Halliburton billions.

Cheney took over as chief executive of Halliburton in 1995. In 1998 he took home $4.4 million in salary and benefits and in 1999 he was paid $1.92 million, according to the company's own financial reports. In May 2000 he cashed in 100,000 Halliburton shares to net another $5.1 million and then sold the rest of his shares in August 2000 for $18.5 million, adding up to a total of almost $30 million in just two years, a tidy sum for a man with no previous experience in running a company, let alone an energy multinational.

In 2000 and 2001 Cheney and his lobbyist, David Gribbin, notch up $1.5 billion in federal loans and insurance subsidies compared to the paltry $100 million that the company received in the five years prior to Cheney's arrival. The federal subsidies support Halliburton's oil services contracts in Algeria, Angola, Bangladesh, and Russia. In addition the company garners $2.3 billion in U.S.

government contracts during that time, or almost double the $1.2 billion it earned from the government in the five years before he arrived.

Not surprisingly, all this work stems from a new scheme to privatize operations of the U.S. military that were drawn up by Halliburton itself under contract to Cheney in 1992.[32]

October 15, 1995: BAGHDAD—Saddam Hussein wins a referendum allowing him to remain in power for seven more years.[33]

November 1995: RIYADH—A truck bomb kills seven at an American-run training center for the Saudi Arabian National Guard.[34]

January 1996: WASHINGTON—The CIA's Counterterrorism Center creates a special unit focusing on Osama bin Laden after his involvement in planning and directing terrorist acts becomes more evident to the U.S. intelligence community.[35]

1996: MANILA—There is an Islamic terrorist conspiracy during 1996 in the Philippines to hijack a dozen airplanes and fly them into CIA headquarters and other buildings. The conspiracy includes a plot for a "bojinka"—a big bang. The information will be discovered on a computer and will be noted in the 1997 trial of Ramzi Yousef, one of the 1993 World Trade Center bombers.[36]

Al Qaeda isn't the only group that wants to use planes as missiles to attack American targets.

Early 1996: KHARTOUM, Sudan—After harboring bin Laden since his 1991 expulsion from Saudi Arabia, Sudan offers to turn al Qaeda's founder over to the Saudis for trial. Saudi Arabia doesn't want him. In May, Sudan throws bin Laden out; he and his family go to Afghanistan.[37]

May 12, 1996: WASHINGTON—Leslie Stahl interviews Madeleine Albright in reference to the economic sanctions against Iraq.

Stahl: We have heard that over half a million children have died. I mean, that's more than died in Hiroshima. And, you know, is the price worth it?

Albright: I think this is a very hard choice. But the price—we think the price is worth it.[38]

<u>1996</u>: Al Qaeda's headquarters and about a dozen training camps move to Afghanistan, where bin Laden forges a close relationship with the Taliban. In this year, al Qaeda kills 19 U.S. soldiers in Saudi Arabia.[39]

<u>1996</u>: RANGOON—Halliburton subsidiary European Marine Contractors (EMC) helps lay the offshore portion of the Yadana natural gas pipeline in Burma. Several human rights organizations allege that tremendous human rights abuses are associated with the project, as thousands of villagers in Burma are forced to work in support of the pipeline and related infrastructure. Many lose their homes due to forced relocation, and there are reports of rape, torture, and killings by soldiers hired by the companies as security guards for the pipelines.[40]

Dick Cheney is CEO of Halliburton at the time.

<u>August 31, 1996</u>: BAGHDAD—In response to a call for aid from the KDP, Iraqi forces launch an offensive into the northern no-fly zone and capture Arbil (Kurdish area).[41]

<u>September 3, 1996</u>: BAGHDAD—The U.S. extends the northern limit of the southern no-fly zone to latitude 33 degrees north, just south of Baghdad.[42]

<u>June 3, 1997</u>: WASHINGTON—Quintessential neoconservatives form the non-profit, "educational" organization: The Project for a New American Century (PNAC). The group supports significant increases in defense spending, and then recommends using it. Noting that the United States stands as the world's preeminent power, the use of the U.S. military is urged to achieve global leadership and to shape a new century favorable to American principles and interests. By early 1998, the group will be aggressively promoting a war in Iraq to depose Saddam Hussein. The 25 inaugural members include: Jeb Bush, Dick Cheney, Steve Forbes, Dan Quayle, Donald Rumsfeld, and Paul Wolfowitz; Richard L. Armitage and Richard Perle join soon thereafter.[43]

<u>January 10, 1998</u>: HOUSTON—During his chairmanship of Halliburton, Cheney criticizes U.S. sanctions against "rogue" nations such as Iran and Libya in a speech. According to a *Washington Post* story, Cheney complains the sanctions "are nearly always motivated by domestic political pressure, the need for Congress to appeal to some domestic constituency."[44]

Dick Cheney doesn't want any sanctions to interfere with Halliburton profits, no matter how hostile the nations are.

January 26, 1998: WASHINGTON—Members of the Project for a New American Century send President Clinton a letter strongly urging him to abandon the current containment policy and remove Saddam Hussein from power. This action, including military steps, is needed to protect our "vital interests" in the Gulf.

The signatures on the letter include Donald Rumsfeld, Paul Wolfowitz, Richard L. Armitage, Richard Perle, as well as William Kristol and Robert Kagan.[45]

Iraq has the second largest oil reserves in the world, but there is no hope of gaining lucrative contracts for American companies in the future due to the 1991 war where the U.S. defeated Iraq. The neocons advocate regime change in Iraq, which would open up billions in oil development and reconstruction contracts for U.S. companies.

April 13, 1998: The U.S. Navy begins the first shipments of Vietnam-era napalm to a disposal site halfway across the country. More than 23 million pounds of the jellied gasoline mixture has been stored at Fallbrook Naval Weapons Facility, about 60 miles north of San Diego.[46]

1998: WASHINGTON—President Bill Clinton and House Speaker Newt Gingrich, R-GA. put together a bipartisan 14-member panel to make sweeping strategic recommendations on how the United States could ensure its security in the 21st century. It is called the Commission on National Security/21st century, and is chaired by former Colorado Senator Gary Hart (D) and former Senator Warren Rudman (R).[47]

May 26, 1998: Afghanistan—Osama bin Laden holds a news conference in Afghanistan declaring war on the United States. Information obtained by senior U.S. policy makers and the intelligence community indicates that bin Laden intends to strike.[48]

June 1998: WASHINGTON—Several sources reveal to the U.S. intelligence community that bin Laden is considering attacks in the United States—targeting cities such as Washington and New York. Senior U.S. officials receive this information a month later.

The U.S. intelligence community consists of the 14 government agencies that conduct the U.S. government's intelligence activities, including the CIA, Treasury Department, Energy Department, State Department, Defense Intelligence

Agency, FBI, National Imagery and Mapping Agency, National Reconnaissance Office, National Security Agency, and the intelligence agencies for the U.S. Air Force, Army, Coast Guard, Marine Corps and Navy.[49]

<u>June 23, 1998</u>: WASHINGTON—"The good lord didn't see fit to put oil and gas only where there are democratic regimes friendly to the United States," says Dick Cheney at a speech at the CATO Institute.[50]

<u>August 7, 1998</u>: Africa—Nearly simultaneous al Qaeda car bombings hit the U.S. embassies in Dar es Salaam, Tanzania, and Nairobi, Kenya, killing 224 people in all. A total of 17 people are indicted for the attacks by al Qaeda, including Osama bin Laden and seven other fugitives.[51]

<u>August 1998</u>: Afghanistan—In retaliation for the car bombings at two U.S. embassies in Africa, President Clinton orders a cruise missile to be fired into al Qaeda's Afghan camp.[52]

Unfortunately, this doesn't stop al Qaeda. It is easier to create a deterrent against an actual country such as Libya or Iraq than a rogue group of terrorists.

<u>August 1998</u>: WASHINGTON—The FBI and the Federal Aviation Administration (FAA) receive information that unidentified Arabs plan to fly an "explosive-laden plane" from an unnamed country into the World Trade Center. The FAA finds the plot "highly unlikely given the state of that foreign country's aviation program." Skeptical FAA officials also believe a flight originating outside the United States would be detected before it reaches its target. The FBI's New York office files away the information.[53]

The plan to use planes as missiles is still in progress, and their favorite target hasn't changed.

<u>September 1998</u>: WASHINGTON—The intelligence community details the infrastructure of al Qaeda in the United States. Also, intelligence information indicates bin Laden's next plan could be to fly an aircraft loaded with explosives into a U.S. airport and then detonate the plane.[54]

<u>September 17, 1998</u>: WASHINGTON—Paul Wolfowitz makes a statement before the House National Security Committee. He rejects the Clinton administration policy of containment of Saddam Hussein, and advocates liberating the Iraqi people from Saddam via regime change. He states that the key lies not in

marching U.S. soldiers into Baghdad, but in helping the Iraqi people to liberate themselves from Saddam. The heart of such action would be to create a liberated zone in Southern Iraq comparable to what the United States and its partners did so successfully in the North in 1991.

Wolfowitz further notes that Russia and France (and not the United States) have lucrative Iraqi oil contracts and that the sought after Southern zone contains the largest oil field in Iraq.[55]

While the vast oil reserves in Iraq are still on his mind, once in the Bush administration, Wolfowitz gives up his "Southern zone" strategy and favors marching U.S. soldiers directly into Baghdad.

October 1998: WASHINGTON—U.S. intelligence officials learn that al Qaeda is trying to establish an operative cell within the United States.[56]

October 31, 1998: BAGHDAD—Iraq ends cooperation with UNSCOM to inspect for weapons of mass destruction, and inspectors withdraw from Iraq.[57]

November 1998: WASHINGTON—The intelligence community is notified that an al Qaeda terrorist cell is trying to recruit a group of five to seven young men from the United States to travel to the Middle East for training.

Intelligence officials also learn that bin Laden and senior associates have agreed to offer a $9 million reward for the assassinations of four top CIA officers.[58]

December 16-19, 1998: BAGHDAD—After U.N. personnel are evacuated from Baghdad, the U.S. and Britain launch a bombing campaign, "Operation Desert Fox," to destroy Iraq's nuclear, chemical, and biological weapons programs.[59]

The U.N. economic sanctions, the end of western firms doing business to support Iraq's weapons programs, and these bombing raids were more effective in eradicating Saddam's illicit weapons, which were amassed during the Reagan/ Bush years, than many realized.

December 1998: WASHINGTON—George Tenet announces in a memorandum to his senior staff at the CIA that they would henceforth be at war with al Qaeda. "I want no resources or people spared," he writes.

In practice, the Sept. 11 Commission will conclude in 2004 that Mr. Tenet's declaration of war, which the CIA director will frequently cite in his public testimony after the attacks, has "little overall effect."[60]

February 19, 1999: AN-NAJAF, Iraq—Grand Ayatollah Sayyid Muhammad Sadiq al-Sadr, the spiritual leader of the Shiite sect, is assassinated in An-Najaf.[61]

1999: WASHINGTON—Since the fall of the Soviet Union, experts have predicted that the next worldwide scourge would be terrorism. There are literally dozens of reports, studies, and court cases in which hijackings, including those that would end up with crashes into buildings, were discussed.

In 1999, the Federal Research Division at the Library of Congress publishes its own report entitled "The Sociology and Psychology of Terrorism: Who Becomes a Terrorist and Why?" which indicates that "Suicide bomber(s) belonging to al Qaeda's Martyrdom Battalion could crash-land an aircraft packed with high explosives (C-4 and semtex) into the Pentagon, the headquarters of the Central Intelligence Agency, or the White House."[62]

More clues about planes used as missiles against marquee U.S. targets.

1999: WASHINGTON—The FBI creates a unit that focuses on bin Laden. By September 10, 2001, about 17 to 19 people are working in that division.[63]

1999–2000: Corrections officials, inmates, and human rights advocates will say in 2004 that physical and sexual abuse of prisoners, similar to what will be uncovered in Iraq in early 2004, takes place in U.S. prisons with little public knowledge or concern.

According to corrections experts, some of the worst abuses are occurring in Texas, whose prisons are under a federal consent decree during much of the time George W. Bush is governor because of violence by guards against inmates and because of overcrowding. A federal district judge, William Wayne Justice, imposes the decree after finding that guards were allowing inmate gang leaders to buy and sell other inmates as slaves for sex.

In a 1999 opinion, Justice writes of the situation in Texas, "Many inmates credibly testified to the existence of violence, rape, and extortion in the prison system and about their own suffering from such abysmal conditions."

In a Texas case beginning in 2000, a prisoner at the Allred Unit in Wichita Falls is repeatedly raped by other inmates, even after he appeals to guards for help, and is allowed by prison staff to be treated like a slave, being bought and sold by various prison gangs in different parts of the prison. The inmate, Roderick Johnson will file a suit against the Texas Department of Criminal Justice and the case will be before the federal 5th Circuit Court of Appeals in New Orleans in

2004, according to Kara Gotsch, public policy coordinator for the National Prison Project of the American Civil Liberties Union.[64]

There is no public evidence that Governor Bush is troubled by this abuse or makes any attempt to rectify the situation.

Spring 1999: WASHINGTON—The intelligence community is notified that bin Laden is planning an attack on a U.S. government facility in Washington.[65]

September 1999: WASHINGTON—Two years before the Sept. 11 attacks, an analysis prepared for U.S. intelligence warns that Osama bin Laden's terrorists could hijack an airliner and fly it into government buildings like the Pentagon.

"Suicide bomber(s) belonging to al Qaeda's Martyrdom Battalion could crash-land an aircraft packed with high explosives (C-4 and semtex) into the Pentagon, the headquarters of the Central Intelligence Agency (CIA), or the White House," the September 1999 report says.[66]

Late 1999: WASHINGTON—Intelligence information raises the possibility of attacks on targets in Washington and New York during the New Year's millennium celebrations.[67]

December 14, 1999: PORT ANGELES—Ahmed Ressam is arrested in Port Angeles, Washington as he tries to enter the United States from Canada. A U.S. Customs Service officer searches his rented car and finds 130 pounds of explosive chemicals and four homemade timing devices. Ressam will later be convicted of conspiracy to detonate a suitcase bomb at the Los Angeles International Airport on New Year's Eve of 1999, the last day before the new millennium. He is yet to be sentenced.[68]

December 17, 1999: WASHINGTON—UNSC Resolution 1284 creates the U.N. Monitoring, Verification and Inspection Commission (UNMOVIC) to replace UNSCOM. Iraq rejects the resolution.[69]

December 1999: HOUSTON—It will be revealed in 2003 that while Vice President Cheney was Halliburton's CEO, the number of its subsidiary companies in offshore tax havens increased from 9 (in 1995) to 44 (in 1999). One of these subsidiaries, Halliburton Products and Services Ltd., incorporated in the Cayman Islands will be used starting in 2000 to get around sanctions on doing business in Iran.[70]

Halliburton's federal taxes drop dramatically from $302 million in 1998 to an $85 million rebate in 1999.[71]

January 2000: KUALA LUMPUR—Khalid al-Midhar and Nawaf Alhamzi—two of the hijackers aboard American Airlines Flight 77, which will crash into the Pentagon in 2001—are seen on a surveillance tape at a meeting in January 2000 at a hotel in Kuala Lumpur, Malaysia. Also at the meeting is Tawfiq al-Atash, who will play a hand in the Cole's bombing U.S. officials will later suspect. The CIA will say it warned the FBI about al-Midhar but the CIA also will not place him on a watch list until August 2001.[72]

March 1, 2000: NEW YORK—Hans Blix becomes the executive chairman of UNMOVIC.[73]

August 2000: WASHINGTON—Dick Cheney leaves his position as Halliburton's CEO to run as Bush's Vice President. Halliburton announces that it is giving Cheney a retirement package worth more than $33.7 million. Under public pressure, Cheney sells company stock worth $30 million.[74]

October 5, 2000: DANBURY, Kentucky—During the 2000 campaign in a broadcasted vice presidential candidates' debate with Joe Lieberman, Cheney asserts that, "the government has absolutely nothing to do" with his financial success as Chairman at Halliburton.[75]

October 6, 2000: JAKARTA—Indonesia Corruption Watch names Kellogg Brown and Root (Halliburton's engineering division) as one of 59 companies using collusive, corrupt, and nepotistic practices in business deals involving former president Suharto's family.[76]

October 12, 2000: ADEN, Yemen—A small boat filled with explosives is detonated next to the USS *Cole* blasting a hole in its side while it is stationed in Aden, Yemen. In the attack, 17 sailors are killed and 39 are injured.[77]

October 2000: According to current and former government officials familiar with terrorism intelligence, who speak on condition of anonymity, one report in August 2001 will have uncorroborated information that two bin Laden operatives meet in October 2000 to discuss a plot to attack the U.S. Embassy in Nairobi using an airplane.

This report will state the operative would either bomb the embassy using the airplane or fly the airplane into it.[78]

October 23, 2000: WASHINGTON—Richard Clarke, the National Security Council adviser who heads U.S. counterterrorism efforts, reports on the USS *Cole* attack, which is very similar to the 1998 attacks on two U.S. embassies. He says Osama bin Laden usually sends people into a country years before an attack in order to lay the groundwork.[79]

October 2000: BAGHDAD—Iraq resumes domestic passenger flights, the first since the 1991 Gulf War.[80]

NOTES TO CHAPTER 6

1 Alan P. Dobson and Steve Marsh, *US Foreign Policy since 1945*, (New York: Routledge, 2001), p. 116.

2 Ibid.

3 *Reuters*, December 29, 1999.

4 "Saddam Hussein's Defiance of United Nations Resolutions," *The White House*, http://www.whitehouse.gov/infocus/iraq/decade/sect2.html.

5 "Gulf War," Wikipedia, http://en.wikipedia.org/wiki/Gulf_War.

6 Ibid.

7 "Saddam's Iraq: Key events," *BBC News*, http://news.bbc.co.uk/1/shared/spl/hi/middle_east/02/iraq_events/html/scuds.stm.

8 Richard Clarke, *Against All Enemies: Inside America's War on Terror*, (New York: Free Press, 2004), p. 64-66.

9 "AMERICA AT WAR: UNDERSTANDING THE CONFLICT", *The Mercury News*, March 21, 2003, p. 5AB.

10 "Iraqi National Congress," http://www.disinfopedia.org/wiki.phtml?title=Iraqi_National_Congress.

11 Robert Scheer (LAT), "Republic of Irony: CIA's man takes over," *The Mercury News*, July 2, 2004, p. 9C.

12 "AMERICA AT WAR: UNDERSTANDING THE CONFLICT",…p. 5AB.

13 Ibid.

14 GAO report, September 2000, http://www.gao.gov/archive/2000/ns00225.pdf.

15 Stephen Green, "Rumsfeld Account Book: Who Armed Saddam?" *CounterPunch*, February 24, 2003, http://www.counterpunch.org/green02242003.html.

16 David Johnston and Jim Dwyer, "Pre-9/11 Files Show Warnings Were More Dire and Persistent," *The New York Times*, April 18, 2004, Section 1, Page 1.

17 Dave Williams, "The Bombing of the World Trade Center in New York City", *International Criminal Police Review*—No 469-471 (1998).

18 Ibid.

19 Barton Gellman and Ann Devroy, "Iraq linked to attempt to kill Bush", *The Mercury News*, May 8, 1993, p. 1A.

20 "AMERICA AT WAR: UNDERSTANDING THE CONFLICT",…p. 5AB.

21 Alan P. Dobson and Steve Marsh, *US Foreign Policy since 1945*, (New York: Routledge, 2001), p. 102.

22 Mark Bowden, "The lesson of Mogadishu," The Wall Street Journal, April 5, 2004, http://www.opinionjournal.com/editorial/feature.html?id=110004911.

23 "AMERICA AT WAR: UNDERSTANDING THE CONFLICT",…p. 5AB.

24 "Mysterious plane crash 'black box' discovered," *The Mercury News*, March 12, 2004, p. 10AA.

25 "Mysterious plane crash 'black box' discovered," *The Mercury News*, March 12, 2004, p. 10AA; and Sudarsan Raghavan, "Witnesses for Rwanda genocide tribunals are intimidated, slain," *The Mercury News*, April 7, 2004, p. 10A.

26 Greg Dropkin, "Bechtel: skeletons in the Iraqi cupboard," April 19, 2003, http://www.labournet.net/world/0304/bechtel1.html.

27 U.S. Joint Inquiry Staff, "Was US informed before attack," *CNN.com*, http://www.mtmi.vu.lt/wtc/questions/02do_they_informed_before2.htm.

28 "AMERICA AT WAR: UNDERSTANDING THE CONFLICT",…p. 5AB.

29 U.S. Joint Inquiry Staff, "Was US informed before attack,"…

30 "AMERICA AT WAR: UNDERSTANDING THE CONFLICT",...p. 5AB.

31 Paul Findley, "Deliberate Deceptions: Facing the Facts About US-Israeli Relationship," Lawrence Hill Books, 1995; and "A List of U.N. SECURITY COUNCIL RESOLUTIONS against Israel," *Middle East News & World Report*, http://www.middleeastnews.com/unresolutionslist.html.

32 Pratap Chatterjee, *Dick Cheney: Soldier of Fortune*, May 2, 2002, http://www.corpwatch.org/issues/PID.jsp?articleid=2469.

33 "AMERICA AT WAR: UNDERSTANDING THE CONFLICT",...p. 6AB.

34 David Johnston and Jim Dwyer,...

35 U.S. Joint Inquiry Staff, "Was US informed before attack,"...

36 Carl Cameron, "Clues Alerted White House to Potential Attacks." Fox news, May 17, 2002, http://www.foxnews.com/story/0,2933,53065,00.html.

37 U.S. Joint Inquiry Staff, "Was US informed before attack,"...

38 Leslie Stahl, "60 Minutes," May 12, 1996.

39 BBC News, "al Qaeda's origins and links", last updated Friday, 16 May, 2003, http://news.bbc.co.uk/1/hi/world/1670089.stm.

40 Earthrights International, http://www.earthrights.org/halliburton/hallintro.shtml.

41 "AMERICA AT WAR: UNDERSTANDING THE CONFLICT",...p. 6AB.

42 Ibid.

43 http://www.newamericancentury.org/.

44 "A Halliburton Primer," *Washingtonpost.com*, July 11, 2002, http://www.washingtonpost.com/wp-srv/onpolitics/articles/halliburtonprimer.html.

45 *Project for a New American Century*, January 16, 1998, http://www.newamericancentury.org/iraqclintonletter.htm.

46 "Vietnam-era napalm finally headed to disposal site," CNN, April 13, 1998, http://www.cnn.com/US/9804/13/napalm.shipments/.

47 Jake Tapper, "We predicted it," Salon.com, September 12, 2001, http://dir.salon.com/politics/feature/2001/09/12/bush/index.html.

48 U.S. Joint Inquiry Staff, "Was US informed before attack,"…

49 Ibid.

50 Richard B. Cheney, "Defending Liberty in a Global Economy," speech at the CATO Institute, June 23, 1998, http://www.cato.org/speeches/sp-dc062398.html.

51 "CARNAGE IN MADRID," *The Mercury News*, March 12, 2004, p. 6AA.

52 U.S. Joint Inquiry Staff, "Was US informed before attack,"…

53 Ibid.

54 Ibid.

55 *Project for a New American Century*, September 18, 1998, http://www.newamericancentury.org/iraqsep1898.htm.

56 U.S. Joint Inquiry Staff, "Was US informed before attack,"…

57 "AMERICA AT WAR: UNDERSTANDING THE CONFLICT",…p. 6AB.

58 U.S. Joint Inquiry Staff, "Was US informed before attack,"…

59 "AMERICA AT WAR: UNDERSTANDING THE CONFLICT",…p. 6AB.

60 David Johnston and Jim Dwyer,…

61 "AMERICA AT WAR: UNDERSTANDING THE CONFLICT",…p. 7AB.

62 Carl Cameron, "Clues Alerted White House to Potential Attacks."…

63 U.S. Joint Inquiry Staff, "Was US informed before attack,"…

64 Fox Butterfield, "Abuse detailed in U.S. prisons," *The Mercury News*, May 8, 2004, p. 3A.

65 U.S. Joint Inquiry Staff, "Was US informed before attack,"…

66 "Report Warned Of Suicide Hijackings," *CBS*, May 17, 2002, http://www.cbsnews.com/stories/2002/05/18/attack/main509488.shtml.

67 U.S. Joint Inquiry Staff, "Was US informed before attack,"….

68 Ibid.

69 "AMERICA AT WAR: UNDERSTANDING THE CONFLICT",…p. 7AB.

70 Erwin Seba, *Reuters*, March 20, 2003.

71 Arianna Huffington, "Holding Dick Cheney 'accountable'," August 5, 2002, http://www.alternet.org.

72 U.S. Joint Inquiry Staff, "Was US informed before attack,"…

73 "AMERICA AT WAR: UNDERSTANDING THE CONFLICT",…p. 7AB.

74 Robert Bryce, "The candidate from Brown and Root," *The Texas Observer*, October 6, 2000.

75 John Rega, "Government Ties Helped Cheney and Halliburton Make Millions," Bloomberg News, October 6, 2000.

76 Ibid.

77 David Johnston and Jim Dwyer,…

78 John Solomon, "Sources: '01 brief warned of attack," *The Mercury News*, April 10, 2004, p. 1A.

79 "U.S. official sees similarities between *USS Cole* blast and embassy attacks," *CNN*, October 23, 2000.

80 "AMERICA AT WAR: UNDERSTANDING THE CONFLICT",...p. 7AB.

7

Neocons II: Recapturing the White House

George W. Bush enters the White House with a gaggle of neoconservatives: Dick Cheney, Donald Rumsfeld, Paul Wolfowitz, Richard Armitage, Douglas Feith, and Richard Perle as an advisor. They are warned about the threat of terrorism by many reports and experts. The primary focus is regime change in Iraq. The threat warnings about an al Qaeda attack become more frequent. The ominous August 6th Presidential Daily Brief is given to Bush. A known terrorist attends flight school in Minnesota. He wants to learn how to fly a 747 but is not interested in learning how to take off or land. The counterterrorism division at FBI Headquarters is busy working on prior incidents and decides to ignore this issue.

On Sept. 11, al Qaeda hijacks four planes. Two planes fly into the twin towers of the World Trade Center, another plane flies into the Pentagon, and the fourth crashes into a field. The neoconservatives, both inside and outside of the Bush administration, immediately build momentum for attacking Iraq. After Sept. 11, sky marshals are added.

The U.S. invades Afghanistan in retaliation for the Sept. 11 attacks and declares that "enemy combatants" are not entitled to the Geneva Convention protections. Prisoner treatment and interrogations become much harsher. The march to war in Iraq accelerates with Vice President Dick Cheney in a fever to remove Saddam Hussein. A Colin Powell speech at the U.N. presents "irrefutable and undeniable" evidence that Iraq is hiding WMD. Halliburton is secretly set up for business in Iraq. After a year of White House resistance, an independent bipartisan commission is authorized to investigate the Sept. 11 tragedy. Aircraft carriers are sent to the Persian Gulf.

November 7, 2000: Al Gore, already hampered by Clinton's Monica Lewinsky scandal, runs into the butterfly ballot snafu, Democratic voter purges, and

Nader's third party challenge in Florida. The voting is followed by an extended legal challenge that allows George W. Bush to sneak into the White House with many Florida ballots, which later reveal Gore's higher vote count in the state, barred from inclusion by the courts.[1]

2000–2001: Millennium bomber Ahmad Ressam testifies, in closed and open court trials relating to his December 1999 arrest for trying to bring bomb-making materials across the Canadian border, that attack plans, including hijackings and attacks on New York City targets, are ongoing.[2]

January 2001: WASHINGTON—At his inauguration, President George W. Bush promises to invigorate sanctions against Iraq.[3]

January 2001: WASHINGTON—President Bush packs his administration with neoconservatives: Secretary of Defense Donald Rumsfeld, Vice President Dick Cheney, and national security advisor Condoleezza Rice. By March, two more neocons will be installed: Richard L. Armitage as Deputy Secretary of State and Paul Wolfowitz as Deputy Secretary of Defense. Also placed into power are neocons Douglas Feith as Undersecretary of Defense for Policy and Richard Perle as the head of a Pentagon advisory panel. Secretary of State Colin Powell is the only significant obstacle in the path of a complete neoconservative takeover of the United States government.

January 25, 2001: WASHINGTON—Richard Clarke was the counterterrorism coordinator for previous presidents, including the first President Bush, and is retained in that position for George W. Bush. After his service, he writes a book, *Against All Enemies*, which will be released in March 2004 and describe his experiences covering terrorism for the presidents. During Bush's first week in office, Clarke writes a memo to Condoleezza Rice urgently asking for a Cabinet-level meeting on the terrorist threat posed by al Qaeda. He doesn't get it—or permission to brief the president directly on the threat—for nearly eight months.[4]

January 25, 2001: WASHINGTON—In her April 8, 2004 public testimony, Dr. Rice will claim that the Bush administration is quite cognizant of the al Qaeda threat, but on this day she refers Clarke to the deputies committee, which is a sub-Cabinet-level committee. Richard Clarke claims that this slows down the process considerably.[5]

The sub-Cabinet decision clearly indicates a low priority for terrorism in the Bush administration.

January 2001: WASHINGTON—One of Cheney's largest projects as Vice President is to coordinate the development of a new National Energy Policy (NEPDG). According to the former climate policy advisor in the EPA, who is present at the task force sessions, Cheney "continually pushes plans to increase…oil supplies while paying little heed to promoting energy efficiency and clean energy resources." Casting as an inevitability that by 2020, the United States will need to import two thirds of its oil, mainly from the Arabic peninsula, the NEPDG recommends "that the President make energy security a priority of our trade and foreign policy."[6]

January 2001: WASHINGTON—According to Treasury Secretary Paul O'Neill in his book, *The Price of Loyalty*, which will be released in January 2004, President Bush is anxious to take action against Saddam Hussein and Iraq in his very first National Security Council meeting.

O'Neill readily agreed to tell his story to the book's author Ron Suskind—and he adds that he'll be receiving no money for his part in the book.

Suskind says he interviewed hundreds of people for the book—including several cabinet members.

"From the very first instance, it was about Iraq. It was about what we can do to change this regime," according to Suskind. "Day one, these things were laid and sealed."

And that comes up at the first National Security Council meeting, says O'Neill, who adds that the discussion of Iraq continues at the next meeting two days later.

Based on his interviews with O'Neill and several other officials at the meetings, Suskind writes that the planning envisioned peacekeeping troops, war crimes tribunals, and even divvying up Iraq's oil wealth.

He obtained one Pentagon document, dated March 5, 2001, and entitled "Foreign Suitors for Iraqi Oilfield contracts," which includes a map of potential areas for exploration.[7]

January 2001: WASHINGTON—Samuel R. Berger, Mr. Clinton's national security adviser, warns his successor, Condoleezza Rice, that "she will be spending more time on terrorism and al Qaeda than any other issue."[8]

Unfortunately, Dr. Rice receives orders from her boss to focus more on Iraq and missile defense. Berger's advice is ignored.

January 2001: WASHINGTON—Bob Woodward won a Pulitzer Price for his Watergate reporting in 1973. Starting in 2002, he will spend a year gaining access to confidential records of over 50 key meetings concerning the Bush administration's war against terrorism, culminating August 2003 in four hours of interviews with President Bush at his ranch in Crawford, Texas.

Newly uncovered documents, which Woodward will unveil on February 28, 2004, illustrate that President Bush neglects to address CIA Director George Tenet's January 2001 warnings about the menace of Osama bin Laden and the proliferation of Weapons of Mass Destruction (WMD). Despite papers, discussions, and a proposed 'action plan' that was never written, nothing is done to reckon with bin Laden's threats. Woodward laconically summarizes the President's unconcern, "He dropped the ball."[9]

January 30, 2001: WASHINGTON—Khalid al-Midhar, an eventual Sept. 11 hijacker, is linked to Khallad, a USS *Cole* bombing suspect. The FBI will claim the CIA never told them; the CIA disputes the claim.

"...if in January 2001, agencies had resumed their search for him or placed him on the TIPOFF watch list, they might have found him before or at the time al-Midhar had applied for a new Visa in 2001. Or they might have been alerted to him when he returned to the United States the following month."—Sept. 11 Commission staff statement.[10]

January 30, 2001: DUBAI, United Arab Emirates—September 11 hijacker Ziad Jarrah is questioned at the Dubai airport at the CIA's request, United Arab Emirates government sources and other Middle Eastern and European intelligence sources will tell CNN. Sources will say he is released because U.S. officials are satisfied but a CIA spokesman denies the agency had anything to do with the questioning, saying it was "flatly untrue." The CIA says it learned of the questioning from CIA officers in the UAE after September 11. The FBI believes Jarrah, who holds a Lebanese passport, will be the hijacker-pilot of United Airlines Flight 93.[11]

January 31, 2001: WASHINGTON—The U.S. Commission on National Security, a bipartisan group evaluating threats facing the country, files its final report today.

Seven Democrats and seven Republicans unanimously approve 50 recommendations. Many of them address the point that, in the words of the commission's executive summary, "the combination of unconventional weapons proliferation with the persistence of international terrorism will end the relative invulnerability of the U.S. homeland to catastrophic attack."

According to the report, "A direct attack against American citizens on American soil is likely over the next quarter century."

The commission recommends the formation of a Cabinet-level position to combat terrorism. The proposed National Homeland Security Agency director would have "responsibility for planning, coordinating, and integrating various U.S. government activities involved in homeland security," according to the commission's executive summary.

The Commission on National Security is supposed to disband after issuing the January 31 report, but Gary Hart and the other commission members get a six-month extension to lobby for their recommendations. Hart spends 90 minutes with Defense Secretary Donald Rumsfeld and an hour with Secretary of State Colin Powell lobbying for the White House to devote more attention to the imminent dangers of terrorism and their specific, detailed recommendations for a major change in the way the federal government approaches terrorism. He and Rudman brief national security advisor Condoleezza Rice on the commission's findings. Gary Hart and Warren Rudman brief top administration officials on the findings of their Commission on National Security.[12]

January 31, 2001: WASHINGTON—Bush administration officials tell former Senators Gary Hart and Warren Rudman that they prefer instead to put aside the recommendations issued in the January report by the U.S. Commission on National Security/21st Century.[13]

Their efforts apparently fall on deaf ears.

February 2001: WASHINGTON—Testifying before Congress, CIA Director George Tenet says "Osama bin Laden and his global network of lieutenants and associates remain the most immediate and serious threat" to U.S. security.

"As we have increased security around government and military facilities, terrorists are seeking out 'softer' targets that provide opportunities for mass casualties," Tenet says.[14]

February 8, 2001: WASHINGTON—The press identifies the names of 22 oil and gas companies whose officials met in secret with the NEPDG. Nineteen of these are among the top 25 energy industry financial contributors to the Republican Party. Among the 19 are Enron, ExxonMobil, BP Amoco, Anadarko Petroleum, Shell Oil, and Chevron.[15]

February 2001: BAGHDAD—U.S. and Britain bomb targets trying to disable Iraq's air defense network. The move has little international support.[16]

February 26, 2001: At a terror conference, L. Paul Bremer says, "The new administration seems to be paying no attention to the problem of terrorism. What they will do is stagger along until there's a major incident, and then suddenly say, 'Oh, my God, shouldn't we be organized to deal with this?' "[17]

Paul Bremer will be President Bush's administrator in Iraq during May 2004 when his statement becomes news, and he will not want it to be used against Bush. However, his statement is dead on.

February, April 2001: BEIRUT—In February and April of 2001, the world's most extreme Islamic terror groups hold meetings in Beirut and Tehran, respectively, to set aside their differences and unite for jihad (holy war) against Israel and the United States. The two unprecedented meetings have over 400 militants in attendance. They call it "the Jerusalem Conference," aiming at uniting behind the Palestinians and winning total Arab control over Jerusalem. The group agrees on a document and the creation of an actual organization now known as "the Jerusalem Project." The document includes the statement: "The only decisive option to achieve this strategy is the option of jihad in all its forms and resistance…America today is a second Israel."

The participants include leaders of Osama bin Laden's al Qaeda terror group, Hamas, Islamic Jihad, Hezbollah, and militants from Egypt, Pakistan, Jordan, Qatar, Yemen, the Sudan, and Algeria. Sources say at least one participant travels to the conference from the United States and returns to the country afterward. U.S. intelligence sources identify two leaders of the Beirut-based Jerusalem Project.[18]

Note that Saddam and Iraqi agents are not cavorting with the Islamic groups.

February 2001: Federal prosecutors tell a court they gained information in September 2000 from Morrocan citizen L'Houssaine Kherchtou that Kherchtou was trained as an al Qaeda pilot in Kenya and attended a meeting in 1993 where an al Qaeda official was conducting a briefing on Western air traffic control procedures.[19]

March 2, 2001: WASHINGTON—Neocon Paul Wolfowitz is sworn in as Deputy Secretary of Defense.

March 2001: WASHINGTON—The Federal Aviation Administration (FAA) informs specific U.S. airlines of threats from suspected terrorists in Middle Eastern nations served by those carriers.[20]

March 2001: WASHINGTON—Representative Mac Thornberry, R-TX, introduces the National Homeland Security Agency Act. Other members of Congress—Representative Wayne Gilchrest, R-MD, John Kyl, R-AR, Dianne Feinstein, D-CA—talk about the issue, and these three and others begin drafting legislation to enact some of the recommendations into law.[21]

This congressional momentum to pursue the issues raised by the National Security Commission will be preempted by the Bush administration's actions in May.

March 2001: WASHINGTON—Sept. 11 Panel officials say in April 2004 the draft reports by the independent commission investigating the Sept. 11 terror attacks show that FBI officials are alarmed throughout 2001 by what they perceive as Attorney General John Ashcroft's lack of interest in terrorism issues and his decision in August 2001 to turn down the bureau's request for a large expansion of its counterterrorism programs.

According to the reports, Ashcroft fails to list combating terrorism as one of the department's priorities in a March 2001 department wide memo. Also, Ashcroft stops flying on commercial airlines for government business in the summer of 2001.[22]

March 26, 2001: WASHINGTON—Neocon Richard L. Armitage is sworn in as Deputy Secretary of State.

April 2001: WASHINGTON—A source with terrorist connections speculates that bin Laden might be interested in using commercial pilots as terrorists. The source warns that embassy bombings should not be the focus of intelligence measures because the operatives want "spectacular and traumatic" attacks, like the first World Trade Center bombing in 1993.

The source doesn't mention when an attack may occur. The information is not disseminated within the intelligence community because the source is speculating and doesn't offer hard information.[23]

April 2001: WASHINGTON—Richard Clarke finally gets a high level meeting on the threat of al Qaeda in April 2001, but the meeting "does not go well." According to Clarke in *Against All Enemies*, Deputy Defense Secretary Paul D. Wolfowitz scowls and asks, "Why are we beginning by talking about this one man, bin Laden?" When Clarke tells him no foe but al Qaeda "poses an immediate and serious threat to the United States," Wolfowitz replies that Iraqi terrorism poses "at least as much" a danger. FBI and CIA representatives back Clarke in saying they have no such evidence.

"I could hardly believe," Clarke writes, that Wolfowitz pressed the "totally discredited" theory that Iraq was behind the 1993 truck bomb at the World Trade Center, a "theory that had been investigated for years and found to be totally untrue."[24]

April 3, 2001: WASHINGTON—Before the Senate Judiciary Committee's Subcommittee on Terrorism and Technology, former Senator Gary Hart sounds a call of alarm, saying that an "urgent" need exists for a new national security strategy, with an emphasis on intelligence gathering.

"Good intelligence is the key to preventing attacks on the homeland," Hart says, arguing that the commission "urges that homeland security become one of the intelligence community's most important missions." The nation needs to embrace "homeland security as a primary national security mission." The Defense Department, for instance, "has placed its highest priority on preparing for major theater war" where it "should pay far more attention to the homeland security mission." Homeland security would be the main purpose of beefed-up National Guard units throughout the country.[25]

April 18, 2001: WASHINGTON—The FAA sends another warning to U.S. airlines that Middle Eastern terrorists might try to hijack or blow up a U.S. plane and that carriers should "demonstrate a high degree of alertness." The warning stems from the April 6, 2001 conviction of Ahmed Ressam over a failed plot to blow up the Los Angeles International Airport during the millennium celebrations.[26]

<u>April-May 2001</u>: WASHINGTON—Briefing articles to top officials contain such headlines as: "Bin Laden Planning Multiple Operations," "Bin Laden Public Profile may Presage Attack," "Bin Laden Network's Plans Advancing."[27]

<u>May 2001</u>: WASHINGTON—President Bush announces his plan for national security almost as if the Hart-Rudman Commission never existed. According to the president, national security efforts need to be seamlessly integrated, and it should be done through the Federal Emergency Management Agency (FEMA).

Nearly four months after the January warnings from Richard Clarke and the Hart-Rudman Commission, Bush directs Cheney, a man with a full plate, to supervise the development of a national counter-terrorism plan while assigning responsibility for dealing with the issue to FEMA, headed by former Bush campaign manager Joe Allbaugh. Bush announces that Cheney and Allbaugh will review the issues and have recommendations for him by October 1, 2001.

The Hart-Rudman Commission specifically recommends that the issue of terrorism is such a threat it needs far more than FEMA's attention. The commission's report, as well as congressional momentum to address it, is essentially put on the shelf at this point.[28]

<u>May 2001</u>: NEW YORK—An Iranian in custody in New York City tells local police of a plot to attack the World Trade Center.[29]

<u>May 2001</u>: DUBAI, United Arab Emirates—Someone calls the U.S. Embassy in the United Arab Emirates saying that a group of bin Laden supporters is in the U.S. planning attacks with explosives. The CIA and the FBI will still be investigating this lead in August 2001 and will not make any progress or suggest any protective measures before the Sept. 11 attacks occur, indicating a very lax attitude regarding the threat of a terrorist attack.[30]

<u>May 29, 2001</u>: Four men are convicted in the bombings of U.S. embassies in Kenya and Tanzania. Witnesses testify at the trial that Osama bin Laden is sending al Qaeda agents to the United States for flight-school training and acquiring planes.[31]

<u>June 4, 2001</u>: GEORGE TOWN—Pakistanis are taken into custody in the Cayman Islands after they are overheard discussing hijacking attacks in New York City. They are questioned and released, and the information is forwarded to U.S. intelligence.[32]

June 2001: WASHINGTON—CIA and FBI meet to go over surveillance of the Malaysia meeting. New York-based FBI Cole investigators are not shown a photograph of Khallad, a USS *Cole* bombing suspect. "...June meeting when three but not all of the photographs are disclosed to FBI agents, and the subsequent description of those events—if all of that had worked the way it could have worked...you could have had a completely different result."—Louis J. Freeh, former FBI Director[33]

June 2001: BERLIN—German intelligence alerts the U.S. Central Intelligence Agency, Britain's MI-6 intelligence service, and Israel's Mossad that Middle Eastern terrorists are training for hijackings and targeting American and Israeli interests.[34]

June 2001: BRUSSELS, Belgium—After his first meeting with NATO heads of state in Brussels in June 2001, Bush outlines the five top defense issues discussed with the closest U.S. allies. Missile defense is at the top of the list, and the only reference to extremists is in Macedonia, where Bush says regional forces are seeking to subvert a new democracy.[35]

June 22, 2001: WASHINGTON—The FAA issues another warning to U.S. airlines. It mentions "unconfirmed reports that American interests may be the target of terrorist threats from extremist groups." The warning also says that hijackings might be used to get the release of Sheik Omar Abdel Rahman, who was convicted in a plot to blow up New York landmarks in 1993.[36]

What were the airlines supposed to do? Whose responsibility was it to reinvigorate the sky marshal program?

June 26, 2001: WASHINGTON—The State Department issues a worldwide caution warning American citizens of possible attacks.

Rice later says that at this time, there is a "threat spike," focusing on possible attacks on U.S. citizens or targets overseas.[37]

Summer 2001: WASHINGTON—Veteran counterterrorism officers privy to reports on al Qaeda threats "were so worried about an impending disaster that one of them tells us that they considered resigning and going public with their concerns," according to a staff report which will be issued by the Sept. 11 commission on March 24, 2004. Senior CIA officials are also frustrated by some Bush appointees who are not familiar with surges in terrorist-threat information and question their veracity, the March 2004 report will say.[38]

<u>Summer 2001</u>: WASHINGTON—As intercepts of reported threats against unspecified targets jump alarmingly in June and July of 2001, the deputy director of central intelligence, John McLaughlin, "felt a great tension" between "the new administration's need to understand these issues and his sense that this was a matter of great urgency," he will tell the Sept. 11 commission.[39]

<u>Summer 2001</u>: WASHINGTON—Attorney General John Ashcroft will not show well when the Sept. 11 commission turns to his department in April 2004.

Acting FBI Director Thomas Pickard says that after he briefed Ashcroft twice on terrorist threats during the summer of 2001, "the attorney general told him he did not want to hear this information anymore."[40]

Does this attitude impact the vigilance of the FBI during the lead up to the Sept. 11 attacks?

<u>July 1, 2001</u>: Senators Dianne Feinstein and Richard Shelby, both members of the Senate Intelligence Committee, appear on CNN's "Late Edition with Wolf Blitzer" and warn of potential attacks by Osama bin Laden. "One of the things that has begun to concern me very much as to whether we really have our house in order, intelligence staff have told me that there is a major probability of a terrorist incident within the next three months," Feinstein says.[41]

<u>July 2, 2001</u>: WASHINGTON—The FBI issues a warning of possible al Qaeda attacks to law enforcement agencies. The message states, "There are threats to be worried about overseas. While we cannot foresee attacks domestically, we cannot rule them out." The FAA, meanwhile, issues another message regarding convicted millennium bomb plotter Ahmed Ressam. Condoleezza Rice tells authorities "there was an intention of using explosives in an airport terminal."[42]

<u>July 4, 2001</u>: WASHINGTON—Presidential counterterrorism advisor Richard Clarke sends a memo to national security advisor Condoleezza Rice outlining steps that had been taken to place the nation on heightened terrorist alert. Among the steps, the memo says, "all 56 FBI field offices were tasked in late June to go to increased surveillance and contact with informants related to known or suspected terrorists in the United States."

On April 9, 2004, portions of the White House memo will be provided by a White House official seeking to portray an administration working aggressively to deter a domestic terror attack. But law enforcement officials will say in April 2004 that Rice's account overstates the scope, thrust, and intensity of activities by the FBI within U.S. borders.

Agents in the summer of 2001 are focused mainly on the threat of overseas attacks, not within the United States, law enforcement officials will say.[43]

July 5, 2001: WASHINGTON—The Bush administration's deliberations and actions in the summer of 2001 with terror warnings mounting shows the government's response is often scattered and inconsistent as the new administration struggles to find a strategy. A review starting in late 2002 based on interviews with current and former officials and preliminary findings of the Sept. 11 panel will verify this confusion.

On July 5, 2001, Dr. Rice and Andrew Card, the president's chief of staff, summon top officials from many domestic agencies to a meeting in the White House Situation Room.

Even though the warnings focus mostly on threats overseas, Rice and Card want the FBI, the FAA, the Customs Service, the INS, and other agencies put on alert inside the United States. When the meeting breaks up, several new security advisories are issued, including an FAA bulletin warning of an increased risk of air hijackings aimed at freeing terrorists imprisoned in the United States.

A congressional inquiry into intelligence activities before Sept. 11 will later find 12 reports over a seven-year period suggesting that terrorists might use airplanes as weapons. And in more than 40 briefings prior to the attacks, Bush is told by CIA Director George Tenet of threats involving al Qaeda, but this one meeting and its advisories is as far as the Bush administration ever goes toward placing the nation on high alert before the attacks of Sept. 11, 2001.

The Pentagon's top priorities this summer are developing a national missile-defense plan and conducting a broad strategy and budget review. Money to finance counterterrorism efforts is limited.

Defense Secretary Donald Rumsfeld spends little time on terrorism issues this summer, aides will later say in interviews. Counterterrorism officials in the Pentagon will later tell the commission that Rumsfeld and his aides "were not especially interested" in their agenda.[44]

July 10, 2001: WASHINGTON—FBI Agent Ken Williams sends a memo to the counterterrorism division at the FBI's Washington headquarters. It outlines a theory that Middle Eastern students at an Arizona flight school could be al Qaeda agents training for hijackings. FBI analysts review the memo but do nothing. The White House, FBI Director Robert Mueller, and Attorney General John Ashcroft will be informed about the memo after the September 11 attacks.[45]

July 2001: WASHINGTON—An aide to the former Taliban foreign minister, Wakil Ahmad Muttawakil, is sent to warn American diplomats and the U.N. that Osama bin Laden is due to launch a huge attack on American soil.

Neither organization heeds the warning, which is given just weeks before the Sept. 11 attacks.

Mr. Muttawakil, who is known to be deeply unhappy with the Arab and other foreign militants in Afghanistan, learns of Osama bin Laden's plan in July.

The attack is imminent, he discovers, and it will be huge. Bin Laden hopes to kill thousands of U.S. citizens.

The minister is deeply worried that the U.S. military would react with deadly vengeance against Afghanistan. His worry is that al Qaeda, the Taliban's guests, are going to destroy the guest house.

He goes first to the American consulate in Peshawar in Pakistan, then to the U.N. But neither warning is heeded.

There are many other occasions where American domestic intelligence fails to heed information, but this is the only known alert that comes from inside the Taliban movement.

At the time, late July 2001, 19 members of al Qaeda are already in place in America, waiting to launch their deadly attacks.[46]

July 2001: WASHINGTON—U.S. intelligence reports another spike in threats related to the July 20-22 G-8 summit in Genoa, Italy. The reports include specific threats against Bush, who is to attend the summit. The head of Russia's Federal Bodyguard Service is quoted as saying that Osama bin Laden has threatened to assassinate President Bush at the summit. "In fact, the CIA goes on…a full-court press to try and deal with these potential attacks and, indeed, manages, through these intelligence activities and liaison activities, to disrupt attacks in Paris, Turkey, and Rome."[47]

July 2001: WASHINGTON—According to CIA Director George Tenet, the threat spikes in this time frame are "blinking red."[48]

July 2001: PHOENIX—The memo from the FBI Phoenix office about Arabs training in U.S. flight schools never reaches headquarters because FBI counterterrorism officials are overwhelmed by the bombing of the USS *Cole* (events October 12, 2000). The memo ends up "sitting on a shelf," according to Fox News sources.[49]

July 21, 2001: GENOA, Italy—U.S. President George W. Bush does not stay with other world leaders at this summit because of fear of a terrorist attack. Condoleezza Rice accompanies Bush on this trip.

Surface-to-air missiles and fighter jets are part of the security to protect the G8 Summit against a suicide attack by terrorists using airplanes.[50]

July 21, 2001: WASHINGTON—After the Sept. 11 attacks, Dr. Rice will claim, "I don't think anybody could have predicted that those people could have taken an airplane and slam it into the World Trade Center…that they would try to use an airplane as a missile." She later retracts the statement in a private session with the Sept. 11 Commission, due to information from Richard Clarke.[51]

Dr. Rice's experience in Genoa, where special precautions were taken to protect against terrorists that might hijack planes and attack a site, is an even greater reason this statement should never have been made. However, with all the warnings of using planes as missiles and mentions of the World Trade Center, the national security advisor to the President remains clueless.

August 6, 2001: WASHINGTON—A document known as the President's Daily Brief (PDB) is presented to the President six days a week. One entitled "Bin Laden Determined to Strike in US" was presented to President Bush on August 6, 2001 (portions marked "x" were blacked out before release):

Clandestine, foreign government, and media reports indicate Bin Laden since 1997 has wanted to conduct terrorist attacks in the U.S. Bin Laden implied in US television interviews in 1997 and 1998 that his followers would follow the example of World Trade Center bomber Ramzi Yousef and "bring the fighting to America."

After US missile strikes on his base in Afghanistan in 1998, Bin Laden told followers he wanted to retaliate in Washington, according to xxxxxxxxxxx service.

An Egyptian Islamic Jihad (EIJ) operative told an xxxxxxxxx service at the same time that Bin Laden was planning to exploit the operative's access to the US to mount a terrorist strike.

The millennium plotting in Canada in 1999 may have been part of Bin Laden's first serious attempt to implement a terrorist strike in the US. Convicted plotter

Ahmed Ressam has told the FBI that he conceived the idea to attack Los Angeles International Airport himself, but that Bin Laden lieutenant Abu Zubaydah encouraged him and helped facilitate the operation. Ressam also said that in 1998 Abu Zubaydah was planning his own US attack.

Ressam says Bin Laden was aware of the Los Angeles operation.

Although Bin Laden has not succeeded, his attacks against the US Embassies in Kenya and Tanzania in 1998 demonstrate that he prepares operations years in advance and is not deterred by setbacks. Bin Laden associates surveilled our Embassies in Nairobi and Dar es Salaam as early as 1993, and some members of the Nairobi cell planning the bombings were arrested and deported in 1997.

Al-Qaeda members—including some who are US citizens—have resided in or traveled to the US for years, and the group apparently maintains a support structure that could aid attacks. Two al-Qaeda members found guilty in the conspiracy to bomb our Embassies in East Africa were US citizens, and a senior EIJ member lived in California in the mid-1990s.

A clandestine source said in 1998 that a Bin Laden cell in New York was recruiting Muslim-American youth for attacks.

We have not been able to corroborate some of the more sensational threat reporting, such as that from a xxxxxxxxxx service in 1998 saying that Bin Laden wanted to hijack a US aircraft to gain the release of "Blind Shaykh" 'Umar 'Abd al-Rahman and other US-held extremists.

Nevertheless, FBI information since that time indicates patterns of suspicious activity in this country consistent with preparations for hijackings or other types of attacks, including recent surveillance of federal buildings in New York...

The FBI is conducting approximately 70 full field investigations throughout the US that it considers Bin Laden-related. CIA and the FBI are investigating a call to our Embassy in UAE [United Arab Emirates] in May saying that a group of Bin Laden supporters was in the US planning attacks with explosives.[52]

<u>August 6, 2001</u>: WASHINGTON—In a May 16, 2002 press briefing, Condoleezza Rice will describe the Aug. 6 brief as merely general information, which isn't as valuable as a warning.[53]

The Aug. 6 memo will not be declassified and available to the public until April 10, 2004. Everyone had to rely on the administration's characterization of the memo.

<u>August 6, 2001</u>: WASHINGTON—The title and 10 references inside this brief indicate planning for an attack on U.S. soil, pointing out Washington and New York (twice), which will be the actual Sept. 11 attack locations.

However, after the Sept. 11 attacks, Dr. Rice will insist for many months—and reiterate on March 24, 2004—that intelligence during the summer pointed exclusively to an attack on foreign soil.[54]

<u>August 6, 2001</u>: WASHINGTON—Testifying before the Sept. 11 Commission on April 8, 2004 under oath, Dr. Rice will claim on eight occasions that the Aug. 6 brief is merely historical information—even though two recent events in the brief suggested planning was in progress and the FBI was conducting many related investigations at the time.[55]

<u>August 6, 2001</u>: WASHINGTON—Dr. Rice will testify before the Sept. 11 panel on April 4, 2004 that "there was nothing in this memo that suggested an attack was coming on New York or Washington, D.C..."[56]

<u>August 6, 2001</u>: WASHINGTON—In April 2004, White House aids and outside experts will say they could not recall a sitting president ever publicly releasing the highly sensitive document, known as a PDB, for presidential daily briefing.[57]

Could this fact have made Dr. Rice feel safe with her characterization of the Aug. 6 brief as exclusively historical and about foreign locations? There will be no intent on the part of the administration to declassify the brief prior to her April 8, 2004 testimony. The momentum to do so will start right after her testimony because several Sept. 11 commission members will dispute Dr. Rice's testimony on the brief.

<u>August 6, 2001</u>: WASHINGTON—On April 11, 2004, President Bush will say that the intelligence briefing he received on al Qaeda one month before the Sept. 11 strike contained no specific "indication of a terrorist attack" on American soil.[58]

<u>August 6, 2001</u>: WASHINGTON—On April 11, 2004, Randy Beers, the senior policy adviser to John Kerry, Bush's likely Democratic opponent, will say that the White House failed to pay proper heed to warnings included in the briefing. Beers will note that he had worked in the National Security Council under four presidents, including Bush, a post that gave him access to such briefings.

"To the knowledgeable reader of the presidential daily brief—and I read it for a number of years when I was in the Clinton White House, and I read it again when I was in the Bush White House, although just the terrorism portions of it—that document was intended to tell the president of the United States that there was a serious problem," he will say.

Some Republicans will also question whether the White House did enough in response to the Aug. 6 report. "Should it have raised more of an alarm bell?" Senator John McCain, an Arizona Republican who is often critical of the Bush administration, will say in April 2004 on NBC's "Meet the Press." "I think, in hindsight, that's probably true."[59]

August 6, 2001: CRAWFORD, Texas—At this time, the U.S. Sky Marshal program doesn't include any sky marshals on domestic flights.[60]

Even though hijacking U.S. planes for attacks against America was mentioned twice in his brief and many times in recent warnings, President Bush was not motivated to even strengthen the air marshal program, a minimal response to such an ominous brief.

Could the obsession with Iraq have distracted Bush and the entire White House from recognizing the seriousness of the terror threats and/or taking actions to protect America?

August 6, 2001: CRAWFORD—After reading the brief, President Bush is still not motivated to have his first cabinet-level meeting on the terror threat from al Qaeda.[61]

August 6, 2001: CRAWFORD—President Bush reviews the Aug. 6 PDB while vacationing in Crawford, Texas. After receiving the warnings, he continues his 30-day vacation, the longest presidential vacation in U.S. history.[62]

August 2001: JERUSALEM—Based on its own intelligence, the Israeli government provides "general" information to the United States in the second week of August that an al Qaeda attack is imminent.[63]

August 2001: MOSCOW—Russian President Vladimir Putin orders his intelligence agencies to alert the United States that 25 suicide pilots are training for attacks on U.S. targets.[64]

<u>August 15, 2001</u>: EAGAN, Minnesota—Instructors at the Pan Am International Flying Academy in Eagan, Minnesota, become suspicious of Zacarias Moussaoui, a French citizen, because he wants to learn how to fly a 747 jet in mid-air but has no interest in learning how to land or take off. Moussaoui has no pilot's license or aviation background. But he shows up with $6,800 in cash and a passion to learn a few flying skills as quickly as possible.

After phoning the local FBI office four times, a flight instructor finally reaches the right FBI agent, relays his suspicions on Moussaoui, and bluntly warns, "Do you realize that a 747 loaded with fuel can be used as a bomb?"[65]

<u>August 16, 2001</u>: EAGAN—FBI agents come, and after ascertaining that Moussaoui's visa is expired, arrest him. The INS agrees to hold Moussaoui for seven to 10 days—exploiting the flexibility in its regulations to protect the public from a potentially dangerous alien.

Minnesota-based FBI agents notify the CIA and the FBI liaison in Paris, seeking further information. French intelligence sources report that Moussaoui is "a known terrorist who has been on their watch list for three years." The CIA alerts its overseas stations that Moussaoui is a "suspect airline suicide hijacker" who might be "involved in a larger plot to target airlines traveling from Europe to the United States."[66]

<u>August 16, 2001</u>: WASHINGTON—The FAA issues a warning to airlines concerning disguised weapons. They are concerned about some reports that the terrorists have made breakthroughs in cell phones, key chains, and pens as weapons.[67]

<u>August 18, 2001</u>: EAGAN—Minneapolis FBI agents send a 26-page memo to headquarters warning that Moussaoui was acting "with others yet unknown" in a hijack conspiracy.[68]

<u>August 19, 2001</u>: WASHINGTON—Bush administration officials and outside experts say that Condoleezza Rice has quickly amassed power and turned out to be a very active and very public foreign policy maker. Dr. Rice, and not Secretary of State Colin Powell, is the first Bush foreign policy official to visit Moscow. Administration officials say that Rice's ascendancy comes as she has aligned herself with more conservative members (neocons) of President Bush's foreign policy team, leaving the State Department feeling 'outnumbered.'[69]

<u>August 21, 2001</u>: MINNEAPOLIS—Minneapolis agents notify headquarters, "If [Moussaoui] seizes an aircraft flying from Heathrow to New York City, it will have the fuel on board to reach D.C."

But when Minneapolis agents seek FBI headquarters' permission to request a search warrant to check out Moussaoui's belongings, an agent at the FBI's Radical Fundamentalist Unit refuses permission. Instead, FBI headquarters insists that Minneapolis agents file a search warrant request under the Foreign Intelligence Surveillance Act (FISA), a 1978 law that created the Foreign Intelligence Surveillance Court to authorize searches of agents of foreign governments and foreign organizations. FISA sets a much lower, easier standard for securing search warrants than is required by other federal courts.

FBI headquarters lawyers incorrectly insist that FISA requires Minneapolis agents to prove that Moussaoui is linked to a foreign power before a search warrant can be issued. French intelligence has hinted that Moussaoui might be linked to Chechen rebels, and Minneapolis agents think that might be sufficient to meet the FISA standard.

However, because the Chechen rebels are not a recognized terrorist group under U.S. law at the time, FBI headquarters insists that Minneapolis agents find evidence connecting the Chechens to a recognized terrorist group. The congressional Joint Intelligence Committee report on pre-September 11 failures will note that "because of this misunderstanding, Minneapolis [FBI agents] spent the better part of three weeks trying to connect the Chechen group to al Qaeda." This "wild goose chase" does nothing except buy time for the hijackers.

The Senate Judiciary Committee will conclude in a 2003 report that "it is difficult to understand how the agents whose job included such a heavy FISA component could not have understood" the FISA law. As FBI agent Coleen Rowley will later complain, the FBI headquarters supervisory special agent handling the Moussaoui case "seemed to have been consistently almost deliberately thwarting the Minneapolis FBI agents' efforts."

As a result of the bungling, Moussaoui's computer is not searched prior to September 11.[70]

<u>August 2001</u>: WASHINGTON—"...all it had to do was put this [Moussaoui] on Intelink. All it had to do was is go out on Intelink and the game's over. It ends. And this conspiracy rolls up," Bob Kerrey, Sept. 11 Commission, former senator from Nebraska in April 2004.[71]

<u>August 2001</u>: WASHINGTON—In April 2004, the commission investigating the Sept. 11 terrorist attacks will conclude that the hijackers would probably have postponed their strike if the U.S. government had announced the arrest of suspected terrorist Zacarias Moussaoui in August 2001 or had publicized fears that he intended to hijack jetliners.

Commission Chairman Thomas Kean will say the conclusion is based on extensive psychological profiles of the Sept. 11 hijackers, who are "very careful and very jumpy."[72]

<u>August 23, 2001</u>: WASHINGTON—In late August, the CIA asks the Immigration and Naturalization Service to put Khalid al-Midhar and Nawaf Alhamzi on a watch list due to his ties to the October 2000 attack on the USS *Cole* in Yemen.

On August 23, the INS informs the CIA that al-Midhar was admitted into the United States as a nonimmigrant visitor on July 4. Al-Midhar will be one of the four hijackers aboard American Airlines Flight 77 that will crash into the Pentagon.[73]

<u>August 2001</u>: EAGAN—Moussaoui has jihadist connections, and has been in a flight school in Minnesota trying to learn the avionics of a commercial jet liner despite the fact that he has no previous training, has no explanation for the funds in his bank account, and has no explanation for why he is in the United States. The FBI doesn't bother to inform Richard Clarke, who heads U.S. counterterrorism efforts, about the development.[74]

<u>August 2001</u>: WASHINGTON—The Moussaoui case is briefed to George Tenet and other top officials under the heading, "Islamist Extremist Learns to Fly."[75]

<u>August 2001</u>: WASHINGTON—Officials are too overwhelmed with intelligence information to tap Zaccarias Moussaoui, who is taken into custody in August, after a Minnesota flight school reports that the alleged 20th hijacker of Sept. 11 was interested in learning how to fly, but not take-off and land.[76]

A rather ominous clue to ignore.

<u>August 2001</u>: WASHINGTON—According to later testimony from supporters of the Patriot Act, the FBI is fatally prevented by excessive concerns about civil liberties from securing a search warrant for Moussaoui's belongings—thereby thwarting the feds from gaining key data on a possible hijacking conspiracy.

Eleanor Hill, the staff director for the Joint Intelligence Committee investigation into pre-September 11 failures, will later observe, "The lesson of Moussaoui was that FBI headquarters was telling the field office the wrong advice. Fixing what happened in this case is not inconsistent with preserving civil liberties."[77]

Late August 2001: WASHINGTON—The FBI is not able to find Khalid al-Midhar or Nawaf Alhamzi.

"Had I been informed by the FBI that two senior al Qaeda operatives that had been in a planning meeting earlier in Kuala Lumpur were now in the United States...I would like to think that I would have...tried to get their names and pictures on the front page of every paper...and caused a successful nationwide manhunt for these two, two of the 19 hijackers."—Richard A. Clarke, former counterterrorism advisor in April 2004[78]

September 4, 2001: WASHINGTON—After eight months in office, President Bush finally holds his first cabinet-level meeting on the al Qaeda threat.[79]

September 4, 2001: WASHINGTON—Just one week before the attacks, presidential counterterrorism advisor Richard Clarke writes to Condoleezza Rice urging "policymakers to imagine a day after a terrorist attack, with hundreds of Americans dead at home and abroad, and ask themselves what they could have done earlier."[80]

Early September: MINNEAPOLIS—An FBI agent in Minneapolis, Minnesota, writes a memo suggesting Zacarias Moussaoui is training to learn to fly planes into buildings. The agent "mentioned the possibility of Moussaoui being that type of person that could fly something into the World Trade Center," FBI Director Robert Mueller will later tell Congress. The FBI notifies the CIA about Moussaoui, but neither agency tells the White House Counterterrorism Security Group. The Federal Aviation Administration, also told about Moussaoui, decides not to warn airlines about a possible threat.[81]

September 6, 2001: WASHINGTON—Five days before the attacks on the World Trade Center and the Pentagon, former Senator Gary Hart again stresses the need for action on the threat of terrorism in a face-to-face meeting with Condoleezza Rice, who in 1984, served as foreign policy adviser to Hart in his bid for the Democratic presidential nomination.

"Her only response was, 'Well, I'll speak to the Vice President about it.' And that was it," according to Hart. "It was disheartening."[82]

September 2001: WASHINGTON—U.S. investigators will confirm in October that a 29-year-old Iranian in custody in Germany's Langenhagen prison made phone calls to U.S. police from his deportation cell that an attack on the World Trade Center is imminent in "the days before the attack." The warning is considered the threat of a madman.[83]

September 2001: WASHINGTON—Condoleezza Rice will claim on April 8, 2004 and many other occasions, "There was no silver bullet that could have prevented the 9/11 attacks."[84]

Was Dr. Rice aware of the many golden opportunities to foil the plot? Should America's national security advisor to the President have been aware of them?

September 10, 2001: WASHINGTON—A CIA plan to strike at al Qaeda in Afghanistan, including support for the anti-Taliban Northern Alliance, is given to the White House. Senator Dianne Feinstein asks for a meeting with Vice President Dick Cheney about al Qaeda. The California Democrat is told that Cheney's staff will need six months to prepare for a meeting.[85]

If the request for a meeting had anything to do with regime change in Iraq, would Cheney's schedule have opened up a little sooner?

September 10, 2001: RIYADH—The National Security Agency intercepts two communications from Afghanistan to Saudi Arabia. "Tomorrow is zero hour," says one. "The match begins tomorrow," says the other. The messages will not be translated until September 12.[86]

September 11, 2001: The attacks begin.

8:46 a.m.: American Airlines Flight 11 from Boston, originally destined for Los Angeles, is hijacked and flies into the North Tower of the World Trade Center.

9:03 a.m.: United Airlines Flight 175 from Boston, originally destined for Los Angeles, is hijacked and flies into the South Tower of the World Trade Center.

9:05 a.m.: President Bush is informed that America is under attack. He remains seated for another five to seven minutes in the elementary school classroom and watches as reporters' cell phones and pagers are ringing.

9:25 a.m.: All domestic flights are grounded by the FAA.

9:45 a.m.: American Airlines Flight 77 from Washington's Dulles International Airport, originally destined for Los Angeles, is hijacked and flies into the Pentagon.

10:05 a.m.: The South Tower of the World Trade Center collapses.

10:05 a.m.: The White House is evacuated.

10:06 a.m.: United Airlines Flight 93 flying from Newark to San Francisco is hijacked with the intent of flying into the Capital, but after passengers confront hijackers, it crashes into a wooded area in Pennsylvania.

10:10 a.m.: A large section of one side of the Pentagon collapses.

10:10 a.m. to 10:15 a.m.: After all four hijacked planes have crashed, Dick Cheney gives the shoot down order. The order never reaches the F-16 pilots who are scrambled to protect Washington.

10:28 a.m.: The North Tower of the World Trade Center collapses.[87]

The Bush administration never seriously expected or prepared for this kind of attack. After the flood of dire warnings, there is no way this horrific tragedy should have been allowed to happen. But it did. And almost 3,000 innocent American civilians lose their lives.

September 11, 2001: WASHINGTON—In the first minutes after the hijacked planes struck the World Trade Center towers on Sept. 11, national security advisor Condoleezza Rice places Richard Clarke in her chair in the Situation Room and asks him to direct the government's crisis response. The next day, Clarke returns to find the subject changed to Iraq. "I realized with almost a sharp physical pain that (Defense Secretary Donald) Rumsfeld and Wolfowitz were going to try to take advantage of this national tragedy to promote their agenda about Iraq," according to Clarke in *Against All Enemies*.[88]

Did the Iraq hawks get the pretext they wanted?

September 11, 2001: WASHINGTON—Barely five hours after American Airlines Flight 77 plowed into the Pentagon, Defense Secretary Donald Rumsfeld is telling his aides to come up with plans for striking Iraq—even though there is no evidence linking Saddam Hussein to the attacks. Aides who are with Rumsfeld in the National Military Command Center on Sept. 11 are taking notes.

At 9:53 a.m., just 15 minutes after the hijacked plane hit the Pentagon, and while Rumsfeld is still outside helping with the injured, the National Security Agency, which monitors communications worldwide, intercepts a phone call from one of Osama bin Laden's operatives in Afghanistan to a phone number in the former Soviet Republic of Georgia.

The caller says he has "heard good news" and that another target is still to come; an indication he knows another airliner, the one that will eventually crash in Pennsylvania, is at that very moment zeroing in on Washington.

It is 12:05 p.m. when the director of Central Intelligence tells Rumsfeld about the intercepted conversation.

Rumsfeld feels it is "vague," that it "might not mean something," and that there is "no good basis for hanging hat." In other words, the evidence is not clearcut enough to justify military action against bin Laden.

But later that afternoon, the CIA reports the passenger manifests for the hijacked airliners show three of the hijackers are suspected al Qaeda operatives.

"One guy is [an] associate of [a] Cole bomber," the notes say, a reference to the October 2000 suicide boat attack on the USS *Cole* in Yemen, which was also the work of bin Laden.

With the intelligence all pointing toward bin Laden, Rumsfeld orders the military to begin working on strike plans. And at 2:40 p.m., the notes quote Rumsfeld as saying he wanted "best info fast. Judge whether good enough hit S.H." [Saddam Hussein] "at same time. Not only UBL" [Osama bin Laden].

No evidence indicates that Iraq was involved in the Sept. 11 attacks. But if these notes are accurate, that doesn't matter to Rumsfeld.

"Go massive," the notes quote him as saying. "Sweep it all up. Things related and not."[89]

September 11, 2001: WASHINGTON—Sunday morning talk shows often make news for days afterward. But the June 15, 2003 edition of NBC's "Meet the Press" will be unusual for the buzz that it won't generate.

Former General Wesley Clark will tell anchor Tim Russert that Bush administration officials had engaged in a campaign to implicate Saddam Hussein in the September 11 attacks—starting that very day. Clark will say that he'd been called on September 11 and urged to link Baghdad to the terror attacks, but declined to do so because of a lack of evidence.

Here is a transcript of the exchange:

CLARK: "There was a concerted effort during the fall of 2001, starting immediately after 9/11, to pin 9/11 and the terrorism problem on Saddam Hussein."

RUSSERT: "By who? Who did that?"

CLARK: "Well, it came from the White House, it came from people around the White House. It came from all over. I got a call on 9/11. I was on CNN, and I got a call at my home saying, 'You've got to say this is connected. This is state-sponsored terrorism. This has to be connected to Saddam Hussein.' I said, 'But—I'm willing to say it, but what's your evidence?' And I never got any evidence."

Wesley Clark's assertion corroborates the CBS Evening News story that will air on September 4, 2002.[90]

September 11, 2001: WASHINGTON—On this fateful day, National Security Adviser Condoleezza Rice is scheduled to outline a Bush administration policy that will address "the threats and problems of today and the day after, not the world of yesterday"—but the focus is largely on missile defense, not terrorism from Islamist radicals.

The address is designed to promote missile defense as the cornerstone of a new national security strategy, and contains no mention of al Qaeda, Osama bin Laden, or Islamist groups, former U.S. officials who have seen the text will say in March 2004.[91]

September 12, 2001: WASHINGTON—A bipartisan commission warned the White House and Congress that a bloody attack on U.S. soil could be imminent.

"We predicted it," Hart says of Tuesday's horrific events. "We said Americans will likely die on American soil, possibly in large numbers—that's a quote (from the commission's Phase One Report) from the fall of 1999."

On Tuesday, Hart says, as he sits watching TV coverage of the attacks, he experiences not just feelings of shock and horror, but also frustration. "I sat tearing my hair out," says the former two-term senator. "And still am."

Warren Rudman generally agrees with Hart's assessment, but adds, "That's not to say that the administration was obstructing."

The White House refers an inquiry on this issue to the National Security Council, which does not return a call for comment.[92]

September 12, 2001: WASHINGTON—According to *Against All Enemies* by Richard Clarke which will be released in March 2004 , the president's counterterrorism coordinator at the time of the attack, Defense Secretary Donald Rumsfeld complains on September 12, 2001—after the administration is certain that al Qaeda is to blame—that "there aren't any good targets in Afghanistan and there are lots of good targets in Iraq." According to Clarke, some members of the Bush administration are very anxious from the beginning to pin the Sept. 11 attacks on Iraq to justify bombing Iraq in order to overthrow Saddam Hussein. However, they have yet to find any evidence that Iraq was supporting al Qaeda.[93]

September 12, 2001: WASHINGTON—Richard Clarke's book details a discussion with President Bush. On the evening of September 12, 2001, Bush wanders alone around the Situation Room in a White House emptied by the previous day's calamitous events. Spotting Richard Clarke, his counterterrorism coordinator, Bush pulls him and a small group of aides into the dark paneled room.

"Go back over everything, everything," Bush says, according to Clarke's account. "See if Saddam did this."

"But Mr. President, al Qaeda did this," Clarke replies.

"I know, I know, but…see if Saddam was involved, Just look. I want to know any shred."

Reminded that the CIA, FBI, and White House staffs had sought and found no such link before, Clarke says, Bush spoke "testily." As he left the room, Bush says a third time, "Look into Iraq, Saddam."[94]

September 12, 2001: WASHINGTON—Initially, the White House will suggest that the Sept. 12, 2001 conversation Richard Clarke describes on March 20, 2004, where President Bush is pressing Clarke on Iraqi involvement, never took place. The administration will say it had no record that Bush had even been in the Situation Room that day and will say the president had no recollection of such a conversation. Although White House officials will stop short of denying the account, they will use it to cast doubt on Clarke's credibility, as they will attempt to debunk the charge that the administration downplayed the threat posed by al Qaeda in the months prior to the Sept. 11 attacks and worried instead about Iraq. One week later, on March 28, 2004, the White House will acknowledge that the conversation did in fact take place.[95]

September 13, 2001: NEW DELHI—In October, U.S. government officials will confirm that India's intelligence agency had some relevant information. Before the attacks, two Islamist radicals with ties to Osama bin Laden were discussing an attack on the White House. India's information is not provided to U.S. intelligence until Sept. 13.[96]

Would it have made any difference? The White House ignored all other warnings.

September 15, 2001: WASHINGTON—Richard Clarke writes a memo to Rice that opens, "When the era of national unity begins to crack in the near future, it is possible that some will start asking questions like did the White House do a good job of making sure that intelligence about terror threats got to FAA and other domestic law enforcement authorities." He describes a July 5, 2001 meeting with the FBI, FAA, the Secret Service, the Customs Service, the Coast Guard, and the INS. "We told them that we thought a spectacular al Qaeda terrorist attack was coming in the near future," and includes, "We could not rule out the possibility that the attack would be in the U.S.," Clarke writes. Dr. Rice will insist for many months—and reiterate on March 24, 2004—that intelligence during the summer pointed exclusively to an attack on foreign soil.[97]

September 20, 2001: WASHINGTON—William Kristol, representing the Project for a New American Century and other parties, writes a letter to the President strongly urging him to remove Saddam Hussein from power in Iraq. The letter argues that this is necessary whether or not Iraq had anything to do with the Sept. 11 attacks.

The letter further requests fully supporting Israel in its fight against terrorism. The 37 signatures on this letter include Richard Perle and Robert Kagan.[98]

September 26, 2001: WASHINGTON—President Bush will announce Thursday new airline safety proposals, including stronger cockpit doors and more sky marshals, as confidence-boosting measures to coax Americans back to flying.

A senior Bush administration official, speaking on condition of anonymity, says the proposals will include strengthened cockpit doors to prevent would-be hijackers from gaining access to the cockpit.

In addition, Bush will announce an expansion of the sky marshals program, which began in the 1970s in reaction to a series of hijackings. Air marshals are armed, plainclothes federal agents who ride on domestic flights.[99]

Good ideas, but a little late.

September 28, 2001: WASHINGTON—Though Vice President Dick Cheney and Secretary of State Colin Powell insist that Saddam Hussein has not been linked to the Sept. 11 attacks, Deputy Defense Secretary Paul Wolfowitz and other administration conservatives are lobbying strenuously to make Saddam a prime target of the anti-terror war. Senator Jesse Helms says we should strike Iraq soon. William Safire calls for it in *The New York Times*. The cover of the current *Weekly Standard* shows a "Wanted" poster of bin Laden and Saddam.[100]

October 2, 2001: WASHINGTON—The Bush administration was reportedly on the verge of announcing Middle East diplomatic offensive that would include U.S. support for Palestinian state before terrorist attacks on September 11. The U.S. intervention in the Middle East conflict, which President Bush sought to play down during first eight months in office, becomes more important as the administration tries to enlist Arab backing in forcing Afghanistan's Taliban rulers to end support of Osama bin Laden. Many moderate Arab states have made it clear that serious American engagement in resolving the Israeli-Palestinian conflict is a condition for their support of the administration's drive to crush terrorism.[101]

October 6, 2001: WASHINGTON—The United States House approves a significant infusion of new spending for nation's intelligence agencies, while backing away from a wide-ranging independent inquiry into the performance of government intelligence leading up to the Sept 11 terrorist attacks.[102]

October 7, 2001: Afghanistan—U.S. and Britain start air strikes on Afghanistan to wage war against the Taliban and al Qaeda in response to the Sept. 11 attacks.[103]

October 8, 2001: WASHINGTON—Former governor of Pennsylvania, Tom Ridge, takes over as director of the Office of Homeland Security. This new office was recommended in the Commission on National Security report provided to Bush administration in January 2001, but there was no presidential interest in this change until after the Sept. 11 attacks.[104]

October 2001: WASHINGTON—Four-star General Wayne Downing is appointed by President Bush to head the White House Office for Combating Terrorism.[105]

October 24, 2001: WASHINGTON—Israeli Foreign Minister Shimon Peres meets in Washington with President Bush and Secretary of State Colin Powell and rebuffs their demand that Israel pull out of Palestinian-controlled areas of West Bank. He says security forces of Yasir Arafat must first arrest men who murdered Israeli Tourism Minister Rehavam Zeevi.[106]

November 8, 2001: Iraq—An article entitled, "Defectors: Iraqi terror camp targeted; U.S. trainees reportedly learned hijacking; site had biological agents" is fed to *The New York Times* (page 5A) by the Iraqi National Congress to support the push to war against Iraq. There is no credible evidence to support these claims by defectors who had a conflict of interest in promoting an invasion to overthrow Saddam Hussein.[107]

November 21, 2001: WASHINGTON—President Bush secretly orders a war plan drawn up against Iraq less than two months after U.S. forces attacked Afghanistan and is so worried the decision will cause a furor he doesn't tell everyone on his national security team, according to *Plan of Attack* by journalist Bob Woodward which will be released in April 2004.

Bush feared that if news got out about the Iraq plan as U.S. forces were fighting another conflict, people would think he was too eager for war, according to the book, which is a behind-the-scenes account of the 16 months leading to the Iraq invasion.

Asked if he told Defense Secretary Donald Rumsfeld on Nov. 21, 2001, to draft an Iraq war plan, the president will state, "I can't remember exact dates that far back."[108]

If the justifications for invading Iraq are solid, and there is no intent of a surprise attack, is it necessary to hide the planning for war?

December 2, 2001: Afghanistan—John Walker Lindh, the Marin County expatriate fighting with Taliban forces in Afghanistan, is captured. He is stripped of clothing and held naked for an extended time; with U.S. soldiers scrawling an expletive on the prisoner's blindfold; and with guards posing for souvenir photos at his side.

Lindh is denied food and proper medical treatment for a gunshot wound during his first days in custody, and is provided only a "single, thin blanket" covering his naked body in a cold metal shipping container in Afghanistan according to court filings.[109]

After Sept. 11 many things changed, including the handling of detainees.

December 16, 2001: Iraq—An article entitled, "Mystery shrouds Atta meeting with Iraqi spy" is fed to *The New York Times* (page 24A) by the Iraqi National Congress to support the push to war with Iraq. There is no credible evidence to support these claims by defectors who had a conflict of interest in promoting an invasion to overthrow Saddam Hussein.[110]

December 20, 2001: Iraq—An article entitled "Evidence of Iraqi weapons: Defector says chemical, nuclear labs functioning in secret" is fed to *The New York Times* (page 22A) by the Iraqi National Congress to support the push to war. There is no credible evidence to support these claims by defectors who had a conflict of interest in promoting an invasion to overthrow Saddam Hussein.[111]

December 2001: WASHINGTON—Kellogg Brown and Root (KBR), a Halliburton subsidiary, secures a 10-year deal with the Pentagon with no cost ceiling to provide support services to the Army. The contract is known as the Logistics Civil Augmentation Program (LOGCAP). This contract is a "cost-plus-award-fee, indefinite-delivery/indefinite-quantity service," which means that the federal government has an open-ended mandate and budget to send KBR anywhere in the world to run humanitarian or military operations for profit.[112]

Halliburton took good care of Dick Cheney, and now it pays off.

December 2001: WASHINGTON—Beginning in late December 2001, President Bush meets repeatedly with Army Gen. Tommy Franks and his war Cabinet to plan the U.S. attack on Iraq even as he and administration representatives insist publicly they are pursuing a diplomatic solution, according to Bob Woodward's *Plan of Attack*.

Bush will later say the secret planning was necessary to avoid "enormous international angst and domestic speculation" and that "war is my absolute last option."[113]

December 2001: WASHINGTON—The Bush administration diverts $700 million from the Afghanistan war fund to prepare for a U.S.-led invasion of Iraq without informing Congress, according to Bob Woodward's *Plan of Attack*.[114]

January 18, 2002: WASHINGTON—Using unusually pointed language, President Bush's chief political adviser Karl Rove suggests Republicans should run on the message that they are the party that can be trusted to successfully fight the war against terrorism.

By keeping the public prepared for a long war, the president keeps up the necessary emotional and practical support the effort requires, but it has a political benefit too, as Bush's popularity and war-time mantle can be extended into this election year and maybe into 2004, when Bush's national security team could serve as actual or virtual surrogates in a possible Bush re-election effort.[115]

The political benefit for a Commander in Chief who is prosecuting a war is not lost on Karl Rove. But the risks involved with sending U.S. troops into an Arab country flies over his head.

January 2002: Among the motives for the Iraq war, according to Richard Clarke, were the politics of the 2002 midterm election. "The crisis was manufactured, and Bush political advisor Karl Rove was telling Republicans to 'run on the war,'" Clarke will write.[116]

January 2002: White House counsel Alberto Gonzales writes to President Bush that in his judgment, the post-Sept. 11 security environment "renders obsolete" the Geneva Convention's "strict limitations on questioning of enemy prisoners and renders quaint some of its provisions," according to *Newsweek* in May 2004.

Secretary of State Colin Powell "hits the roof" when he reads the memo and fires off his own note to the president, warning that the new rules "will reverse over a century of U.S. policy and practice" and have "a high cost in terms of negative international reaction."[117]

We learn in 2004 that Gonzales wins this battle.

January 24, 2002: WASHINGTON—U.S. President George W. Bush announces plans for a $48 billion increase in defense spending to fight the war on terror.

The increase—of nearly 15%—will be the largest rise in U.S. military spending in 20 years, he says in a speech to military reserve officers.

"I have no ambition whatsoever to use this as a political issue…"[118]

<u>January 29, 2002</u>: WASHINGTON—Bush delivers his State of the Union speech.

"Iraq continues to flaunt its hostility toward America and to support terror. The Iraqi regime has plotted to develop anthrax, and nerve gas, and nuclear weapons for over a decade."

President Bush refers to Iraq, North Korea, and Iran, as an "axis of evil."[119]

<u>Early 2002</u>: WASHINGTON—Vice President Dick Cheney asks the CIA to check out the rumor that Iraq was shopping for Uranium ore in Niger.[120]

<u>Early 2002</u>: From the earliest days at the Bagram military base in Afghanistan, detainees report that U.S. interrogators routinely cover prisoners' heads with black hoods, strip them of their clothing or force them to kneel or stand in uncomfortable positions for long periods. The Pentagon later investigates reports that two prisoners died while in U.S. custody at Bagram.[121]

<u>February 7, 2002</u>: WASHINGTON—Halliburton subsidiary KBR pays $2 million to settle a lawsuit with the Justice Department, which alleges that the company defrauded the government in the mid-1990's by over-billing expenses.[122]

<u>February 2002</u>: NIAMEY, Niger—The CIA dispatches Joseph Wilson, a retired ambassador who has held senior positions in several African countries and Iraq, to Niger to investigate claims that Saddam Hussein's government had shopped there for uranium ore that could be processed into weapons-grade material. He reports back that Niger officials say they knew of no such effort. His report will later be confirmed by U.S. intelligence officials.[123]

<u>February 2002</u>: WASHINGTON—A congressional inquiry, by members of both the House and Senate intelligence committees, is launched in February 2002 amid growing concerns that failures by U.S. intelligence had allowed 19 al Qaeda members to enter the United States, hijack four airliners, and kill almost 3,000 people.[124]

<u>2002</u>: NFL player Pat Tillman walks away from a $3.6 million contract offer from the Arizona Cardinals so he can serve his country as a member of the U.S. Army's elite Rangers unit.[125]

<u>February 2002</u>: WASHINGTON—The CIA concludes that the rumor that Iraq was shopping for Uranium ore in Niger, checked out for Vice President Cheney, appears to be false.[126]

<u>March 7, 2002</u>: WASHINGTON—The Bush administration decides to terminate its unequivocal support for Prime Minister Ariel Sharon's hard-line strategy and declares that his approach will likely fail. The administration officials are alarmed by Sharon's recent comment that Palestinians must be 'hit hard' because they will only negotiate after they are beaten. The administration decides to respond strongly to Sharon, lest he interpret Washington's silence as implicit permission to intensify the conflict or declare an all-out war. Secretary of State Colin Powell's comments to House subcommittee asking Israel to a take a 'hard look' at its policies are the sharpest criticism to date of Sharon's tough policy.[127]

<u>March 2002</u>: WASHINGTON—David M. Walker, the Comptroller General of the GAO, as well as Judicial Watch, launch lawsuits against Vice President Dick Cheney because he refuses to turn over to Congress documents that reveal the identities of industry executives involved in the National Energy Strategy.[128]

<u>April 2002</u>: BAGHDAD—Saddam Hussein suspends oil exports to protest Israeli incursions into Palestinian territories. Despite calls by Saddam Hussein, no other Arab countries follow suit. Exports resume after 30 days.[129]

<u>April 2002</u>: WASHINGTON—"You go back to the John Walker Lindh case and…you discover that, when he was arrested, he was stripped, roughed up and photographed, twice, by people," journalist Seymour Hersh will say May 9, 2004 on CNN's "Late Edition With Wolf Blitzer." "In other words, the idea of using photographs to humiliate somebody was started in Afghanistan."

An April 2002 court filing releases one photo of a naked and blindfolded Lindh, his hands and legs shackled and his body bound by heavy tape to a stretcher. In another photo U.S. soldiers scrawled an expletive across his blindfold and posed with him for "souvenir photographs."

"Had Lindh not thrown his lot in with al Qaeda and the Taliban, he would not have suffered the deprivations of low temperatures, 'inadequate' food and water, and 'little cover'," government prosecutors write in one court filing.

The Bush administration's insistence that Lindh renounce any charges of abuse will be echoed in the reluctance to reveal detailed information about the

Abu Ghurayb abuses in 2004, says William Aceves, who studied the case for a 2002 legal report.

"There does seem to be somewhat of a pattern there of trying to minimize these situations and not get them out in the open," Aceves says.[130]

May 2002: NEW YORK—The U.N. Security Council agrees to overhaul the sanctions regime, replacing a blanket ban on a range of goods with "smart" sanctions targeted at military and dual-use equipment.[131]

May 15, 2002: WASHINGTON—The White House approves of the Republican congressional campaign committee's plan to use a photograph of President Bush taken on September 11 as part of a GOP fundraising effort, a move Democrats call "nothing short of grotesque."

The National Republican Senatorial Committee and the National Republican Congressional Committee are offering the picture, along with photos of the president during his State of the Union address and at his inauguration, to donors who contribute at least $150 and attend a fund-raising dinner with Bush and the first lady next month.

"We know it's the Republicans' strategy to use the war for political gain, but I would hope that even the most cynical partisan operative would have cowered at the notion of exploiting the September 11 tragedy in this way," says Terry McAuliffe, chairman of the Democratic National Committee, in a written statement.[132]

May 16, 2002: WASHINGTON—At her statement at the White House Condoleezza Rice says, "I don't think anybody could have predicted that these people would take an airplane and slam it into the World Trade Center...that they would try to use...a hijacked airplane as a missile."

Intelligence reports had detailed such plans as much as five years before 9/11. She will retract this statement at a private session with the Sept. 11 Commission on February 7, 2004.[133]

May 17, 2002: WASHINGTON—"Had I known that the enemy was going to use airplanes to kill on that fateful morning, I would have done everything in my power to protect the American people," Mr. Bush says at the White House on Friday. It is his first public comment on revelations this week that he was told August 6, 2001 that bin Laden wanted to hijack planes and attack America.

The Vice President has repeatedly asked Congress not to investigate the intelligence failures. But with the new commotion, the White House now says it will cooperate with an investigation if it's done the right way.[134]

It's easy to understand why the White House didn't want an investigation.

May 20, 2002: WASHINGTON—Vice President Dick Cheney says he will advise President Bush against turning over to Congress the August 6, 2001 Presidential Daily Brief that warned of possible hijacking of airplanes by terrorists, and insists the investigation into the September 11 attacks should be handled by Congressional intelligence committees, not an independent commission. The brief has ignited a political uproar over whether or not the nation could have anticipated attacks on World Trade Center and Pentagon.[135]

May 22, 2002: WASHINGTON—The Senate Governmental Affairs Committee unanimously approves a bill that will create a commission with sweeping powers to investigate Sept. 11 terrorist attacks. The commission will consist of 14 prominent citizens, half Republican and half Democrats, and no current officeholder. The administration's position is that narrower inquiry, like that already being undertaken in House and Senate intelligence committees, is preferable.[136]

May 22, 2002: WASHINGTON—Tom Daschle, the Senate majority leader, calls for an independent commission to investigate government action before Sept. 11 terrorist attacks and criticizes the Bush administration's 'intransigence' to sharing information with Congress. Administration officials and Congressional Republicans step up their opposition to an independent commission.[137]

May 26, 2002: WASHINGTON—President Bush's opposition to having an independent commission to investigate intelligence and law enforcement lapses before Sept. 11 represents reversal of practice of past presidents, who have generally pressed for independent investigations into calamitous events and political embarrassments.[138]

June 2, 2002: HOUSTON—Halliburton announces that the SEC has begun a probe into the company's booking of cost overruns on energy-related construction jobs. This practice accounts for the overruns as revenue, even if customers have not yet approved the charges, and inflated Halliburton profits by almost $100 million in 1998 in a manner similar to the Enron accounting scandal.

In a *Washington Post* story, Halliburton says a shift in its mix of business mandates the new accounting policy, and that it conforms to generally accepted accounting principles. The accounting change was approved by Halliburton auditor Arthur Andersen.[139]

June 2002: WASHINGTON—General Wayne Downing, head of the White House Office for Combating Terrorism, resigns.

According to Richard Clarke, Wayne Downing quit the White House in frustration at the administration's continued bureaucratic response to the terrorist threat.[140]

He is replaced by retired Air Force Gen. John Gordon, an expert in nuclear security.

2002: The INC orchestrates a coordinated propaganda campaign during 2002 that exaggerates and fabricates intelligence on Iraq, and feeds the misinformation to news agencies and magazines in the U.S., Britain, and Australia.

The group, led by Ahmed Chalabi, has close contacts to Vice President Dick Cheney and Secretary of Defense Donald Rumsfeld, both of which are strong supporters of the invasion. The assertions in the information that is fed to the media supporting President Bush's claims that Saddam Hussein should be removed because he is linked to al Qaeda, he is developing nuclear weapons, and he already has biological and chemical weapons.

By channeling this information through many news organizations and officials, the INC creates an impression that multiple sources are confirming the various justifications of war. However, many of the allegations come from a few defectors, and are either not confirmed by any credible intelligence or vigorously contested by the governmental intelligence agencies. This continuous flow of fictitious information helped move public opinion toward the use of preemptive force in Iraq.

A letter will be sent in June 2002 from the Iraqi National Congress (INC), a former Iraqi exile group led by Ahmed Chalabi, to the Senate Appropriations Committee listing 108 articles based upon information provided by the Iraqi National Congress's Information Collection Program, which is funded by the United States to collect information in Iraq. Following are some examples of the faulty claims circulated by the INC:

> *Saddam cooperated with bin Laden and was involved in the Sept. 11 terrorist attacks.*
> Intelligence officials say there is no evidence of an operational relationship

between Iraq and al Qaeda, and no evidence of Saddam being involved in the attacks.

Iraq trained Islamists in hijacking techniques and prepared them for operations against the United States.
Two senior U.S. officials claim there is no evidence to support this claim.

Iraq had mobile biological warfare facilities and hid banned weapons production and storage facilities in Saddam's palaces.
No such facilities or vehicles have been located.

Iraq held 80 Kuwaitis captured in the 1991 Persian Gulf War in a secret underground prison in 2000.
No Kuwaiti prisoners have been found.

Iraq could launch toxin-armed Scud missiles at Israel that could kill 100,000 people and was aggressively developing nuclear weapons.
No Iraq Scud missiles have been found and there is no evidence of any nuclear program in Iraq.[141]

July 11, 2002: Judicial Watch files suit on behalf of shareholders against Dick Cheney and 13 other Halliburton directors, as well as Halliburton itself and its accounting firm, Arthur Andersen LLP and Arthur Andersen Worldwide. The suit charges Cheney and Halliburton with fraudulent accounting practices and misleading press releases resulting in the overvaluation of the company's shares, leading to shareholder losses. The lawsuit alleges Halliburton overstated revenues by $445 million from 1999 through the end of 2001.

Two shareholders, Stephen S. Stephens of Indiana and Lyle and Deanna J. Lionbarger of New Mexico, are listed as plaintiffs. The suit is filed in U.S. District Court in Dallas.

Despite the ongoing investigation and the previous revelations about cost overruns, Halliburton continues to receive government contracts worth billions.[142]

July 15, 2002: HOUSTON—*Newsweek* publishes an article, "Halliburton CEO says Cheney knew about firm's accounting practices," revealing that Dick Cheney was aware that the firm was counting projected cost-overrun payments as revenues during his watch.[143]

July 26, 2002: WASHINGTON—The House votes, 193-188, over White House objections, to create an independent commission to investigate performance of nation's intelligence agencies with regard to the Sept. 11 terrorist attacks. Twenty-five Republicans break party lines in an unexpected early morning vote on an amendment giving the intelligence agencies biggest funding increase since the cold war. The measure is backed by the families of the victims, but the commission's scope is far narrower than original proposal by Representative Tim Roemer.[144]

Summer 2002: WASHINGTON—According to an editorial, the United States spots a Pakistani plane picking up North Korean missile parts in the summer of 2002, despite Pakistan's claim that it ended such exchanges with North Korea. These actions are not those of reliable partner, and Washington must make it clear to General Pervez Musharraf that continuing such behavior will not be tolerated.[145]

Why doesn't President Bush do anything about Pakistan's nuclear proliferation?

July/August 2002: WASHINGTON—Just as the focus on Dick Cheney's role in alleged accounting violations at Halliburton starts to build, the Bush administration turns the nation's attention to Iraq.[146]

Ironically, Bush will need to find other distractions in 2004 due to the Iraq debacle.

August 26, 2002: NASHVILLE—Dick Cheney delivers a speech to the Veterans of Foreign Wars in Nashville, warning that "seated atop of 10 percent of the world's oil reserves, Saddam Hussein could then be expected to seek domination of the entire Middle East, take control of a great portion of the world's energy supplies,…and subject the United States to nuclear blackmail."[147]

In Dick Cheney's mind, there is a rock-solid link between oil reserves and the need to conquer Iraq.

September 10, 2002: WASHINGTON—Senator Richard Shelby, the ranking Republican on the Senate Intelligence Committee, says he will not oppose an independent commission to investigate events leading up to September 11 terrorist attacks citing fears that Congress will adjourn before all facts are unearthed.[148]

September 12, 2002: WASHINGTON—President Bush tells skeptical world leaders gathered at a U.N. General Assembly session to confront the "grave and gathering danger" of Iraq—or stand aside as the United States acts.[149]

An Iraq report released by the White House in conjunction with President Bush's speech to the U.N. claims that Iraq is training international terrorists in airplane hijacking at a facility south of Baghdad called Salman Pak. At the time, several intelligence officials tell Knight Ridder and CBS News, among others, that the allegation isn't true and that the facility probably is used by the Iraqis for counterterrorism training. Later inspections will find no facilities.[150]

September 19, 2002: WASHINGTON—In a statement to the Senate Armed Services Committee, Donald Rumsfeld says, "There are a number of terrorist states pursuing weapons of mass destruction, but no terrorist state poses a greater or more immediate threat to the security of our people than the regime of Saddam Hussein and Iraq."[151]

September 24, 2002: LONDON—British Prime Minister Tony Blair publishes a dossier on Iraq's military capability. The report claims that Iraq is continuing to produce chemical and biological weapons and is trying to acquire uranium for nuclear weapons from Africa.[152]

British intelligence cites the Niger uranium claim in an unclassified report, based in part on unsubstantiated postings on the Internet.[153]

September 25, 2002: WASHINGTON—President Bush's national security adviser says al Qaeda operatives have found refuge in Baghdad, and accuses Iraqi President Saddam Hussein's regime of helping Osama bin Laden's followers develop chemical weapons.

Condoleezza Rice's statements, aired in a broadcast interview, are the strongest yet alleging contacts between al Qaeda and the Iraqi government. Previously, evidence of the two working together was tenuous, or came from unreliable sources.

She makes her accusations as the Bush administration continues to make its case to a skeptical world that Saddam should be removed from power, by force if necessary.

The widely held view has been that while Saddam and bin Laden both oppose the United States, their motivations are too different for them to work together. Saddam seeks secular power. However, bin Laden's drive comes from religious motivations and his opposition to the U.S. military presence in Saudi Arabia and the Arab world.

"No one is trying to make an argument at this point that Saddam Hussein somehow had operational control of what happened on Sept. 11, so we don't want to push this too far, but this is a story that is unfolding, and it is getting clearer, and we're learning more," Rice says.

She suggests that details of the contacts will be released later.

After Sept. 11, officials in the Czech Republic said Mohamed Atta, believed to have led the suicide hijacking attacks, had met with an Iraqi intelligence agent in Prague, which some viewed as a link between Iraq and the attacks. But U.S. officials have since said they doubt the meeting took place.

The Iraqi government has been linked to other groups labeled terrorist by the United States, primarily those that oppose Iran and Israel.[154]

October 2, 2002: WASHINGTON—Congress passes a resolution authorizing the use of armed forces against Iraq under certain conditions [diplomatic efforts fail].[155]

If it were known at the time that Iraq had no weapons of mass destruction and there was no connection between Saddam Hussein and the Sept. 11 attacks, would Congress have authorized the use of force for regime change in Iraq anyway?

October 11, 2002: WASHINGTON—The White House raises fresh objections to the terms of the independent commission to investigate Sept 11 attacks just hours after Congressional Republicans and Democrats reach an accord on the terms. Some officials say they suspect the real White House objection is to having the commission at all.[156]

October 12, 2002: WASHINGTON—Senators John McCain, Arizona Republican, and Joseph L Lieberman, Connecticut Democrat, accuse the White House of deliberately sabotaging their efforts to create an independent investigation of Sept. 11 attacks, suggesting that the Bush administration is afraid the commission might turn up embarrassing government mistakes. Senator McCain declares, "Every bureaucracy in this town is scared to death of an investigation."[157]

October 12, 2002: BALI—Bombs kill 202 people in nightclubs on the Indonesian island of Bali. Authorities blame Jemaah Islamiyah, a Southeast Asian terror group linked to al Qaeda.[158]

October 13, 2002: WASHINGTON—A *Washington Post* article describes Vice President Dick Cheney as the "fulcrum of foreign policy," and that his influence for a pro-war policy comes to the fore on the eve of a possible conflict with Iraq.[159]

October 16, 2002: WASHINGTON—Ariel Sharon has complicated the U.S. war on terrorism. The Israeli leader's determination to retaliate for Palestinian suicide attacks with overwhelming force has angered Arab allies and inflamed anti-American hatred among Muslims around the world. After the two leaders meet today in Washington, Bush needs to strike a hard bargain with Sharon before the Israeli Prime Minister's policies derail the administration's effort to build support for a war against Iraq.

The U.S. should gain a commitment to ease the Israeli army's occupation of the West Bank, and a tacit assurance that Israel will not retaliate against Iraq should Saddam Hussein fire Scud missiles into Israeli cities, which he did 39 times during the Gulf War. The U.S. needs to calm the fears of Arab leaders that an Israeli attack on Iraq could destabilize their regimes and possibly drag them into a wider war.[160]

October 21, 2002: PRAGUE, Czech Republic—Czech intelligence officials eliminate a previously intimated link between al Qaeda terrorists and the Iraqi regime of Saddam Hussein.

Senior Czech intelligence officials claim that they now have "no confidence" in their earlier report of direct meetings in Prague between Mohammed Atta, leader of the Sept. 11 hijackers, and an Iraqi diplomat stationed in Prague.

"Quite simply, we think the source for this story may have invented the meeting that he reported. We can find no corroborative evidence for the meeting and the source has real credibility problems," a high-ranking source close to Czech intelligence tells UPI.[161]

October 2002: WASHINGTON—CIA Director George Tenet urges Bush's deputy national security advisor to delete a reference to the Niger uranium caper in a speech the president plans to give since there was no evidence to support the claim. He does.[162]

October 2002: WASHINGTON—Despite widespread doubts within the CIA and the State Department, the allegation that Iraq sought uranium in an African nation [Niger] resurfaces in a classified intelligence document that is sent to Congress.[163]

Dick Cheney was very interested in tying Iraq to uranium from Niger. Did he encourage this deception?

October 2002: WASHINGTON—The public version of the U.S. intelligence community's key prewar assessment of Iraq's illicit arms programs is released in October 2002, but it is stripped of dissenting opinions, warnings of insufficient information and doubts about deposed dictator Saddam Hussein's intentions, a review of the document and its once-classified version shows.

As a result, the public is given a far more definitive assessment of Iraq's plans and capabilities than President Bush and other U.S. decision-makers received from their intelligence agencies.

The two documents are replete with differences. For example, the public version declares that "most analysts assess Iraq is reconstituting its nuclear weapons program" and says "if left unchecked, it probably will have a nuclear weapon within this decade."

But it fails to mention the dissenting view offered in the top-secret version by the State Department's intelligence arm, the Bureau of Intelligence and Research, known as the INR.

A Knight Ridder comparison of the two documents shows that although the top-secret version was heavily qualified with caveats about some of its most important conclusions about Iraq's illicit weapons programs, those caveats are omitted from the public version.

The caveats included the phases: "we judge that," "we assess that," and "we lack specific information on many key aspects of Iraq's WMD programs."

These phrases, according to current and former intelligence officials, long have been used in intelligence reports to stress an absence of hard information and underscore that judgments are extrapolations or estimates.[164]

Was Vice President Cheney, who spent a great deal of time with the CIA during this time period, involved with this deception?

October 2002: WASHINGTON—According to the Wall Street Journal, Halliburton officials meet informally with representatives of Vice President Cheney's office in October 2002 to figure out how best to jumpstart Iraq's oil industry following a war.[165]

Publicly, Dick Cheney maintains that he has had no involvement whatsoever with Halliburton since becoming Vice President.

October 24, 2002: WASHINGTON—Defense Secretary Donald Rumsfeld and key aides assign a small intelligence unit to search for information on Iraq's hostile intentions or links to terrorists that the nation's spy agencies may have overlooked. Rumsfeld and Deputy Defense Secretary Paul Wolfowitz feel frustrated that they are not receiving undiluted information on the capacities of Saddam Hussein and his suspected ties to terrorist organizations. Rumsfeld's inner circle claims there are numerous intelligence findings indicating links between Iraq and senior Qaeda leaders.

Critics say top civilian policy makers are intent on politicizing the intelligence to fit their hawkish views on Iraq. Many parties in the intelligence agencies say Saddam cannot be directly linked to Osama bin Laden and al Qaeda, and that the two are unlikely to make common cause against United States. Some senior intelligence analysts at the CIA contend that Saddam is contained and is unlikely to unleash any weapons of mass destruction unless he is attacked.[166]

October 25, 2002: CAIRO—Anti-American demonstrations in Cairo, Egypt reflect deep fear in the Arab world that if the U.S. attacks Iraq, it will then impose long-term military control. At issue is the prospect that the American government, backed by its military, may exert daily administrative control over a large swath of Arab soil for a long period. The idea summons up angry emotions in the region where sensitivities about a colonial past run deep.[167]

November 2002: BAGHDAD—U.N. weapons inspectors return to Iraq for the first time since 1998, backed by a tough U.N. Security Council resolution that Baghdad reluctantly accepts. The resolution threatens serious consequences if Iraq is in "material breach" of its terms.[168]

2002–2003: WASHINGTON—Adding to the momentum for war, according to Bob Woodward, is the pressure from advocates of war inside the administration. Vice President Dick Cheney, whom Woodward describes as a "powerful, steamrolling force," leads that group and has what some of his colleagues believe is a "fever" about removing Saddam by force.

Also according to Woodward, the relationship between Cheney and Secretary of State Colin Powell becomes so strained that Cheney and Powell are barely on speaking terms. Cheney engages in a bitter and eventually winning struggle over Iraq with Powell, an opponent of war who believes Cheney is obsessively trying to establish a connection between Iraq and the al Qaeda terror network and treats ambiguous intelligence as fact.

The Vice President believes Powell is mainly concerned with his own popularity and told friends at a dinner he will host celebrating the outcome of the war that Powell was a problem and "always had major reservations about what we were trying to do…"

Powell believes Cheney and his allies—his chief aide, Lewis "Scooter" Libby, Deputy Defense Secretary Paul Wolfowitz, and Undersecretary of Defense for Policy Douglas Feith, and what Powell calls Feith's "Gestapo" office—have established what amounts to a separate government.[169]

2002–2003: WASHINGTON—Dick Cheney's wife Lynne is a senior fellow at the American Enterprise Institute (AEI), which exerts considerable influence in Washington. It is one of the leading architects of the Bush administration's foreign policy and one of the leading voices pushing the administration's plan for "regime change" through a war in Iraq. The AEI has received funding from the Bechtel Foundation.[170]

Why would Bechtel be so anxious for a war in Iraq?

November 2, 2002: WASHINGTON—The Congressional deal to create an independent commission to probe the Sept. 11 terrorist attacks is stalled, with Democrats, some Republicans, and families of attack victims charging that the Bush administration undermines the idea it only reluctantly embraced. Administration officials and Congressional Republicans say they want the commission structured to produce a bipartisan result. An almost completed deal was suddenly undone in October after Representative Porter Goss, the Republican involved in the talks, got a call from Vice President Dick Cheney. The impasse shows how sensitive the issue of intelligence lapses before Sept. 11 remains for the Bush administration.[171]

November 8, 2002: DAMASCUS—Syria, which has long centered foreign policy around its leadership of countries against Israel, fears being isolated in the region if a pro-U.S. government is installed in Iraq.

Damascus also fears being next on the U.S. list.[172]

November 13, 2002: WASHINGTON—The House, voting mostly along party lines, rejects bill, 215-203, to establish an independent commission to investigate Sept. 11 terrorist attacks.[173]

November 14, 2002: WASHINGTON—The White House, yielding to intense pressure from families of the Sept. 11 victims, agrees to a Congressional compromise that will create an independent commission to investigate the terrorist attacks. The House immediately approves the bill to establish the commission on a 366-to-3 vote. The 10-member commission is charged with providing the nation a most comprehensive examination of vulnerabilities that made the attacks possible.[174]

November 14, 2002: WASHINGTON—Kristin Breitweiser of Middletown, Patty Casazza of Colt's Neck, and Lorie Van Auken and Mindy Kleinberg of East Brunswick, are the four "Jersey girls."

On Capitol Hill, these stay-at-home moms from the New Jersey suburbs are gaining prominence as savvy World Trade Center widows who came to Washington as part of a core group of politically active relatives of Sept. 11 victims. They have forced Congress and a very reluctant White House to create the independent commission—a panel that will bring official Washington to its knees in April 2004 when Condoleezza Rice will testify in public after months of President Bush's refusals.

"They call me all the time," says Thomas Kean, the panel's chairman and a former Republican governor of New Jersey. "They monitor us, they follow our progress, they've supplied us with some of the best questions we've asked. I doubt very much if we would be in existence without them."[175]

November 15, 2002: WASHINGTON—The Bush administration has been pressing Israel and the Palestinian leadership to embrace an ambitious plan for reciprocal steps toward creating a Palestinian state. Painstakingly negotiated with the U.N., the European Union and Russia, the administration's so-called road map was thought by those who conceived it to have a better chance of success than the administration's previous forays into Middle East arena. However, hopes of securing any agreement this year on the plan have now evaporated with the talk of war in Iraq, in pending elections in Israel caused by the collapse of Prime Minister Ariel Sharon's broad coalition, and the increasingly dire living conditions of many Palestinians.[176]

November 2002: WASHINGTON—Ousted Treasury Secretary Paul O'Neill will be a guest on a CBS "60 Minutes" broadcast in January 2004, along with Ron Suskind, the author of a book for which O'Neill was the primary source.

Within six months of taking office, Bush pushed a trillion dollars worth of tax cuts through Congress. And O'Neill thought that should have been the end of it. After the Sept. 11 attacks and the war in Afghanistan, the budget deficit was growing. So at a meeting with the vice president after the mid-term elections in 2002, O'Neill argues against a second round of tax cuts.

"Cheney, at this moment, shows his hand," according to Suskind. "He says, 'You know, Paul, Reagan proved that deficits don't matter. We won the mid-term elections, this is our due.'...O'Neill is speechless..."

In the end, the President, with an additional push from Karl Rove, follows Cheney's instructions. And nine days after a meeting in which O'Neill made it clear he could not publicly support another tax cut, the Vice President will call and ask him to resign.[177]

November 22, 2002: WASHINGTON—The question of who should lead a post-Saddam Hussein Iraq is a matter of deep disagreement within the administration of President George W. Bush.

The neoconservative hawks around Pentagon chief Donald Rumsfeld and Vice President Dick Cheney lobby heavily for the Iraqi National Congress (INC), and especially its leader, Ahmed Chalabi.

However, Middle East specialists in the State Department and their colleagues at the CIA have generally favored former military officers who are believed to retain influence in Iraq's army.

But what has really given Chalabi political muscle in Washington is the enthusiastic backing he receives from a group of neocons closely identified with Israel's Likud Party and associated with the American Enterprise Institute and the Project for a New American Century (PNAC).

Rumsfeld and Cheney, charter members of the PNAC, recruited their top foreign policy aides heavily from these two groups, while the American Enterprise Institute's Richard Perle, who heads Rumsfeld's Defense Policy Board, has been friends with Chalabi for some 20 years.[178]

Late 2002: Former CIA counter-terror director Cofer Black tells a congressional committee in late 2002 that with respect to detainee interrogations after Sept. 11, "the gloves came off."[179]

December 3, 2002: WASHINGTON—In a BBC interview, Mr. Wolfowitz claims ordinary Iraqis will greet American troops as liberators. In the vision endorsed by Mr. Wolfowitz, a transformed Iraq would not only help secure oil supplies and reduce the threat to Israel. It could also become a democratic model, which other Arab countries would emulate.[180]

This is also President Bush's vision. Will American troops be greeted as liberators?

December 2002: For more than a hundred years, major powers have battled to control the enormous source of wealth and strategic power of Middle East oil, and the reserves in Iraq are especially attractive to the big international oil companies for three reasons: huge reserves, high quality, and low production costs.

Iraq's oil is generally of high quality because it has high carbon content, lightness, and low sulfur content. It is especially suitable for refining into the high-value products and commands a premium on the world market.

Iraq's oil is very plentiful. The country's proven reserves in 2002 were listed at 112.5 billion barrels, about 11% of the world total. With little exploration since the nationalization of the industry in 1972, many promising areas remain unexplored. Experts believe that Iraq has potential reserves substantially above 200 billion barrels.

The U.S. Department of Energy states, "Iraq's oil production costs are amongst the lowest in the world, making it a highly attractive oil prospect." This is because Iraq's oil comes in enormous fields that can be tapped by relatively shallow wells, producing a high "flow rate."[181]

December 2002: WASHINGTON—The congressional inquiry into the Sept. 11 attacks completed its work, but publication of the report is delayed due to "vigorous discussions" with administration officials over which parts of it could be declassified.[182]

December 2002: KABUL, Afghanistan—An Afghan captive freezes to death in a CIA-run lockup in Kabul, Afghanistan after he is doused with water and shackled overnight to a wall in an exposed cell with the temperature plummeting. The prisoner dies, according to U.S. intelligence sources, after Afghan guards punish him for being unruly.

An Afghan named Mullah Habibullah and a taxi driver named Dilawar both die after they were interrogated at the Bagram air base and detention camp north of Kabul, the Afghan capital, in December 2002. Army pathologists rule both cases homicides due to "blunt force injuries" to the legs. As of May 2004, no one has been publicly charged or reprimanded, and a Pentagon official will say at that time that both cases remain under investigation.[183]

<u>December 2002</u>: Defense Secretary Donald Rumsfeld is presented with a request by Army Maj. Gen. Geoffrey Miller to use a broad range of extraordinary "non-doctrinal" questioning techniques on a specific al Qaeda detainee at the U.S. naval station at Guantánamo Bay, Cuba, a general with the Pentagon's Judge Advocate General's office will say in May 2004 on condition of anonymity.[184]

<u>December 7, 2002</u>: WASHINGTON—The Bush administration's response to terrorism against Israel, combines sympathy and pledges of support with calls for restraint in military retaliation. The tension between the two impulses reflects Bush's concern that Israel do nothing to stir anti-Israel passions in Middle East and Europe that might undermine support for a possible war against Iraq. He calls for restraint, and is hoping that his proposed 'road map' of reciprocal steps by Palestinians and Israel makes progress.[185]

Bush's road map for the Holy Land became road kill long ago.

<u>December 7, 2002</u>: BERLIN—The leftwing Berlin daily, *die tageszeitung*, says it has obtained a copy of part of the document handed by Baghdad to the U.N. on December 7, 2002, which supplies details of its weapons programs. The extract includes a list of foreign companies supplying Iraq including 80 that are German, 24 from the U.S., and 17 from Britain.

The report blows apart an unwritten agreement between the U.N., governments and industry that companies which contributed, wittingly or unwittingly, to Iraq's arms build-up should not be named. The U.N. weapons inspection mission in New York spent several days purging the Iraqi declaration of company names.

In a dispatch from Geneva, the newspaper says the copy of the Iraqi report it has obtained was made from the original handed over by the authorities in Baghdad and shipped to New York via Cyprus.

One U.N. diplomat who has read the report says that the German correspondent must have at least seen parts of the Iraqi declaration, which was supposed to remain secret after it was handed over on December 7.[186]

<u>December 17, 2002</u>: WASHINGTON—The Egypt-United States relationship is under strain as the Bush administration prepares for a possible invasion of Iraq. President Hosni Mubarak makes it clear that an attack on Iraq could let loose a virulently radical backlash across the region that is already incensed by the Israeli crackdown in West Bank and Gaza Strip.[187]

December 21, 2002: WASHINGTON—At a White House meeting, CIA Deputy Director John McLaughlin presents the case for President Bush that Iraq has weapons of mass destruction.

McLaughlin's version uses communications intercepts, satellite photos, diagrams, and other intelligence. "Nice try," Bush says when the CIA official finishes, according to the Bob Woodward's *Plan of Attack.* "I don't think this quite—it's not something that Joe Public would understand or would gain a lot of confidence from."

He then turns to Tenet, McLaughlin's boss, and says, "I've been told all this intelligence about having WMD and this is the best we've got?"

"It's a slam-dunk case," Tenet says, throwing his arms in the air. Bush presses him again. "George, how confident are you?"

"Don't worry, it's a slam-dunk," Tenet repeats.

Tenet will later tell associates he should have said the evidence on weapons was not ironclad, according to Woodward.[188]

George Tenet maintained that he was privately trying to hold administration officials back off their claims of evidence against Iraq. Was the "slam dunk" comment really part of this conversation, or was it invented later so that Tenet could fall on his sword to help save his boss?

Late December 2002: WASHINGTON—When asked personally by the president, Powell agrees to make the U.S. case against Saddam at the U.N. in February 2003, a presentation White House communications director Dan Bartlett describes as "the Powell buy-in." Bush wants someone with Powell's credibility to present the evidence that Saddam possesses weapons of mass destruction, a case the president had initially found less than convincing when presented to him by John McLaughlin.[189]

December 30, 2002: WASHINGTON—A competitor to Halliburton is brushed off by the Defense Department:

"They basically told us that there wasn't going to be any oil well fires." Bob Grace, President of GSM Consulting shows "60 Minutes" a letter from the Department of Defense saying, "The department is aware of a broad range of well firefighting capabilities and techniques available. However, we believe it is too early to speculate what might happen in the event that war breaks out in the region."

The letter is dated Dec. 30, 2002, more than a month after the Army Corps of Engineers began talking to Halliburton about putting out oil well fires in Iraq.[190]

Was there ever any doubt that Halliburton would be first in line for lucrative business in the event of an invasion of Iraq?

<u>2002–2003</u>: WASHINGTON—Richard Perle, chairman of the defense policy board, an advisory panel to the Pentagon, lobbies aggressively to promote a war in Iraq. Like a broken record, Perle keeps repeating, "The Iraqis will welcome the liberators with open arms."[191]

<u>January 2003</u>: WASHINGTON—By early January 2003, Bush has made up his mind to take military action against Iraq, according to *Plan of Attack* by Bob Woodward. But Bush is so concerned that the government of his closest ally, British Prime Minister Tony Blair, might fall because of his support for Bush's war that he delays the war's start until March 19 in Washington—March 20 in Iraq—because Blair asks him to seek a second resolution from the U.N.

Before the war with Iraq, Powell bluntly tells Bush that if he sends U.S. soldiers there "you're going to be owning this place." Powell and his deputy and closest friend, Richard Armitage, used to refer to what they called "the Pottery Barn rule" on Iraq: "You break it, you own it," according to Woodward.[192]

Should the Commander in Chief have considered such advice?

<u>January 2003</u>: WASHINGTON—Senior U.S. officials never found any evidence that Saddam's secular police state and Osama bin Laden's Islamist terrorism network were in league. That verdict is in a secret report by the CIA's Directorate of Intelligence that is updated in January 2003, on the eve of the war.[193]

Do Bush and Cheney share this information with the public prior to the war?

<u>January 2003</u>: WASHINGTON—Richard Clarke quits as counterterrorism coordinator to the President because the Bush administration is more interested in starting a war in Iraq, which will increase terrorism, than in fighting terrorism.[194]

<u>January 17, 2003</u>: MOSCOW—Iraq signs a new development deal with Stroitransgaz, a Russian oil and gas construction company worth $3.4 billion, to develop block four in Iraq's Western Desert.

It also initials two more agreements with Russian companies and starts negotiations with Zarubezhneft, Russia's umbrella company for state holdings abroad, on the giant Bin Umar field, Reuters news agency quotes Iraq's oil ministry as saying.[195]

What are Dick Cheney and the other neocons willing to do to get these lucrative contracts to fall into the hands of American companies?

January 28, 2003: NEW YORK—Chief weapons inspector Hans Blix delivers a harsh report to the U.N. Security Council, accusing Baghdad of failing to come to a "genuine acceptance" of disarmament.[196]

January 28, 2003: WASHINGTON—President Bush in his State of the Union address claims that Saddam Hussein might possess enough chemical and biological material to kill millions of people, and warns of "a day of horror like none we have ever known."[197]

Bush also says, "The British government has learned that Saddam Hussein recently sought significant quantities of uranium from Africa [Niger]." In clearing the speech, the CIA first resisted the inclusion of the infamous 16 words, but then relented.[198]

By including the claim—which was previously debunked and excluded from a presidential speech for that reason—in the widely viewed State of the Union address, the administration can strengthen its public case for the war against Iraq. If anyone questions the evidence, the White House can back away from the statement later, after the war is already started, in a small article that will attract little notice. Did Dick Cheney twist George Tenet's arm in order to pull off this stunt?

January 28, 2003: TAMPA—Norman Schwarzkopf wants to give peace a chance.

The general who commanded U.S. forces in the 1991 Gulf War says he hasn't seen enough evidence to convince him that his old comrades Dick Cheney, Colin Powell, and Paul Wolfowitz are correct in moving toward a new war now. He thinks U.N. inspections are still the proper course to follow. He worries about the cockiness of the U.S. war plan, and even more about the potential human and financial costs of occupying Iraq.

The hero of the last Gulf War worries about the Iraqi leader, but would like to see some persuasive evidence of Iraq's alleged weapons programs.

He hasn't seen that yet, and so—in sharp contrast to the Bush administration—he supports letting the U.N. weapons inspectors drive the timetable, "I think it is very important for us to wait and see what the inspectors come up with, and hopefully they come up with something conclusive."

"It's obviously not a black-and-white situation over there" in the Mideast, he says. "I would just think that whatever path we take, we have to take it with a bit of prudence…"

"The Rumsfeld thing…that's what comes up," when Schwarzkopf calls old Army friends in the Pentagon, he says. He thinks Rumsfeld and the people around him lack the background to make sound military judgments by themselves—and don't include the Army.

Schwarzkopf expresses concern about the task the U.S. military might face after a victory. "What is postwar Iraq going to look like, with the Kurds and the Sunnis and the Shiites? That's a huge question, to my mind. It really should be part of the overall campaign plan."

"I would hope that we have in place the adequate resources to become an army of occupation," he warns, "because you're going to walk into chaos."[199]

Did the Iraq hawks heed any of this advice?

January 30, 2003: WASHINGTON—Consider al Qaeda terrorists, funded by Osama bin Laden's millions and with access to Saddam Hussein's hidden stockpiles of chemical and biological weapons, launching a massive attack against the United States.

In making his case for possible war with Iraq, President Bush warns such a day might come if America fails to act, but there is no known evidence of a link between Washington's chief villains.

"Ideologically and logically, they cannot work together," Gen. Hamid Gul, the former chief of Pakistan's spy agency InterServices Intelligence, tells The Associated Press. "Bin Laden and his men considered Saddam the killer of hundreds of Islamic militants," a reference to Saddam's relentless crackdowns on domestic political rivals, especially the Shiites…

In his State of the Union address Tuesday, Bush used the alleged link between Saddam and al Qaeda as a major argument in his push for a tough stance on Iraq. The president offered no new evidence, but said Secretary of State Colin Powell would present the U.S. case to the U.N. next week.

A Taliban commander tells The Associated Press at the time that despite Saddam's battle with the United States, bin Laden would not relocate to Iraq if kicked out of Afghanistan because "he has differences with Saddam. He is not a good Muslim. Saddam does not care about Islam like Osama." The commander refuses to be identified for fear of reprisal.[200]

January 31, 2003: WASHINGTON—George Tenet and Secretary of State Colin Powell agree there's no evidence to use the uranium story in Powell's speech before the U.N.[201]

Getting the unsubstantiated evidence into the State of the Union speech was apparently enough of a victory for the Iraq hawks.

January 31, 2003: BAGHDAD—Hans Blix, who days ago delivered a broadly negative report on Iraq's cooperation with international inspectors, challenges several of Bush administration's assertions about Iraqi cheating and the notion that time is running out for disarming Iraq through peaceful means. He seems determined to dispel any impression that his report was intended to support the Bush administration's campaign to build world support for a war to disarm Saddam Hussein. He also takes issue with Secretary of State Colin Powell's claim that inspectors found Iraqi officials hiding and moving illicit materials within and outside of Iraq to prevent their discovery. He further disputes the administration's allegations that his inspection agency might have been penetrated by Iraqi agents. He also says he has seen no persuasive indications of Iraqi ties to al Qaeda.[202]

Early 2003: Rumsfeld personally approves very harsh interrogation techniques for suspected Taliban and al Qaeda detainees to extract more information about the Sept. 11 attacks and help prevent future ones, defense officials will say in May 2004.[203]

February 5, 2003: UNITED NATIONS—In a presentation to the U.N., with CIA Director George Tenet seated directly behind him, Secretary of State Colin Powell claims that the United States has "irrefutable and undeniable" evidence that Iraq is hiding weapons of mass destruction.[204]

Powell also claims that three human sources have described Iraq's mobile germ-weapons labs and a fourth has revealed a mobile bio-warfare research facility. The Defense Information Agency had already concluded that the defector who described the mobile research lab was a fabricator; but an alert on that went unnoticed.

CIA Director George Tenet will later acknowledge that official government assessments of Iraq included information from known fabricators and promises to initiate an investigation.[205]

Secretary of State Colin Powell charges that Iraq has repeatedly conspired to conceal banned weapons and is allowing al Qaeda to operate in Baghdad.[206]

Colin Powell had excellent credibility with world leaders, a situation that President Bush was anxious to exploit. But did Powell really believe the nonsense that he was proclaiming to the world? Tenet knew this evidence was unsubstantiated, but he just sat there, as if he supported everything that was said. No evidence has ever come forth to substantiate the al Qaeda link or the hiding of weapons that Hans Blix refutes.

Mid-February 2003: WASHINGTON—Randy Beers takes over as counterterrorism coordinator to the President.[207]

February 2003: WASHINGTON—Intermediaries for ousted dictator Saddam Hussein make numerous attempts to open secret contacts with the Bush administration to head off a U.S.-led invasion of Iraq, but the administration rebuffs or ignores every effort, U.S. officials, who requested anonymity, will say in November 2003.

A Lebanese-American businessman, Imad El Haje, relays word that Saddam will allow U.S. experts and troops into Iraq to verify that he has no weapons of mass destruction, the officials will say.

El Haje sends his message through a Department of Defense official, F. Michael Maloof, who is involved in a Pentagon effort to find links between Saddam and Osama bin Laden, and Richard Perle, the head of a Pentagon advisory panel who is a leading advocate of invading Iraq.

U.S. officials will say none of the approaches went anywhere.

"They were all non-starters because they all involved Saddam staying in power."

"More than 5,000 [U.S.] troops were being proposed [to search for weapons]."

Perle agrees to pursue the matter if he receives approval from the administration, but the go-ahead never comes.[208]

These overtures were non-starters because getting rid of the weapons wasn't the main issue. If Saddam stays in power, how would Dick Cheney accomplish his goals?

February 2003: WASHINGTON—Former U.N. weapons inspector Scott Ritter will say in February 2004 that the Israeli intelligence community was well aware that Iraq had no weapons of mass destruction prior to the March 2003 the invasion.

Ritter, a former marine, was a weapons inspector in Iraq from 1991 to 1998 and a vocal critic of the Bush administration's policy on Iraq.

"That's the only conclusion you can reach," Ritter said in an interview with Y-Net in Washington. "Israeli intelligence reached it years ago…"[209]

February 2003: WASHINGTON—The GAO's lawsuit against Cheney for refusing to turn over to Congress documents that reveal the identities of industry executives involved in the National Energy Strategy is abandoned after Republican threats to cut the GAO's $440 million budget.

But the Judicial Watch legal efforts on the same issue continue.[210]

February 2003: *Parade* magazine publishes "The World's 10 Worst Dictators" each year after consulting with human rights organizations. In February 2003, the worst dictator in the world is Kim Jong II of North Korea. The second worst dictator in 2003 is Crown Prince Abdullah of Saudi Arabia. The third worst dictator is Saddam Hussein of Iraq.[211]

For military action, President Bush skips over the first two without explanation and plans to remove number three on the list.

February 27, 2003: JERUSALEM—The Israelis are hoping that an American war on Iraq will usher in a new Middle East of comfortable Israeli-Arab relations. The Oslo agreement inspired a similar hope, but faded over time.[212]

March 3, 2003: San Diego—The USS *Nimitz* departs San Diego to become the sixth U.S. aircraft carrier sent to the gulf. Each carrier contains approximately 75 aircraft, with about 50 attack planes.[213]

March 4, 2003: WASHINGTON—U.S. officials announce the deployment of 60,000 more soldiers to the gulf. The U.S. Army's 1st Armored Division with 160 tanks and the 1st Calvary Division's 15,000 soldiers are the biggest units.[214]

March 8, 2003: A total of 40 U.N. resolutions critical of Israel have been deflected by U.S. (the only dissenting party) vetoes over the last 30 years.[215]

March 9, 2003: Dr Mohamed ElBaradei, executive director International Atomic Energy Agency, announces the discovery of a forgery in the document that purports to show Iraq trying to buy uranium from Niger. The document was quoted in report from British intelligence services in 2002 as Britain and U.S. sought to build their case for disarming Iraq.[216]

This information arrives before the war begins, but gets lost on page 13 while the impact of the claim in the State of the Union speech stills resonates with the American public.

<u>March 2003</u>: A March 2003 report from *The New York Times* on Camp Delta in Guantánamo Bay, Cuba cites U.S. officials saying that the techniques of interrogation there were "not quite torture, but as close as you can get."[217]

These "enemy combatant" detainees are hooded, receive the "stress and duress" techniques, are provided with no lawyers, and can be held forever. The Bush administration openly admits that they are not provided with any protections covered by the Geneva Convention.

<u>March 2003</u>: Joseph Wilson questions the claim of the infamous 16 words about uranium and Niger in Africa in the president's State of the Union message last January.

"In mid-March, just days before the war, I said in a TV interview with CNN that I believed the administration knew more about the Niger allegations than it was saying."[218]

<u>March 12, 2003</u>: WASHINGTON—Halliburton, the Texas company which has been awarded the Pentagon's contract to put out potential oil-field fires in Iraq and which is bidding for postwar construction contracts, is still making annual payments to its former chief executive, current Vice President Dick Cheney.

The payments, which appear on Mr. Cheney's 2001 financial disclosure statement, are in the form of "deferred compensation" of up to $1 million (£600,000) a year.[219]

<u>March 2003</u>: WASHINGTON—Former Ambassador Joseph C. Wilson IV will tell Knight Ridder on April 29, 2004 that Vice President Dick Cheney's office mounted a campaign to discredit him, including calls to reporters revealing that his wife was an undercover CIA officer, after he challenged President Bush's claim that Saddam Hussein had secretly tried to buy uranium in Africa for nuclear weapons.

"According to a number of sources from different walks of life, there was a meeting held in March 2003 in the offices of the vice president...chaired by either the vice president himself or more likely Scooter Libby, in which the decision was made to do a 'work-up' on me," Wilson will say. "In other words, to find out everything they could about me."

Lewis "Scooter" Libby is Cheney's chief of staff.

"They clearly came across my wife's name and they decided to put my wife's name out on the street" as part of a "campaign to drag my wife into the public square and beat her to get at me," Wilson will say.[220]

NOTES TO CHAPTER 7

1 Ed Villiamy, "Now it's unofficial: Gore did win Florida", *The Observer*, December 24, 2000, http://www.guardian.co.uk/US_election_race/Story/0,2763,415400,00.html.

2 U.S. Joint Inquiry Staff, "Was US informed before attack," *CNN.com*, http://www.mtmi.vu.lt/wtc/questions/02do_they_informed_before2.htm.

3 "AMERICA AT WAR: UNDERSTANDING THE CONFLICT", *The Mercury News*, March 21, 2003, p. 7AB.

4 Barton Gellman, "Book: al Qaeda ignored by Bush", *The Mercury News*, March 22, 2004, p. 3A.

5 AP, "Rice vs. Clark," *The Mercury News*, April 9, 2004, p. 17A.

6 Jeremy Simons, "How Bush and Co. Obscure the Science," *The Washington Post*, July 13, 2003; and U.S. Dept. of Energy, Report of the national Energy Policy Group, Chapter 8: "Strengthening Global Alliances," http://www.whitehouse.gov/energy.

7 *60 Minutes*, "Bush sought 'Way' to oust Saddam?" *CBS.News.com*, January 12, 2004.

8 David Johnston and Jim Dwyer, "Pre-9/11 Files Show Warnings Were More Dire and Persistent," *The New York Times*, April 18, 2004, Section 1, Page 1.

9 "BOB WOODWARD SPEAKS TO NSU STUDENTS ABOUT 'BUSH AT WAR'," Nova Southeastern University, February 28, 2003, http://www.nova.edu/cwis/ia/pubaffairs/news/jan-march2003/woodward-speaks.html.

10 David Johnston and Jim Dwyer,…

11 U.S. Joint Inquiry Staff, "Was US informed before attack,"…

12 Jake Tapper, "We predicted it," Salon.com, September 12, 2001, http://dir.salon.com/politics/feature/2001/09/12/bush/index.html; Full report: http://usinfo.state.gov/topical/pol/terror/01013102.htm.

13 Ibid.

14 U.S. Joint Inquiry Staff, "Was US informed before attack,"...

15 "Top GOP Donors in Energy Industry Met Cheney Panel," *The New York Times*, March 1, 2002; and "Energy Firms were Heard on Air Rules," *The New York Times*, March 2, 2002.

16 "AMERICA AT WAR: UNDERSTANDING THE CONFLICT",...p. 7AB.

17 "Bremer: Don't use remarks against Bush," *The Mercury News*, May 3, 2004, p. 8A.

18 Carl Cameron, "Clues Alerted White House to Potential Attacks." Fox news, May 17, 2002, http://www.foxnews.com/story/0,2933,53065,00.html.

19 "Report Warned Of Suicide Hijackings," *CBS*, May 17, 2002, http://www.cbsnews.com/stories/2002/05/18/attack/main509488.shtml.

20 U.S. Joint Inquiry Staff, "Was US informed before attack,"...

21 Jake Tapper, "We predicted it,"...

22 Philip Shenon, "Draft describes Ashcroft's apathy," *The Mercury News*, April 13, 2004, p. 3A.

23 U.S. Joint Inquiry Staff, "Was US informed before attack,"...

24 Barton Gellman, "Book: al Qaeda ignored by Bush",...

25 Jake Tapper, "We predicted it,"...

26 U.S. Joint Inquiry Staff, "Was US informed before attack,"...

27 David Johnston and Jim Dwyer,...

28 Jake Tapper, "We predicted it,"...

29 Carl Cameron, "Clues Alerted White House to Potential Attacks."...

30 "Complete Text of 2001 Memo", *The Mercury News*, April 11, 2004, p. 5A.

31 U.S. Joint Inquiry Staff, "Was US informed before attack,"...

32 Carl Cameron, "Clues Alerted White House to Potential Attacks."…

33 David Johnston and Jim Dwyer,…

34 Carl Cameron, "Clues Alerted White House to Potential Attacks."…

35 Robin Wright, "2001 Focus: Missile Shield," *The Mercury News*, April 1, 2004, p. 3A.

36 U.S. Joint Inquiry Staff, "Was US informed before attack,"…

37 Ibid.

38 Dan Eggen and Walter Pincus, "Terror wasn't top issue for Bush, ex-advisor says", *The Mercury News*, March 25, 2003, p. 1A.

39 David Johnston and Todd S. Purdum, "Concerns about bin Laden never coalesced", *The Mercury News*, March 25, 2003, p. 15A.

40 Shannon McCaffrey, "Ashcroft rips Clinton effort on anti-terror," *The Mercury News*, April 14, 2004, p. 1A.

41 "CNN Late Edition with Wolf Blitzer," CNN.com/Transcripts, July 1, 2001, http://www.cnn.com/TRANSCRIPTS/0107/01/le.00.html.

42 U.S. Joint Inquiry Staff, "Was US informed before attack,"…

43 *The New York Times*, "White House provides memo on FBI orders before Sept. 11," *The Mercury News*, April 10, 2004, p. 3A.

44 David Johnston and Eric Schmitt, "Anti-terror efforts had leveled off in mid-'01," *The Mercury News*, April 4, 2004, p. 1A.

45 U.S. Joint Inquiry Staff, "Was US informed before attack,"…

46 Kate Clark, "Taliban 'warned U.S. of huge attack," BBC, September 7, 2002, http://news.bbc.co.uk/2/hi/south_asia/2242594.stm.

47 U.S. Joint Inquiry Staff, "Was US informed before attack,"…

48 David Johnston and Jim Dwyer,…

49 Carl Cameron, "Clues Alerted White House to Potential Attacks."...

50 "G8 Summit Death Shocks Leaders," *CNN.com*, July 21, 2001, http://www.cnn.com/2001/WORLD/europe/07/20/genoa.protests/; and David Johnston and Jim Dwyer,...

51 Walter Pincus, Dana Milbank, Washington Post, "In rush to defend White House, Rice trips over own words," *San Francisco Chronicle*, March 26, 2004, page A-4.

52 "Complete Text of 2001 Memo",...

53 "National Security Advisor Holds Press Briefing," May 16, 2002, http://www.whitehouse.gov/news/releases/2002/05/20020516-13.html.

54 Ken Fireman, "White House reacts to accuser," *The Mercury News*, March 26, 2004, p. 1A.

55 Full Dr. Rice transcript: http://www.nytimes.com/2004/04/08/politics/08RICE-TEXT.html.

56 Ron Hutcheson, "Memo warned of hijackings," *The Mercury News*, April 11, 2004, p. 1A.

57 AP, "Bush: Aug. 6 brief didn't foretell 9/11", *MSNBC News*, April 11, 2004, http://msnbc.msn.com/id/4700899/.

58 Adam Nagourney and Philip Shenon, "Bush downplays terror briefing," *The Mercury News*, April 12, 2004, p. 1A.

59 Ibid.

60 Full Dr. Rice transcript.

61 Ron Hutcheson, "Memo warned of hijackings," *The Mercury News*, April 11, 2004, p. 1A.

62 From Elizabeth Wilner, Mark Murray, and Huma Zaidi, "First Read," *MSNBC News*, April 9, 2004, http://www.msnbc.msn.com/id/4667930/#040904.

63 Carl Cameron, "Clues Alerted White House to Potential Attacks."...

64 Ibid.

65 James Bovard, "Moussaoui myths," *The Washington Times*, September 7, 2003, http://www.washtimes.com/commentary/20030906-110344-4296r.htm.

66 Ibid.

67 U.S. Joint Inquiry Staff, "Was US informed before attack,"…

68 James Bovard, "Moussaoui myths," *The Washington Times*, September 7, 2003, http://www.washtimes.com/commentary/20030906-110344-4296r.htm.

69 Jane Perlez, "Rice on front line in foreign policy role," *The New York Times*, August 19, 2001, Section 1, Page 10.

70 James Bovard, "Moussaoui myths,"…

71 David Johnston and Jim Dwyer,…

72 "Panel says hijacker alert might have halted plan," *The Mercury News*, April 17, 2004, p. 5A.

73 U.S. Joint Inquiry Staff, "Was US informed before attack,"…

74 Full Dr. Rice transcript.

75 David Johnston and Jim Dwyer,…

76 Carl Cameron, "Clues Alerted White House to Potential Attacks."…

77 James Bovard, "Moussaoui myths," *The Washington Times*, September 7, 2003, http://www.washtimes.com/commentary/20030906-110344-4296r.htm.

78 David Johnston and Jim Dwyer,…

79 Ron Hutcheson, "Memo warned of hijackings," *The Mercury News*, April 11, 2004, p. 1A.

80 Dan Eggen and Walter Pincus, "Terror wasn't top issue for Bush,…"

81 U.S. Joint Inquiry Staff, "Was US informed before attack,"…

82 Ron Hutcheson, "Make or break moment for Rice," *News-leader.com*, April 4, 2004, http://www.news-leader.com/today/0404-Makeorbrea-54952.html.

83 Carl Cameron, "Clues Alerted White House to Potential Attacks,"…

84 Full Dr. Rice transcript.

85 U.S. Joint Inquiry Staff, "Was US informed before attack,"…

86 Ibid.

87 http://www.september11news.com/AttackImages.htm, and Shannon McCaffrey, "U.S. was ill-prepared on Sept. 11," *The Mercury News*, June 18, 2004, p. 1A.

88 Barton Gellman, "Book: al Qaeda ignored by Bush",…

89 "Plans For Iraq Attack Began On 9/11," *CBSNews.com*, September 4, 2002, http://www.cbsnews.com/stories/2002/09/04/september11/printable520830.shtml.

90 "Media Silent on Clark's 9/11 Comments: Gen. says White House pushed Saddam link without evidence," *Fairness & Accuracy in Reporting*, June 20, 2003, http://www.fair.org/press-releases/clark-iraq.html.

91 Robin Wright, "2001 Focus: Missile Shield," *The Mercury News*, April 1, 2004, p. 3A.

92 Jake Tapper, "We predicted it,"…

93 Ted Bridis, "Details of 2001 threats on Iraq", *The Mercury News*, March 20, 2004, p. 8A.

94 Ibid.

95 Eric Lichtblau, "Rice: Bush did ask about Iraq," *The Mercury News*, March 29, 2004, p. 1A.

96 Carl Cameron, "Clues Alerted White House to Potential Attacks,"…

97 Ken Fireman, "White House reacts to accuser," *The Mercury News*, March 26, 2004, p. 1A.

98 *Iraq Watch*, http://www.iraqwatch.org/perspectives/pnac-letter-9-20-01.htm.

99 Reuters News Service, "Bush plans to add more sky marshals," *HoustonChronicle.com*, September 26, 2001, http://www.chron.com/cs/CDA/ssistory.mpl/special/terror/impact/1062414.

100 David Plotz, "Osama, Saddam, and the Bombs," *MSN*, September 28, 2001, http://slate.msn.com/id/116232/.

101 Jane Perlez and Patrick E. Tyler, "Before Attacks, U.S. Was Ready To Say It Backed Palestinian State," *The New York Times*, Section A, Page 1.

102 Alison Mitchell, "A NATION CHALLENGED: INTELLIGENCE GATHERING; House Votes for More Spy Aid And to Pull in Reins on Inquiry," *The New York Times*, October 6, 2001, Section B, Page 5.

103 Clyde Haberman, "An Overview: October 7, 2001; A Mission Begun; a Defiant bin Laden and Another Crisp, Clear Day," *The New York Times*, October 8, 2001, Section B, Page 1.

104 Steven Thomma and William Douglas, "Bush insists war is justified," *The Mercury News*, April 14, 2004, p. 1A.

105 http://slate.msn.com/id/2080099/.

106 Tim Weiner, "Israel rebuffs U.S. demand to end its West Bank raids," *The New York Times*, October 24, 2001, Section A, Page 8.

107 Jonathon S. Landay and Tish Wells, "Exiles built case for war in news media", *The Mercury News*, March 16, 2004, p. 1A.

108 "Woodward book: Bush hid Iraq war plan," *MSNBC*, April 16, 2004, http://www.msnbc.msn.com/id/4756962/.

109 Jim Puzzanghera, "Abuse foreshadowed in Lindh case," *The Mercury News*, May 15, 2004, p. 3A.

110 Jonathon S. Landay and Tish Wells, "Exiles built case for war in news media",...

111 Ibid.

112 "In Tough Times, a Company Finds Profits in War," *The New York Times*, July 13, 2002; and Pratap Chatterjee, "The War on Terrorism's Gravy Train," May 2, 2002, http://www.corpwatch.org.

113 William Hamilton, "Book: War plans set as Bush spoke of diplomacy," *The Mercury News*, April 17, 2004, p. 1A.

114 "Book alleges diversion of funds for Iraq war," *The Mercury News*, April 20, 2004, p. 4A.

115 Mark Halperin, "Rove: Republicans Benefit from War Credentials," *ABC News*, http://abcnews.go.com/sections/politics/DailyNews/Rove_020118.html.

116 Barton Gellman, "Book: al Qaeda ignored by Bush",…

117 Tom Hamburger, "Senators want top-level probe," *The Mercury News*, May 17, 2004, p. 1A.

118 "Big Boost for U.S. Military spending," BBC News, January 24, 2002, http://news.bbc.co.uk/1/hi/world/americas/1778681.stm.

119 "President delivers State of the Union address," www.whitehouse.gov, January 29, 2002.

120 Editorial, "Tale of twisted intelligence, a timeline: Who knew what and when?" *The Mercury News*, July 16, 2003, p. 6B.

121 Don Van Natta Jr., "Harsh tactics more routine in prisons, experts say," *The Mercury News*, May 7, 2004, p. 1AA.

122 Department of Defense, Criminal Investigative Service, *Press Release*, February 7, 2002.

123 Richard Leiby and Dana Priest, "A spy undone: Few knew secret of diplomat's wife," *The Herald*, October 12, 2003.

124 Shaun Waterman, "White House 'delayed 9-11 report'," *United Press International*, July 25, 2003, http://www.upi.com/view.cfm?StoryID=20030723-064812-9491r.

125 Mark Emmons and David E. Early, "Athlete's Life, Soldier's Death," *The Mercury News*, April 24, 2004, p. 1A.

126 Editorial, "Tale of twisted intelligence, a timeline: Who knew what and when?"…

127 David E. Sanger, "Bush officials end support of Sharon's tough stance," *The New York Times*, March 7, 2002, Section A, Page 8.

128 "Top GOP Donors in Energy Industry Met Cheney Panel,"…

129 "AMERICA AT WAR: UNDERSTANDING THE CONFLICT",…p. 8AB.

130 Jim Puzzanghera, "Abuse foreshadowed in Lindh case,"…

131 AMERICA AT WAR: UNDERSTANDING THE CONFLICT",…p. 8AB.

132 Kelly Wallace, "WH defends GOP plan to sell Bush 9-11 photo," *CNN.com*, May 15, 2002, http://www.cnn.com/2002/ALLPOLITICS/05/14/wh.fundraising.flap/.

133 KENNETH R. BAZINET and THOMAS M. DeFRANK, "White House retreat on 9/11 claims," NYDailyNews.com, March 27, 2004, http://www.nydailynews.com/03-27-2004/news/wn_report/story/177783p-154700c.html.

134 "Report Warned Of Suicide Hijackings,"…

135 Alison Mitchell, "Cheney Rejects Broader Access To Terror Brief," *The New York Times*, May 20, 2002, Section A, Page 1.

136 David Stout, "A NATION CHALLENGED: CONGRESSIONAL ACTION; Panel Votes for Wide Scrutiny Into Attacks," *The New York Times*, May 22, 2002, Section A, Page 13.

137 Alison Mitchell, "TRACES OF TERROR: CONGRESS; DASCHLE IS SEEKING A SPECIAL INQUIRY ON SEPT. 11 ATTACK," *The New York Times*, May 22, 2002, Section A, Page 1.

138 David E. Rosenbaum, "Washington Memo; Bush Bucks Tradition on Investigation," *The New York Times*, May 26, 2002, Section 1, Page 18.

139 "A Halliburton Primer," *Washingtonpost.com*, July 11, 2002, http://www.washingtonpost.com/wp-srv/onpolitics/articles/halliburtonprimer.html.

140 "Playing into al Qaeda's hands," *The Mercury News*, March 28, 2004, p. 1P.

141 Jonathon S. Landay and Tish Wells, "Iraqi exiles fed exaggerated tips to news media," *The Mercury News*, March 16, 2004 p. 1A.

142 "A Halliburton Primer,"...

143 "Halliburton CEO says Cheney knew about firm's accounting practices," *Newsweek*, July 15, 2002.

144 Alison Mitchell, "TRACES OF TERROR: THE INVESTIGATION; House Votes for Independent Inquiry on Intelligence Agencies' Actions on Sept. 11," *The New York Times*, July 26, 2002, Section A, Page 18.

145 Editorial, "Nuclear Duplicity From Pakistan," *The New York Times*, December 2, 2002, Section A, Page 20.

146 *The New York Times*, July 20, 2002 and August 1, 2002; and San *Francisco Chronicle* August 1, 2002.

147 Cheney speech, http://www.whitehouse.gov/news/releases/2002/08/20020826.html.

148 Alison Mitchell, "THREATS AND RESPONSES: PERSPECTIVES—In Senate, a Call for Answers And a Warning on the Future; CIA and FBI Faulted," *The New York Times*, September 10, 2002, Section A, Page 1.

149 AMERICA AT WAR: UNDERSTANDING THE CONFLICT",...p. 8AB.

150 Jonathon S. Landay, Warren P. Strobel and John Walcott, "Misinformation, poor planning had serious impact," *The Mercury News*, March 21, 2004, p. 1A.

151 John Daniszewski, "Bombings against U.S. on rise after weeks of declining fatalities," *The Mercury News*, March 15, 2004 p. 7A.

152 Karl Kahler, "Weapons claim unravels: Charges led to Saddam's downfall, political tempest," *The Mercury News*, January 30, 2004, p. 1AA.

153 Editorial, "Tale of twisted intelligence, a timeline: Who knew what and when?"…

154 AP, "Bush Administration Links Iraq, al Qaeda," *CBSNews.com*, September 26, 2002, http://www.cbsnews.com/stories/2002/09/26/national/main523326.shtml.

155 State Department, October 10, 2002, http://usinfo.state.gov/regional/nea/iraq/text/1010res.htm.

156 David Firestone, "THREATS AND RESPONSES: TOWARD AN INQUIRY; White House Blocks Deal By Congress On 9/11 Panel," *The New York Times*, October 11, 2002, Section A, Page 19.

157 Ibid.

158 CARNAGE IN MADRID," *The Mercury News*, March 12, 2004, p. 6AA.

159 *The Washington Post*, October 13, 2002.

160 Romesh Ratnesar "Why Bush Can't Give Sharon What He Wants," *Time*, October 16, 2002, http://www.time.com/time/world/article/0,8599,365172,00.html.

161 "Czechs retract Iraq terror link," NewsMax Wires, October 21, 2002, http://www.newsmax.com/archives/articles/2002/10/20/102425.shtml.

162 Editorial, "Tale of twisted intelligence, a timeline: Who knew what and when?"…

163 Ibid.

164 Jonathan S. Landay, "Public report of Iraq threat minimized dissenting views," *The Mercury News*, February 10, 2004, p. 5A.

165 Thaddeous Herrick, "U.S. Wants to work in Iraq," *Wall Street Journal*, January 16, 2003.

166 Eric Schmitt and Thom Shanker, "THREATS AND RESPONSES: A CIA RIVAL; Pentagon Sets Up Intelligence Unit," *The New York Times*, October 24, 2002, Section A, Page 1.

167 Daneil J. Wakin, THREATS AND RESPONSES: AN ARAB VIEW; Anger Builds and Seethes as Arabs Await American Invader," *The New York Times*, October 25, 2002, Section A, Page 14.

168 "AMERICA AT WAR: UNDERSTANDING THE CONFLICT",...p. 8AB.

169 William Hamilton, "Book: War plans set as Bush spoke of diplomacy,"...

170 Media Transparency, http://www.mediatransparency.org/recipients/aei.htm.

171 Carl Hulse, "THREATS AND RESPONSES: THE INQUIRY; How a Deal Creating an Independent Commission on Sept. 11 Came Undone," *The New York Times*, November 2, 2002, Section A, Page 8.

172 Daniel J. Wakin, "THREATS AND RESPONSES: THE ARABS; Syria Fears Isolation More Than War," *The New York Times*, November 8, 2002, Section A, Page 14.

173 David Firestone, "House Approves Domestic Security Bill," *The New York Times*, November 14, 2002, Section A, Page 32.

174 David Firestone, "THREATS AND RESPONSES: THE INQUIRY; White House Gives Way On a Sept. 11 Commission; Congress Is Set to Create It," *The New York Times*, November 15, 2002, Section A, Page 19.

175 Sheryl Gay Stolberg, *The New York Times*, "'Jersey girls' a driving force behind 9/11 panel," startribune.com, April 1, 2004, http://www.startribune.com/stories/484/4698533.html.

176 Steven R. Weisman, "U.S. Still Trying to Unfold Mideast Road Map," *The New York Times*, November 15, 2002, Section A, Page 13.

177 *60 Minutes*, "Bush sought 'Way' to oust Saddam?"...

178 Jim Lobe, "Battle of the old Middle East hands," *Asia Times*, November 22, 2002, http://www.atimes.com/atimes/Middle_East/DK22Ak04.html.

179 Daniel Sneider, "Prisoner abuse is not an aberration," *The Mercury News*, May 9, 2004, p. 5P.

180 Barny Mason, "Analysis, Is Wolfowitz waiting for war?" *BBC News*, December 3, 2003, http://news.bbc.co.uk/1/hi/world/middle_east/2539443.stm.

181 James A. Paul, "Oil in Iraq: The heart of the Crisis," Global Policy Forum, December 2002, http://www.globalpolicy.org/security/oil/2002/12heart.htm.

182 Shaun Waterman, "White House 'delayed 9-11 report'," ...

183 Bob Drogin, "More inmate deaths emerge," *The Mercury News*, May 16, 2004, p. 1A.

184 "Official: Rumsfeld OK'd questioning," *The Mercury News*, May 21, 2004, p. 6A.

185 Steven R. Weisman, "TERROR IN AFRICA: DIPLOMACY; Concern and caution: U.S. continues to urge Israeli restraint," *The New York Times*, December 7, 2002, Section A, Page 15.

186 John Hooper in Berlin and Suzanne Goldenberg in Washington, "Germany was 'key supplier' of Saddam supplier," *The Guardian*, December 18, 2002, http://www.guardian.co.uk/Iraq/Story/0,2763,861902,00.html.

187 Clifford Krauss, "Egypt-U.S. relationship is strained by Iraq crisis," *The New York Times*, December 17, 2002, Section A, Page 16.

188 William Hamilton, "Book: War plans set as Bush spoke of diplomacy,"...

189 Ibid.

190 "All in the Family," 60 Minutes, *CBSNews.com*, September 17, 2003, http://www.cbsnews.com/stories/2003/04/25/60minutes/main551091.shtml.

191 David Plotz, Julia Turner, and Avi Zenilman, "The *Slate* Field Guide to Iraq Pundits," MSN, March 14, 2003, http://slate.msn.com/id/2080099/.

192 William Hamilton, "Book: War plans set as Bush spoke of diplomacy,"...

193 Warren P. Strobel, Jonathon S. Landay and John Walcott, "More Doubts of Iraq links to al Qaeda," *The Mercury News*, March 3, 2004, p. 11A.

194 http://www.disinfopedia.org/wiki.phtml?title=Richard_A._ Clarke&printable=yes.

195 "Russia strikes oil deal with Iraq," *CNN.com*, January 17, 2003, http://edition.cnn.com/2003/WORLD/europe/01/17/russia.iraq.oil/.

196 "AMERICA AT WAR: UNDERSTANDING THE CONFLICT",…p. 8AB.

197 Karl Kahler, "Weapons claim unravels:…"

198 Editorial, "Tale of twisted intelligence, a timeline: Who knew what and when?"…

199 Thomas E. Ricks, "Desert Caution: Once 'Stormin' Norman,' Gen. Schwarzkopf Is Skeptical About U.S. Action in Iraq," *The Washington Post*, January 28, 2003, p. C01.

200 AP, "Nightmare Scenario: Iraq, al Qaeda Linked," *FoxNews.com*, January 30, 2003, http://www.foxnews.com/story/0,2933,77046,00.html.

201 Editorial, "Tale of twisted intelligence, a timeline: Who knew what and when?"…

202 Judith Miller and Julia Preston, "THREATS AND RESPONSES: THE INSPECTOR; Blix Says He Saw Nothing to Prompt a War," *The New York Times*, January 31, 2003, Section A, Page 10.

203 "Official: Rumsfeld OK'd questioning,"…

204 Karl Kahler, "Weapons claim unravels:…"

205 Jonathon S. Landay, Warren P. Strobel and John Walcott,…

206 AMERICA AT WAR: UNDERSTANDING THE CONFLICT",…p. 9AB.

207 http://www.disinfopedia.org/wiki.phtml?title=Richard_A._ Clarke&printable=yes.

208 Jonathan S. Landay and Warren P. Strobel, "Feelers were dismissed by Bush officials," *The Mercury News*, November 6, 2003, p. 9A.

209 Jerusalem Post staff, "Israel knew Iraq had no WMDs'," *Iraq Net*, February 2, 2004, http://www.iraq.net/displayarticle1571.html.

210 Peter Brand and Alexander Bolton, "GOP Threats Halted GAO Cheney Suit," The Hill, February 19, 2003, http://www.thehill.com.

211 David Wallechinsky, "The World's 10 Worst Dictators," *Parade*, February 22, 2004, page 4.

212 James Bennet, "THREATS AND RESPONSES: THE MIDDLE EAST; Israel Says War on Iraq Would Benefit The Region," *The New York Times*, February 27, 2003, Section A, Page 12.

213 AMERICA AT WAR: UNDERSTANDING THE CONFLICT",…p. 9AB.

214 Ibid.

215 "30 Years of U.S. UN Vetoes," *Information Clearing House*, March 8, 2003, http://www.informationclearinghouse.info/article2000.htm; and "U.S. Vetoes of UN resolutions Critical of Israel," *Jewish Virtual Library*, http://www.us-israel.org/jsource/UN/usvetoes.html.

216 Felicity Barringer, "THREATS AND RESPONSES: DOCUMENTS; Forensic Experts Uncovered Forgery on Iraq, an Inspector Says," *The New York Times*, March 9, 2003, Section 1, Page 13.

217 Daniel Sneider, "Prisoner abuse is not an aberration,"…

218 Joseph Wilson IV, "White House officials went after me and my wife, a CIA operative, after I questioned their claim that Saddam was pursuing nuclear weapons. Here's how they did it, and why it was so important to them," *The Mercury News*, May 2, 2004, p. 1P.

219 Robert Bryce and Julian Borger, "Cheney is still paid by Pentagon contractor," *The Guardian*, March 12, 2003, http://www.guardian.co.uk/Iraq/Story/0,2763,912515,00.html.

220 Jonathan S. Landay, "Ex-diplomat: Cheney's office orchestrated smear campaign," *The Mercury News*, April 30, 2004, p. 5A.

8

Shock and Awe I: A Quick Victory in Iraq

President Bush ignores Secretary of State Colin Powell's advice, "You break it, you own it," and invades Iraq. Saddam's army is no match for the superpower, and retreats without much of a fight. U.S. prestige declines due to Bush's unilateral move. A neoconservative celebrates the demise of the U.N. Baghdad falls, making the mission appear to be a success. Anarchy results, looting is rampant, museum artifacts are stolen, but the oil ministry and oil fields are protected by U.S. troops. Bush declares "Mission Accomplished." Major no-bid contracts in Iraq go to Halliburton, Bechtel, and other companies with connections to the Bush administration.

The mistreatment of prisoners spreads from Guantánamo Bay, Cuba to Iraq. The Red Cross alerts U.S. officials but little is changed. Bush makes an offer to terrorists "Bring them on." The U.S. appoints the Iraqi Governing Council, a puppet government, which contains many exiles friendly to the U.S.

Early March 2003: WASHINGTON—In his prime-time press conference, which focuses almost solely on Iraq, President Bush mentions Sept. 11 eight times. He refers to Saddam Hussein many more times than that, often in the same breath with Sept. 11.

Bush never pins blame for the attacks directly on the Iraqi president, but the overall effect is to reinforce an impression that persists among much of the American public: that the Iraqi dictator did play a direct role in the attacks.

The White House appears to be encouraging this false impression, as it seeks to maintain American support for a possible war against Iraq. And it's working.

A recent *New York Times*/CBS poll shows that 45 percent of Americans believe Saddam was "personally involved" in Sept. 11.

In a January 2003 Knight Ridder poll, 44 percent of Americans thought that either "most" or "some" of the Sept. 11 hijackers were Iraqi citizens. The correct answer is zero.

"Going to war with improper public understanding is risky," says Richard Parker, a former U.S. ambassador to several Mideast countries. "If it's a failure, and we get bogged down, this is one of the accusations that [Bush] will have to face when it's all over…"[1]

<u>March 15, 2003</u>: WASHINGTON—President George Bush, following several days of negotiations with British Prime Minister Tony Blair, promises to adopt a long-deferred peace plan for a Palestinian state as soon as the Palestinians choose a new prime minister. He says, "There can be no peace for either side in the Middle East unless there is freedom for both." Blair, moments later, hails Bush's announcement as showing an "obligation of even-handedness" on the eve of possible war against Iraq.[2]

<u>March 15, 2003</u>: WASHINGTON—Randy Beers quits as counterterrorism coordinator to the President after just one month in the position for the same reason as Richard Clarke—the Bush administration is more interested in starting a war in Iraq, which will increase terrorism, than in fighting terrorism.

He tells Richard Clarke, "They still don't get it."[3]

<u>March 16, 2003</u>: Azores—President Bush and leaders of Britain and Spain meet in Azores and issue an ultimatum to the U.N. Security Council declaring diplomacy to win support for disarming Iraq will end on March 17. They make it clear military action to depose President Saddam Hussein will begin imminently, with or without U.N. endorsement. Bush is critical of France for threatening to veto any resolution authorizing the use of force.[4]

<u>March 17, 2003</u>: WASHINGTON—President Bush gives Saddam Hussein a 48-hour deadline to leave Iraq or the U.S. will use military force. The move comes after a decision not to seek another U.N. Security Council resolution.[5]

<u>1999–2003</u>: Violence that accelerated in 1999 continues in the Democratic Republic of Congo (DRC). Of the 20 million inhabitants of eastern DRC, 2.27 million have been displaced and 3.5 million have died, 2.5 million due to the conflict. The situation for women is especially desperate due to systematic rape,

maternal mortality, and infant mortality. For the children born in the conflict, 75% will not reach the age of two.[6]

This is the most severe humanitarian issue in the world during March 2003.

March 18, 2003: BAGHDAD—As U.N. nuclear inspectors race out of Iraq, some of them are angry at the Bush administration for cutting short their work, bad-mouthing their efforts, and making false claims about evidence about WMD. None of the nuclear-related claims by the Bush administration has held up to scrutiny, inspectors say. From suspect aluminum tubes to aerial photographs to documents—revealed to be forgeries—that claimed to link Iraq to uranium from Niger, inspectors say they chased U.S. leads that went nowhere and wasted valuable time in their efforts to determine the extent of Saddam Hussein's arsenal of weapons.

Recent inspection teams include a new batch of U.S. nuclear scientists from Lawrence Livermore and Los Alamos national laboratories. A U.N. official says these inspectors arrived as hawks but will leave as doves, after finding Iraq "a ruined country, not a threat to anyone." It is a view radically different from that of the administration.

The nuclear inspectors traveled through the Iraqi countryside for months. They found the Iraqi weapons infrastructure, built at great expense in the 1980's, to be in a state of decay. They sought out out-of-the-way machine shops of companies where Iraqi scientists might be congregated. But they found no sign of an organized nuclear weapons program.

Responding to the U.S. emphasis on underground facilities, the inspectors worked their way through the mud beneath a petroleum plant and visited an irrigation reservoir dug into the inside of a mountain. Neither contained anything suspicious.

Some of the inspectors are suspicious of U.S. motives. Some believe that recent flights of U.S. U-2 spy planes are intended to help the military draw up target lists, not to aid the inspectors in their search for weapons of mass destruction.[7]

U.S. Image Plummets

	Favorable view of the U.S.		
	'99-00	2002	Today
	%	%	%
Britain	83	75	48
France	62	63	31
Germany	78	61	25
Italy	76	70	34
Spain	50	--	14
Poland	86	79	50
Russia	37	61	28
Turkey	52	30	12

1999/2000 trends provided by Office of Research, U.S. Department of State

March 18, 2003: Anti-war sentiment and disapproval of President Bush's international policies continue to erode America's image among the publics of its allies. U.S. favorability ratings have plummeted in the past six months in countries actively opposing war, such as France, Germany, and Russia, as well as in countries that are part of the "coalition of the willing."

In Great Britain, favorable views of the U.S. have declined from 75% in mid-2002 to 48% in March 2003. In Italy, the proportion of respondents holding favorable views of the United States has declined from 70% to 34% in the same period. In Spain, only 14% have a favorable opinion of the United States. Favorable views of the U.S. in Germany have dropped from 78% (1999-2000) to 61% (2002) to 25% (March 2003). In France, favorable views of the U.S. dropped from 63% in 2002 to 31%.

More generally, criticisms of U.S. foreign policy are almost universal. Overwhelming majorities disapprove of President Bush's foreign policy and the small boost he received in the wake of Sept. 11 has disappeared. As a consequence, publics in seven of the eight nations surveyed believe that American policies have a negative effect on their country. Only the British are divided on this issue.[8]

March 19, 2003: BAGHDAD—Bush starts the war by launching dozens of Tomahawk cruise missiles and 2,000-pound bombs at Saddam and other leadership targets in Baghdad. He calls Iraq "an outlaw regime that threatens the peace with weapons of mass murder."[9]

March 19, 2003: WASHINGTON—During a one-month period beginning on this day, the United States launches 50 air strikes using precision-guided munitions on a broad array of senior Iraqi leaders during the early days of the war. None of the strikes is successful and some cause significant civilian casualties, according to senior military and intelligence officials.

The broad scope of the campaign, its failures, and the civilian casualties will not be acknowledged by the Bush administration.[10]

March 21, 2003: WASHINGTON—Richard Perle, chairman of the defense policy board, an advisory panel to the Pentagon, notes shortcomings of the U.N. and celebrates its demise as the unilateral invasion of Iraq begins.[11]

March 24, 2003: The grenades that a U.S. serviceman is accused of throwing into three tents at Camp Pennsylvania in Kuwait bring back a term commonly used in Vietnam: "fragging," the killing of an American by another American during war.[12]

Due to the absence of the military draft, fragging has been rare since the Vietnam War.

March 24, 2003: WASHINGTON—A senior House Democrat asks the Defense Department to investigate the business dealings of Richard N. Perle, the head of an influential Pentagon advisory board who is also an adviser to Global Crossing, the large telecommunications company that is seeking to overcome Pentagon objections to its proposed sale to Asian investors.

"I am aware of several potential conflicts that warrant your immediate review," Representative John Conyers Jr. of Michigan says in a letter to the Pentagon's inspector general.

Mr. Perle was appointed by Defense Secretary Donald H. Rumsfeld in 2001 to head the Defense Advisory Board, an influential group of unpaid advisers to the administration. By law, Mr. Rumsfeld is ultimately responsible for deciding whether the Pentagon should grant permission to Global Crossing to complete its sale.[13]

March 26, 2003: WASHINGTON—In a letter to the Army Corps of Engineers, Representative Waxman asks why the administration has entered into a new multi-million dollar contract with Kellogg Brown & Root, a Halliburton subsidiary, for extinguishing oil fires in Iraq without any competition or notice to Congress.[14]

March 2003: WASHINGTON—Richard Perle steps down as chairman of the defense policy board. The move follows news reports questioning whether his work with a company seeking favor with the Pentagon is a conflict of interest for such a senior adviser. Perle has consistently insisted he did nothing wrong.[15]

March 30, 2003: WASHINGTON—On "This Week with George Stephanopoulos:"

MR. STEPHANOPOULOS:…And is it curious to you that given how much control U.S. and coalition forces now have in the country, they haven't found any weapons of mass destruction?

SEC. RUMSFELD: Not at all. If you think—let me take that, both pieces—the area in the south and the west and the north that coalition forces control is substantial. It happens not to be the area where weapons of mass destruction were dispersed. We know where they are. They're in the area around Tikrit and Baghdad and east, west, south and north somewhat.[16]

March 31, 2003: WASHINGTON—A *New York Times* editorial says the federal committee investigating the Sept. 11 terrorist attacks is being starved for funding by the White House, which was reluctant to support its creation in the first place. The author of the editorial wonders if the White House is resorting to budgetary starvation as a tactic to hobble any politically uncontrolled inquiry into possible intelligence failures or shortcomings.[17]

Late March 2003: The Swiss-based International Committee of the Red Cross (ICRC) which will make 29 visits to coalition-run prisons and camps in Iraq between late March 2003 and November 2003, will repeatedly present its reports of mistreatment to prison commanders, U.S. military officials in Iraq, and members of the Bush administration in Washington.[18]

While some individuals will be dealt with after the fact, there will be no attempt to investigate or reform the culture that will spawn such broad abuses during the entire remainder of calendar 2003.

April 1, 2003: NEW YORK—Relatives of those who died in the Sept. 11 terror attacks, as well as some survivors, finally get a chance to testify as the first witnesses before the government panel investigating the attacks. The first day is heavy on the emotions, causing some members of the commission to sigh, wince, or shed tears. It reveals frustration and anger among some family members over the investigation's progress. Witness after witness either asks or implies the key questions: Who, if anyone, will ever be held responsible for failing to stop attacks? Does the commission have the authority to truly make changes? Will a world focused on the new war in Iraq have any interest in the facts surrounding the Sept 11 attacks?[19]

April 5, 2003: A failed strike targeting Gen. Ali Hasan al-Majid, a top official known as Chemical Ali, in a residential area of Basra fails, but kills 17 civilians instead.[20]

April 9, 2003: BAGHDAD—The United States occupies Baghdad and jubilant Iraqis topple the 40-foot statue of Saddam.[21]

At this moment, it appears as if the U.S. troops will in fact be the liberators welcomed with open arms.

April 10, 2003: BAGHDAD—Baghdad is the scene of widening anarchy as jubilation accompanying the fall of Saddam Hussein gives way to violence and looting. A suicide bombing attack on a checkpoint manned by American marines leaves at least four of them severely injured. Saddam Hussein, before his fall, had promised a wave of suicide bombings against American forces. The power vacuum in the city appears almost complete, with no immediate prospect of new order rising from the old. Bands of looters have free run of wide areas on both banks of the Tigris, breaking into at least six government ministries and setting several afire, and attacking luxurious mansions of Saddam's two sons and other members of his ruling elite. The looting is done in plain view of American units, without fear of any American response. American troops are kept busy battling pockets of resistance.[22]

April 10, 2003: BAGHDAD—The National Museum of Iraq is destroyed only 48 hours after American troops enter Baghdad in sufficient force to topple Saddam Hussein's government, and at least 170,000 artifacts of ancient Mesopotamian civilizations are carried away by looters. Museum officials says thousands of looters broke in early on April 10 and stayed until dusk on April 11 and were interrupted by American forces for only about half an hour the first day.[23]

"The people who came in here knew what they wanted. These were not random looters," Donny George, the director general of Iraq's state board of antiquities, says in front of the museum as he holds up four glass cutters—red-handled with inch-long silver blades—that he found on the floor of the looted museum.

Among the most valuable stolen pieces are the vase of Warka, from 3200 B.C., and the Basiqi, a bronze Acadian statue.

Even though few items are taken from the main collection, the damage is grave, George says. "What we have lost and what has been broken is priceless. We will never put a number on it."

"Human civilization was here," he said. "There may have been other museums in the world that have small pieces of this story, but there was no collection so detailed with the evidence of human civilization."

"We have lost masterpieces from the Syrian and Sumerian ages, from 5,000 years ago," George says. He turns to a soldier, points his finger and says, "You are too late."

George says he was shocked that the United States began guarding the country's Ministry of Oil before the museum, saying that told him where the American priorities stood. The American Archeological Association had appealed to Pentagon officials prior to the war to spare the museum during the war and protect it afterward.

The military perspective is that it did all it could to protect the museum at the time. During the looting, "the fighting was still going on. The Republican Guard headquarters are across the street, and they were far from secure," Army Maj. Michael Donovan said. "Frankly, we were here to protect people and property, but in the early days we had to choose, and we chose people."[24]

And the oil ministry.

April 10, 2003: WASHINGTON—Bush administration press secretary Ari Fleischer comments about weapons of mass destruction, "That is what this war is all about."[25]

April 15, 2003: WASHINGTON—A question-and-answer session with Defense Secretary Donald Rumsfeld includes a map showing developments in Iraq, as American focus turns westward toward Syria.[26]

With the war in Iraq going well so far, are there plans being made for Syria to be the next target for the neocons to pursue?

April 17, 2003: SAN FRANCISCO—San Francisco-based Bechtel Corp. has forged lasting political bridges, raising worries it enjoyed an unfair advantage in the bidding to lead the biggest reconstruction since World War II.

The recent deal it won could be worth more than its projected $680 million price tag, because the winning bidder is expected to become the front-runner for future business as the United States invests up to $100 billion to help rebuild Iraq.

Bechtel's critics worry that by limiting the bidding to Bechtel and five other U.S. companies, the federal government might not be getting competitive pricing.

"We are concerned that the government seems to be handpicking their buddies for these contracts," says Seth Morris, research associate for the Washington-based Project on Government Oversight.

The other companies invited to submit bids were Pasadena-based Parsons Corp., Fluor Corp., Louis Berger Group Inc., and Washington Group International Inc. A subsidiary of Halliburton Co., which was formerly run by Vice President Dick Cheney, was invited to bid but removed itself amid a flood of cronyism charges.

The government limited the field to an exclusive group for security reasons, as well as a desire to start the work quickly, spokesman Luke Zahner says. But such explanations don't quell suspicions that politics were at play.

A Bechtel senior vice president, Jack Sheehan, has sat on the Defense Policy Board formed to advise Defense Secretary Donald Rumsfeld, who himself lobbied for one of Bechtel's projects in 1983. And President Bush appointed Bechtel Chairman Riley Bechtel to the Export Council in February.

The company has also backed its personal contacts within Washington with sizable campaign contributions. Bechtel gave $1.3 million to political candidates from 1999 through 2002, according to the Center for Responsive Politics.[27]

Bechtel Board member George Shultz also has very strong ties with the neocons in the Bush administration, and Bechtel financially supported "education" groups that promoted the war in Iraq.

April 18, 2003: WASHINGTON—Pro-Israel activists are wondering if Israel will have an ally leading Iraq as the war effort ends and the United States launches its rebuilding process.

For the moment, those activists are hoping Ahmed Chalabi, a leader of the Iraqi National Congress opposition group, becomes a major player in the new Iraqi government.

Chalabi has strong ties with the White House and Pentagon and he also has a strong following in the American Jewish community.

"There's no track record of anyone else in Iraqi leadership having a relationship with the Jewish community," says Tom Neumann, executive director of the Jewish Institute for National Security Affairs (JINSA).

"Because Saddam was so anti-Israel, the hope is that all of Saddam's policies will be revisited, including his relationship with Israel and the United States," Neumann says. "There's no reason for the Iraqi people to have a problem with Israel…"

However, his analysis is contradicted by history. Iraqi antagonism toward Israel predates Saddam by several decades, as Iraqi army units invaded Israel during its 1948 War of Independence.[28]

April 24, 2003: WASHINGTON, UNITED NATIONS—The United States will not permit U.N. weapons inspectors to return to Iraq, saying the U.S. military has taken over the role of searching for Saddam's weapons of mass destruction.

In simultaneous briefings in New York and Washington, both the White House and the U.S. ambassador to the U.N. say they see no role in postwar Iraq for the U.N. weapons inspection teams.[29]

April 30, 2003: HOUSTON—Even with the Iran-Libya sanctions in place, Halliburton continues to operate in Iran. It pays the Department of Commerce $15,000 to settle allegations that the company has broken anti-boycott provisions of the U.S. Export Administration Act for an Iranian-related transaction, without admitting wrongdoing. Halliburton also continues to do business in Libya throughout Cheney's tenure.[30]

April 30, 2003: WASHINGTON—Representative Waxman asks Defense Secretary Rumsfeld about evidence that Halliburton has profited from business with three nations known for their support of terrorism: Iran, Iraq, and Libya.

The letter sent to Rumsfeld notes the foreign subsidiaries set up by Halliburton to circumvent restrictions on U.S. firms working in these countries. The company paid a $3.8 million fine in 1995 for nuclear-related exports to Libya, but apparently is still working there.[31]

May 1, 2003: WASHINGTON—President Bush addresses the nation to proclaim the end of major combat operations in Iraq on board the USS *Abraham Lincoln* with the "MISSION ACCOMPLISHED" banner in the background.[32]

<u>May 2003</u>: (CBS) Soon after the last bomb of the Iraqi invasion was dropped, the United States begins the business of rebuilding the country. And it's very big business. The U.S. will spend approximately $25 billion to repair Iraq by the end of next year—and billions more after that.

The earliest contracts were given to a few favored companies. And some of the biggest winners in the sweepstakes to rebuild Iraq have lots of very close friends in the Bush Administration.

One is Halliburton, the Houston-based energy services and construction giant whose former CEO, Dick Cheney, is now vice president of the United States.

Even before the war in Iraq, the Pentagon had secretly awarded Halliburton subsidiary Kellogg Brown & Root a two-year, no-bid contract to put out oil well fires and to handle other unspecified duties involving war damage to the country's petroleum industry. It is worth up to $7 billion.

Not everyone thought the award to Halliburton was a good deal for the government. Bob Grace is president of GSM Consulting, a small company in Amarillo, Texas, that has fought oil well fires all over the world. Grace worked for the Kuwait government after the first Gulf War and was in charge of firefighting strategy for the huge Bergan Oil Field, which had more than 300 fires.

Last September, when it looked like there might be another Gulf war and more oil well fires, he began contacting the Pentagon. Grace was told they weren't interested in letting a contract for oil well fires, even though they had secretly started talks with Halliburton to do just that over a month before.

"From what I've read in the papers, they're charging $50,000 a day for a five-man team. I know there are guys that are equally as qualified as the guys that are over there that'll do it for half that," Grace says.

However, Grace and his friends are no match for Halliburton when it comes to landing government business. Last year alone, Halliburton and its Brown & Root subsidiary delivered $1.3 billion worth of services to the U.S. government.[33]

<u>May 2003</u>: WILKES-BARRE, Pa.—Hossam Shaltout, a Canadian citizen and permanent U.S. resident, is seeking $350,000 from the government through the Army Claims Service for "torture and other personal injuries" at Camp Bucca.

The Egyptian-born Shaltout entered Iraq in January 2003 as a member of a peace organization called Rights and Freedom International. The organization tried to persuade Iraqi leaders to step down to avoid war with the United States.

He is held prisoner in southern Iraq in May 2003, according to his account, which will surface in May 2004:

Detainees there are beaten and sexually humiliated by their American jailers. Widespread mistreatment by soldiers in the detention center is as inhumane as the treatment in Abu Ghurayb prison in Baghdad.

Camp Bucca is a "torture camp," where soldiers beat and humiliate prisoners, including having them lie naked atop each other or pose in sexual positions. Soldiers also tie groups of naked prisoners together.

Shaltout considers himself a "peacemaker" but the soldiers at Camp Bucca pressure him to admit to being Saddam Hussein's "right-hand man." He refuses to confess during daily interrogations.

They hogtie Shaltout's hands and legs and place scorpions on his body.

The word "Canadian" is written on his white shirt and he is "interrogated and tortured on a daily basis." Gun muzzles are put to his head and body.

Several soldiers under the direction of 320th Military Police Master Sgt. Lisa Girman, of Hazleton, Pa., place handcuffs and leg irons on him. Girman beats him in the face and knees him in the groin after he goes on a hunger strike.

Shaltout is released later in the month.

Girman, 35, a Pennsylvania state police trooper, did not return phone messages seeking comment. A military public-affairs officer in Iraq had no immediate comment about Shaltout's claim.

Girman is among four soldiers with the Ashley, Pa.-based 320th Military Police Battalion accused of beating prisoners in May 2003. She will be found guilty of one count each of abuse of prisoners and failing to safeguard them.

Girman will be given an other-than-honorable discharge in connection with a May 12, 2003 incident at Camp Bucca. By accepting the Army's punishment, she will avoid court-martial and a potential prison sentence.

Shaltout is an aerospace engineer and an exporter for an American company that distributes global-positioning equipment and he is able to afford psychological treatment. Many other prisoners freed from camps in Iraq are not so lucky.

"Their lives will be destroyed," according to Shaltout.[34]

May 2003: BAGHDAD—Saddam Hussein warns his Iraqi supporters to be wary of joining forces with jihadist and other foreign Arab fighters entering Iraq to battle American troops, according to a document he wrote after losing power. The document, which will be found with Saddam when he is arrested in December 2003 and whose content is revealed by unidentified Bush administration officials, provides additional evidence challenging the administration's contention of close cooperation between Saddam's government and terrorists from al Qaeda. Administration officials say Saddam apparently believed foreign Arabs, eager for holy war against West, had a different agenda from Baathists, who were eager for their own return to power in Baghdad.[35]

May 2003: Army Maj. Gen. Antonio M. Taguba's March 3, 2004 prisoner abuse report will find that several detainees are beaten at Camp Bucca, a detention site in Iraq, in May 2003. Soldiers responsible for those abuses will be charged and punished in late 2003. However, nothing will be done to make clear to military police elsewhere that this is not to be tolerated.[36]

May 7, 2003: WASHINGTON—Patrick Lang, former head of Middle Eastern affairs in the Defense Intelligence Agency, says that he hears from those still in the intelligence world that when experts wrote reports that were skeptical about Iraq's WMD, "they were encouraged to think it over again." Lang says, "In this administration, the pressure to get the product 'right' is coming out of OSD (the Office of the Secretary of Defense)." He added that intelligence experts had cautioned that Iraqis would not necessarily line up to cheer U.S. troops and that the Shiite clergy could be a problem. "The guys who tried to tell them that came to understand that this advice was not welcome," he said.[37]

May 8, 2003: HOUSTON—Halliburton admits having paid $2.4 million in bribes to a Nigerian official in return for tax breaks.[38]

May 12, 2003: BAGHDAD—Paul Bremer, of the U.S. State Department, replaces retired Lt. General Jay Garner as head of interim administration.[39]

May 2003: The U.S. de-Baathification project, started soon after Paul Bremer's arrival, causes many thousands of teachers and doctors, as well as army soldiers to lose their jobs. Will these people want to support the U.S. and the new regime? As angry fired soldiers wander around, holding weapons but not jobs, can peace and security be expected?[40]

May-June 2003: BAGHDAD—There is mistreatment of prisoners during interrogations by the 205th Military Intelligence Brigade at Camp Cropper detention facility, on the outskirts of Baghdad International Airport during May and June of 2003.

After several visits to Camp Cropper, where they interviewed Iraqi prisoners, officials of the International Committee for the Red Cross (ICRC) in early July

2003 will cite at least 50 incidents of abuse reported to have taken place in a part of the prison under the control of military interrogators.

In one example to be cited to U.S. officers in Baghdad in July by committee officials, a prisoner is beaten during interrogation, as part of an ordeal in which he was hooded, cuffed, threatened with torture and death, urinated on, kicked in the head, lower back and groin, "force-fed a baseball which was tied into the mouth using a scarf and deprived of sleep for four consecutive days."

A medical examination of the prisoner by the committee's doctors "revealed hematoma in the lower back, blood in urine, sensory loss in the right hand due to tight handcuffing with flexi-cuffs, and a broken rib," a final report by the Red Cross panel will say when it is presented to U.S. officials in February 2004.

"Sometimes they treated them good, and sometimes they didn't treat them so good," Staff Sgt. Floyd Boone, a military police officer, will say of the military intelligence interrogators from the 205th Brigade at Camp Cropper. He and other members of the military police were not permitted to watch the interrogations, but he remembers "all the noise, yelling and screaming" from trailers where interrogators from the 205th brigade took Iraqi prisoners for questioning before returning them to the custody of the military police.

After the ICRC complaints, the military interrogation site at Camp Cropper where the abuses took place was closed. It remains unclear whether any disciplinary action was taken at the time against members of the 205th Brigade.[41]

<u>May 30, 2003</u>: HOUSTON—Halliburton says that it has agreed to pay $6 million to settle 20 shareholder lawsuits accusing it of using deceptive accounting practices while Vice President Dick Cheney led the company. The company says costs of the settlement will not affect second-quarter results.

Halliburton doesn't admit to any wrongdoing.[42]

<u>June 6, 2003</u>: A military investigator will later conclude that low-ranking Marines repeatedly struck two defenseless Iraqis at Camp Whitehorse in June, and one of the detainees, Nagem Sadoon Hatab, dies after he is left disabled and naked under a scorching sun.

According to two reports obtained by the *Los Angeles Times* in 2004, Marine Col. William V. Gallo is critical of the death investigation, claiming the dead Iraqi's bodily fluids were mishandled by investigators and were destroyed on the way to a laboratory for analysis.

In October 2003, two of the Marines will be charged with negligent homicide in connection with the June 6, 2003, death of Hatab.

The news of this event will first be reported in 2004 when the two Marines will face a general court martial, but all charges of negligent homicide will be dropped.[43]

June 2003: BAGHDAD—At Camp Cropper, near Baghdad's airport, detainee No. 7166 is shot and killed as he tries to crawl under a barbed-wire fence in an escape attempt commanders knew about a day earlier.[44]

June 2003: WASHINGTON—The Pentagon assures Congress in writing that military interrogations of detainees worldwide are not violating constitutional stipulations against cruel and unusual punishment.[45]

June 18, 2003: KABUL, Afghanistan—A former Afghan local military commander named Abdul Wali dies during interrogation by a CIA retiree who had been rehired as a private contractor according to U.S. intelligence officials. Wali dies at a U.S. facility near Asadabad in the Kunar province three days after his capture, officials will report in 2004.[46]

June 22, 2003: AN-NAJAF, Iraq—Many locals object to U.S. administrator Paul Bremer's cancellation of the first mayoral election out of concern that unacceptable fundamentalists or Baathists could win power.[47]

How does canceling an election promote freedom and democracy?

June 24, 2003: BAGHDAD—The administration is considering a plan to mortgage future Iraqi oil revenue to pay the expenses of U.S. contractors, such as Halliburton and Bechtel, now operating in Iraq—despite past administration claims that Iraq's oil "belongs to the Iraqi people."[48]

July 2, 2003: WASHINGTON—President Bush says that American troops under fire in Iraq aren't about to pull out, and he challenges those tempted to attack U.S. forces, "Bring them on."

"We got the force necessary to deal with the security situation," President Bush says of U.S. troops in Iraq.

More than 65 U.S. troops have died in Iraq since Bush declared on May 1 that major combat has ended.[49]

How many U.S. troops will die after this open invitation for terrorists to enter Iraq's porous borders and kill Americans?

July 7, 2003: WASHINGTON—The Bush administration acknowledges the claim that Iraq tried to buy uranium in Africa [Niger] is erroneous.[50]

By now the war is already started, thanks in part to the uranium claim—known to be false at the time—made in the State of the Union address. Polls confirm that the unsubstantiated claims made by the administration during the march to war had a profound impact on public opinion. This after-the-fact acknowledgment is merely a minor nuisance for the White House. So, for the Niger deception campaign—it's "mission accomplished."

July 8, 2003: WASHINGTON—After Judicial Watch gains a lower court ruling to force the White House to disclose the names of nongovernmental officials who were consulted by the task force in 2001, the U.S. Court of Appeals for the District of Columbia Circuit affirms the lower court judge's order and rejects Cheney's bid to keep all of the workings of the task force secret. Cheney appeals to the Supreme Court.[51]

In the Supreme Court, Cheney will have his duck-hunting friend Justice Antonin Scalia—who would not recuse himself—to push for a reversal.

July 9, 2003: WASHINGTON—The commission investigating the Sept. 11 terror attacks says its work is hampered by the failure of executive branch agencies, especially the Pentagon and the Justice Department, to respond to requests for documents and testimony. The commission also says the Bush administration's refusal to allow officials to be interviewed without the presence of colleagues could impede the probe. Chairman Thomas Kean suggests there is 'intimidation.' He and vice chairman Lee Hamilton release a statement to bring public pressure on the White House to expedite the "monumental" task.[52]

July 10, 2003: WASHINGTON—President Bush says that the intelligence agencies read and cleared his State of the Union speech [in reference to the 16 words regarding Saddam getting uranium from Niger].[53]

July 11, 2003: WASHINGTON—CIA Director George Tenet accepts full responsibility for the reference to Iraq seeking uranium from Niger, saying "these 16 words should never have been included in the text written for the president."[54]

What Tenet doesn't say is who pressured the CIA to include the claim.

July 13, 2003: WASHINGTON—After watching George Tenet "walk the plank" for the president, national security advisor Condoleezza Rice and Defense Secretary Donald Rumsfeld dismiss the sacrifice as much to do about nothing. They defend Bush's speech as technically accurate. "The British government did say that," Rice says.[55]

These two are suggesting that it was acceptable for the President to include the 16 words even though the U.S. had determined the claim to be unfounded.

July 13, 2003: BAGHDAD—The U.S. appointed 25-member Iraqi Governing Council takes office.[56]

The U.S. placed Ahmed Chalabi onto this council even though he hadn't been in Iraq for 45 years and had no support there. Is this the beginning of democracy for Iraq, or a puppet government that won't take hold?

July 14, 2003: WASHINGTON—In a July 14 column, syndicated newspaper journalist and CNN contributor Robert Novak names former Ambassador Joseph Wilson's wife, Valerie Plame, as a CIA operative on weapons of mass destruction, citing Bush administration sources.

Novak reveals on CNN's "Crossfire" that he learned Plame's identity from two senior Bush administration officials in the course of researching an article about Wilson. He denies that anyone in the administration called him to leak the information.

But sources tell CNN that Novak was among as many as six journalists who were told Plame's name. The *Washington Post* reports that the disclosure came from two top administration officials.

Sources told CNN that Plame works in the CIA's Directorate of Operations—the part of the agency in charge of spying—and worked in the field for many years as an undercover officer.[57]

July 14, 2003: WASHINGTON—Democratic presidential candidates offer a near-unified assault on President Bush's credibility in his handling of the Iraq war. They cite his use of unsubstantiated evidence in supporting the looming invasion of Iraq in his State of the Union address in January. They also criticize his administration for what has happened in postwar Iraq, especially the continued deaths of American military personnel. Many attribute this to Bush's failure to enlist the help of the U.N. in conducting the war.[58]

July 19, 2003: WASHINGTON—The FBI is investigating the origin of forged documents indicating that Iraq was seeking uranium from Niger, and one candidate for the forgeries is an Iraqi opposition group, U.S. officials say.

The documents ended up "tainting" intelligence on Iraq's weapons programs and undermining the credibility of U.S. intelligence reports, say officials who speak on the condition of anonymity.

An official says the documents include a letter about the purchase of some 500 tons of uranium ore, supposedly signed by Niger's president, Mamadou Tandja. The signature was found to have been faked.[59]

When generating pro-war propaganda, the Iraqi National Congress would stoop to any level.

July 22, 2003: BAGHDAD—Both of Saddam's sons, Qusay and Uday, are killed in a gun battle with U.S. troops.[60]

July 24, 2003: WASHINGTON, (UPI)—A member of the independent commission to investigate the Sept. 11, 2001 terror attacks accuses the Bush administration of deliberately delaying publication of an earlier congressional inquiry into the attacks.

Former Senator Max Cleland, D-Georgia, tells UPI that the White House did not want the report made public before launching military action in Iraq. He says the administration feared publication might undermine its case for war, which was based in part on the allegation that Iraqi leader Saddam Hussein had supported Osama bin Laden. The related possibility that Iraq might supply al Qaeda with weapons of mass destruction would also be discounted with a timely release of the report.

"The administration sold the connection (between Iraq and al Qaeda) to scare the pants off the American people and justify the war," says Cleland. "There's no connection, and that's been confirmed by some of bin Laden's terrorist followers…What you've seen here is the manipulation of intelligence for political ends."

Cleland accuses the administration of deliberately delaying the report's release to avoid having its case for war undercut.

"Had this report come out in January like it should have done, we would have known these things before the war in Iraq, which would not have suited the administration."[61]

<u>July 2003</u>: WASHINGTON—Joseph Wilson, who was acting U.S. ambassador to Iraq just before the Persian Gulf War of 1991, alleges White House officials revealed his wife's identity to Robert Novak in retaliation for his exposing flaws in prewar intelligence on Iraq.[62]

NOTES TO CHAPTER 8

1 Linda Feldmann, "The impact of Bush linking 9/11 and Iraq, *The Christian Science Monitor*, March 14, 2003, http://www.csmonitor.com/2003/0314/p02s01-woiq.html.

2 Steven R. Weisman, "Bush promises to adopt plan for Mideast," *The New York Times*, March 15, 2003, Section A, Page 1.

3 "Playing into al Qaeda's hands," *The Mercury News*, March 28, 2004, p. 1P.

4 David E. Sanger, "THREATS AND RESONSE: DIPLOMACY; Bush and 2 allies seem set for war to depose Hussein," *The New York Times*, March 17, 2003, Section A, Page 1.

5 AMERICA AT WAR: UNDERSTANDING THE CONFLICT", *The Mercury News*, March 21, 2003, p. 9AB.

6 http://www.genocideprevention.org/ituri_dr_congo_2003.htm.

7 Dan Stober, "Nuclear inspectors reportedly angry", *The Mercury News*, March 18, 2003, p. 14A.

8 "America's image further erodes, Europeans want weaker ties," March 18, 2003, *The Pew Research Center*, http://people-press.org/.

9 Karl Kahler, "Weapons claim unravels: Charges led to Saddam's downfall, political tempest," *The Mercury News*, January 30, 2004, p. 1AA.

10 Douglas Jehl and Eric Schmidt (NYT), "Targeted strikes in Iraq war largely failed, officials say," *The Mercury News*, June 13, 2004, p. 12A.

11 Richard Perle, "Thank God for the death of the UN," *The Guardian*, March 21, 2003, http://www.guardian.co.uk/Iraq/Story/0,2763,918812,00.html.

12 Jessica Wehrman, "Fragging Stirs Memories of Vietnam," *Scripps Howard News Service*, March 24, 2003 05:57.

13 Stephen Labaton, "Democrat Seeks Inquiry on Bankrupt Firm's Adviser," *The New York Times*, March 24, 2003, http://www.truthout.org/cgi-bin/artman/exec/view.cgi?archive=3&num=266&printer=1.

14 "Questions on Iraq Oil Fire Contracts Awarded without Competition or Notice to Congress," Government Reform Minority Office, March 26, 2003, http://www.house.gov/reform/min/inves_admin/admin_contracts.htm.

15 "Perle Resigns," *ABC News*, February 25, 2004, http://abcnews.go.com/sections/wnt/Investigation/ perle_resignation_040225.html.

16 Donald Rumsfeld, "This Week with George Stephanopoulos," U.S. Department of Defense, March 30, 2003, http://www.dod.gov/news/Mar2003/ t03302003_t0330sdabcsteph.html.

17 Undercutting the 9/11 Inquiry," *The New York Times*, March 31, 2003, Section A, Page 12.

18 Bob Drogin, "Red Cross report details abuse, mistaken detentions in Iraq," *The Mercury News*, May 11, 2004, p. 7A.

19 David W. Chen, "A NATION AT WAR: 9/11 INQUIRY; Beyond Numbers, 9/11 Panel Hears Families' Anguish," *The New York Times*, April 1, 2003, Section A, Page 1.

20 Douglas Jehl and Eric Schmidt (NYT), "Targeted strikes in Iraq war...

21 "A divisive war, an elusive peace," *The Mercury News*, March 19, 2004, p. 4AA.

22 John F. Burns, "A NATION AT WAR: THE IRAQIS; Looting and a Suicide Attack As Chaos Grows in Baghdad," *The New York Times*, April 11, 2003, Section A, Page 1.

23 Ibid.

24 Matthew Schofield and Nancy A. Youssef, "Museum looting likely well-executed theft, officials say," *The Mercury News*, April 16, 2003, http://www.mercurynews.com/mld/mercurynews/news/special_packages/iraq/ 5648587.htm.

25 Nicholas D. Kristof, "Missing in Action: Truth" *The New York Times*, May 6, 2003, Section A, p. 31.

26 "A NATION AT WAR: FOR THE RECORD | A WARNING, AND A PROGRESS REPORT; Taking Issue With Syria, and an Update From Central Command," *The New York Times*, April 15, 2003, Section A, Page 12.

27 Michael Liedtke, "Bechtel's political clout helps land Iraq reconstruction bid," *The Wichita Eagle*, April 18, 2003, http://www.kansas.com/mld/kansas/business/5662973.htm.

28 Matthew E. Berger, "Pro-Israel activists courting Iraqi opposition leader," Jewish Bulletin of Northern California, April 18, 2003, http://www.jewishsf.com/bk030418/1b.shtml.

29 Caroline Overington and Marian Wilkinson, "Bush bars UN weapons team from Iraq," *smh.com.au*, April 24, 2003, http://www.smh.com.au/articles/2003/04/23/1050777306319.html.

30 Jason Leopold, *Online Journal*, http://www.onlinejournal.com, April 20, 2003.

31 "Questions on Halliburton Ties to Countries that Sponsor Terrorism," Government Reform Minority Office, April 30, 2003, http://www.house.gov/reform/min/inves_admin/admin_contracts.htm.

32 Dana Bash, "White House pressed on 'mission accomplished' sign," CNN Washington Bureau, October 29, 2003.

33 "All in the Family," 60 Minutes, *CBSNews.com*, September 17, 2003, http://www.cbsnews.com/stories/2003/04/25/60minutes/main551091.shtml.

34 Bonnie Adams, "Ex-inmate at another Iraq jail also describes 'a torture camp'," *The Mercury News*, May 8, 2004, p. 21A.

35 James Risen, "THE STRUGGLE FOR IRAQ: INTELLIGENCE; Hussein Warned Iraqis to Beware Outside Fighters, Document Says," *The New York Times*, January 14, 2004, Section A, Page 1.

36 Thom Shanker and Dexter Filkins, "U.S. reprimands prison supervisors," *The Mercury News*, May 4, 2004, p. 1A.

37 Nicholas D. Kristof, "Missing in Action: Truth" *The New York Times*, May 6, 2003, Section A, p. 31.

38 Oliver Burkeman, "Cheney firm paid millions in bribes to Nigerian official," The Guardian, May 9, 2003.

39 "A divisive war, an elusive peace,"…

40 Robin Wright, "U.S. may ease policies to win back Iraqi Sunnis," *The Mercury News*, April 22, 2004, p. 12A.

41 Douglas Jehl, "Abuses surfaced months earlier," *The Mercury News*, May 15, 2004, p. 16A.

42 AP, "Company News; Halliburton aggress to pay $6 million to settle 20 suits," *The New York Times*, May 31, 2003, Section C, Page 4.

43 Kevin Sack (LAT), "2 Marines to face trial in abuse," *The Mercury News*, May 22, 2004, p. 13A.

44 Bob Drogin, "More inmate deaths emerge," *The Mercury News*, May 16, 2004, p. 1A.

45 Don Van Natta Jr., "Harsh tactics more routine in prisons, experts say," *The Mercury News*, May 7, 2004, p. 1AA.

46 Bob Drogin, "More inmate deaths emerge,"…

47 David Rohde, "The World: Managing Freedom in Iraq; America Brings Democracy: Censor Now, Vote Later," *The New York Times*, June 22, 2003, Section 4, Page 1.

48 "Army Corps Questioned on Plans to Mortgage Iraq Oil to Fund Reconstruction," Government Reform Minority Office, June 24, 2003, http://www.house.gov/reform/min/inves_admin/admin_contracts.htm.

49 Luke Frazza, "Bush: 'Bring on' attackers of U.S. troops," *USA Today*, July 2, 2003,
http://www.usatoday.com/news/world/iraq/
2003-07-02-bush-iraq-troops_x.htm.

50 Karl Kahler, "Weapons claim unravels:…"

51 Henri E. Cauvin, "Cheney Loses ruling on Energy Panel Records," *The Washington Post*, July 9, 2003.

52 Philip Shenon, "9/11 COMMISSION SAYS U.S. AGENCIES SLOW ITS INQUIRY," *The New York Times*, July 9, 2003, Section A, Page 1.

53 Editorial, "Tale of twisted intelligence, a timeline: Who knew what and when?" *The Mercury News*, July 16, 2003, p. 6B.

54 Ibid.

55 Ibid.

56 "A divisive war, an elusive peace,"…

57 "Bush welcomes probe of CIA leak," *CNN.com*, February 11, 2004, http://www.cnn.com/2003/ALLPOLITICS/09/30/wilson.cia/.

58 Adam Nagourney, "Democrats Say Bush's Credibility Has Been Damaged," *The New York Times*, July 14, 2003, Section A, Page 11.

59 Bill Gertz, "FBI probing forged papers on Niger uranium," *The Washington Times*, July 19, 2003, http://www.washtimes.com/national/20030719-120154-5384r.htm.

60 "A divisive war, an elusive peace,"…

61 Shaun Waterman, "White House 'delayed 9-11 report'," *United Press International*, July 25, 2003, http://www.upi.com/view.cfm?StoryID=20030723-064812-9491r.

62 Novak: 'No great crime' with leak," *CNN.com*, October 1, 2003, http://www.cnn.com/2003/ALLPOLITICS/09/29/novak.cia/index.html.

9

An Elusive Peace:
Welcomed with Open AK-47s

The glow of the spring victory gives way to an increasingly violent insurgency in the summer of 2003. General Miller is brought to Iraq from Guantánamo Bay, Cuba to stress harsher treatment of prisoners to get better intelligence. The sexual humiliation of detainees quietly begins. Saddam Hussein is captured, but the violence continues. Treasury Secretary Paul O'Neill supplies documents for a book critical of the Bush administration and his character assassination begins. An investigation of prisoner abuse begins quietly. The two primary reasons for the war, stockpiles of WMD and the link between Saddam and al Qaeda, gradually evaporate.

The Bush administration rewards Pakistan after learning that it was transferring nuclear technology to North Korea, Iran, and Libya. Dick Cheney's former company, Halliburton, is embroiled in accusations of price gouging, kickbacks, and bribery. Spain's new prime minister pulls his troops out of Iraq as the "coalition of the willing" begins to crumble. Criminal charges are filed against six MPs for detainee abuse. Richard Clarke releases his book accusing the Bush administration of ignoring terror threats and eroding the war on terror with the invasion of Iraq. His character assassination begins. U.S. soldiers shut down Cleric Muqtada al-Sadr's newspaper and an explosion of violence follows. Under pressure, Condoleezza Rice testifies under oath and claims that the Aug. 6th brief is not a warning. The brief is declassified and her credibility disintegrates.

The U.S. military makes bold threats in two battles and then backs down handing major victories to the insurgents. Comparisons to the Vietnam War begin in Washington. Kidnappings begin in Iraq and the Sunnis and the Shiites unite against the foreign occupation. Iraqi public opinion turns decidedly against the U.S. occupation.

<u>1917 & 2003</u>: Is there a resemblance between the occupation of Iraq by the United Kingdom roughly a century ago and that of the United States in 2003?

"Our armies do not come into your cities and lands as conquerors or enemies, but as liberators...It is [not] the wish of [our] government to impose upon you alien institutions," says General Frederick Stanley Maude, the British commander who occupied Baghdad in 1917. Does this sound familiar?

In both cases, foreign troops were able to sweep from the south of the country to the capital in a matter of weeks. In both cases, their governments disclaimed any desire to rule Iraq directly and install Iraqi governments with at least the appearance of popular legitimacy.

In both cases, imposing law and order proved much harder than achieving the initial military victory: British troops were being picked off by gunmen throughout 1919, and massive air power was used to quell a major insurrection in the summer of 1920, which left 450 British personnel dead.

In both cases, there were times when it was tempting to pull out altogether. Also in both cases, the presence of substantial oil reserves was not a wholly irrelevant factor.[1]

<u>August 2003</u>: The United States is facing an upsurge of violence in Iraq. Fear that the war is not going well is on the rise and Saddam Hussein still hasn't been captured.

، Major Gen. Geoffrey Miller, the Guantanamo commander, is dispatched to Iraq. In order to fight the insurgency, he recommends that the United States "rapidly exploit internees for actionable intelligence," according to the investigation carried out by Major Gen. Antonio Taguba in 2004.

According to Miller "it is essential that the guard force be actively engaged in setting the conditions for successful exploitation of the internees." The investigators learn that military intelligence and CIA interrogators told the guards to "loosen this guy up for us," or to "make sure he gets the treatment," all intended "to get them to talk." This role for MPs is in direct violation of standing procedure.

Major Gen. Antonio Taguba, in his March 3, 2004 report on prisoner abuse at Abu Ghurayb, will question these interrogation methods. Many Iraqi detainees have been taken into custody as criminals or in sweeps after attacks on U.S. troops. "These are not believed to be international terrorists or members of al Qaeda, Anser Al Islam, Taliban, and other international terrorist organizations," the report points out.[2]

After these new instructions from General Miller, the prisoner abuse situation at Abu Ghurayb takes a turn for the worse.

<u>August 14, 2003</u>: In a Wall Street Journal article, Richard Perle argues forcefully for the Air Force proposal to lease 100 Boeing 767 tanker aircraft to refuel war planes in flight and for building more long range bombers.

Senator John McCain (R-Arizona), chair of the Senate Commerce and Transportation Committee, accuses Boeing of refusing to reveal its pricing policy or to disclose its communications with the Defense Department. He calls the lease arrangement a waste of money, a sweetheart deal for Boeing, and "one of the most unsavory, inside, military-industrial complex deals."

The Congressional Budget Office says the price of leasing the planes is $5.7 billion over what it would cost to buy them outright.[3]

There is no mention in the article that Richard Perle is one of the main architects of Bush administration foreign policy while he is linked to armament corporations.

<u>August 20, 2003</u>: WASHINGTON—A Jessica Stern editorial observes that the bombing of the U.N. headquarters in Baghdad is the latest evidence that the U.S. has taken a country that was not a terrorist threat and turned it into one. It notes that the aftermath of the war has been precisely what the Bush administration previously described as a breeding ground for terrorists. It also says the effect of the war in fostering terrorism beyond Iraq's borders may be even more worrisome than the situation inside Iraq.[4]

And not to long after this article, terrorism in Saudi Arabia explodes.

<u>Summer 2003</u>: Photos taken in the summer of 2003 through the winter at the Abu Ghurayb prison will be seized in 2004 for a criminal investigation. They show Iraqis stripped of their clothes, piled on top of one another and in positions that simulate sexual acts. One picture shows a female U.S. soldier holding a leash tied around the neck of a naked Iraqi, who lies on the floor of the prison.[5]

<u>2003</u>: BAGHDAD—At Iraq's Camp Bucca, a detainee is shot through the chest in 2003 while throwing rocks at a guard tower. The Army rules the killing a "justifiable shooting," but a Red Cross team that witnesses the incident at the facility in southern Iraq concludes that "at no point" does the prisoner pose a serious threat to guards.[6]

<u>September 14, 2003</u>: WASHINGTON—Vice President Cheney says on NBC's "Meet the Press" that success in Iraq means "we will have struck a major blow right at the heart of the base, if you will, the geographic base of the terrorists who had us under assault now for many years, but most especially on Sept. 11."[7]

Cheney is still pushing the link between Iraq and the Sept. 11 attacks, hoping that repetition will suffice when supporting evidence is missing.

<u>September 17, 2003</u>: WASHINGTON—President Bush says that there is "no evidence" that Iraq's Saddam Hussein was involved in the September 11, 2001 terrorist attacks, disavowing a link that had been hinted previously by his administration. In stating this position, Bush is clarifying an issue long left vague by his administration. He also appears to be correcting what Cheney said three days prior. A *Washington Post* poll in August 2003 found that 69 percent of Americans thought it at least likely that Saddam had a role in the attacks on the World Trade Center and the Pentagon.[8]

This public opinion created fertile ground for the Bush administration to suggest a link between Saddam and the terrorist attacks in order to justify the war, even though there was never any valid evidence to support the link.

<u>September 23, 2003</u>: WASHINGTON—House Speaker Dennis Hastert, R-Illinois, calls Bush's U.N. speech "comprehensive and compelling" and calls on other nations to pitch in with the reconstruction of Iraq and the defeat of terrorism.

"Now the international community needs to step up to the plate and help the United States finish the job," Hastert says.

"The fact is, the president's eleventh-hour, halfhearted appeal to the United Nations, and his continuing I-told-you-so tone, have made it more difficult to secure international assistance in building a safe, stable and self-governing Iraq," says Senator Joe Lieberman, D-Connecticut.

Lieberman, a prominent Democratic supporter of the war, calls on Bush to turn over Iraq's administration to an international authority within 60 days.[9]

<u>September 29, 2003</u>: WASHINGTON—The *Washington Post* quotes a senior administration official who will say in 2004 that two top White House officials called at least six journalists and disclosed Plame's CIA status, saying "Clearly it was meant purely and simply for revenge."[10]

<u>October 3, 2003</u>: Army Maj. Gen. Antonio M. Taguba's March 3, 2004 prisoner abuse report will find that between October and December 2003 at the Abu Ghurayb facility in Iraq, the military police are told by military intelligence officers to soften up the prisoners so they will talk more freely in interrogations conducted by intelligence officials.

The Taguba report will state "Military intelligence interrogators and other U.S. Government Agency interrogators actively requested that MP guards set physical and mental conditions for favorable interrogation of witnesses." According to the report, one civilian interrogator, a contractor from a company called CACI who is attached to the 205th Military Intelligence Brigade, "clearly knew his instructions" to the military police equates to physical abuse.

A series of photographs taken by American soldiers in Abu Ghurayb, dating back to October 3, 2003, showing acts of sexual humiliation and other forms of abuse will be seized as evidence in 2004. The photographs support the conclusions of the Taguba report, which will find that "between October and December, 2003, at the Abu Ghurayb Confinement Facility, numerous incidents of sadistic, blatant and wanton criminal abuses were inflicted on several detainees" by members of the 800th Military Police Brigade. "This systemic and illegal abuse of detainees was intentionally perpetrated by several members of the military police guard force."

The report will also say abuses were also committed by members of the 325th Military Intelligence Battalion, the 205th Military Intelligence Brigade, and the Joint Interrogation and Debriefing Center.[11]

This is the time period during which many of the notorious and humiliating Abu Ghurayb actions occurred and photos were taken—over six months after high-level U.S. authorities were alerted that prisoner abuses were occurring in Iraq.

<u>October 2003</u>: WASHINGTON—Military intelligence officers at the Abu Ghurayb prison in Iraq direct military police to take clothes from prisoners, leave detainees naked in their cells and make them wear women's underwear, part of a series of abuses that are openly discussed at the facility, according to Sgt. Samuel Provance, a military intelligence soldier working at the prison at the time.

He voices his disapproval as early as October 2003.[12]

<u>October 2003</u>: The International Committee of the Red Cross says that it regularly visited Abu Ghurayb and frequently complained to U.S. officials about the abuses over a period of many months.[13]

October 2003: An Iraqi prisoner is "hooded, handcuffed in the back, and made to lie face down" on what investigators believe is the engine hood of a vehicle while he is being transported. He is hospitalized for three months for extensive burns to his face, abdomen, foot and hand. The incident is described in a Red Cross report which will be released in May 2004.[14]

October 13, 2003: Defense Secretary Donald Rumsfeld poses a question in an Oct. 13, 2003, internal memo, "Are we capturing, killing or dissuading more terrorists every day than the *madrasahs* and radical clerics are recruiting, training and deploying against us?"[15]

October 18, 2003: WASHINGTON—Former President George H. W. Bush, gives the 2003 George Bush Award for Excellence in Public Service to anti-Iraq war Democrat Senator Edward Kennedy.

Ever since the current President Bush went adventuring in Iraq, much to his father's dismay, the policy schism between father and son has been well known. Now the father reveals the depth of his disagreement with his uninformed son.[16]

October 20, 2003: TOLEDO, Ohio—After an eight-month investigation, the Toledo Blade publishes a series of articles revealing the Tiger Force platoon's brutal sweep through 40 Vietnamese villages where civilians were tortured and killed in 1967.[17]

October 21, 2003: WASHINGTON—U.S. troops in Iraq are responsible for at least 20 "legally questionable" civilian deaths in Baghdad since May 1 and are not doing enough to avoid harming bystanders, Human Rights Watch concludes in one of the most detailed analyses of civilian casualties resulting from the U.S.-led occupation.[18]

October 24, 2003: WASHINGTON—Scott McClellan, the chief White House spokesman, specifically denies that any of three prominent White House officials—Karl Rove, Vice President Cheney's Chief of Staff Lewis Libby or National Security Council official Elliott Abrams—had leaked the identity of a CIA agent or authorized such leaks. President Bush has said he hopes the Justice investigators get to the bottom of the case, but he also noted that it is possible the person responsible for the leak will never be identified.[19]

A few months later, Lewis Libby and another Cheney staffer will be identified as the culprits.

October 26, 2003: BAGHDAD—The evidence for White House claims of illicit weapons before the invasion of Iraq fades on inspection. Among the closely held internal judgments of the Iraq Survey Group, overseen by David Kay as special representative of CIA Director George Tenet, are that Iraq's nuclear weapons scientists did no significant arms-related work after 1991, that facilities with suspicious new construction proves benign, and that equipment of potential use to a nuclear program remains under seal or in civilian industrial use.[20]

October 27, 2003: WASHINGTON—A leaked Defense Department memo claiming new evidence of an "operational relationship" between Osama bin Laden and Saddam Hussein's former regime is mostly based on unverified claims that were first advanced by a top Bush administration official, Undersecretary of Defense for Policy Douglas Feith, more than a year ago—and were largely discounted at the time by the U.S. intelligence community, according to current and former U.S. intelligence officials.[21]

October 27, 2003: WASHINGTON—In reference to the Douglas Feith October 27, 2003 document, George Tenet says the CIA, "did not clear the document. We did not agree with the way the data was characterized in the document."[22]

November 3, 2003: On an obscure federal web site devoted to the war on terrorism, the Bush administration quietly begins a public campaign to bring the draft boards back to life. The site is recruiting volunteers to fill vacancies on the 2,000 local and appeal boards supporting the military draft.

With more troops needed in Iraq, some experts are suggesting a return to the draft. Bills to reactivate the draft have already been submitted in both houses of Congress.

"They don't want us to have to do it," agrees Dan Amon, a spokesman for the Selective Service. "But they want us to be ready to do it at the click of a finger."[23]

When rumors of a draft start to circulate during 2004, an election year, the posting for these volunteers will be dropped from the web site.

November 5, 2003: WASHINGTON—President Bush struggles with the political consequences for a president who has said little about mounting casualties of occupation. Democratic Senator Tom Daschle says deference must be paid to the dead and wounded. The Bush administration bans media coverage of coffins arriving at Dover Air Force Base.[24]

In Britain, fallen soldiers returning from Iraq are honored publicly.

November 2003: BAGHDAD—Iraqi Manadal Jamaidi dies during interrogation by a CIA officer and a contractor translator at Abu Ghurayb prison. According to sources, Jamaidi slumps over and dies during questioning, and an autopsy indicates internal injuries are the cause of death. The case was among the three homicides that Army Maj. Gen. Donald Ryder will cite as under investigation in May 2004.[25]

November 15, 2003: BAGHDAD—Paul Bremer and the Iraqi Governing Council agree on a plan to transfer power to the provisional Iraqi government on July 1, 2004.[26]

November 17, 2003: Afghanistan—In the two years since the war in Afghanistan, opium production has soared 19 fold and become a major source of the world's heroin.

"There is a palpable risk that Afghanistan will again turn into a failed state, this time in the hands of drug cartels and narco-terrorists," Antonio Maria Costa, executive director of the U.N. Office on Drugs and Crime, writes in a grim new report on Afghanistan.

The Pentagon is making the same misjudgment in both Afghanistan and Iraq: It fatally underestimates the importance of ensuring security.[27]

November 25, 2003: WASHINGTON—Representative Waxman, Senator Lieberman, and Representative Dingell ask the Dept. of Defense Inspector General to investigate the high gasoline prices being charged by Halliburton and the appropriateness of using $725 million from the Development Fund for Iraq to pay these inflated fuel costs.[28]

November 26, 2003: BAGHDAD—Iraqi Maj. Gen. Abid Hamad Mahalawi collapses and dies in U.S. custody after alleged mistreatment during interrogation near the western Iraqi city of Al-Qaim. A U.S. intelligence official will say in 2004 that CIA operatives had questioned Mahalawi but they were not present when he died.[29]

<u>November 27, 2003</u>: WASHINGTON—Amid fears that it can no longer meet a spring deadline, the independent commission investigating the Sept. 11 attacks is coming under increasing pressure to seek an extension of its work into the 2004 election season.

The White House, which opposed the commission's formation for more than a year, successfully fought to impose a deadline that is five months before the November elections.[30]

<u>December 2003</u>: It has will be reported that a former Iraqi general, Abed Hamed Mowhoush, dies during U.S. interrogations late in 2003.[31]

<u>December 13, 2003</u>: Ahmad Khalil Ibrahim Samir al-Ani, a former Iraqi intelligence officer, who was said to have met with the suspected leader of the Sept. 11 attacks will tell American interrogators the meeting never happened, according to United States officials familiar with classified intelligence reports.[32]

<u>December 13, 2003</u>: TIKRIT, Iraq—Saddam Hussein is captured hiding in a "spider hole" near Tikrit.[33]

<u>December 13, 2003</u>: AN-NAJAF, Iraq—One of the most important men in Iraq these days is Grand Ayatollah Ali Sistani. He keeps a low profile in this holy city of an-Najaf for Shiite Muslims. Like other clerics, Sistani spent most of the 1990s under house arrest. As other clerics died or were assassinated, many of their followers turned to Sistani.

He has the largest group of religious followers in Iraq, and with that comes access to financial contributions. He is the most influential cleric in the country, and perhaps the most powerful man in Iraq. With a few words he can create significant opposition to the U.S. military occupation.

Sistani hasn't opposed the U.S. occupation, which removed Saddam Hussein from power. He speaks for the interests of 15 million Shiites, who were brutally repressed by the dictator and who make up 60 percent of Iraq's population.

The 73-year-old Sistani objects to the American plan for local leaders to select delegates to a transitional government by July. He insists on direct elections instead, as he did in a religious edict he issued in June that declared "fundamentally unacceptable" any effort to write a constitution without directly electing its drafters.

Sistani warns that the constitution must be consistent with Islamic law and Sistani's agents insist that Iraq's judges be drawn from the Hawza, the religious council of scholars he helps preside over. Ignoring Sistani could be a big mistake.

"In the long term, power lies with Sistani and not with the coalition," says Joost Hiltermann, director of the Amman office for the International Crisis Group, a non-partisan conflict-resolution group. "When a person like Sistani speaks out in public, as he very rarely does, for a person like him to have to back down would be a tremendous loss of face."

"It's a matter of national pride for Iraqis that the political process not be imposed by outsiders or the U.S. generally," Hiltermann says.

"We support him very strongly. He's our spiritual leader. We will sacrifice our souls under his feet," says Adnan Khalil Ibrahim, 42, a retired high school chemistry teacher.

Iraqi Shiites trust Sistani.[34]

December 18, 2003: A soldier who will be accused in March 2004 of abusing prisoners at the Abu Ghurayb facility in Iraq writes to his family that military intelligence officers are pleased with how the Iraqis are being treated, according to correspondence that will be provided by the soldier's family in May 2004.

"We have had a very high rate with our style of getting them to break," the soldier, Staff Sgt. Ivan L. "Chip" Frederick II, writes according to a Dec. 18 e-mail. "They usually end up breaking within hours."

Frederick also writes that he questions some of the abuses. "I questioned this and the answer I got was: This is how military intelligence wants it done."[35]

January 8, 2004: The Carnegie Endowment of International Peace, a non-partisan research institution, claims in a 61-page report that Iraqi weapons programs threatened regional and global security in the long run, but they weren't an immediate danger to the United States in 2003—a key reason the Bush administration gave for going to war. The study claims that intelligence agencies failed to make an accurate assessment of the status of Saddam's illicit weapons and missile programs.

The report accuses President Bush and top officials of "systematically" misrepresenting the threats posed by those programs, even beyond the evidence presented by what it deemed faulty intelligence analyses. Among the findings, intelligence assessments after 2002, coupled with the creation of a separate intelligence cell in the Pentagon, "suggest that the intelligence community began to be unduly influenced by policymakers views sometime in 2002." The report recommends that Congress create an independent, blue-ribbon panel to assess the quality and handling of intelligence on Iraq before the war.[36]

January 11, 2004: WASHINGTON—Ousted Treasury Secretary Paul O'Neill is a guest on CBS "60 Minutes" broadcast, along with Ron Suskind, the author of a book for which O'Neill was the primary source. O'Neill says on the program that the administration was preparing plans to move against Iraq "from the very beginning."

He also describes a conflict with Vice President Dick Cheney and Karl Rove on the tax cuts.[37]

The book is critical of President Bush and results in harsh personal attacks against O'Neill from Republicans.

January 12, 2004: WASHINGTON—The Treasury Department is launching an investigation into how a document—marked "secret" and outlining plans for a post-Saddam Iraq—from the very early days of the Bush administration became part of a CBS "60 Minutes" broadcast Sunday night.

Ousted Treasury Secretary Paul O'Neill, now an outspoken critic of the Bush administration, sparked a fury of controversy in Washington and was the target of the investigation.

Ron Suskind says O'Neill gained proper authorization to all 19,000 Government documents used as sources for the book he wrote.[38]

January 13, 2004: A member of the 800th Military Police Brigade tells superiors about prisoner abuses at the Abu Ghurayb prison and turns over photographs.[39]

The prisoner abuse case begins to unfold when Spec. Joseph Darby returns to Abu Ghurayb from leave and hears about a shooting at the prison's "hard site," which contains Tier 1A, according to military investigators. He asks the MP in charge of the tier's night shift, Spec. Charles Graner, if he had any photographs of the cell where the shooting took place.

According to Darby Graner handed him two CDs of photographs.

"I thought the discs just had pictures of Iraq, the cell where the shooting occurred," Darby will tell investigators.

Instead, Darby will say, he views hundreds of photographs showing naked detainees being abused by U.S. soldiers.

"It was just wrong," Darby will say. "I knew I had to do something."[40]

January 14, 2004: BAGHDAD, Iraq—The U.S. commander in Iraq, Army Lt. Gen. Richard Sanchez, opens a criminal investigation of prison abuse. Defense Secretary Donald Rumsfeld and President Bush are informed of the allegations in general terms.[41]

Spec. Jeremy Sivits tells military authorities a harrowing tale of abuse, including an episode in which a guard used a nightstick to beat an Iraqi detainee who had been shot in the legs and handcuffed to a bed.

As the prisoner screamed "Mister, mister, please stop," military police Cpl. Charles Graner struck him twice with the police baton, according to fellow guard Sivits.

An atmosphere is described in which a group of military police repeatedly laughed, joked, and mocked Iraqi detainees as they stripped them naked, struck and kicked them, and forced them to hit one another.

According to Sivits, Graner told him not to say anything.

Sivits first became aware of the abuse, and began photographing much of it, on Oct. 3, 2003.

Graner was striking inmates, and Sgt. Javal Davis was running across the floor and jumping on them when they were handcuffed, naked and piled on the floor in a pyramid, according to Sivits.

"A couple of the detainees kind of made an 'ah' sound as if this hurt them or caused them some type of pain when Davis would land on them," he says. "After Davis had done this, Davis then stomped on either the fingers or toes of the detainees. When he stomped the detainees, they were in pain, because the detainees would scream loudly."[42]

This interview will become public on May 14, 2004.

January 14, 2004: Democratic presidential candidate Wesley Clark criticizes the timing of an investigation of former Treasury Secretary Paul O'Neill and suggests that President Bush is more concerned with "political security" than national security.[43]

January 16, 2004: Central Command says in a news release, "An investigation has been initiated into reported incidents of detainee abuse at a Coalition Forces detention facility. The release of specific information concerning the incidents could hinder the investigation."[44]

January 17, 2004: Sanchez advises the commander of military prisons in Iraq, Army Reserve Brig. Gen. Janis Karpinski, that there are serious deficiencies in her command; she will later be suspended.[45]

January 19, 2004: WASHINGTON—In a new book about the Bush administration, former Treasury Secretary Paul O'Neill describes Vice President Dick Cheney as the leader of a "Praetorian Guard" around the president, cutting him off from dissenting opinions.

It was Cheney who told O'Neill he was fired in 2002.[46]

January 20, 2004: WASHINGTON—In his State of the Union address, President Bush says, "We are seeking all of the facts—already the Kay report identified dozens of weapons of mass destruction-related program activities and significant amounts of equipment that Iraq concealed from the U.N. Had we failed to act, the dictator's weapons of mass destruction programs would continue to this day."

Bush also describes wonderful progress with peace and freedom for Iraq. Bush says, "America will never seek a permission slip to defend the security of our country."[47]

From what threat to the security of our country is Bush defending us?

January 21, 2004: BAGHDAD—CIA officers in Iraq warn that the Shiite majority could launch a violent revolution unless their desires for a direct election are met, starkly contradicting the upbeat assessment that President Bush gave in his State of the Union address the day before. Meanwhile, Iraq's Kurdish minority is pressing its demand of autonomy and shares of oil revenue.[48]

January 22, 2004: On National Public Radio, Vice President Dick Cheney claims that two truck trailers recovered in Iraq are "conclusive evidence" that Saddam had a biological weapons program. CIA Director George Tenet will refute this claim on March 9, 2004[49]

January 23, 2004: WASHINGTON—The former chief U.S. arms inspector in Iraq, David Kay, resigns and says he has concluded that Iraq had no chemical or biological weapons at the start of the war in March 2003. He believes that Iraq had illicit weapons at the end of the 1991 Persian Gulf War, but that U.N. inspections and Iraq's own decisions "got rid of them."[50]

January 23, 2004: HOUSTON—Halliburton fires employees who allegedly took kickbacks from a Kuwaiti subcontractor helping to supply U.S. troops in Iraq, the company says.

The Wall Street Journal reports that two employees of Halliburton subsidiary KBR accepted up to $6 million in kickbacks from the unnamed Kuwaiti firm. The company doesn't discuss specifics of the charges.

The kickback allegations involve KBR's contract to supply U.S. Army troops in Iraq, not its separate contract to rebuild Iraqi oil facilities and deliver gasoline to civilians.

In a separate matter, pentagon auditors are seeking a criminal probe into findings that KBR and Kuwaiti firm Altanmia Marketing Co. overcharged by $61 million for fuel deliveries.[51]

January 26, 2004: WASHINGTON—The White House retreats from its once-confident claims that Iraq had weapons of mass destruction.[52]

January 26, 2004: WASHINGTON—Senator Joe Lieberman, a Democratic presidential hopeful, urges an investigation or congressional hearings "on the intelligence that some of us saw directly, and the statements that the administration was making and the emphasis the administration was putting on weapons of mass destruction."[53]

January 26, 2004: Reports surface that photos were taken of partially unclothed prisoners and of soldiers hitting detainees in Iraq.[54]

January 27, 2004: WASHINGTON—When President Bush is asked if he believes that U.S. troops will find banned weapons in Iraq, he says only that Saddam was a "gathering threat."[55]

January 27, 2004: WASHINGTON—Thomas Kean says his independent commission investigating Sept. 11 terror attacks needs an extension of its mandate until at least July. House Speaker Dennis Hastert opposes any bill to extend the May 27 deadline, an extension Bush opposes.[56]

January 30, 2004: WASHINGTON—President Bush says that he won't back calls for an independent investigation of intelligence failures surrounding Saddam Hussein's alleged weapons of mass destruction stockpiles despite increasing demands for one by some U.S. lawmakers.[57]

January 31, 2004: Maj. Gen. Antonio Taguba is appointed chief investigator of the prison abuse scandal.[58]

February 2, 2004: Maj. Gen. Antonio M. Taguba and his team visit Abu Ghurayb to investigate prisoner abuse.[59]

February 2, 2004: WASHINGTON—Bowing to political pressure, President Bush will name a bipartisan, independent commission this week to review prewar U.S. intelligence about Iraq's weapons programs, administration sources say. There will be no public report from the commission prior to the November elections—the due date is early to middle 2005.[60]

February 2, 2004: ISLAMABAD—Pakistan's top nuclear scientist, Abdul Qadeer Khan, tells investigators that he helped North Korea design and equip facilities for making weapons-grade uranium with the knowledge of senior military commanders, including General Pervez Musharraf, Pakistan's president, according to a friend of Khan's and a senior Pakistani investigator.

Khan also tells investigators that Gen. Mirza Aslam Beg, the Pakistani army chief of staff from 1988 to 1991, was aware of assistance that Khan was providing to Iran's nuclear program and that two other army chiefs, in addition to Musharraf, knew and approved of his efforts on behalf of North Korea, the same individuals say.[61]

February 2, 2004: WASHINGTON—The U.S. Secretary of State, Colin Powell, reveals the first cracks of doubt from within the Bush administration about the decision to go to war against Iraq, acknowledging he might not have supported an invasion had he known Saddam Hussein had no weapons of mass destruction.

Mr. Powell's admission that the "absence of a stockpile changes the political calculus" is the first public sign that the Bush administration may be having second thoughts on its decision to wage war.[62]

February 3, 2004: WASHINGTON—Colin Powell's admission yesterday that the absence of weapons stockpiles had weakened Bush's argument that Iraq was a direct and urgent threat had clearly irritated the White House. After some communication with, and undoubtedly some prodding from the administration, Powell revises yesterday's comment about going to war with Iraq with a response coordinated with the White House, "The bottom line is this: The President made the right decision."[63]

The isolated Powell frequently struggles between loyalty to his boss versus frankly describing situations as he sees them. Does he belong in this administration?

February 4, 2004: ISLAMABAD—In a televised address, Pakistan's top nuclear scientist Abdul Qadeer Khan admits providing nuclear weapons expertise and equipment to Iran, Libya and North Korea, saying he had done so without authorization from the Pakistani government.

The national hero will likely keep the money he made from the deals and escape punishment. Khan agreed to address the nation in return for assurances that he would not be prosecuted. The deal included his dropping the charges that the military was involved.[64]

While it is inconceivable that the military and President Musharraf were unaware of the missiles for nuclear technology dealing that spanned decades, the allegations would create complications for both Musharraf and the Bush administration, which wanted to retain Musharraf as an ally in the war on terror. The deal appears to be a neat "win-win-win" where Khan is not punished, Musharraf is off the hot seat with the international community as well as Khan's many fans in Pakistan, and Bush gets to keep his ally. In return for the Bush administration's looking the other way with respect to Pakistan's proliferation of WMD, Musharraf's part of the deal appears to include a more vigorous effort to catch Osama bin Laden. A more intensive hunt for bin Laden will occur soon after the deal.

February 4, 2004: WASHINGTON—Under pressure, the White House reverses itself and says it will support a request from the independent commission investigating Sept 11 attacks for an extension until late July.[65]

February 6, 2004: WASHINGTON—Former Treasury Secretary Paul O'Neill has been cleared of wrongdoing in the use of classified documents as source material for a book that portrays President Bush in an unflattering light, Treasury Department sources tell CNN.

The investigation by the department's inspector general found that though O'Neill did receive classified material from the department after his resignation, the lapse was the fault of the department, not O'Neill, the sources say.[66]

<u>February 5, 2004</u>: WASHINGTON—UPI quotes federal law-enforcement officials as saying they have "developed hard evidence of possible criminal misconduct by two employees of Vice President Dick Cheney's office" related to the leak that Valerie Plume was a CIA agent.[67]

<u>February 6, 2004</u>: WASHINGTON—President Bush signs an executive order creating an "independent" commission to review Iraq and other intelligence failures. Bush is to personally appoint the commission members, and there will be no public report from the commission prior to the November elections—the due date is March 31, 2005. The commission will report to the President, not the public or Congress, and its findings may never be publicly reported.[68]

Why is it so important to the President that the public be shielded from this investigation prior to his reelection bid?

<u>February 6, 2004</u>: WASHINGTON—CIA Director George Tenet acknowledges for the first time that American spy agencies may have overestimated Iraq's illicit weapons capacities, in part because of failure to penetrate inner workings of Iraqi government. However, he says intelligence analysts never portrayed Iraq as presenting an imminent threat to the United States before American invasion.[69]

<u>February 7, 2004</u>: WASHINGTON—Rice, who has refused to testify before the panel investigating the Sept. 11 attacks under oath and in public, meets with the commission privately for four hours.

"She corrects [herself] in our private interview by saying, 'I could not anticipate that they would try to use an airplane as a missile,' but acknowledging that the intelligence community could anticipate it," Richard Ben-Veniste says.[70]

<u>February 10, 2004</u>: KABUL—The multi-billion-dollar business that is fed by Afghanistan's vast opium fields is damaging the country's national security, economy and reputation, President Hamid Karzai says.

"Trafficking and production of heroin helps terrorism," according to Mr. Karzai. This could "destroy Afghanistan."

The irony is that the Taliban reduced opium production to 185 tons in 2001. After the American invasion, the production has mushroomed to 3,600 tons in 2003.[71]

Is this a precursor to the quality of nation building that can be expected in Iraq?

<u>February 10, 2004</u>: WASHINGTON—At this time the media learns that the public version of the October 2002 U.S. intelligence community's key prewar assessment of Iraq's illicit arms programs was stripped of dissenting opinions, warnings of insufficient information, and doubts.[72]

<u>February 13, 2004</u>: WASHINGTON—"President Bush is defining himself as a war president. It is endemic to everything he says and does and that's the overriding definitional tone," says Mike Frank, a government expert from the Heritage Foundation.

"The main strategy for Bush is he wants people to look at him as a war president," Democratic strategist Peter Fenn points out.[73]

<u>February 15, 2004</u>: WASHINGTON—Due to articles recently published by the Toledo Blade, military investigators will begin interviewing former soldiers of the elite Tiger Force platoon accused of slaughtering scores of unarmed civilians in the Vietnam War.

As part of the new inquiry, the Army has appointed an investigator to look into why the original Army inquiry was dropped in 1975 with no charges filed. Secretary of Defense Donald Rumsfeld was in the same position at the time the inquiry was squashed.[74]

<u>February 18, 2004</u>: WASHINGTON—Richard Perle, a lightning rod for critics of the Bush administration's policies, resigns from the Defense Policy Board. Perle is a leading figure of the "neoconservative" ideological school, a major advocate of the war in Iraq, and has strong views on wielding U.S. military power.

Last March, Perle resigned as chairman of the same board amid accusations of conflict of interest. Perle has consistently insisted he did nothing wrong.[75]

<u>February 22, 2004</u>: WASHINGTON—The Department of Defense continues to pay millions of dollars for information from the former Iraqi opposition group that produced some of the exaggerated and fabricated intelligence President Bush used to argue his case for war.

The Pentagon has set aside $3+ million this year for the Iraqi National Congress (INC), led by Ahmed Chalabi, say two senior U.S. officials.

Chalabi, who lobbied for years for a U.S.-backed military effort to topple Saddam, is publicly committed to making peace with Israel and providing American military bases in the heart of the oil-rich Middle East.

The State Department and the CIA, which soured on Chalabi in the 1990s, viewed the INC's information as highly unreliable.[76]

February 25, 2004: LONDON—The British government, in a sudden reversal, will not prosecute Katharine Gun, the government intelligence translator who admitted leaking the top-secret request by the U.S. National Security Agency for help in bugging U.N. diplomats during the Iraq war debate last year. Gun claims she acted to expose the U.S. attempt to undermine the U.N. debate.[77]

February 26, 2004: WASHINGTON—President Bush and Vice President Cheney place strict limits on the private interviews they will grant to the federal commission investigating the Sept. 11 attacks, saying that they will meet only with the panel's top two officials and that Bush will submit to only a single hour of questioning.

Also, Condoleezza Rice, the national security adviser, rejects the commission's request that she testify in public about the intelligence reports that reached her desk before the Sept. 11 attacks.[78]

February 26, 2004: WASHINGTON—The Senate is expected to approve a two-month extension for the commission investigating the Sept. 11 terrorist attacks. The Bush administration agrees to the extra time.[79]

February 29, 2004: HOUSTON—There are accusations against Halliburton for everything from price gouging to bribery, but as allegations of widespread wrong-doing at the Houston company mount, investors don't seem to care.

Halliburton has been in the spotlight due to its past ties with Vice President Dick Cheney, who was the company's chairman from 1995 to 2000, and because of its receipt of a multibillion no-bid contract to rebuild Iraq's oil industry. It is also facing allegations that it overcharged by millions of dollars for its services, including feeding U.S. troops and delivering fuel.

Outside of Iraq, the company's alleged involvement in the payment of $180 million in bribes to win a contract in the 1990s for a natural gas project in Africa is under investigation by U.S., French and Nigerian officials.[80]

March 2, 2004: ISLAMABAD—A *Washington Post* commentary delves deeper into the Khan-Musharraf deal and concludes, "It is inconceivable Mr. Khan, for three decades, could have indulged in such extensive nuclear proliferation with-out the knowledge and acquiescence of ISI and the military high command. Mr.

Musharraf was army chief of staff prior to seizing the presidency in October 1999.

What did Mr. Musharraf know—and when did he know it—are the kind of questions Pakistani journalists are well-advised not to ask."[81]

March 2, 2004: BAGHDAD—Coordinated blasts strike Shiite Muslim shrines in Baghdad and the southern Iraqi city of Karbala, killing at least 181 people.[82]

March 3, 2004: WASHINGTON—The Bush administration's claim that Iraqi leader Saddam Hussein had ties to al Qaeda appears to have been based on very weak intelligence.

Nearly a year after U.S. and British soldiers invaded Iraq, no evidence has turned up to verify allegations of Saddam's links with al Qaeda. Many key parts of the Bush administration's case either have proved false or seem increasingly doubtful. A secret report by the CIA's Directorate of Intelligence that was updated in January 2003, on the eve of the war, tells a different story.

There never was any evidence that Saddam's secular police state and Osama bin Laden's Islamist terrorism network were in league.

Much of the evidence that is now available indicates that Iraq and al Qaeda had no close ties, despite repeated contacts between the two. It turns out that the terrorists who administration officials claimed were links between the two had no direct connection to either Saddam or bin Laden. Also, a key meeting between an Iraqi intelligence officer and one of the leaders of the Sept. 11 terrorist attacks probably never happened.

But before the war and since, Bush and his aides, especially Dick Cheney, claimed "overwhelming evidence" of links that have turned out to be baseless.[83]

March 3, 2004: WASHINGTON—President Bush's re-election team unveils his first campaign advertisements on Wednesday and they in part use the events of Sept. 11, 2001, to focus on his "steady leadership" during turbulent times.

Two ads refer to the tragedy of Sept. 11, 2001, as the Bush campaign seeks to present Bush as a tried and tested leader who has risen to the challenge. One ad, entitled "Tested," shows, among other images, a damaged building from the World Trade Center ruins behind an American flag.[84]

March 3, 2004: Maj. Gen. Antonio M. Taguba's early findings suggest members of the 372nd Military Police Company and intelligence operatives are the prisoner abusers.[85]

<u>March 5, 2004</u>: WASHINGTON—Firefighters and some relatives of those killed during the Sept. 11, 2001, terrorist attacks say they were furious about Bush-Cheney campaign ads featuring fleeting images of a destroyed World Trade Center and of firefighters carrying a flag-draped coffin. The nation's firefighters union calls on the campaign to pull the television ads.

Some of the Sept. 11 families find the ads acceptable, but the strongest comments come from families of Sept. 11 victims that are not.

"I think it's outrageous that he should use our grief to promote his candidacy," says Wright Salisbury of Lexington, Mass., whose son-in-law was killed in New York. "I understand why he's doing this. He's trying to cover himself with the flag. He's trying to justify the war in Iraq by saying it had something to do with 9/11."[86]

The Bush administration does not permit the flag-draped coffins returning from Iraq to be seen at all, but a Sept. 11 flag-draped coffin can be used in his campaign ad.

<u>March 8, 2004</u>: BAGHDAD—The Iraqi Governing Council signs an interim constitution that returns power to Iraqis June 30, 2004, with elections in January 2005.[87]

Will the Iraqi people accept this action by a council hand-picked by the United States? Will the U.S. turn over complete sovereignty to the Iraqis on June 30, 2004?

<u>March 9, 2004</u>: WASHINGTON—In comments to the Senate Armed Services Committee, CIA Director George Tenet rejects recent assertions by Vice President Dick Cheney that Iraq cooperated with the al Qaeda terrorist network and that the administration had proof of an illicit Iraqi biological warfare program.

At first Tenet defends the administration, but after sharp questioning, Tenet reverses himself, saying there had been instances when he had warned administration officials that they were misstating the threat posed by Iraq. While not wanting to be pinned down on all occasions where he privately corrected administration officials, Tenet did offer that he had told Cheney that the Vice President was wrong in saying that two truck trailers recovered in Iraq were "conclusive evidence" that Saddam had a biological weapons program. Cheney made the assertion on National Public Radio January 22, 2004.

In another case, Cheney cited an article in the Weekly Standard, a conservative magazine, as "the best source of information" on cooperation between Saddam and al Qaeda. The article was based upon a top-secret memorandum written by Undersecretary of Defense for Policy Douglas Feith, the third highest Pentagon official and a key proponent of the war. Tenet says the CIA, "did not clear the document. We did not agree with the way the data was characterized in the document." Tenet says he plans to speak to Cheney about the CIA's view of the document.[88]

Why didn't George Tenet take some action to help give the American public a more accurate picture of the Iraqi threat prior to the invasion?

March 9, 2004: WASHINGTON—President Bush will answer all the questions of a federal commission investigating the Sept. 11 attacks, a White House spokesman says, suggesting that the president will be more flexible in his approach to the commission.[89]

March 11, 2004: MADRID—Simultaneous explosions rock three train stations in Madrid, Spain, killing over 200 people, and wounding more than 1,400 people in Spain's worst terror attack. Initially blamed on the separatist group ETA, the attack appears to be linked to al Qaeda.[90]

March 14, 2004: WASHINGTON—On CBS's "Face the Nation," Secretary of Defense Donald Rumsfeld reiterates his claim that neither he nor President Bush called Iraq an imminent threat. Then he's confronted with his September 19, 2002 statement, "There are a number of terrorist states pursuing weapons of mass destruction but no terrorist state poses a greater or more immediate threat to the security of our people than the regime of Saddam Hussein and Iraq." Rumsfeld responds that we still might find weapons of mass destruction in Iraq.[91]

March 15, 2004: MADRID—Spain's newly elected Socialist Prime Minister, Jose Luis Rodriguez Zapatero, offers a scathing criticism of the American-led war in Iraq and pledges to break with the policies of his predecessor and shift Spain's allegiance away from Washington to Paris and Berlin. He promises to withdraw Spain's 1,300 troops from Iraq prior to June 30, 2004 unless there is a U.N. mandate.[92]

Withdrawing Spain's troops from Iraq would have the unfortunate consequence of rewarding the terrorists. However, Zapatero's election was in protest to Spain's deployment of troops in Iraq, a move by Spain's current Prime Minister Jose Maria Aznar that was disapproved by 90% of the country's population. Aznar's decision to make a dramatic move against the wishes of his own people set up Zapatero's dilemma: He could ignore the main issue that placed him into office or reward the militants who committed the greatest act of terrorism against Spain in its history.

<u>March 16, 2004</u>: The diplomat whose wife was identified as a CIA operative questions the credibility of the Bush administration in an article entitled, "The Pinocchio Presidency."[93]

<u>March 16, 2004</u>: Recent polls indicate that the plummeting image of the United States in other countries recovered somewhat after the war started, but then eroded again when illicit weapons weren't found.[94]

<u>March 18, 2004</u>: WASHINGTON—Secretary of State Colin Powell announces that the United States will give Pakistan easier access to military weapons and equipment, despite questions about the Pakistani military's role in selling nuclear secrets to other nations. The Bush administration pledges $3 billion in aid to Pakistan over the next five years, and forgives almost $1.5 billion in debt. This is their reward for cooperation in the war on terror.[95]

Was this also an award for Pakistan's prominent role in the proliferation of weapons of mass destruction to rogue nations, or does that not matter?

<u>March 18, 2004</u>: BERKELEY—Joseph Wilson, the former diplomat who clashed with the Bush administration over its use of faulty intelligence to justify the war in Iraq, says that the United States would be blamed "forever" by the Arab world if it failed to create a functioning democracy in Iraq.

"The mess that's left over is our mess," Wilson says in a speech at the University of California-Berkeley. "We own it."

Wilson says journalists failed to ask hard questions about the administration's justifications for going to war, particularly Secretary of State Colin Powell's speech to the U.N. Security Council in 2003.

"Did anybody bother to go out and ask an inspector his interpretation of what Powell said?" asks Wilson, who was deputy chief of mission at the U.S. Embassy in Baghdad from 1988 to 1991.

Wilson says he spoke with a weapons inspector after Powell's speech and the inspector told him, "Powell's got nothing."[96]

March 19, 2004: WASHINGTON—President Bush's prized "coalition of the willing"—the three-dozen countries that are contributing military forces in Iraq—appears suddenly to be losing some of its will.

First Spain said it was getting out, then Poland threatened to leave early, and now the South Korean Ministry of Defense announces that it will not send its troops to the area of Iraq that U.S. commanders had requested, although it says it would position them elsewhere in Iraq.[97]

March 20, 2004: Brig. Gen. Mark Kimmitt announces in Baghdad that criminal charges have been brought against six members of an Army Reserve military police unit for prisoner abuses that occurred in November and December.[98]

March 20, 2004: WASHINGTON—Richard Clarke, former counterterrorism coordinator at the time of the Sept. 11 attacks, releases his book *Against All Enemies*, which reveals a strong desire by President Bush, Vice President Cheney, Defense Secretary Rumsfeld and others to attack Iraq in retaliation to Sept. 11 even though there was no evidence of Iraqi involvement in the attacks.[99]

March 24, 2004: WASHINGTON—White House officials react fiercely to Richard Clarke's accusation that terror wasn't their top issue. Condoleezza Rice claims that Clarke sharply changed his view of the administration's war on terror. However, she is refusing to testify publicly under oath before the commission on the Sept. 11 attacks.[100]

March 25, 2004: The U.S. is reducing the size of foreign military bases and plans to construct a network of smaller bases closer to potential trouble spots such as the Middle East.[101]

March 26, 2004: WASHINGTON—This week's testimony and media blitz by former White House counterterrorism chief Richard Clarke has placed his former boss, national security adviser Condoleezza Rice, in the spotlight.

Deputy Secretary of State Richard Armitage contradicted Rice's claim that the White House had a strategy before Sept. 11 for military operations against al Qaeda and the Taliban. The CIA contradicted Rice's earlier assertion that Bush had requested a CIA briefing in the summer of 2001 because of elevated terrorist threats. And Rice's assertion this week that Bush had told her on Sept. 16, 2001, that "Iraq is to the side" appeared to be contradicted by an order signed by Bush on Sept. 17 directing the Pentagon to begin planning military options for an invasion of Iraq.

Rice has contradicted Vice President Dick Cheney's assertion that Clarke was "out of the loop" and his suggestion that Clarke had been demoted. Rice has also given various conflicting accounts. She criticized Clarke for being the architect of failed Clinton administration policies, but also said she had retained Clarke so the Bush administration could continue to pursue Clinton's terrorism policies.[102]

March 27, 2004: WASHINGTON—Senator John Kerry accuses the White House of engaging in character assassination against the administration's former counter-terrorism chief and calls on President Bush's top national security adviser to testify under oath before a commission investigating the Sept. 11 terrorism attacks.

In his toughest reaction to last week's testimony before the special commission, Kerry says accusations from Bush allies that the former aide, Richard Clarke, is lying are part of a White House pattern of attacks against its detractors.

"It's interesting, every time somebody comes up and says something that this White House doesn't like, they don't answer the questions about it or show the truth about it. They go into character assassination mode," he says.[103]

March 28, 2004: WASHINGTON—When asked why he didn't include criticism of the administration's handling of terror while he was still working for the White House, Richard Clarke replies, "no one asked me what I thought about the president's invasion of Iraq. And the reason I am strident in my criticism of the president of the United States is because by invading Iraq...the president of the United States has greatly undermined the war on terrorism."

Clarke's book comports with other accounts that key administration officials appeared unduly focused on Iraq in the months before the Sept. 11 attacks—and then leaped to the conclusion that Iraq was somehow involved.

Randy Beers, who served as counterterrorism chief after Clarke, has voiced the same complaint and is now foreign-policy advisor to Democratic presidential candidate John Kerry, D-Mass. Flynt Leverett, a former CIA analyst and Middle East specialist who left Bush's National Security Council staff a year ago, also agrees.

"Clarke's critique of administration decision-making and how it did not balance the imperative of finishing the job against al Qaeda, vs. what they wanted to do in Iraq is absolutely on the money," Leverett says.[104]

<u>March 28, 2004</u>: BAGHDAD—U.S. soldiers shut down Cleric Muqtada al-Sadr's popular Baghdad newspaper and padlock the doors after the occupation authorities accused it of printing lies that incited violence. Thousands of angered Iraqis protest the closing, demonstrating the hostility many feel toward the United States.

"No, no, America!" and "Where is democracy now?" scream protesters who hoist banners and shake clenched fists in a hastily organized rally against the closing of the newspaper, Al-Hawza, a radical Shiite weekly.

Under a law passed by occupying authorities in June, a news organization's license can be revoked if it publishes or broadcasts material that incites violence or civil disorder or "advocates alterations to Iraq's borders by violent means."

But the letter outlining the reasons for taking action against Al-Hawza did not cite any material that directly advocated violence. Several Iraqi journalists say that means there is no basis to shut Al-Hawza down.[105]

Would this action come back to haunt the effort to maintain peace?

<u>March 28, 2004</u>: WASHINGTON—Initially, the White House suggested that the Sept. 12, 2001 conversation Richard Clarke described on March 20, 2004, where President Bush was pressing Clarke on Iraqi involvement with the Sept. 11 attacks, never took place. Today the White House acknowledges that the conversation did take place.[106]

<u>March 29, 2004</u>: WASHINGTON—The chairman and vice chairman of the independent commission investigating the Sept. 11 attacks say that they will ask Condoleezza Rice to testify under oath in any future questioning because of discrepancies between her statements and those made in sworn testimony by Bush's former counterterrorism chief, Richard Clarke.

The White House declined to respond to Kean's comments.[107]

<u>March 30, 2004</u>: HOUSTON—Halliburton has reaped billions in military contracts from the U.S. invasion of Iraq so far, but improprieties in their dealings have also given Vice President Dick Cheney's former company high-profile headaches.

Pentagon auditors have criticized Halliburton's estimating, spending and subcontracting, and they plan to begin withholding up to $300 million in payments next month. The Justice Department is investigating allegations of overcharges, bribes and kickbacks. Democrats have accused the company of war profiteering.

"The entire Halliburton affair represents the worst in government contracts with private companies: influence peddling, kickbacks, overcharging and no-bid deals," Senator Frank Lautenberg, D-N.J., says.

Bush administration officials say Vice President Cheney has nothing to do with awarding contracts to Halliburton.

Halliburton reported making $3.6 billion in revenue from Iraq contracts last year. Executives say the company is taking in about $1 billion a month from its work in Iraq, bringing its total revenue so far to about $6 billion.[108]

March 30, 2004: WASHINGTON—Bowing to political pressure, President Bush agrees to allow national security advisor Condoleezza Rice to testify publicly and under oath to the commission investigating the Sept. 11 terrorist attacks.

In addition to letting Rice testify, Bush and Cheney agree to answer questions from all 10 commission members in a joint private session. Previously, the White House had insisted that Bush and Cheney would speak only with the commission's chair and vice chair.[109]

April 1, 2004: AL-FALLUJAH—Four Americans working for a security company are ambushed and killed, and an enraged mob then jubilantly drags the burned bodies through the streets of downtown AL-Fallujah, hanging at least two corpses from a bridge over the Euphrates River.

The violence is one of the most brutal outbursts of anti-American rage since the Iraq war began more than a year ago. Since the war in Iraq began, AL-Fallujah has been a flash point of violence. Of all the places in Iraq, it is where anti-American hatred is the strongest.

In November, an American helicopter was shot down outside the town, killing 16. Townspeople danced on the wreckage.[110]

April 1, 2004: WASHINGTON—In the latest legal challenge to the secrecy surrounding Vice president Dick Cheney's energy task force, a federal judge orders the Bush administration to release thousands of pages of records on the panel's deliberations. Activists accuse the vice president of colluding with energy corporations.[111]

April 1, 2004: WASHINGTON—The commission investigating the Sept. 11 attacks say that it is pressing the White House to explain why the Bush administration had blocked nearly 11,000 pages of classified foreign policy and counterterrorism documents from former President Clinton's files from being turned over to the panel's investigators.[112]

April 1, 2004: BAGHDAD, Iraq—A top U.S. administrator in Iraq says that the deaths and mutilation of four American contractors in AL-Fallujah "will not go unpunished," and a U.S. general vows an "overwhelming" response. U.S. troops, however, remain outside the city, and commanders say they will act "at the time and place of our choosing."[113]

April 2, 2004: WASHINGTON—The White House agrees to allow the independent commission investigating the Sept. 11 attacks to review thousands of Clinton administration national-security documents that the White House acknowledged this week it had withheld from the panel, the commission says.

The Bush White House had previously decided to block transfer of three-quarters of the nearly 11,000 pages of material, according to former Clinton aides who said they were concerned that so many of the documents had been withheld from the panel.[114]

April 4, 2004: WASHINGTON—The leaders of the independent commission investigating the Sept. 11 terrorist attacks agree that evidence gathered by their panel shows the attacks could probably have been prevented.

"The whole story might have been different," Mr. Kean, a former Republican governor of New Jersey, says on the NBC News program "Meet the Press." He outlines a series of intelligence and law enforcement blunders in the months and years before the attacks.

Despite allegations from several Congressional Republican leaders that Mr. Clarke is not telling the truth, he receives new support for his account from a prominent Senate Republican, Richard G. Lugar of Indiana, chairman of the Senate Foreign Relations Committee.

On the ABC News program "This Week," Mr. Lugar says he did not recall any contradictions between Mr. Clarke's testimony to the Sept. 11 commission and information he had previously provided to the joint Congressional investigation of the attacks. Asked if he would join his Republican colleagues in attacking Mr. Clarke's credibility, Senator Lugar replies, "I wouldn't go there."[115]

April 4, 2004: BAGHDAD—A Shiite militia uprising against the American-led occupation ricochets across Iraq impacting the Shiite slum of Sadr City on the capital's outskirts and igniting the holy city of An-Najaf and at least two other cities.

Seven American soldiers are killed in Sadr City, one of the worst firefights for the American forces since Baghdad fell.

Within hours of a call by Muqtada al-Sadr, a firebrand Shiite cleric, to his followers to "terrorize your enemy," his militiamen, said to number tens of thousands across Iraq, took up arms in the streets of Baghdad, An-Najaf, Kufa and Amara.

The insurgency stretches a force of 130,000 American troops from the minority Sunni population to the majority Shiites. Privately, senior American officers have said that prospects for success in Iraq would plummet if the insurgency spread into the Shiite population, which includes 15 million Iraqis.

Until now, powerful Shiite clerics have urged their followers to protest peacefully. But today, Mr. al-Sadr's veiled threats to stir public disorder erupt into carefully orchestrated violence.[116]

Was the closing of al-Sadr's newspaper worth the price?

April 5, 2004: WASHINGTON—As of today, 607 U.S. service members have died since the beginning of military operations in Iraq last year, according to the Department of Defense. Of those, 417 died as a result of hostile action and 190 died of non-hostile causes.

The British military has reported 58 deaths; Italy, 17; Spain, eight; Bulgaria, five; Ukraine, three; Thailand, two; Denmark, El Salvador, Estonia and Poland have reported one each.

Since May 1, 2003 when President Bush declared that major combat operations in Iraq had ended, 469 U.S. soldiers have died.[117]

April 6, 2004: Lt. Gen. David McKiernan, commander of U.S. ground forces in Iraq, approves issuing letters of reprimand for prisoner abuse to six military police officers and non-commissioned officers, two of who are relieved of duty.[118]

April 6, 2004: AR-RAMADI, Iraq—In one of the most violent days in Iraq since the fall of Saddam Hussein, intense combat spreads to at least four more cities, killing at least 13 Marines.[119]

April 6, 2004: BAGHDAD, Iraq—Three days of violent clashes have shaken the already fractious and fragile political process that is supposed to result in a sovereign Iraq in less than 90 days.

As U.S. troops battle insurgents in AL-Fallujah, Ar-Ramadi, Baghdad and other cities in a third day of fierce fighting around Iraq, officials express concern that a popular uprising could erode U.S. control of the country.

"We've reached a moment of truth here with both AL-Fallujah and al-Sadr," says a senior U.S. official involved in Iraq policy, referring to the Shiite Muslim cleric, Muqtada al-Sadr, whose militia members began clashing with the Americans on Sunday. "We have to get both right or there are serious questions about whether this political transition can go forward."[120]

April 7, 2004: WASHINGTON—Comparisons to the Vietnam War fill the debate on Capitol Hill as lawmakers watch the spreading violence in Iraq and talk about the possibility of sending more U.S. soldiers.

Senator Robert Byrd of West Virginia becomes the second senior Democratic senator this week to declare that Iraq is becoming another Vietnam. Senator Edward Kennedy, D-Mass., was the first. Both served in the Senate throughout the Vietnam War.

Republican senators dispute the analogy, with at least two charging that such talk inspires Iraqi insurgents and heightens the danger they pose to U.S. soldiers.[121]

April 8, 2004: BAGHDAD—In an ominous turn, kidnappers seize 13 foreign hostages and threaten to burn three Japanese captives alive if Tokyo doesn't withdraw its troops.[122]

April 8, 2004 9:00 AM EST: WASHINGTON—National security advisor Condoleezza Rice testifies before the Sept. 11 Commission in public, under oath, for three hours. Some of the exchanges:

BEN-VENISTE. Well, my only question to you is whether you told the president.

RICE. "Dick Clarke had told me…that there were al Qaeda cells in the United States.

…There was no recommendation that we do something about this; the FBI was pursuing it. I really don't remember…whether I discussed this with the president."

LEHMAN. Were you told that the U.S. Marshal program had been changed to drop any U.S. Marshals on domestic flights?

RICE. I was not told that.

LEHMAN. Were you aware that I.N.S. had quietly internally halved its internal security enforcement budget?

RICE. I was not made aware of that. I don't remember being made aware of that, no.

Republican commissioner John Lehman asked whether before 9/11 she was aware that the Saudis—with whom the Bush administration continues a close relationship—were barring U.S. access to al Qaeda suspects. Again, Rice replied, "I don't remember anything of that kind."[123]

Does it make sense that the presidential national security advisor doesn't know whether or not air marshals are in use on domestic flights?

April 8, 2004: WASHINGTON—Rice insists that she and the president did all they reasonably could to address the "frustratingly vague" threats despite being hobbled by longstanding legal and bureaucratic barriers, but all the commissioners aren't satisfied.

Former Clinton administration Deputy Attorney General Jamie Gorelick lists some of the panel's earlier witnesses who said they were never alerted to the possible danger:

"Secretary Mineta, the Secretary of Transportation, had no idea of the threat," she says. "The administrator of the FAA, responsible for security on our airlines, had no idea.… You indicate in your statement that the FBI tasked its field offices to find out what was going on out there. We have no record of that. The Washington field office international-terrorism people say they never heard about the threat."

This, Gorelick suggests, was a failure of leadership at the highest reaches. "You get a greater degree of intensity when it comes from the top," she says.[124]

April 10, 2004: WASHINGTON—President Bush invaded Iraq hoping to spread democracy across the Middle East, but after the worst week of violence since Saddam Hussein was overthrown, he is now struggling to avoid a costly, humiliating defeat.[125]

April 10, 2004: WASHINGTON—Under pressure from the Sept. 11 Commission, the Bush administration declassifies the August 6, 2001 Presidential Daily Brief warning that al Qaeda was preparing an attack on U.S. soil, possibly using airplane hijacking.[126]

Condoleezza Rice's credibility takes a beating when this memo turns out to be almost exactly what she said it was not.

<u>April 10, 2004</u>: AMMAN, Jordan—A long row of battered taxicabs lines a street Friday in downtown Amman, waiting to carry eager young Iraqi exiles home to battle.

Emboldened by news accounts of Islamic militiamen fighting U.S.-led forces, many Iraqis say they are keen to replenish the uprising that has left hundreds of their compatriots dead.

Shiite and Sunni Muslims, age-old rivals now united against the foreign occupiers, taunt each other about which sect is punishing the Americans more.[127]

<u>April 11, 2004</u>: BAGHDAD—At first, Washington's blame for violence rested with "remnants" of Saddam Hussein's regime, then with a few "Saddam loyalists" and "foreign terrorists," later with the "Sunni triangle," and then, Sunnis in general. When the fighting spread last week to Shiite areas, Washington blamed a single "outlaw" Iraqi Shiite leader, Muqtada al-Sadr.

The Bush administration's prosecution of the war includes critical mistakes that triggered a bloody week and created a situation where there may be no good options left.

Bush failed to exploit American influence immediately after the fall of Saddam to broaden the international role and stakes in Iraq. Under orders, Paul Bremer destroys the existing Iraqi institutions, including the army. The administration was too slow to move closer to Sistani on the issue of Iraqi elections. The U.S. troops closed al-Sadr's newspaper.[128]

Washington will later place all of the blame on Jordanian terrorist Abu Musab al-Zarqawi.

<u>April 11, 2004</u>: WASHINGTON—Bush for the first time suggests that others in his administration might not have done enough to head off the Sept. 11 attacks. "That's what the 9/11 commission should look into, and I hope it does," he says.[129]

<u>April 13, 2004</u>: WASHINGTON—President Bush schedules a rare prime-time television news conference to help counter a potential crisis of confidence in his leadership on two fronts: the Iraq war and the investigation into government counterterrorism preparedness before Sept. 11, 2001.

He dodges the question as to why it was necessary for him and Cheney to appear together in front of the Sept. 11 Commission instead of separately, as requested. Clinton and Gore agreed to appear separately.

He frequently stumbles when answering questions, lapsing into awkward silences as he searches for words.

When asked to cite his biggest mistake at this news conference, Bush is stumped. He says, "I wish you would have given me this question ahead of time so that I [Karl Rove] could plan for it."

Bush firmly insists that the United States must "stay the course" in Iraq—with more troops if necessary. "As I have said to those who have lost loved ones, we will finish the work of the fallen."[130]

In a war that lacks both legitimacy and any hope for an exit, this commitment to the fallen—the "Vietnam syndrome"—is now resurrected by Bush as a last resort to extend the Iraq war and its tragedies.

April 13, 2004: BAGHDAD, Iraq—American commanders had said they planned to 'kill or capture' Muqtada al-Sadr, but concede privately that any raid into An-Najaf would risk provoking more anti-American violence.[131]

April 14, 2004: WASHINGTON—George Tenet and his deputies at the CIA were presented in August 2001 with a briefing paper labeled "Islamic Extremist Learns to Fly" about the arrest days earlier of Zacarias Moussaoui, but they did not act on the information, the independent commission investigating the Sept. 11 attacks says in 2004.

An interim report by the panel's staff, offering a stinging assessment of the CIA under Tenet's leadership, is made public at a hearing where Tenet discloses that he had little contact with President Bush during much of the summer of 2001, a period when intelligence agencies were warning of a dire terrorist threat.[132]

April 14, 2004: WASHINGTON—In a major shift of U.S. policy, President Bush embraces an Israeli proposal to withdraw unilaterally from Gaza, recognizing that Israel can permanently retain some of the occupied West Bank, and says Palestinian refugees will not have the right to return to Israel under any final peace settlement.

With the announcement, Bush sweeps away decades of U.S. insistence that any final peace settlement must require a return to Israel's 1949 borders. The new stand also softens longstanding U.S. objections to Israel's settlements in Palestinian territory and to Israel's construction of a fence to separate Palestinian and Israeli areas.

The new position also enrages Palestinians.

By siding so unequivocally with Sharon, Bush risks inflaming the Muslim world against America even further. His stance also adds stress to America's strained ties with Europe, whose capitals are far more sympathetic to the Palestinians than the United States.[133]

Will the Arab anger caused by this policy change exacerbate the war on terror and the Iraq war?

<u>April 14, 2004</u>: SAN JOSE—Senator Dianne Feinstein, a San Francisco Democrat who sits on the U.S. Senate Select Intelligence Committee, says Bush should have returned to the White House from his Texas ranch after reading the Aug. 6, 2001, Presidential Daily Brief that warned al Qaeda had been operating for years in the United States, had been conducting surveillance of federal buildings in New York City, and was considering hijacking airliners.

"This, to me, sounded the alarm bell," Feinstein says.

Feinstein also has sharp words for Bush on the Iraq war, saying she felt misled into voting for it because of faulty intelligence that exaggerated the threat posed by Saddam Hussein.

"I don't believe that if the mission had been based on regime change there would have been 77 votes in the United States Senate to authorize use of force," she says. "There certainly would not have been my vote. And there may not even have been a majority of votes."[134]

<u>Mid-April 2004</u>: Major General Geoffrey Miller, the former commander of the U.S. detention center for terror suspects at Guantánamo Bay, Cuba, is placed in command of the entire Iraqi prison system. With harsh treatment of prisoners at Guantánamo Bay widespread, and with Miller's 'get tough' comments in August 2003 preceding the worst of the abuse at Abu Ghurayb prison, he makes an interesting choice to bring the situation under control.

<u>April 15, 2004</u>: JERUSALEM—Israel's largest daily newspaper headlines its main story "Sharon Got It All." Speaking of the Palestinians, Sharon tells the newspaper, "They were dealt a lethal blow."

"Things will look, I think, much brighter," Sharon's spokesman Raanan Gissin says. He says no U.S. president had given such a clear statement of support "in 56 years of Israel's existence."[135]

<u>April 15, 2004</u>: SHANGHAI—It is said, a Chinese student tells Dick Cheney, "You are the most powerful vice president in U.S. history…"

"Well," Cheney begins, "that's not a question that I had anticipated."[136]

Even the student's statement falls short of Cheney's true power in the Bush administration.

<u>April 15, 2004</u>: BAGHDAD—Saddam Hussein didn't scare electrical engineer Jamal Polatov away. Neither did the U.S. air strikes that shattered the Iraqi army, nor the suicide bombings, drive-by shootings and grenade attacks that have bedeviled the U.S. occupation of Iraq for nearly a year.

But today, the Russian native leaves for Moscow, joining a growing exodus of contract workers fleeing shadowy insurgents trying to drive out the foreigners. The insurgents' latest tactic—taking hostages—is working.[137]

<u>April 15, 2004</u>: BAGHDAD—Foreign contractors scramble to catch planes leaving Iraq, even as three Japanese hostages are released and the Pentagon announces it is beefing up U.S. forces in Iraq by extending tours of duty.[138]

<u>April 16, 2004</u>: WASHINGTON—President Bush's top political advisor, Karl Rove, says that he regrets the use of the "Mission Accomplished" banner as a backdrop for the president's landing on an aircraft carrier last May to mark the end of major combat operations in Iraq.[139]

<u>April 16, 2004</u>: WASHINGTON—The Bush administration accepts the outlined proposal by U.N. envoy Lakhdar Brahimi to dissolve the American-appointed Iraqi Governing Council and replace it with caretaker government of prominent Iraqis when sovereignty is restored on July 1. The U.N. will take the lead in appointing the transition government's leaders under the Brahimi plan.[140]

After several tries, the Bush administration is finally admitting that any U.S. political proposal in Iraq is doomed to failure.

<u>April 17, 2004</u>: GAZA CITY, Gaza Strip—Israeli helicopter gunships incinerate a car carrying Hamas leader Abdel Aziz Rantisi, killing the firebrand militant and two bodyguards less than a month after his predecessor, Sheik Ahmed Yassin, met the same fate.

The Israeli airstrike comes four hours after a Palestinian suicide bombing killed an Israeli border police officer at the main crossing between the Gaza Strip and Israel. And it follows by only three days a triumphal visit to Washington by Prime Minister Ariel Sharon, during which President Bush endorsed the Israeli leader's plan to withdraw troops and Jewish settlers from Gaza while laying claim to large settlement blocs in the West Bank.[141]

April 18, 2004: HANOI, Vietnam—The Vietnamese people have some friendly advice for the United States: Don't make the same mistake twice. Get out of Iraq—before it's too late.

"It seems like the United States is going to be stuck in Iraq just like they got stuck in Vietnam years ago," says Colonel Tran Nhung, who writes for Quan Doi Nhan Dan, Vietnam's military daily. "No country in the world will accept a foreign invasion—this is a fundamental truth…"

"Everyone in the world can see that the United States went to Iraq for oil," says Hoang Van Thinh, a 27-year-old Hanoi resident. "And they had a political motive as well: to expand their influence in the Middle East."[142]

April 18, 2004: WASHINGTON—There were 87 deaths by hostile fire in the first 15 days of the month, more than in the opening two weeks of the invasion, when 82 Americans were killed in action.

The last time U.S. troops experienced a comparable two-week loss in combat was October 1971, two years before U.S. ground involvement ended in Vietnam.

"Even Vietnam was a more conventional war than this," says Charles Moskos, a sociologist with Northwestern University who specializes in the military and worked as a correspondent in the Vietnam War.

"Here in Iraq, there are no battle lines," he says. "It's all over…"[143]

April 18, 2004: GAZA CITY, Gaza Strip—Tens of thousands of Palestinians escort the corpse of Hamas leader Abdel Aziz Rantisi through the streets of Gaza City amid condemnation of Israel for his assassination and warnings that fracturing the militant group could fuel greater extremism…

Rantisi's assassination occurs only three days after President Bush met with Israeli Prime Minister Ariel Sharon and announced a shift in U.S. Middle East policy. The timing cements the views of many Palestinians that the United States and Israel had colluded in the killing, marking a potentially dangerous turning point for the United States, according to Palestinian leaders and analysts.[144]

Will this event help the U.S. win the hearts and minds of Iraqis?

April 18, 2004: BAGHDAD—With no sign of a breakthrough in talks with rebels in AL-Fallujah and An-Najaf, the leader of the U.S. occupation appears to move closer to a military showdown, saying the rebels' failure to submit to U.S.

demands would necessitate action against those who "want to shoot their way to power."

Also today, Spain's prime minister orders the withdrawal of Spanish soldiers from Iraq as soon as possible.[145]

April 19, 2004: BAGHDAD—Far more than in any other conflict in U.S. history, the Pentagon is relying on private security companies to perform crucial jobs once entrusted to the military.

The contractors race around Iraq in armored cars, many outfitted with the latest in high-end combat weapons. They give the appearance of private, for-profit militias—by several estimates, a force of roughly 20,000 on top of an official U.S. military presence of 130,000.

By some recent government estimates, payments to private security companies could claim up to 25 percent of the $18 billion budgeted for reconstruction, a huge and mostly unanticipated expense.[146]

The private security companies pay much better than the military, and provide their employees with better equipment.

April 19, 2004: WASHINGTON—President Bush asserts that Iraq "will be free and democratic and peaceful" as he names veteran diplomat John Negroponte—the United States' top diplomat at the U.N.—to be America's first ambassador to post-Saddam Hussein Iraq.[147]

April 19, 2004: AMMAN, Jordan—In a surprise move, King Abdullah II postpones a White House meeting with President Bush this week, citing questions about the U.S. commitment to the Middle East peace process.

The announcement by one of Washington's closest allies comes amid Arab anger at Bush for endorsing an Israeli proposal to withdraw from the Gaza Strip and parts of the West Bank in exchange for U.S. concessions on keeping Jewish settlements on other land claimed by the Palestinians.

The rift between the Bush administration and its moderate Arab allies over Bush's statement on Israeli settlements is one of the worst to emerge in years—and has exacerbated the already tense relations between the United States and Arab countries over the war in Iraq.

The White House denies U.S. support for Israel angered the Arab ally.[148]

April 19, 2004: WASHINGTON—Ralph Nader, the independent presidential hopeful, calls for the withdrawal of all U.S. troops from Iraq in six months.[149]

April 20, 2004: WASHINGTON—Spain and Honduras already have announced that they are removing their troops from Iraq earlier than scheduled. The Dominican Republic will withdraw its 302 soldiers from Iraq early, in the next few weeks, Gen. José Miguel Soto Jiménez says. The administration is pressing to keep other members of the 30-plus nations in the coalition from following suit.

Both Secretary of State Colin Powell and National Security Adviser Condoleezza Rice have been calling coalition members to check the level of their resolve, administration officials say.

One senior administration official acknowledges, "It tells you where we are today—a year into this—that they have to call to keep this glued together…"[150]

How far away is the military draft?

April 21, 2004: WASHINGTON—Intense combat in Iraq is chewing up military hardware and consuming money at an unanticipated rate—depleting military coffers, straining defense contractors and putting pressure on Bush administration officials to seek a major boost in war funding long before they had hoped.[151]

April 21, 2004: WASHINGTON—Paul Bremer is moving to rehire former members of Iraq's ruling Baath Party and senior Iraqi military officers fired after the ouster of Saddam Hussein, in an effort to undo the damage of its two most controversial policies in Iraq, according to U.S. officials.

Ironically, the two policies were the first actions taken by Bremer, who brought them from Washington, when he arrived in Baghdad to assume leadership of the U.S.-led occupation in May 2003.

The first move to revise policy on former Baathists will be to reinstate about 11,000 teachers and hundreds of professors fired after Saddam's ouster last year, U.S. officials say.[152]

April 21, 2004: BAGHDAD—The suicide attacks in Basra on Wednesday shatter a week of relative calm in Iraq, bringing anger, mourning and upheaval to a mostly Shiite southern city that has been spared the worst of the violence in the yearlong U.S. occupation.

Officials in Basra say the death toll from the attacks reaches 68, including as many as 23 children on their way to school. About 200 people, among them four British soldiers, are wounded in five explosions.[153]

<u>April 22, 2004</u>: WASHINGTON—The Iraqi National Congress (INC) may have violated restrictions against using taxpayer funds to lobby when it campaigned for U.S. action to oust Saddam Hussein, according to documents. If true, it means that U.S. taxpayers paid to have themselves convinced that it was necessary to invade Iraq.

Federal law prohibits the use of U.S. government funds for lobbying on financial matters, such as government contracts. A grant agreement between the Iraqi group and the State Department also prohibited lobbying and propagandizing.

Individuals who held senior positions with the Iraqi National Congress set up a non-profit group, the Iraq Liberation Action Committee, to lobby for U.S. action in Iraq.

The Iraqi National Congress leader, Ahmed Chalabi, is a member of the Iraqi Governing Council in Baghdad and has been pushed by some Pentagon (Donald Rumsfeld and Paul Wolfowitz) and White House (Dick Cheney) officials as the next leader of Iraq.[154]

<u>April 22, 2004</u>: An Internet-driven rumor mill about the possible return of a military draft is forcing Pentagon officials to step up denials that such plans are in the works.

Defense Secretary Donald Rumsfeld tries to quell rumors with denials, but an avalanche of bad news in Iraq leaves many, including members of Congress, unconvinced.

April has been the deadliest month for U.S. soldiers since the war began, Spain is preparing to withdraw its troops, and at least 20,000 soldiers have had their deployments extended—facts that have fueled a growing barrage of myths, rumors and conspiracy theories via e-mails and Web postings.[155]

The Pentagon is having considerable difficulty deploying sufficient troops in Iraq, the National Guard and reserve units have been sent to war like never before, troops that have served honorably in Iraq for their full 12 months are getting extended another 3 months, expensive private security firms are picking up the slack, and Congress is talking up the draft. Do the stepped up denials of a return to the draft indicate that this issue is being deferred until after the election—in the same manner as the cost of the war?

<u>April 22, 2004</u>: Pat Tillman, the Leland High graduate and overachieving NFL player who walked away from a multimillion-dollar contract so he could serve his

country as a member of the U.S. Army's elite Rangers unit, is killed in action Thursday in southeastern Afghanistan.

He was 27.[156]

To add insult to injury, it turns out that Tillman is the victim of "friendly fire."

April 22, 2004: The Pentagon bans the photographing of dead soldiers' home-comings at all military bases. However, hundreds of photographs of flag-draped coffins at Dover Air Force Base are released on the Internet by a Web site (www.thememoryhole.org) dedicated to combating government secrecy.

Earlier this week, the Seattle Times published a similar photo taken by a military contractor, who was later fired for taking photos of coffins of war dead being loaded onto a transport plane in Kuwait.

Tami Silicio's photo of flag-draped caskets appears on the front page of the Seattle Times. Her husband, a co-worker, also is fired. The contractor, Maytag Aircraft, says Silicio of Seattle and her husband, David Landry, have "violated Department of Defense and company policies."

The firing underscores the stringency with which the Pentagon and the Bush administration have pursued a policy to ban news organizations from taking photographs or news footage of the homecomings of the war dead.[157]

April 22, 2004: WASHINGTON—The Bush administration's plans for a new caretaker government in Iraq will place severe limits on its sovereignty, including only partial command over its armed forces and no authority to enact new laws, administration officials say.

With only 10 weeks left before the June 30 handover, the White House doesn't know who will govern Iraq or how they will be selected.[158]

April 22, 2004: BAGHDAD—The American authorities issue another series of blunt warnings to the insurgents in Fallujah that if they don't lay down their arms, United States soldiers will attack within days.

However, the U.S. faces a dilemma because an attack could further inflame the Sunnis.[159]

This continues the no-win situation. If the U.S. doesn't respond to the violence it sends a message of weakness that will likely embolden the insurgents. But if the response damages too many religious sites and/or claims too many civilian Iraqi lives, with such images flowing across Arab satellite TV, it could ignite a broader rebellion and demolish any hopes of accomplishing the mission of nation building.

April 23, 2004: BAGHDAD—As the security situation deteriorates across their country, Iraqi public opinion is turning sharply against the Americans. Paul Bremer addresses them on TV suggesting that the mission in Iraq might fail unless ordinary Iraqis rise up.

"If you do not defend your beloved country, it will not be saved," he says.

Bremer seems to be shifting the responsibility to the Iraqis by essentially admitting that American military power might not be enough. He announces an immediate injection of $500 million to build roads and schools in the hopes that this will help the situation.[160]

April 23, 2004: JERUSALEM—Israeli Prime Minister Ariel Sharon says that he is no longer bound by a promise to the United States to avoid harming Palestinian leader Yasser Arafat. The White House objects, saying Sharon should continue to honor the pledge.

The quick response reflects the Bush administration's concern that Sharon's statement will further inflame anti-American passions in the region. There has been a strong Arab backlash against Bush's endorsement of Sharon's plan to withdraw Israeli troops and settlers from the Gaza Strip but keep several large settlements in the West Bank.[161]

April 25, 2004: The Bush administration is receiving heat for allegedly ignoring the threat of Islamic radicalism before Sept. 11 and then retaliating in the wrong place, Iraq. Craig Unger, author of *HOUSE OF BUSH, HOUSE OF SAUD: The Secret Relationship Between the World's Two Most Powerful Dynasties*, suggests an explanation. He says that President George W. Bush's circle and the ruling family of Saudi Arabia are way too close. "Never before," Unger concludes, "has an American president been so closely tied to a foreign power that harbors and supports our country's mortal enemies…"

A Saudi investor bailed out Harken Energy, George W. Bush's less-than-stellar oil company.

Saudis donated millions of dollars to Bush family charities. Mahfouzes and bin Ladens bought into the Carlyle Group, the private equity firm that counted the elder George Bush and former Secretary of State James A. Baker III as paid-up advisers in the 1990s. Unger claims that Saudi interests have paid not less than $1.477 billion to persons and entities in the Bush circle.[162]

<u>April 28, 2004</u>: UNITED NATIONS—U.N. Secretary-General Kofi Annan warns that U.S. military action in the embattled city of Fallujah could stiffen the resistance and make it harder to end the occupation.

"The more the occupation is seen as taking steps that harm the civilians and the population, the greater the ranks of the resistance grow," Annan tells a news conference.[163]

<u>April 28, 2004</u>: Rising concern over violence in the Middle East gives investors a reason to sell. The quagmire in Iraq unnerves investors and causes the stock market to plunge, overriding any otherwise positive economic news.[164]

NOTES TO CHAPTER 9

1 Niall Ferguson, "An ephemeral empire, built on sand," *The Mercury News*, April 25, 2004, p. 1P.

2 Daniel Sneider, "Prisoner abuse is not an aberration," *The Mercury News*, May 9, 2004, p. 5P.

3 Thomas Donnelly and Richard Perle, "Gas Stations in the Sky," Wall Street Journal, August 14, 2003, http://www.frontpagemag.com/Articles/ReadArticle.asp?ID=9391.

4 Jessica Stern, "How America Created a Terrorist Haven," *The New York Times*, August 20, 2003, Section A, Page 21.

5 Elisabeth Bumiller and Eric Schmitt, "Bush 'sorry' for abuse, vows Rumsfeld will stay," *The Mercury News*, May 7, 2004, p. 1A.

6 Bob Drogin, "More inmate deaths emerge," *The Mercury News*, May 16, 2004, p. 1A.

7 Dana Milbank, "Bush Sept. 11, Iraq not linked," *The Mercury News*, September 18, 2004, p. 14A.

8 Ibid.

9 CNN, "Bush U.N. speech draws mixed, partisan reviews," *CNN.com*, September 23, 2003, http://www.cnn.com/2003/ALLPOLITICS/09/23/sprj.irq.un.washington.reax/.

10 "Trail of a leak," *The Mercury News*, May 2, 2004 p. 3P.

11 James Risen, "Prisoner abuse probes widen," *The Mercury News*, May 3, 2004, p. 1A.

12 Josh White and Scott Higham (WP), "Interrogators directed prison police, officer says," *The Mercury News*, May 20, 2004, p. 17A.

13 Elisabeth Bumiller and Eric Schmitt, "Bush 'sorry' for abuse,…"

14 Bob Drogin, "Red Cross report details abuse, mistaken detentions in Iraq," *The Mercury News*, May 11, 2004, p. 7A.

15 Sumana Chatterjee, "Tough questions about war," *The Mercury News*, May 13, 2004, p. 6A.

16 Georgie Anne Geyer, "Bush Sr.'s 'message' to Bush Jr.," *The Boston Globe*, October 18, 2003, http://www.boston.com/news/globe/editorial_opinion/oped/articles/2003/10/18/bush_srs_message_to_bush_jr/.

17 Michael D. Sallah and Mitch Weiss, "Investigators will question ex-GIs about killing spree," Toledoblade.com, February 15, 2004, http://www.toledoblade.com/apps/pbcs.dll/article?AID=/20040215/SRTIGERFORCE/102150175.

18 Bryan Bender, "Rights report finds high risk for civilians," The Mercury News, October 21, 2003, p. 11A.

19 Dan Eggen, "Bush's Press Aide, Rove Questioned in Leaks Probe," *Washington Post*, October 24, 2003, page A08.

20 Barton Gellman, "Nuclear-Iraq case withers," *The Mercury News*, October 26, 2003, p. 18A.

21 Michael Isikoff and Mark Hosenball, "Case Decidedly Not Closed," *MSNBC*, November 19, 2003, http://msnbc.msn.com/id/3540586/.

22 Jonathan S. Landay, "CIA Chief contradicts Cheney, rejecting Iraq link to al Qaeda," *The Mercury News*, March 10, 2004, p. 1A.

23 Dave Lindorff, "Oiling up the draft machine?" Salon.com, November 3, 2003, http://fairuse.1accesshost.com/news1/salon1.html.

24 Elisabeth Bumiller, "Issue for Bush: How to Speak Of Casualties?" *The New York Times*, November 5, 2003, Section A, Page 1.

25 Bob Drogin, "More inmate deaths emerge,"…

26 A divisive war, an elusive peace," *The Mercury News*, March 19, 2004, p. 4AA.

27 Nicholas D. Kristof, "A Scary Afghan Road," *The New York Times*, November 15, 2003, Section A, Page 13.

28 "DOD Asked to Investigate Use of Development Fund to Pay Inflated Fuel Prices," Government Reform Minority Office, November 5, 2003, http://www.house.gov/reform/min/inves_admin/admin_contracts.htm.

29 Bob Drogin, "More inmate deaths emerge,"...

30 Mercury News Wire Services, "Sept. 11 investigators might miss deadline," *The Mercury News*, November 27, 2003, p. 4A.

31 Shannon McCaffrey and Sumana Chatterjee, "Pentagon probes inmate deaths," *The Mercury News*, May 5, 2004, p. 1A.

32 James Risen, "A REGION INFLAMED: INQUIRY; Iraqi Agent Denies He Met 9/11 Hijacker in Prague Before Attacks on the U.S.," *The New York Times*, December 13, 2004, Section A, Page 10.

33 "A divisive war, an elusive peace,"...

34 Maureen Fan, "Iraq's Silent Leader," *The Mercury News*, December 13, 2003, p. 1A.

35 Sewell Chan and Michael Amon, "Army checking charges of Iraqi prisoner abuse," *The Mercury News*, May 2, 2004, p. 16A.

36 Drew Brown, "Report: Iraq war was not needed," *The Mercury News*, January 8, 2004, p. 12A.

37 *60 Minutes*, "Bush sought 'Way' to oust Saddam?" *CBS.News.com*, January 12, 2004.

38 "Treasury wants O'Neill papers probed," CNN, January 13, 2004.

39 "Timeline of prisoner abuse," *The Mercury News*, May 8, 2004, p. 21A, citing *Associated Press*, *The Los Angeles Times*, *The New York Times*.

40 Scott Higham and Joe Stephens (WP), "Guards: Abuse was to punish or amuse," *The Mercury News*, May 22, 2004, p. 1A.

41 Ibid.

42 Richard A. Serrano, "Soldier identifies leaders, details abuses at prison," *The Mercury News*, May 14, 2004, p. 1A.

43 "Clark blasts quick investigation of O'Neill," *The Mercury News*, January 14, 2004, p. 8A.

44 "Timeline of prisoner abuse,"…

45 Ibid.

46 Drew Brown, "Cheney describes O'Neill as a big disappointment," *Los Angeles Times*, January 19, 2004.

47 www.whitehouse.gov.

48 Warren P. Strobel and Jonathon S. Landay, "CIA warning of uprising counters Bush's address," *The Mercury News*, January 22, 2004, p. 12A.

49 Jonathan S. Landay, "CIA Chief contradicts Cheney,…"

50 Richard W. Stevenson, "IRAQ ILLICIT ARMS GONE BEFORE WAR, INSPECTOR STATES," *The New York Times*, January 24, 2004, Section A, Page 1.

51 AP, "Halliburton in Iraq Kickback Flap," *CBSNews.com*, January 23, 2004, http://www.cbsnews.com/stories/2004/01/23/iraq/main595556.shtml.

52 Terence Hunt, "White House backs away from claims of Iraq Weapons," *The Mercury News*, January 27, 2004, p. 9A.

53 AP, "White House retreats on claims of stockpiles of hidden weapons," *The London Free Press*, January 27, 2004.

54 "Timeline of prisoner abuse,"…

55 Karl Kahler, "Weapons claim unravels: Charges led to Saddam's downfall, political tempest," *The Mercury News*, January 30, 2004, p. 1AA.

56 Philip Shenon, "9/11 Commission Says It Needs More Time to Complete Report," *The New York Times*, January 28, 2004, Section A, Page 1.

57 Bush Won't Demand Intelligence Probe," Fox News, January 30, 2004, http://www.foxnews.com/story/0,2933,109960,00.html.

58 "Timeline of prisoner abuse,"…

59 Ibid.

60 CNN, "Sources: Bush to order WMD intelligence inquiry," Monday, February 2, 2004, http://edition.cnn.com/2004/US/02/01/sprj.nirq.iraq.wmd/.

61 John Lancaster and Kamran Khan, "Pakistan army chiefs knew of technology export, scientist says," *The Mercury News*, February 3, 2004, p. 9A.

62 Suzanne Goldenberg, "Powell rows back on doubts over invasion," *The Guardian*, February 4, 2004, http://www.guardian.co.uk/Iraq/Story/0,2763,1140426,00.html.

63 Richard W. Stevenson, "Powell and White House Get Together on Iraq War," *The New York Times*, February 4, 2004, Section A, Page 11.

64 John Lancaster and Kamran Khan, "Pakistan scientist admits dealing nuclear secrets," *The Mercury News*, February 5, 2004, p. 3A.

65 Philip Shenon, "Bush, in Reversal, Supports More Time for 9/11 Inquiry," *The New York Times*, February 5, 2004, Section A, Page 21.

66 "O'Neill cleared in use of classified documents," *CNN*, February 6, 2004.

67 "Trail of a leak," *The Mercury News*, May 2, 2004 p. 3P.

68 "President Bush Announces Formation of Independent Commission," February 6, 2004, http://www.whitehouse.gov/news/releases/2004/02/20040206-3.html.

69 Douglas Jehl, "TENET CONCEDES GAPS IN CIA DATA ON IRAQ WEAPONS," *The New York Times*, February 6, 2004, Section A, Page 1.

70 KENNETH R. BAZINET and THOMAS M. DeFRANK, "White House retreat on 9/11 claims," NYDailyNews.com, March 27, 2004, http://www.nydailynews.com/03-27-2004/news/wn_report/story/177783p-154700c.html.

71 Andrew North, "The drugs threat to Afghanistan," *BBC News*, February 10, 2004, http://news.bbc.co.uk/1/hi/world/south_asia/3476377.stm.

72 Jonathan S. Landay, "Public report of Iraq threat minimized dissenting views," *The Mercury News*, February 10, 2004, p. 5A.

73 David Paul Kuhn, "Bush Strategy: A war president," *CBSNews.com*, February 13, 2004, http://www.cbsnews.com/stories/2004/02/12/politics/main599984.shtml.

74 Michael D. Sallah and Mitch Weiss, "Investigators will question ex-GIs…"

75 "Perle Resigns," *ABC News*, February 25, 2004, http://abcnews.go.com/sections/wnt/Investigation/perle_resignation_040225.html.

76 Jonathan S. Landay, Warren P. Strobel and John Walcott, "Unreliable group keeps U.S. support," *The Mercury News*, February 22, 2004, p. 18A.

77 Patrick E. Tyler, "The struggle for Iraq: Allies; Britain drops charges in leak of U.S. memo," *The New York Times*, February 26, 2004, Section A, Page 13.

78 "Bush, Cheney restrict time with Sept. 11 panel," *The Mercury News*, February 26, 2004, p. 4A.

79 Philip Shenon, "Extension of the 9/11 Panel Is Said to Hinge on Speaker," *The New York Times*, February 27, 2004, Section A, Page 18.

80 Rachel Beck, "Halliburton stock strong despite controversy," *The Mercury News*, February 29, 2004, p. 5F.

81 Arnaud de Borchgrave, "What did Musharraf know?" *Washington Post*, commentary.

82 "CARNAGE IN MADRID," *The Mercury News*, March 12, 2004, p. 6AA.

83 Warren P. Strobel, Jonathon S. Landay and John Walcott, "More Doubts of Iraq links to al Qaeda," *The Mercury News*, March 3, 2004, p. 11A.

84 Jim Rutenburg, "First Bush ads focus on 9/11 'steady leadership'," *Reuters*, March 3, 2004.

85 "Timeline of prisoner abuse,"…

86 Wayne Washington and Anne E. Kornblut, "9/11 images in Bush ads hit," *The Boston Globe*, March 5, 2004, http://www.boston.com/news/nation/articles/2004/03/05/911_images_in_bush_ads_hit/.

87 "A divisive war, an elusive peace,"…

88 Jonathan S. Landay, "CIA Chief contradicts Cheney,…"

89 Kirk Semple, "Bush will answer all questions from the 9/11 panel, aide says," *The New York Times*, March 9, 2004.

90 CARNAGE IN MADRID,"…

91 John Daniszewski, "Bombings against U.S. on rise after weeks of declining fatalities," *The Mercury News*, March 15, 2004 p. 7A.

92 Elaine Sciolino, "Spain puts chill on U.S. relations," *The Mercury News*, March 16, 2004, p. 1A.

93 Joe Wilson, "The Pinocchio Presidency," Salon.com, March 16, 2003, http://www.salon.com/opinion/feature/2004/03/16/wilson_iraq/index_np.html.

94 "A Year after Iraq War: Mistrust of America in Europe Ever Higher, Muslim Anger Persists," *The Pew Research Center*, March 16, 2004, http://people-press.org/.

95 "U.S. improves ties with Pakistan," *The Mercury News*, March 19, 2004, page 3A.

96 Laura Kurtzman, "Arabs will blame U.S. 'forever' if Iraq falls apart, critic says," *The Mercury News*, March 18, 2004, page 19A.

97 AP, "Less will among 'Coalition of willing'," *USA Today*, March 19, 2004, http://www.usatoday.com/news/world/iraq/2004-03-19-iraq-coalition_x.htm.

98 "Timeline of prisoner abuse,"…

99 Ted Bridis, "Details of 2001 threats on Iraq," *The Mercury News*, March 20, 2004, p. 8A.

100 Dan Eggen and Walter Pincus, "Terror wasn't top issue for Bush, ex-advisor says", *The Mercury News*, March 25, 2003, p. 1A.

101 Bradley Graham, "U.S. plans foreign network of smaller, scattered bases", *The Mercury News*, March 25, 2004, p. 10A.

102 Walter Pincus, Dana Milbank, Washington Post, "In rush to defend White House, Rice trips over own words," *San Francisco Chronicle*, March 26, 2004, page A-4.

103 James Kuhnhenn, "Kerry assails attacks on Sept. 11 testimony," *The Mercury News*, March 28, 2004, p. 5A.

104 Glenn Kessler, "Bush's focus on Iraq at issue," *The Mercury News*, March 28, 2004, p. 5A.

105 Jeffrey Gettleman, "U.S. closes Shiite paper; angry Iraqis flood streets," *The Mercury News*, March 29, 2004, p. 1A.

106 Eric Lichtblau, "Rice: Bush did ask about Iraq," *The Mercury News*, March 29, 2004, p. 1A.

107 Philip Shenon and Richard W. Stevenson, "Panel wants Rice under oath," *The Mercury News*, March 30, 2004, p. 5A.

108 Matt Kelly, "Iraq contracts give Halliburton headaches," *The Associated Press*, March 30, 2004, 4:04 ET, http://www.uslaboragainstwar.org/article.php?id=4062.

109 Jim Puzzanghera, "Rice will testify publicly on terrorism," *The Mercury News*, March 30, 2004, p. 1A.

110 Jeffrey Gettleman, "4 from U.S. Killed in Ambush from Iraq; Mob Drags Bodies," *The New York Times*, April 1, 2004, Section A, Page 1.

111 David Savage, "Release of records ordered from Cheney's energy panel," *The Mercury News*, April 2, 2004, p. 4A.

112 Philip Shenon and David E. Sanger, "Sept. 11 panel wants records," *The Mercury News*, April 2, 2004, p. 3A.

113 Sameer N. Yacoub, "Strong response promised in Iraq," *The Mercury News*, April 2, 2004, p. 1A.

114 Philip Shenon, "Sept. 11 panel to get some documents," *The Mercury News*, April 3, 2004, p. 3A.

115 Philip Shenon, "Leaders of 9/11 Panel Say Attacks Were Probably Preventable," *The New York Times*, April 5, 2004, Section A, Page 16.

116 John F. Burns, "THE STRUGGLE FOR IRAQ: UPRISING; 7 U.S. Soldiers Die in Iraq as a Shiite Militia Rises Up," *The New York Times*, April 5, 2004, Section A, Page 1.

117 AP, "U.S. Military Deaths in Iraq," *The New York Times*, April 5, 2004, 7:21 PM ET.

118 "Timeline of prisoner abuse,"...

119 Matthew Schofield and David Swanson, "14 U.S. Soldiers Die as Shiites Revolt: Coordinated ambushes batter Marine patrols," *The Mercury News*, April 7, 2004, p. 1A.

120 Sewell Chan and Robin Wright, "Violence obstructs road to Iraq self-rule," *The Mercury News*, April 7, 2004, p. 1A.

121 Sumana Chatterjee, "Vietnam War haunts debate," *The Mercury News*, April 8, 2004, p. 3A.

122 Lee Keath, "Insurgents seize 3 Iraqi cities," *The Mercury News*, April 9, 2004, p. 1A.

123 Full Dr. Rice transcript: http://www.nytimes.com/2004/04/08/politics/08RICE-TEXT.html.

124 David Von Drehle, "Rice testimony narrows focus," *The Mercury News*, April 9, 2004, p. 1A.

125 Warren P. Strobel, "Reverses in Iraq pressure Bush," *The Mercury News*, April 11, 2004, p. 1A.

126 Complete Text of 2001 Memo", *The Mercury News*, April 11, 2004, p. 5A.

127 Hannah Allam, "Iraqi exiles trek home to join battle," *The Mercury News*, April 10, 2004, p. 18A.

128 Shibley Telhami, "They Don't Like U.S.," *The Mercury News*, April 11, 2004, p. 1P.

129 Adam Nagourney and Philip Shenon, "Bush downplays terror briefing," *The Mercury News*, April 12, 2004, p. 1A.

130 Steven Thomma and William Douglas, "Bush insists war is justified," *The Mercury News*, April 14, 2004, p. 1A; AP, "Full text of Bush news conference," *The Seattle Times*, April 14, 2004, http://seattletimes.nwsource.com/html/nationworld/2001902649_bushtext14.html.

131 John F. Burns, "THE STRUGGLE FOR IRAQ: NEGOTIATION; LEADING SHIITES AND REBEL MEET ON IRAQ STANDOFF," *The New York Times*, April 13, 2004, Section A, Page 1.

132 Philip Shenon and Eric Lichtblau, "Panel slams CIA chief for lack of action," *The Mercury News*, April 15, 2004, p. 1A.

133 William Douglas, "Bush backs Israel on territory issues," *The Mercury News*, April 15, 2004, p. 1A.

134 Laura Kurtzman, "Feinstein calls on Bush to apologize," *The Mercury News*, April 15, 2004, p. 6A.

135 James Bennet, "Shift in U.S. policy fuels Palestinian anger," *The Mercury News*, April 16, 2004, p. 3A.

136 Tim Johnson, "Questioning Cheney," *The Mercury News*, April 16, 2004, p. 1AA.

137 Robert Moran, Soraya Sarhaddi Nelson and Ken Moritsugu, "As tensions rise, diplomat slain; 3 Japanese freed," *The Mercury News*, April 16, 2004, p. 1AA.

138 Carol Rosenberg, "Hostage crisis causing exodus of foreigners," *The Mercury News*, April 16, 2004, p. 1AA.

139 Rove admits regret over 'Mission Accomplished'," *The Mercury News*, April 17, 2004, p. 8A.

140 Steven R. Weisman and David E. Sanger, "THE STRUGGLE FOR IRAQ: DIPLOMACY; U.S. OPEN TO PLAN THAT SUPPLANTS COUNCIL IN IRAQ," *The New York Times*, April 16, 2004, Section A, Page 1,

141 Laura King and Fayed Abu Shammaleh, "Israel kills Hamas leader," *The Mercury News*, April 18, 2004, p. 1A.

142 Ben Stocking, "To Hanoi, Iraq is Bush's Vietnam," *The Mercury News*, April 18, 2004, p. 1A.

143 Drew Brown, "U.S. battle deaths in Iraq are worst since Vietnam War," *The Mercury News*, April 18, 2004, p. 21A.

144 Molly Moore and John Ward Anderson, "Palestinians mourn Hamas chief's death," *The Mercury News*, April 19, 2004, p. 3A.

145 John F. Burns and Christine Hauser, "U.S. forces brace for showdown," *The Mercury News*, April 19, 2004, p. 1A.

146 *The New York Times*, "Reliance on private security in Iraq unique," *The Mercury News*, April 19, 2004, p. 13A.

147 Robert Moran, "Iraqi rebels urged to lay down arms in key city," *The Mercury News*, April 20, 2004, p. 1A.

148 Jamal Halaby, "Jordan King puts off meeting with Bush," *The Mercury News*, April 20, 2004, p. 9A.

149 Maria Recio, "Nader says troops should leave Iraq," *The Mercury News*, April 20, 2004, p. 6A.

150 Thom Shanker and David E. Sanger, "U.S. plan includes extra soldiers," *The Mercury News*, April 21, 2004, p. 1A.

151 Jonathon Weisman, "Ferocity of Iraq combat straining U.S. was funding," *The Mercury News*, April 21, 2004, p. 8A.

152 Robin Wright, "U.S. may ease policies to win back Iraqi Sunnis," *The Mercury News*, April 22, 2004, p. 12A.

153 Ian Fisher, "Death toll rises to 68 in Iraqi suicide attacks," *The Mercury News*, April 22, 2004, p. 1A.

154 Warren P. Strobel and Jonathan S. Landay, "Exile group crossed line on lobbying, U.S. believes," *The Mercury News*, April 23, 2004, p. 1AA.

155 Dana Hull, "Pentagon denies need to revive military draft," *The Mercury News*, April 23, 2004, p. 1A.

156 Mark Emmons and David E. Early, "Athlete's Life, Soldier's Death," *The Mercury News*, April 24, 2004, p. 1A.

157 Bill Carter, "Coffin pictures published despite ban by Pentagon," *The Mercury News*, April 23, 2004, p. 1A.

158 Steven R. Weisman, "White House says Iraq Sovereignty Could be Limited," *The New York Times*, April 23, 2004, Section A, Page 1.

159 Ian Fisher and Steven R. Weisman, "Americans Issue a Blunt Warning to Rebels in Iraq," *The New York Times*, April 24, 2004, Section A, Page 1.

160 Edward Wong, "Policy Barring Ex-Baathists From Key Iraq Posts Is Eased," *The New York Times*, April 23, 2004, Section A, Page 10.

161 John Ward Anderson, "Sharon may target Arafat," *The Mercury News*, April 24, 2004, p. 14A.

162 James Buchan, "Bush too chummy with Saudi elite, book alleges," *The Mercury News*, April 25, 2004, p. 18E.

163 Reuters, "U.S. Offensive in Iraq May Hurt Transition—Annan," April 28, 2004 10:05 PM ET.

164 Stocks fall on worries over Mideast 'quagmire'," *The Mercury News*, April 29, 2004, p. 5C.

10

Shock and Awe II:
Grisly Images

Grisly images of prisoner abuse are shown on television around the world. President Bush tries to blame the mistreatment on a "few bad apples." International outrage of the mistreatment follows. The violence continues with many American soldiers dying due to lack of proper armor and equipment. Many prisoner abuse investigations begin. There are multiple incarceration facilities involved with the abuse over a long period of time. The military starts scrambling to find more troops for Iraq. The strain creates rumors of another military draft.

As the abuse probe widens, there are at least 25 detainee deaths in U.S. custody. More photos and videos are released. Nicholas Berg is beheaded in retaliation for the prisoner abuse. Bush says Donald Rumsfeld is doing a "superb job." It is estimated that 70 to 90 percent of the prisoners in Iraq were detained by mistake. CIA and military intelligence units are also implicated in the abuse scandal. The sabotage of Iraqi oil distribution facilities causes world oil and gas prices to spike.

Support for the war erodes. Amnesty International and Human Rights Watch both release annual reports critical of American interventions and noting that the Iraq war has increased the threat of terrorism. The Pentagon still reserves the right to ignore the Geneva Convention for detainees in Iraq.

April 28, 2004: NEW YORK—CBS obtained photos, which were taken late in 2003 at Abu Ghurayb prison near Baghdad where American soldiers were holding hundreds of prisoners captured during the invasion and occupation of Iraq. They are shown on "60 Minutes II" and prompt a worldwide outcry.

U.S. military police stacked Iraqi prisoners in a human pyramid and attached wires to one detainee to convince him he might be electrocuted, according to graphic images.[1]

237

CBS finally runs their story after two weeks of "discouragement" from Gen. Richard Myers, chairman of the Joint Chiefs of Staff.

April 29, 2004: WASHINGTON—A Pentagon intelligence report claims that Saddam's secret service (M14) had planned the insurgency even before the fall of Baghdad. In the past, American officials have described the insurgents as some unorganized combination of foreign fighters, Islamist jihadists, former Baathists, and common criminals.[2]

In spite of the new report, the unorganized combination of disparate groups is still probably the most accurate overall assessment.

April 29, 2004: Despite their safety concerns, the majority of Iraqis wants U.S. and British troops to leave Iraq within the next few months.

"There's a sense of disillusionment," Gallup's director of international polling, Richard Burkholder, says. "They had higher expectations of us. If we can sweep their army aside in a matter of weeks, why can't we stabilize their country? We're a victim of their high expectations."

And 70% of the Iraqis fear for their safety if they are seen assisting the coalition.[3]

April 29, 2004: BAGHDAD, Iraq (AP)—The Pentagon announces that American forces will pull back in AL-Fallujah, and an all-Iraqi force will enter the city Friday and provide security. It will consist of up to 1,100 Iraqi soldiers led by a former general from Saddam Hussein's military.

During a ceremony marking the official end of the Spanish mission, Spain's defense minister says Madrid will not send any more soldiers to Iraq.

Secretary of State Colin Powell acknowledges that support among Americans for the war is declining. "When lives are lost people start to wonder about it, and it is reflected in the polls," Powell said.[4]

April 29, 2004: BAGHDAD, Iraq (AP)—When she was 13, she had a schoolgirl crush on Adam Estep. It was so strong she filled six diaries with fantasies about him. In a tiny bottle she kept a pink shard of spoon from Baskin-Robbins that had touched his lips.

In February 2004, she married him. Two months later, 20 year old Demara Estep is a widow.

Sgt. Adam Estep, 23, of Campbell, CA, who graduated from Prospect High School in 1999, was killed in Iraq on Thursday. A rocket-propelled grenade hit his vehicle near Baghdad. He died on the way to the hospital.

"If by some chance I don't make it back, well, I want you to be happy," he wrote in mid-April, in one of the last letters she received. "I love you, Demara, more than I can say or do anything about. Take care of yourself and please do whatever you can to be happy. Until then, I'll be back as soon as I can."

He signed it, "Your ever loving husband and collector of your kisses, Adam."

They had so little time together.[5]

April 29, 2004: WASHINGTON—The State Department releases its annual "Patterns of Global Terrorism" report for 2003. The 199-page report says the number of terrorist attacks had declined 45 percent since 2001, dropping to its lowest level in 34 years.

Deputy Secretary of State Richard L. Armitage says, "Indeed, you will find in these pages clear evidence that we are prevailing in the fight."

Vice President Dick Cheney questions whether Democratic presidential candidate John Kerry is qualified to conduct a war against terrorism.

However, errors began to become apparent in early May when many parties called in to the State Department to complain that the report didn't seem right.

Instead, both the number of incidents and the toll in victims increased sharply, the department will say in June 2004. Among the mistakes, according to department spokesman Richard Boucher, was the fact that only part of 2003 was taken into account.

Secretary of State Colin Powell will blame the "very embarrassing" report on data collection mistakes, not political considerations.[6]

April 30, 2004: President Bush says he is disgusted by photos showing American soldiers laughing and holding their thumbs up as naked Iraqi detainees are forced into sexually abusive and humiliating positions. He also claimed that the actions of a handful should not taint those who serve honorably.

The British military says that they are investigating new allegations that their soldiers abused a prisoner in Iraq. Their Ministry of Defense confirms that military authorities are considering whether to prosecute eight soldiers for allegedly abusing prisoners.[7]

April 30, 2004: AL-FALLUJAH, Iraq—U.S. Marines begin withdrawing from this volatile city, taking up positions a few miles away as commanders begin to hand over responsibility for pursuing insurgents to a new Iraqi brigade led by former officers who served in Saddam Hussein's military.

It is a major strategy shift for the U.S. military after a month-long struggle. But the offensive drew condemnation from many quarters of Iraq's fractious population and appeared to raise tensions between majority Shiites and the Sunni minority that dominated Saddam's government.

"In AL-Fallujah, the Americans shake hands with you with the right and shoot with the left," Ahmed Abdul Ghafour Samarrae, a Sunni sheik, told about 600 worshipers at the Umm al-Qurra Mosque in Baghdad.[8]

April 30, 2004: WASHINGTON—"There was no debate about the wisdom of going to war," says one senior administration official, who spoke on the condition of anonymity. "No discussion of pros and cons, of what might happen, no planning for the unexpected. It was just something we were going to do."

It didn't have to be this way, critics inside and outside the administration say. Top Bush administration officials ignored and sometimes belittled pre-invasion warnings from their military, intelligence and foreign-policy professionals—warnings that were right on.

Shortly before the war, Gen. Eric Shinseki, then the U.S. Army chief of staff, told Congress that it would take "several hundred thousand" American soldiers to pacify and stabilize Iraq. He was rebuked by Deputy Secretary of Defense Paul Wolfowitz, who called the estimate "wildly off the mark."

An intensive State Department-led planning effort called "The Future of Iraq Project," was ignored by Pentagon planners, according to State Department officials and other participants.

Now that the intervention in Iraq is crumbling, even Robert Kagan and William Kristol, two neoconservatives who strongly supported the invasion, write an article in the Weekly Standard magazine critical of the strategy of current policymakers.

"It is clear there have been failures in planning and in execution," they write.[9]

President Bush invaded Iraq on behalf of the neocons, including Robert Kagan and William Kristol, who must be smarting from the dismal results. Not surprisingly, they push the blame for the mess in Iraq onto the Bush administration. Where will the neocons in the administration, such as Dick Cheney, Donald Rumsfeld, Douglas Feith, and Paul Wolfowitz, and the President himself, push the blame?

<u>April 30, 2004</u>: An editorial says a costly miscalculation at the Pentagon has left American soldiers in Iraq in thin-skinned Humvees, nearly defenseless against rocket-propelled grenades, roadside bombs, and AK-47 rifle fire they face daily. It says tanks would have saved lives in battle zones like Fallujah and An-Najaf, and notes that the Pentagon has finally ordered thousands of armored vehicles to be sent to Iraq. It says every effort must be made to speed the movement of this badly needed equipment to minimize future American casualties.[10]

Converting the thin-skinned Humvees to armored vehicles isn't expected to be completed until November 2004.

<u>May 1, 2004</u>: On the anniversary of President Bush's "Mission Accomplished" speech, First Lt. Paul Rieckhoff, who recently returned from combat in Iraq, speaks in a radio spot responding to Bush's "stay the course" weekly address.

"The people who planned this war were not ready for us," he says in his address. "There were not enough vehicles, not enough ammunition, not enough medical supplies, not enough water."

"Well, it is time for a change," Lieutenant Rieckhoff says in his address. "Our troops are still waiting for more body armor. They are still waiting for better equipment. They are still waiting for a policy that brings in the rest of the world and relieves their burden."

He continues, "I got an e-mail from a guy who used to be in my platoon recounting to me a story about an R.P.G. round that came through the center of his Humvee and blew apart a kid next to him."

As part of a light infantry unit, his men did not use heavy armored vehicles, Lieutenant Rieckhoff says, but they still needed transportation.

There were some 500 soldiers in his battalion but only two or three armored Humvees. The soldiers "would pretty much draw straws as to who was going to ride in the armor who was going to ride in the other ones."[11]

<u>May 1, 2004</u>: AL-FALLUJAH, Iraq—Masked men carrying rocket-propelled grenade launchers and waving Iraqi flags ride through the deserted streets, claiming victory in the withdrawal this week of U.S. Marines after a month-long siege of the city.

Despite the coalition's insistence their exit was not a retreat, local religious leaders call a victory prayer at a battle-scared mosque.

"The Americans have been pushed out by true soldiers, heroic men," says Shaker Adnan, 35, who wore the burgundy beret and dark camouflage of the Fallujah Brigade, the new proxy security force assembled by the coalition. "If the

Americans were men, they would have never retreated. This triumph came from God."[12]

May 1, 2004: BAGHDAD—The deputy commander of the U.S. Army's intelligence force is leading an investigation into interrogation practices at an Army-run prison where Iraqi detainees were allegedly beaten and sexually abused, U.S. officials announce. The move came after allegations that military guards abused prisoners at the request of military intelligence operatives.

Brig. Gen. Janis L. Karpinski, in a telephone interview from her home, describes a high-pressure atmosphere that encourages successful interrogations. In 2003, a month before the alleged abuses occurred a team of military intelligence officers from the detention facility at Guantánamo Bay, Cuba, came to Abu Ghurayb. "Their main and specific mission was to get the interrogators—give them new techniques to get more information from detainees," she says.

Saturday, Arabic satellite television networks repeatedly broadcast photographs of naked prisoners being humiliated. The images are being broadcast around the world and drawing widespread condemnation.

In March 2004, the Army charged six military police officers with the physical and sexual abuse of 20 prisoners at Abu Ghurayb in November and December.

"I won't defend my soldiers," an officer writes, on the condition of anonymity. "They knew better."

The officer adds, "I am extremely disappointed in the way the Army has handled the entire situation and feel the leadership has been made the scapegoat for a few individuals. I think the leadership problems go much higher than the brigade commander."[13]

May 2, 2004: BAGHDAD, Iraq—A U.S. contractor taken hostage by militants last month escapes from his captors and runs into the arms of a group of passing U.S. troops, on a day when nine U.S. soldiers die in violence across central and northern Iraq.[14]

The hostage's escape is a rare piece of good news coming from Iraq.

May 2, 2004: BAGHDAD, Iraq—Gen. Richard B. Myers, chairman of the Joint Chiefs of Staff, says the Iraqi General Jassim Mohammed Saleh who had been selected to lead a new Iraqi security force in AL-Fallujah was not likely to take charge after all. His selection to secure the city was condemned by the Shiite majority.[15]

The flip flop on who will take responsibility of AL-Fallujah indicates the level of confusion vexing the U.S. military.

May 2, 2004: Inquiries into the abuse of Iraqi detainees by U.S. military guards have revealed a much broader pattern of command failures than initially acknowledged by the Pentagon and the Bush administration.

The main Army investigation of abuse finds that key military intelligence officers and civilian employees may have actively encouraged acts of abuse and humiliation by U.S. enlisted personnel against Iraqi detainees at Abu Ghurayb.

The Taguba report essentially finds that the military police were told to soften up the prisoners so they would talk more freely in interrogations conducted by intelligence officials.

The report and other documents reveal a collapse of the command structure in the prison. Mid-level military intelligence officers were allowed to bypass the normal chain of command to issue questionable orders to enlisted personnel.

In addition, the report says abuses were also committed by members of the 325th Military Intelligence Battalion, the 205th Military Intelligence Brigade and the Joint Interrogation and Debriefing Center.[16]

May 3, 2004: BAGHDAD, Iraq—American military commanders say that they have selected a new commander for the Iraqi security force in AL-Fallujah, dropping a general who had been accused of involvement in widespread repression under Saddam Hussein.

The American commanders say they have chosen Muhammad Latif, a former intelligence officer, to lead the Iraqi security force. Unlike the man he is replacing, Maj. Gen. Jassim Muhammed Saleh, Latif appears to have been regarded as an opponent of Saddam.

Recent deaths bring the U.S. toll to 153 since April 1—including 15 in May. At least 755 U.S. military personnel have died in Iraq since the war began in March 2003.

The continuing violence creates doubt about the ability of the coalition and the United Nations to install a political process in Iraq.

Because of the violence, only 13 of the country's 18 governing regions are currently able to nominate members of the commission. The electoral process is contingent upon an improved security situation.[17]

May 3, 2004: WASHINGTON—The Bush administration is struggling with damage-control due to the mounting global backlash against the United States after prisoner abuse images are seen, U.S. officials say. The quest for a strong response follows the devastating fallout and criticism well beyond the Islamic world, from Brazil and Britain to Hong Kong.

The military's investigative 53-page report into the abuses of detainees in Iraq, by Army Maj. Gen. Antonio M. Taguba, describes broader problems in the prison system throughout Iraq, and it suggests that these problems had contributed to abuses of prisoners over many months, even after earlier offenses were reported and punished.

The report cites several cases of "riots, escapes (at least 27) and shootings" of prisoners over many months, adding that "the same types of deficiencies" were found repeatedly, but that "little to nothing was done."

Among the problems at Abu Ghurayb, the report says, is "a potentially dangerous contingent" of Iraqi guards who have given inmates contraband, weapons, and information and helped at least one inmate to escape. Lack of training appears to have been one of the problems.

In the criminal portion of the investigation, six U.S. military police face charges of assault, cruelty, indecent acts and maltreatment of detainees.

The Taguba report also indicates that military police may have been used to "soften up" detainees in Afghanistan before interrogations there.[18]

May 4, 2004: WASHINGTON—Suffering rising casualties and a growing threat of more violence, the United States abandons plans to reduce its military force in Iraq sometime this summer and says it will keep about 135,000 soldiers there for at least 1 ½ more years.

In addition, U.S. commander Gen. John P. Abizaid asks that fresh troops arrive with a larger percentage of heavy tanks and armored fighting vehicles than had been planned; an acknowledgment of the violent prowess of the insurgency.

Maintaining the unexpectedly high troop levels in Iraq represents a major change in the military force structure, straining the U.S. military's worldwide resources and incurring billions of dollars in additional costs.

Even worse, the widening prisoner-abuse scandal has cemented Iraqis' mistrust of American authorities.[19]

May 4, 2004: WASHINGTON—As investigations into U.S. military abuse of Iraqi captives gather steam, Pentagon officials reveal that they had investigated the deaths of 25 prisoners overseas and labeled two of them homicides.

At the United Nations, Secretary of State Colin Powell seeks to quell the anger in the Arab world and, in an interview with CNN's "Larry King Live," compares the abuse case to the U.S. massacre of Vietnamese civilians at My Lai.

"I'm deeply concerned about the horrible image that this has sent around the world," Powell says.

Senate Majority Leader Bill Frist, R-TN, calls the abuse disgusting and degrading and questions why Congress has been kept in the dark.

Senator John Warner, R-VA, chair of the Senate Armed Services Committee, calls the incidents the most "serious a problem of breakdown in discipline as I've ever observed."

"Who is responsible for what happened?" asks Senator Joseph Biden, the top Democrat on the Senate Foreign Relations Committee.

Making his first remarks about the abuse at the Abu Ghurayb prison, Rumsfeld calls the actions "totally unacceptable and un-American." He says an internal Pentagon report that describes the prisoners as being beaten, sodomized and drenched in phosphoric liquid and cold water left him "deeply disturbed." Rumsfeld pledges that those responsible would be brought to justice.

Since the release of the humiliating photos, other Iraqis are alleging that they, too, have been beaten.

A European diplomat for the U.N. says, "The damage is overwhelming."

New revelations Tuesday about prisoner deaths in Afghanistan and Iraq are adding to the firestorm, and officials are continuing to investigate 10 deaths and 10 assaults. A third homicide is ruled justifiable by authorities.[20]

May 4, 2004: BAGHDAD, Iraq—The U.S. commander overseeing Army-run prisons in Iraq says that the population of overcrowded Abu Ghurayb prison will be cut by more than half and that he had ordered military intelligence operatives to stop placing hoods over prisoners' heads as an interrogation tactic.[21]

May 4, 2004: WASHINGTON—Defense Department officials say that since Sept. 11, they turned to private sources to meet the burgeoning need for linguists, translators and ultimately people to question prisoners for intelligence gathering.

But critics say relying on non-military personnel undermines the threat of punishment. While U.S. soldiers allegedly involved in the acts face a military court-martial or other sanctions, the legal status and possible penalties for private workers are far less certain.

Even before the abuses at the Iraqi prison became public, several lawmakers had raised concerns about the accountability of private security companies operating in Iraq. Military officials have said they had little choice but to turn to private firms such as CACI and the San Diego-based Titan Corp., also under investigation in the Army's report.[22]

Will the desire to occupy foreign countries where the U.S. is unwelcome, which triggered a shortage of personnel and swelled the ranks of private contractors eventually lead to a return of the military draft?

May 5, 2004: WASHINGTON—Michael Moore goes on TV to denounce the Walt Disney Co.'s refusal to allow its Miramax division to distribute his new documentary, "Fahrenheit 9/11," while in Washington. Disney was denounced for quashing dissent.[23]

May 5, 2004: WASHINGTON—In interviews on two Arab television stations, Bush calls the prison abuses "abhorrent" but stops short of apologizing. In an Oval Office meeting, he angrily reprimands Rumsfeld over the scandal.

Lawmakers from both parties in Congress continue to voice outrage, and many push for Rumsfeld to take responsibility and resign. In Baghdad, many Iraqis call for the executions of all Americans who abused prisoners.

The number of prisoner deaths in Iraq and Afghanistan known to be under investigation or blamed on U.S. forces rose from 10 to 14.

Virtually every Iraqi man and woman interviewed say U.S. soldiers who took part in the sexual humiliation of Muslim prisoners should be put to death.

"They promised to liberate us, give us freedom—that's their slogan. But there is no safety here," says Manal Abed, 24, who stayed home all year rather than work as a biologist because she's afraid of crime and U.S. troops in Baghdad.

"If it goes all the way to Rumsfeld, then he should resign," Senator Joseph Biden says on NBC's "Today" show. "Who is in charge? I mean, look, every single, solitary decision made, almost since the fall of Saddam Hussein, has been mistaken."[24]

May 5, 2004: LONDON—The British are struggling with an Iraqi prisoner-abuse scandal of their own. British soldiers have been accused of mistreating, and in at least 12 cases, killing, Iraqi prisoners. The most horrific of the allegations is that a 17-year-old Iraqi boy drowned after British troops beat him and then forced him to attempt to swim in a river.

The British scandal finds a more willing, and outraged, audience. Millions of Britons opposed the war in the first place, and see the scandal as proof that it was doomed to go wrong.[25]

<u>May 6, 2004</u>: Army Field Manual 34-52 lists 20 acceptable tactics for interrogations of prisoners, with the most effective of all, "the direct approach," which is the direct questioning of a prisoner without resorting to coercion of any kind.

The manual asserts that direct questioning of prisoners was 85 to 95 percent effective during World War II and 90 to 95 percent effective during Vietnam. But during the U.S. campaign against terror and, more recently, the U.S.-led occupation of Iraq, military intelligence experts say the direct approach has often been ignored.

Several prisoners' rights advocates and former Army interrogators agree that interrogation techniques have grown more aggressive since Sept. 11. They now include some of the harsh techniques used in Abu Ghurayb prison that generated the scandal.

The methods now include the use of strobe lights and loud music, shackling prisoners in awkward positions for long hours and manipulating levels of pain medication. However, the U.S. commander in charge of military jails in Iraq, Maj. Gen. Geoffrey D. Miller, says that several harsh interrogation techniques will now be forbidden in Iraq.

"We will no longer, in any circumstances, hood any of the detainees," Miller says. "We will no longer use stress positions in any of our interrogations. And we will not use sleep deprivation in any of our interrogations."

"Clearly, keeping people sleep-deprived for four days or forced standing—a notorious torture technique, though it seems very innocuous—it is clear that those things would be prohibited in the United States by the Eighth Amendment," Tom Malinowski, the Washington advocacy director for Human Rights Watch says.

However, last June, the Pentagon assured Congress in writing that military interrogations of detainees worldwide had not violated constitutional stipulations against cruel and unusual punishment.

After release from Bagram, Saif-ur Rahman says that during his first night of detention, he was stripped naked, doused with cold water and forced to sleep in a freezing cell.[26]

<u>May 6, 2004</u>: CAIRO, Egypt—The photographs have dominated news media, political and private discussion in the Middle East. Those already primed to

believe the worst about the United States say they now have the pictures to prove it.

If the prisoners had simply been beaten or subjected to the types of physical torture thought to be common in Arab jails, the reaction might have been less severe and the inmates would have been left with some dignity intact, says Sarah Sirgany, a writer. But by stripping the prisoners naked and posing them in ways designed to insinuate homosexual behavior, the American guards at Abu Ghurayb violated some of the oldest and most deeply held prohibitions in the Arab world.[27]

May 6, 2004: WASHINGTON—President Bush says that he is sorry for the abuse of Iraqi prisoners by U.S. soldiers, but vows that the man in charge of the U.S. military, Defense Secretary Donald Rumsfeld, will remain in his job.

The International Committee of the Red Cross says that it had regularly visited Abu Ghurayb and had frequently complained to U.S. officials over the past several months about the abuses.[28]

May 7, 2004: WASHINGTON—"There are other photos that depict incidents of physical violence towards prisoners, acts that can only be described as blatantly sadistic, cruel and inhuman," Defense Secretary Donald Rumsfeld says. "There are many more photographs and indeed some videos. Congress and the American people and the rest of the world need to know this."

In a rare occurrence, the Republican-controlled Congress is holding the Bush administration accountable for a mistake.

"Our central task here today is to get at the facts in this difficult situation, no matter where they lead, no matter how embarrassing they may be," says Senator John Warner, R-VA, chair of the Senate Armed Services Committee.

An internal Pentagon investigation cataloged alleged prisoner abuses ranging from beatings to sexual assault. Some of them may be revealed in the photographs and videos that have not been made public.

In Geneva, the International Red Cross says it had warned U.S. officials of abuse of prisoners in Iraq more than a year ago.

"We were dealing here with a broad pattern, not individual acts. There was a pattern and a system," says Pierre Kraehenbuehl, director of operations for the International Committee of the Red Cross.

Amnesty International says in a letter to President Bush that the abuses at Abu Ghurayb amounted to war crimes. The human rights group says it had documented abuses by U.S. personnel against detainees in Iraq and Afghanistan for the last two years.

"We're talking about rape and murder here. We're not just talking about giving people a humiliating experience," says Senator Lindsey Graham, R-S.C., a member of the Armed Services Committee. He does not elaborate.[29]

<u>May 8, 2004</u>: Spec. Sabrina D. Harman, a military police officer accused of abusing detainees at the Abu Ghurayb prison in Iraq, says she was assigned to break down prisoners for interrogation. She claims there were no rules and little training.

"They would bring in one to several prisoners at a time already hooded and cuffed," Harman says by e-mail from Baghdad. "The job of the MP was to keep them awake, make it hell so they would talk."

"The person who brought them in would set the standards on whether or not to 'be nice'," she says. If the prisoner didn't give what they wanted, it was all taken away…Sleep, food, clothes, mattresses, cigarettes were all privileges and were granted with information received."

Harman is accused of photographing and videotaping detainees who were ordered to strip and masturbate in front of other prisoners and soldiers, according to a charge sheet obtained by the *Washington Post*. She is also charged with posing for a picture with a corpse; with striking several prisoners by jumping on them as they lay in a pile; and with attaching wires to a prisoner's hands while he stood on a box with his head covered. She told him he would be electrocuted if he fell off the box, according to the documents.

"The Geneva Convention was never posted and none of us remember taking a class to review it," Harman says. "The first time reading it was two months after being charged. I read the entire thing highlighting everything the prison is in violation of. There's a lot."

In his investigation into abuse at the prison, Taguba used a portion of Harman's sworn statement to conclude that prisoners had been abused. Harman "stated…regarding the incident where a detainee was placed on box with wires attached to his fingers, toes, and penis, 'that her job was to keep detainees awake'."[30]

<u>May 9, 2004</u>: WASHINGTON—Major General Charles H. Swannack Jr., the commander of the 82nd Airborne Division, and Army Colonel Paul Hughes, who last year was the first director of strategic planning for the U.S. occupation

authority in Baghdad, both indicate that the U.S. is winning the tactical battles, but losing strategically, and therefore losing the war.

The Iraqi people feel less safe than under Saddam. Both the reconstruction efforts, and the process to create an interim government and voter rolls are frequently stopped in their tracks.

Some high-ranking officers are recommending, off the record, that Defense Secretary Donald Rumsfeld and Deputy Defense Secretary Paul Wolfowitz are the problem and should be replaced. Rumsfeld has generated anger in the military for his meddling in logistical details, ignoring good advice, and making blunders. And this frustration isn't even related to the massive prisoner abuse scandal that has his head on the line.[31]

May 9, 2004: DUSHANBE, Tajikistan—Heroin producers in Afghanistan are cultivating opium poppies and yielding scores of 2.2-pound bags of heroin they smuggle out of Central Asia. Much of the proceeds are funding al Qaeda and other terrorists.

A Western-led campaign against opium growing and heroin laboratories has been a complete failure, and drug-control experts say the number of processing facilities in Afghanistan has mushroomed since the U.S. invasion in late 2001.

"There's absolutely no threat to the labs inside Afghanistan," says Maj. Avaz Yuldashov of the Tajikistan Drug Control Agency. "Our intelligence shows there are 400 labs making heroin there, and 80 of them are situated right along our border."

Some 200,000 acres of opium poppies have been planted in Afghanistan and the country's late-summer harvest will produce three-fourths of the world's heroin. That will mean a windfall for al Qaeda, which is said to be regrouping in the mountains of Central Asia.

"Drug trafficking from Afghanistan is the main source of support for international terrorism now," Yuldashov says. "That's quite clear."

"The connection is absolutely obvious to us," says Col. Alexander Kondratiyev, a senior Russian officer who has served with border guards in Tajikistan for nearly a decade. "Drugs, weapons, ammunition, terrorism, more drugs, more terrorism—it's a closed circle."[32]

May 9, 2004: BAGHDAD, Iraq—Spc. Jeremy Sivits, a 24-year-old military police officer from Pennsylvania, will be court-martialed here May 19. He will be the first U.S. soldier to face trial in the prisoner abuse at Abu Ghurayb prison, military officials say.

The urgency of his trial and the kind of proceedings he faces indicate there is a deal with prosecutors that could include testifying against other soldiers.

At a briefing with a U.S. military lawyer, an Iraqi reporter demanded to know why Sivits is not being turned over to an Iraqi court.

"It will be a trial with a United States judge," the U.S. lawyer says.

The Iraqi reporter asks, "No Iraqi participation?"

"No," the U.S. official answers. "This is a United States military court-martial."[33]

May 9, 2004: WASHINGTON— A series of new photos shows U.S. guards using German shepherd dogs threatening to attack a naked Iraqi prisoner at the Abu Ghurayb prison in Baghdad in December 2003.

Although U.S. officials claimed last week that the problems were aberrations, Senator Lindsey Graham, R-SC, a former chief prosecutor for the Air Force, says on NBC's "Meet the Press" that "it's clear to me that we had systemic failure" within the military and that "we just don't want a bunch of privates and sergeants to be the scapegoats here."

No Pentagon or administration officials appear on TV shows this Sunday, after a week in which officials were subjected to stiff questioning and lectures from members of the armed services and intelligence committees.[34]

May 9, 2004: LONDON—One of British Prime Minister Tony Blair's close political allies, Lord David Puttnam, told a TV interviewer over the weekend that Blair had become so closely associated with bad news from Iraq that he should step down. And the crisis over the treatment of prisoners weakens Blair as Bush's principal ally in Iraq.

Britain's Sunday Times says soldiers from the Royal Regiment of Fusiliers face prosecution after photos surfaced showing Iraqi prisoners being forced to engage in sex acts. A Ministry of Defense press officer says the abuse occurred last year and that the investigation file has been forwarded to military prosecutors.

Another pending case is the death last year of a hotel clerk after a brutal interrogation session by British soldiers in Basra. Last week, Adam Ingram, the armed forces minister, said 33 criminal investigations had been conducted into civilian deaths, injuries or ill treatment and that of those, 12 were still active and six had been referred for possible prosecution.[35]

<u>May 9, 2004</u>: BAGHDAD—The State Department confirms that Nicholas Berg's body was found Saturday near an overpass in Baghdad. A U.S. intelligence official says the body of the American was found without a head.[36]

<u>May 10, 2004</u>: WASHINGTON—One senior military official says military-intelligence officers felt pressure from their superiors—both military and civilian—to "turn up the heat" on Iraqi prisoners after early interrogations had not yielded much useful information.

"Most of the people that were picked up were the wrong ones," says a U.S. intelligence official speaking on condition of anonymity. "They were either too low-level to know much, they didn't know about anything other than the stuff they were doing themselves or they weren't involved in any bad stuff." The detainees they were "squeezing" did not have the information desired.

Lawmakers from both parties are unhappy at Rumsfeld's reluctance to share information. Many blame him and his top aides for failing to plan adequately for the occupation of Iraq and the problems that U.S. soldiers have suffered through in Iraq.

However, Karl Rove, President Bush's chief political adviser, opposes getting rid of Rumsfeld because he believes that firing the defense secretary or other top officials would put the Bush administration's Iraq policy in the spotlight.

Therefore, with Secretary of State Colin Powell, Gen. Richard Myers, chairman of the Joint Chiefs of Staff, and CIA Director George Tenet standing nearby and flanked by Vice President Dick Cheney and Secretary of Defense Rumsfeld, Bush delivers an unqualified endorsement of his defense secretary.

"You are doing a superb job," Bush tells Rumsfeld in front of reporters, his strongest defense of him yet. "You are a strong Secretary of Defense, and our nation owes you a debt of gratitude."

Minutes after praising Rumsfeld, Bush gets a firsthand look at more alarming pictures of U.S. soldiers mistreating Iraqi captives.

The evidence collected by military investigators includes shots of naked Iraqi women. Taguba, who investigated the treatment of Iraqi captives, says in his report that other abuses included a male guard having sex with a female detainee and male captives being sodomized with some kind of pole or stick.[37]

<u>May 11, 2004</u>: WASHINGTON—Coalition military intelligence officials estimate that 70 to 90 percent of prisoners detained in Iraq since the war began "had been arrested by mistake," according to a confidential Red Cross report given to the Bush administration earlier this year.

The report cites more than 250 allegations of mistreatment, which it said U.S. officials had failed to halt, despite repeated complaints from the International Committee of the Red Cross (ICRC).

The Swiss-based ICRC made 29 visits to coalition-run prisons and camps between late March and November 2003. Reports of detainee mistreatment were repeatedly presented to prison commanders, U.S. military officials in Iraq and members of the Bush administration in Washington.

The ICRC report also says that Iraqi families of suspects usually were told so little that most arrests resulted "in the de facto 'disappearance' of the arrestee for weeks or even months." Also, more than 100 "high-value detainees" were held for five months at the Baghdad airport, "in strict solitary confinement" in small cells for 23 hours a day.

Such conditions "constituted a serious violation" of the Third and Fourth Geneva Conventions, which set minimum standards for treatment of prisoners of war and civilian internees, the report says.[38]

May 11, 2004: BAGHDAD, Iraq—An Islamist Web site posts a videotape graphically showing the decapitation of an American, Nicholas Berg, in Iraq, in what the killers call revenge for the American mistreatment of Iraqi prisoners at Abu Ghurayb prison.

"I knew he was decapitated before," Michael Berg, his father, tells the Associated Press after the videotape was shown. "That manner is preferable to a long and torturous death. But I didn't want it to become public."

The militants threaten more bloodshed due to the abuse to the Muslim men and women in Abu Ghurayb prison. "You will receive nothing from us but coffin after coffin slaughtered in this way."

Berg's death comes amid a surge in the number of foreigners killed and kidnapped here in recent days.

During Berg's second trip to Iraq, he was arrested by Iraqi police while riding in a taxi at a checkpoint in the northern city of Mosul. His family members learned of the arrest on March 31, when FBI agents told them he was in an Iraqi jail.

On April 5, the family filed a federal suit claiming Berg was being held illegally by the U.S. military in Iraq. On April 6, he was released, his family says, and began making plans to return home.[39]

There is nothing that Nicholas Berg, or any other Americans, could have done that would have justified such a savage act, but it was definitely triggered by the prisoner abuse scandal, and it may not be the end of the retaliation.

<u>May 11, 2004</u>: WASHINGTON—The officer, Maj. Gen. Antonio Taguba, tells the Senate Armed Services Committee that it has been against the Army's doctrine for another Army general to recommend last summer that military guards "set the conditions" to help Army intelligence interrogators extract information from prisoners.

Taguba spars with Stephen Cambone, the Undersecretary of Defense for intelligence, as senators try to shed some light on whether the Pentagon's pursuit for better intelligence to combat Iraqi insurgents contributed to the detainee abuse there.

Lt. Gen. Keith Alexander, head of military intelligence for the Army, says he believed that the abuses were carried out by "a group of undisciplined military police," and that he had seen no evidence that military intelligence officers had told them what to do.

Those assertions were greeted with skepticism from even some Republicans on the committee.[40]

<u>May 12, 2004</u>: ORLANDO, Fla.—Senator John Kerry strongly suggests that Bush is partly to blame for abuses at the Abu Ghurayb prison.

"They dismiss the Geneva Convention, starting in Afghanistan and Guantánamo Bay, so that the status of prisoners both legal and moral becomes ambiguous at best," the senator tells radio host Don Imus. This amounts to "major failures in command."

Kerry proposes immediately ousting Defense Secretary Donald Rumsfeld. He says dismissing Rumsfeld during wartime will not hinder efforts in Iraq and Afghanistan, and offers up a few candidates to replace the defense secretary: GOP Senators John McCain of Arizona and John Warner of Virginia, and Senator Carl Levin, D-Michigan, a staunch war critic.

"The fact is that we need a change in policy."[41]

<u>May 12, 2004</u>: WASHINGTON—Republican and Democratic senators have pointed questions for Defense Secretary Donald Rumsfeld.

What are the plans for the hand-over of sovereignty to Iraqis? Why not abide by the Geneva Convention? Who's responsible for civilian contractors in Iraq? Why aren't there enough flak jackets and armored Humvees to protect the forces?

Due to the bad news, lawmakers are exerting stronger oversight of U.S. policy on Iraq, says Senator John Warner, R-VA, the chair of the Senate Armed Services Committee.

Senator Richard Durbin, D-Ill., challenges Rumsfeld for permitting the abuse of detainees at Abu Ghurayb prison, which violated international rules set by the Geneva Convention.

Senator Patrick Leahy, D-VT asks Rumsfeld to answer a question that the secretary posed in an Oct. 13, 2003, internal memo, "Are we capturing, killing or dissuading more terrorists every day than the *madrasahs* and radical clerics are recruiting, training and deploying against us?"

"Al Qaeda wasn't in Iraq when we started this war. They are there now," Leahy says. "How do you answer the question you posed last October?"

Rumsfeld responds, "I don't know of any way that one can calculate that. Our folks are doing the best job they can."[42]

May 12, 2004: WASHINGTON—All afternoon, a procession of somber senators and House members file into secure rooms in the Capitol and House Rayburn Office Building to view about 1,800 images, many of them duplicates, along with some video clips. The lawmakers file out stunned, even though they had already seen some of the images before.

"What we saw is appalling," the Senate majority leader, Bill Frist, R-TN, tells reporters.

The photos "sear the soul," says Senator Barbara Boxer, D-CA

"It's a sad day when Congress is called to see these photos," says a grim Representative Nancy Pelosi, D-San Francisco, the House minority leader.

Among the most upsetting images is a video clip of a male detainee repeatedly banging into a cell door, until he collapses. Senator Joe Lieberman, D-CT, says it appeared that the man had a rope lashed around his waist, and that someone was pulling him toward the door.

Some say the pictures make them doubt that the mistreatment was limited to a handful of low-level soldiers.

"Some of it is clearly individuals acting in a rogue manner," says Senator Lindsey Graham, R-S.C. "Some of it has an elaborate nature to it that makes me very suspicious of whether or not others were directing or encouraging."

The images include women who were apparently being forced to expose their breasts, says Senator Ben Nighthorse Campbell, R-CO. He also says the photos show dogs snarling at cowering prisoners. Other lawmakers say some prisoners appeared to have dog bite wounds and abrasions.

"It is totally vulgar behavior," says Campbell, who served in a police unit in the Air Force. "It just really bothered me that it could be our military people doing that."[43]

<u>May 12, 2004</u>: BAGHDAD, Iraq—The U.S. military orders courts-martial for two additional U.S. soldiers accused of abusing naked prisoners at the Abu Ghurayb prison. Charged with violating five counts of the Uniform Code of Military Justice are Sgt. Javal Davis, 26, of Maryland and Staff Sgt. Ivan L. Frederick II, 37, of Buckingham, Va.

The charging documents allege that Frederick:

- Stacked several nude prisoners in a pyramid.

- Posed for a picture sitting atop a prisoner who was bound and stuffed between two hospital stretchers.

- Hooding of a prisoner, connecting wires to his hands, and telling him he would be electrocuted if he fell off it.

- Ordered prisoners to masturbate in front of other prisoners, and photographed the acts.

- Ordered two detainees to fight.

- Watched while other soldiers took pictures of prisoners masturbating in a public corridor of Abu Ghurayb.[44]

<u>May 13, 2004</u>: WASHINGTON—At least one CIA employee has been disciplined for threatening a detainee with a gun during questioning, U.S. officials say.

In the case of Khalid Shaikh Mohammad, CIA interrogators used a technique known as "water boarding," in which a prisoner is strapped down, forcibly pushed under water and made to believe he might drown.

These techniques were authorized by a set of secret rules for the interrogation of high-level al Qaeda prisoners that were endorsed by the Justice Department and the CIA. The rules were adopted by the Bush administration after the Sept. 11 attacks for handling detainees and may have established a precedent throughout the government that officials could deal harshly with detainees.

The methods employed by the CIA are so severe that senior officials of the FBI directed bureau agents to steer clear of many interviews of the high-level detainees, counterterrorism officials say.

After Sept. 11, President Bush signed a series of directives authorizing the CIA to conduct a covert war against Osama bin Laden's al Qaeda network, but it is not clear whether the White House approved any specific rules for interrogations.[45]

May 13, 2004: WASHINGTON—With war expenditures in Iraq and Afghanistan now approaching $5 billion a month, next year's total cost "is $50 billion to $60 billion," Deputy Defense Secretary Paul Wolfowitz tells senators. "If you look at our operations in Iraq and Afghanistan, it's a big bill." Wolfowitz stresses that the Pentagon would seek additional spending early next year.

Under questioning from Senator Jack Reed, D-R.I., Wolfowitz and Gen. Peter Pace, the vice chairman of the Joint Chiefs of Staff, acknowledge that some of the Bush administration's approved interrogation techniques could be interpreted as violating the Geneva Convention.[46]

May 14, 2004: WASHINGTON—After a bombardment of international and domestic criticism, the Pentagon announces that virtually all coercive interrogation practices, like forcing prisoners to crouch for long periods or depriving them of sleep, are now barred in Iraq.

Defense Secretary Donald Rumsfeld's deputy, Paul Wolfowitz, acknowledges at a Senate hearing Thursday that hooding prisoners or forcing them to crouch naked for 45 minutes is inhumane.

The changes appear to affect only operations in Iraq, and would not change interrogation methods at the U.S. base at Guantánamo Bay, Cuba, where harsher approaches have been authorized.

Seven criminal charges are filed against Cpl. Charles A. Graner including conspiracy to maltreat detainees, dereliction of duty for willfully failing to protect detainees from abuse, cruelty and maltreatment, maltreatment of detainees, assaulting detainees, committing indecent acts, adultery and obstruction of justice.[47]

May 15, 2004: WASHINGTON—Secretary of Defense Donald Rumsfeld and Stephen A. Cambone, the Undersecretary of Defense for intelligence, authorized the expansion of a secret program that permitted harsh interrogations of detained members of al Qaeda. They allowed these methods, including degrading and sexually humiliating practices, to be used against prisoners at the Abu Ghurayb prison in Iraq in 2003, according to an article in the New Yorker by Seymour Hersh.

"According to interviews with several past and present American intelligence officials," Hersh wrote, "the Pentagon's operation, known inside the intelligence community by several code words, including Copper Green, encouraged physical coercion and sexual humiliation of Iraqi prisoners in an effort to generate more intelligence about the growing insurgency in Iraq."

Rumsfeld has previously said the techniques were carried out by lower-level forces without the approval of senior commanders. Today, officials in the Bush administration say they are aware of no high-level decision to use highly coercive interrogation techniques on Iraqi prisoners.[48]

<u>May 16, 2004:</u> With unleaded gas starting at $2.05 a gallon, frustrations from motorists in Michigan are similar to the rest of the country, "It's ridiculous," says one patron of a Sunoco gas station, "Outrageous," says another.[49]

One of the costs of the Iraq war, due to insurgent sabotage of oil fields and distribution facilities, can be seen at the gas pump.

<u>May 16, 2004</u>: WASHINGTON—An Afghan captive froze to death in a CIA-run lockup in Kabul, Afghanistan, in 2002. At Iraq's Camp Bucca, a detainee was shot through the chest in 2003 while throwing rocks at a guard tower. At Camp Cropper, near Baghdad's airport, detainee No. 7166 was shot and killed in June 2003 as he tried to crawl under a barbed-wire fence in an escape attempt that commanders had known about a day earlier.

All were deaths in U.S. custody and were largely ignored by outsiders prior to the prisoner abuse scandal. At least 18 cases of deaths of detainees while in U.S. custody in Iraq and Afghanistan since 2002 have been identified by the *Los Angeles Times*. The deaths occurred either from detainee mistreatment or shootings during prison unrest.

The CIA has been connected to as many as five of the deaths. Independent human rights groups argue that more detainees have died than the military has revealed. Only one low-ranking soldier has been tried and convicted for shooting an unarmed prisoner. He was demoted to private and discharged from the Army (facing no jail time).

Until the prison-abuse scandal erupted two weeks ago, the Pentagon only permitted the Red Cross to visit America's foreign detention camps and prisons. Reporters, lawyers, and other human rights groups were given no access, and little information on who was being held was disclosed.

But faced with the prison uproar, Army Maj. Gen. Donald Ryder told a Senate hearing earlier this month that the military had investigated 25 deaths in custody over the past 18 months.

Amnesty International and other human rights groups still insist that the military isn't providing complete information.

In reference to Afghan Mullah Habibullah and a taxi driver named Dilawar, "There's been no public accounting of these two cases," says Kenneth Roth, executive director of Human Rights Watch. "That sends the signal that the Bush administration is not terribly serious about upholding international law."[50]

May 16, 2004: WASHINGTON—The Supreme Court is weighing whether detainees at the Guantánamo Navy base should have access to federal courts to challenge their confinement and whether two U.S. citizens held as "enemy combatants" have any legal rights.

The Justice Department has argued that the detainees do not have any legal rights. And in wartime the courts should have no say in how the executive branch and military handle captives.

But the images of abused detainees in Iraqi prisons and harsh treatment on some captives in Guantánamo Bay may sway the Supreme Court to offer some protections for the detainees.

"The justices don't live in solitary confinement, and this will certainly have an impact on them," says Eugene Fidell, director of the non-partisan National Institute of Military Justice. "They have already expressed their doubts about these cases."

Several justices are clearly troubled by the Guantánamo camp, which is shrouded in secrecy and now holds about 600 detainees.

Justice Ruth Bader Ginsburg asked government lawyers last month if "mild torture" of a detainee authorized by the executive branch would trigger some judicial review.

Not necessarily, said Deputy Solicitor Paul Clement, "You have to trust the executive to make quintessential military judgments."[51]

May 16, 2004: WASHINGTON—The May 24, 2004 edition of *Newsweek* says in January 2002 White House counsel Alberto Gonzales wrote to President Bush that, in his judgment, the post-Sept. 11 security environment "renders obsolete" the Geneva Convention's "strict limitations on questioning of enemy prisoners and renders quaint some of its provisions."

Secretary of State Colin Powell "hit the roof" when he read the memo, according to the magazine, and fired off his own note to the president, warning that the new rules "will reverse over a century of U.S. policy and practice" and have "a high cost in terms of negative international reaction."

The New Yorker article says the interrogation methods were part of a secret "special-access program" that gave advance approval to capture, interrogate or kill "high-value targets."

In a statement, Pentagon officials harshly criticize the report, calling it "outlandish, conspiratorial and filled with error and anonymous conjecture." But the Pentagon would not say flatly whether the program exists.

"I think there's been a lack of accountability up the chain," says Senator Carl Levin of Michigan, the ranking Democrat on the Armed Services Committee. "All the focus has been on the few at the bottom that we've seen pictures of. It goes way further up than that, both on the military and the civilian side."[52]

May 17, 2004: BAGHDAD, Iraq—In a further setback to the U.S. effort to stabilize Iraq before the June 30 hand-over of limited sovereignty, a suicide bomber kills the president of the Iraqi Governing Council and at least six other people.

The suicide attack, just before 10 a.m., shoots a sooty plume of dense smoke into the sky over Baghdad, shattering windows in houses and on cars down the block and sending hot metallic shards for hundreds of yards.[53]

May 17, 2004: An artillery shell containing the nerve agent sarin exploded near a U.S. military convoy in Baghdad recently, releasing a small amount of the deadly chemical and slightly injuring two ordnance disposal experts, a top U.S. military official in Iraq says.

Weapons experts caution that this did not necessarily mean that Saddam possessed hidden stockpiles of chemical munitions. Experts familiar with Iraq's chemical weapons program say the shell was likely a leftover from Saddam's pregulf war stockpile.

The Saddam Hussein government claimed that all leftover chemical munitions had been destroyed in accordance with U.N. Security Council requirements. It is possible that some munitions were overlooked, hidden or stolen.

Army Brig. Gen. Mark Kimmitt says he believed that whoever rigged the shell as a roadside bomb didn't know it contained chemicals. He says the bomb was "virtually ineffective as a chemical weapon."[54]

May 17, 2004: WASHINGTON—The Pentagon announces it will move 3,600 soldiers from their garrisons in South Korea to Iraq this summer.

The decision to move troops from a unit stationed long term in South Korea underscores how much the military is straining to provide enough forces for Iraq while also meeting its other commitments around the world.

A senior military official says the troop levels in Iraq could remain as high as 138,000 for the next year.[55]

May 18, 2004: WASHINGTON—Interrogators from military intelligence and other government agencies told guards at the Abu Ghurayb prison to deprive detainees of sleep and food, and to strip detainees and make them sleep naked in their cells, but their orders stopped well short of the abuse at the center of the prison scandal, guards and investigators testify at the preliminary hearing.

A transcript of the hearing obtained by *The New York Times* suggests that interrogators gave guards orders to treat detainees harshly to get them to talk.[56]

May 18, 2004: WASHINGTON—Deputy Defense Secretary Paul Wolfowitz acknowledges that he and other officials had failed to fully appreciate the strength of the enemy fully.

"The real killers, who number in the thousands, were much tougher people, I think, than anyone imagined," he says.[57]

No one imagined? There was a loud chorus of claims that U.S. troops would be up against a fierce urban resistance in Iraq prior to the invasion. Dr. Wolfowitz, and his fellow neocons, merely chose not to listen to anyone but themselves.

May 18, 2004: WASHINGTON—The U.S. Army is scraping up soldiers for duty in Iraq wherever it can find them because it has been stretched so thin.

The Army confirms that it had pulled the files of some 17,000 people in the Individual Ready Reserve, the nation's pool of former soldiers, for review.

The Army is also considering a plan to close its premier training center at Fort Irwin in the Mojave Desert so the 11th Armored Cavalry Regiment will be available for combat duty in Iraq.

Troops from these sources would be in addition to the 3,600 soldiers from South Korea that will be rotating to Iraq this summer.[58]

May 18, 2004: KARBALA, Iraq—An American general says in an interview in Karbala that the military would press its campaign against al-Sadr.

"He is going to either have his militia lay down their arms, or we're going to defeat them," says Army Brig. Gen. Mark P. Hertling, assistant division commander for support in the 1st Armored Division, which is trying to crush al-Sadr's forces in Karbala and An-Najaf.[59]

<u>May 18, 2004</u>: WASHINGTON—The Pentagon is finally cutting off funds for the former Iraqi exile group that supplied defectors who provided exaggerated, fabricated and unsubstantiated information on Iraq's weapons programs and said Iraqis would greet U.S. troops as liberators, U.S. officials say.

The Iraqi National Congress was informed Friday that the $335,000 monthly payment it has received from the Defense Intelligence Agency would stop in June, the officials say.[60]

<u>May 19, 2004</u>: BAGHDAD, Iraq—U.S. ground forces and aircraft attack a village in Iraq's western desert before dawn, striking what Iraqi witnesses say is a wedding celebration but U.S. officials call a way station for foreign terrorists.

Video footage from the scene shows fresh graves and the corpses of several children. The images of civilian casualties are broadcast widely on Arab television.

U.S. officials acknowledge that their troops attacked in the area, but say they fired in response to hostile fire and later recovered weapons, large amounts of cash and other evidence of an insurgent supply route.

Iraqis interviewed on an APTN video say revelers had fired volleys of gunfire into the air in a traditional wedding celebration before the attack took place.

The deputy police chief of a nearby city says 42 to 45 people died, including 15 children and 10 women.[61]

<u>May 19, 2004</u>: BAGHDAD, Iraq—A tearful Army Spec. Jeremy Sivits apologizes in court to the victims and the Iraqi people after being sentenced to one year in prison. "I let everybody down," he says.

Sivits provides a detailed account of the mistreatment he witnessed and is sentenced after pleading guilty to four criminal counts and promising that he will testify against six other accused Americans.[62]

<u>May 19, 2004</u>: WASHINGTON—At a Senate Armed Services Committee, Senator John Warner, R-VA, committee chairman, discloses that the Pentagon had found another disk containing photos of abuse at Abu Ghurayb.

Gen. John Abizaid, the top commander in the Middle East, speaks in somber tones as he assesses the situation in Iraq, offering a sometimes grim view of the challenge in bringing stability to Iraq.

"It could very well be more violent than we are seeing today, so it's possible that we might need more forces," he says, adding that he hopes more countries will contribute troops.[63]

<u>May 20, 2004</u>: WASHINGTON—In one terrible day, Israeli forces kill unarmed Palestinian protesters, and Arab news reports claim that a U.S. Army helicopter killed 40 people at a wedding party in Iraq.

Three facts may make these two mistakes into a powerful recruiting tool for Osama bin Laden and other Islamist terrorists: Christian or Jewish troops kill Arabs, they use American-made weapons, and the attacks and casualties are shown on television.

The failure of the U.S. occupation to bring stability to Iraq, the Iraq prison-abuse scandal and Bush's past support for Israel's tactics against Palestinians are not painting a good picture.

Several analysts and former officials with long experience in the Middle East say they couldn't remember a time when events in the region seemed more out of control and America's standing in the region seemed lower.[64]

<u>May 20, 2004</u>: WASHINGTON—Sgt. Samuel Provance says intelligence inter-rogators told military police to strip down prisoners, leave them naked, and make them wear women's underwear as a way to help "break" them. The same interro-gators in the 205th Military Intelligence Brigade would then talk about the abuse with Provance and flippantly dismiss it because the Iraqis were considered "the enemy," he says.

He maintains he voiced his disapproval as early as October 2003.

The 205th Military Intelligence Brigade's top officers have declined to com-ment publicly, not answering repeated phone calls and e-mail messages. Pro-vance, a member of the 302nd Military Intelligence Battalion's A Company, signed a non-disclosure agreement at his base in Germany on Friday. But he says he wants to discuss Abu Ghurayb because he feels the intelligence community is covering up the abuses.[65]

<u>May 20, 2004</u>: The top American general in Afghanistan orders a sweeping review of secretive U.S. jails in the country amid mounting allegations of prisoner abuse, a military spokesman says.[66]

<u>May 20, 2004</u>: BAGHDAD, Iraq—American soldiers and intelligence officers send Iraqi police inside the home of Ahmed Chalabi, confiscating computers, weapons and other equipment.

A senior British official with the coalition says the raid was conducted to arrest as many as 15 people on charges that "involve fraud, kidnapping and associated matters." Chalabi is not among those named in arrest warrants.

Chalabi, a member of the Iraqi Governing Council, says he had severed ties with the U.S.-led coalition after the raid, which his colleagues on the U.S.-appointed council have condemned.

News photographs taken after the raid show ransacked rooms and a framed portrait of Chalabi with a bullet hole in the head.

Until recently, Chalabi and his INC enjoyed unusual access to and support from neoconservative officials in the Pentagon and Vice President Dick Cheney's office. The INC received $33 million from the State Department from 2000 to 2003, according to a General Accounting Office report.

Intelligence suggested that Chalabi's security chief, Arras Habib, might have given Iran information about American military activities and political plans in Iraq.

Chalabi was undermining United Nations special representative Lakhdar Brahimi's efforts to form an interim government by June 30. He also irked U.S. officials when he refused to turn over files the INC had seized from Saddam Hussein's intelligence services and he bitterly opposed the U.S. policy reversal to rehabilitate some members of Saddam's Baath Party.

Also, there is mounting evidence that Iraqi defectors supplied by the INC fed the administration exaggerated, fabricated or unproved information on Iraq's suspected weapons programs.

The officials say support for Chalabi in Washington has largely evaporated. Rumsfeld would not comment Thursday when a reporter asked if he had lost confidence in Chalabi.[67]

May 20, 2004: WASHINGTON—President Bush goes to Capitol Hill to rally Republicans. He did not address the prisoner abuse scandal, calls for Donald Rumsfeld's resignation, or the raid by authorities on the Baghdad offices and home of Ahmed Chalabi.

While Republicans publicly rally around Bush, the House Democratic leader, Representative Nancy Pelosi of San Francisco, unleashes some of her toughest criticism yet on the president.

"I believe that the president's leadership in the actions taken in Iraq demonstrate an incompetence in terms of knowledge, judgment and experience in making the decisions that would have been necessary to truly accomplish the mission without the deaths to our troops and the cost to our taxpayers," she tells reporters. She later adds, "The emperor has no clothes. When are people going to face the reality? Pull this curtain back."[68]

May 21, 2004: WASHINGTON—Fresh allegations of prison abuse are contained in statements taken from 13 detainees shortly after a soldier reported the incidents to military investigators in mid-January. They include prisoners being ridden like animals, sexually fondled by female soldiers and forced to retrieve their food from toilets.

The detainees said they were savagely beaten and repeatedly humiliated sexually by U.S. soldiers on the night shift at Tier 1A in Abu Ghurayb, according to copies of the statements obtained by the *Washington Post*. Some said they were pressed to denounce Islam or were force-fed pork and liquor.

"They forced us to walk like dogs on our hands and knees," said Hiadar Sabar Abed Miktub al-Aboodi, detainee No. 13077. "We had to bark like a dog, and if we didn't do that they started hitting us hard on our face and chest with no mercy. After that, they took us to our cells, took the mattresses out and dropped water on the floor, and they made us sleep on our stomachs on the floor with the bags on our head, and they took pictures of everything."

"They said we will make you wish to die and it will not happen," said Ameen Saeed Al-Sheik, detainee No. 151362. "They stripped me naked. One of them told me he would rape me. He drew a picture of a woman to my back and makes me stand in shameful position holding my buttocks."

Kasim Mehaddi Hilas, detainee No. 151108, said he watched as Graner and others sodomized a detainee with a phosphoric light. "They tied him to the bed," Hilas said.

Mustafa Jassim Mustafa, detainee No. 150542, told military investigators he also witnessed the phosphoric-light assault. He said it was around the time of Ramadan, the holiest period of the Muslim year, when he heard screams coming from a cell below.[69]

May 21, 2004: WASHINGTON—The U.S. government is investigating how Iraqi National Congress leader Ahmed Chalabi obtained highly classified American intelligence that was then passed to Iran. Senior administration officials, speaking on condition of anonymity, says the compromised intelligence is "highly classified and damaging."

The two U.S. officials say that evidence suggests that Arras Habib, Chalabi's security chief, is a longtime agent of Iran's intelligence service and that he is suspected of giving classified U.S. intelligence to officials in Iran, with whom Chalabi has long had close ties. Habib is now a fugitive.

"The bottom line here is that much of the information the administration had about Iraq may have come from an Iranian agent," says the intelligence official. "If that's true, this is a huge scandal."[70]

May 21, 2004: WASHINGTON—The chairman of the Joint Chiefs of Staff, Gen. Richard B. Myers, tells the House Armed Services Committee that, far from calming violence in Iraq, the June 30 turnover is likely to usher in more turmoil, comments echoed by Army Chief of Staff Gen. Peter Schoomaker.

"The threat will continue to intensify after June 30," Myers says.

The ranking Democrat on the Armed Services Committee, Representative Ike Skelton of Missouri, asks Myers, "Are we on the brink of failure?"

"I don't think so," Myers replies. "It is going to be tough. But I think we are on the brink of success."

Representative Ellen Tauscher, D-Walnut Creek, asks Myers whether U.S. forces in Iraq "could get out safely if we were told we had to leave."

"We have the authority under United Nations resolutions to stay in Iraq," Myers says. "We are *not* going to be asked to leave."[71]

May 22, 2004: BAGHDAD, Iraq—A military lawyer for a soldier charged in the Abu Ghurayb prisoner-abuse case testifies that a captain at the prison near Baghdad said the highest-ranking U.S. military officer in Iraq was present during some "interrogations and/or allegations of the prisoner abuse," according to a recording of a military hearing obtained by the *Washington Post*.

The lawyer says he was told that Lt. Gen. Ricardo Sanchez and other senior military officers were aware of what was taking place on Tier 1A of Abu Ghurayb. The lawyer, Capt. Robert Shuck, also says a sergeant at the prison was prepared to testify that intelligence officers told him the abuse of detainees on the cellblock was "the right thing to do."

A Defense Department official says that statements by defense lawyers or their clients should be treated with "appropriate caution."[72]

May 22, 2004: TUNIS, Tunisia—Seeking unity in an increasingly divided Arab world suffering what one diplomat calls a "period of despair," leaders of 22 Middle Eastern, Persian Gulf and North African nations meet for the Arab League summit.

A resolution to be presented today reportedly condemns the prisoner abuse as "inhuman" and "immoral." It also denounces "terrorist bombings" that have killed innocent Iraqis and the heavy use of force by U.S.-led coalition soldiers.

It reportedly criticizes President Bush for recent statements supporting Israeli Prime Minister Ariel Sharon's "unilateral disengagement" plan, under which Israel would evacuate settlements in the Gaza Strip while consolidating its hold on some West Bank settlements.[73]

May 22, 2004: Shirin Ebadi, the first Muslim woman and first Iranian to win the Nobel Peace Prize, says that the United States' military occupation of Iraq is harming development of democracy in that country.

At a news conference before her Saturday night speech at Stanford University, Ebadi says the United States must get out of Iraq and allow the United Nations to help the Iraqis establish the will of the people. The ongoing military presence "becomes a machine for producing violence," which further unites fundamentalists and undermines human-rights advocates, she says.

The Iranian human-rights lawyer was named the 2003 Nobel Peace laureate for championing democracy and the rights of women and children in the Islamic republic. Ebadi, also Iran's first female judge, was repeatedly imprisoned as she fought for religious freedom and free speech.[74]

May 23, 2004: The Stress of war:
31% Male Vietnam veterans have experienced post-traumatic stress disorder.
27% Female Vietnam veterans have experienced the disorder.
600+ Soldiers have been diagnosed with the disorder since the war in Iraq started.
15.6 Suicide rate per 100,000 soldiers during the Vietnam War.
3.6 Suicide rate per 100,000 soldiers during the 1991 Persian Gulf War.
17.3 Suicide rate per 100,000 soldiers during the Iraq war.[75]

May 23, 2004: AL-KUFAH, Iraq—U.S. forces raid the Sahla mosque in Al-Kufah where they say insurgents store weapons, and the military says at least 32 fighters loyal to radical Shiite cleric Muqtada al-Sadr were killed during the first U.S. incursion into the holy city.

U.S. soldiers smashed the gate to the mosque complex with an armored vehicle and killed people inside, mosque employee Radhi Mohammed says. An Associated Press photographer saw bloodstains on the ground indicating that someone was dragged for at least 10 yards. There also was blood in mosque bathrooms.[76]

May 23, 2004: WASHINGTON—"We're going to be there no matter what," Gen. John Abizaid, commander of U.S. troops in the Middle East, tells Congress in response to questions regarding a new U.N. resolution on the length of U.S. occupation in Iraq.[77]

May 24, 2004: BAGHDAD, Iraq—Bodies keep coming into Baghdad's main morgue. Some are dropped onto the blood-splattered concrete floor. Others lie naked on metal gurneys in a hallway, waiting for autopsies.

There is no precise count for Iraq as a whole on how many people have been killed, nor is there a breakdown of deaths caused by the different sorts of attacks. The U.S. military, the occupation authority and Iraqi government agencies say they do not have the ability to track civilian deaths.

Iraq is not a more dangerous place than during the worst years of Saddam Hussein's leadership. At least 300,000 people were killed by security forces—many from the massacres that followed rebellions—and buried in mass graves during the dictator's 23-year rule, U.S. officials say.

But an Associated Press survey of morgues in Baghdad and the provinces of Karbala, Kirkuk and Tikrit found 5,558 violent deaths recorded since May 1, 2003 to April 30, 2004.

The AP's survey was merely a sampling intended to assess the levels of violence. Figures for violent deaths in the months before the war showed a far lower rate.

"Before the war, there was a strong government, strong security. There were a lot of police on the streets and there were no illegal weapons," Kais Hassan, director of statistics at Baghdad's Medicolegal Institute, said during an AP reporter's visit to the morgue. "Now, there are few controls. There is crime, revenge killings, so much violence."

The death toll recorded by the Baghdad morgue was an average of 357 violent deaths each month from May through April. That contrasts with an average of 14 a month for 2002 (prior to the U.S. invasion), Hassan's documents show.

The toll translates into an annual homicide rate of about 76 killings for every 100,000 people. By comparison, Bogotá, Colombia, reported 39 homicides per 100,000 people in 2002, while New York City had about 7.5 per 100,000 in 2003.[78]

May 24, 2004: WASHINGTON—"The United States…is gambling regardless of what it does; if a prolonged military presence threatens to de-legitimize the new Iraqi government, a premature and abrupt withdrawal could create a security vacuum encouraging disorder, even civil war," warns a new study published by the Strategic Studies Institute at the U.S. Army War College in Carlisle, Pa.

The report compares the U.S. wars in Vietnam and Iraq and finds that "the differences greatly outnumbered the similarities."

Nevertheless, it says, Vietnam holds important lessons for Bush because the United States faces a dilemma in Iraq similar to the one it faced in South Vietnam 40 years ago. No local government is likely to survive without massive U.S. military support, but that support undermines the government's legitimacy.[79]

The differences do outnumber the similarities, but are some of these differences of the nature to increase the likelihood of a Vietnam-like quagmire?

May 24, 2004: AR-RAMADI, Iraq—The U.S. military insists that there was no wedding in the village of Mogr el-Deeb that was attacked last Wednesday.

But a video that Associated Press Television News (APTN) shot a day after the attack shows fragments of musical instruments, pots and pans, and brightly colored beddings used for celebrations, scattered around the bombed-out tent.

There was also a video of the wedding itself. The bride arrives in a white pickup truck and is quickly ushered into a house by a group of women. Outside, men recline on brightly colored silk pillows as boys dance to tribal songs.

The videotape obtained Sunday by APTN captures a wedding party that survivors say was later attacked by U.S. planes early Wednesday, killing up to 45 people.

An AP reporter and photographer, who interviewed more than a dozen survivors a day after the bombing, were able to identify many of them on the wedding party video which runs several hours.[80]

May 24, 2004: CARLISLE, Pa.—President Bush promises to give Iraqis "full sovereignty" on June 30 and he also vows to demolish the Iraqi prison that serves as a reminder of prisoner abuse. The speech is part of a White House effort to counter fears that Iraq is spinning out of control.

However, with a little more than five weeks to go before the handoff to an interim Iraqi government, U.S. officials do not know who will take over in Iraq or how long U.S. troops will stay.

Bush says the 138,000 U.S. soldiers will remain in Iraq under U.S. command "as long as necessary" without presenting any exit strategy.[81]

Bush tries to portray the prisoner abuse scandal as just a few bad MPs in one prison that will be resolved when Abu Ghurayb prison is razed. He also doesn't answer the questions of how security will be achieved, how Iraq's infrastructure will be rebuilt or elections held without security, how much it will all cost, or who has the final say on whether U.S. troops should enter an Iraqi city in the event of violence.

Without offering any changes, Bush is essentially saying that his current plan is good enough.

<u>May 24, 2004:</u> NEW YORK—In an early-evening speech before the prestigious Council of Foreign Relations in New York City, Nader says Iraq faces a choice between two futures. In one, he says, Iraq could stay on its current course and remain a "puppet regime" under Washington's control. Or, he says, "We could declare a set date for corporate and military withdrawal—let's say the end of the year."

Nader calls for the withdrawal of U.S. corporations, such as Halliburton, that have won lucrative contracts in Iraq and for Bush's impeachment, saying he prosecuted a war under false pretenses. "To say Bush has exaggerated the threat of Saddam Hussein is pretty much commonly accepted," Nader says. "The fabrications, deceptions and prevarications rise to high crimes and misdemeanors and warrant impeachment proceedings in the House of Representatives."[82]

Nader didn't clearly outline an exit plan that would avoid dire consequences, but maybe there isn't one.

<u>May 24, 2004:</u> WASHINGTON—The top U.S. officer in Iraq, Lt. Gen. Ricardo S. Sanchez, will leave his command this summer, to be replaced by Gen. George W. Casey Jr., senior Pentagon officials say.

Pentagon officials say that rotating Sanchez out of Iraq in no way reflects Sanchez's handling of the widening prisoner-abuse scandal at Abu Ghurayb prison outside of Baghdad, which was under his authority.

But this move comes only one day after the *Washington Post* announced that a captain will be testifying that Sanchez was present and knew of the abuse, and it is now unclear where Sanchez will go.[83]

<u>May 24, 2004:</u> UNITED NATIONS—The United States and Britain introduce a draft Security Council resolution that pledges a transfer of power to an interim government in Iraq on June 30.

But, while it calls for "close coordination" between Iraq's new government and the foreign troops, it does not set a date for their withdrawal or explicitly give Iraqis the power to order their departure.

France, Germany and several other Security Council countries have made it clear that they want a more precise date to reconsider the force and more direct language entitling Iraqis to order the departure of foreign troops.[84]

May 24, 2004: Michael Moore's "Fahrenheit 9/11," a scathing indictment of White House actions surrounding the Sept. 11 attacks, is the first documentary to win the Cannes Film Festival's *Palme d'Or* since Jacques Cousteau and Louis Malle's "The Silent World" in 1956. The *Palme d'Or* is the most prestigious prize at Cannes.[85]

May 25, 2004: WASHINGTON—Support for the war has hit its lowest point in California, according to a Field Poll released today.

In April 2003, 58 percent of Californians said the war was worth the costs, while 35 percent said it was not. In polling of 514 California adults from last Tuesday to Sunday, just 31 percent said the war was worth the costs and 63 percent said it was not. The margin of polling error was 4.5 percentage points.

"The war is like a ball and chain that is dragging the president down," says Field Poll director Mark DiCamillo. Women in particular were down on Iraq: just 27 percent believed it was worth the costs.

A survey released Monday by the National Annenberg Election Survey showed that just 40 percent of Americans think Iraq was worth going to war over, with 54 percent saying it wasn't. In the poll of 1,997 people, 39 percent said they approved of Bush's handling of the situation in Iraq; 57 percent disapproved.

Among Americans, nearly two-thirds believe the president does not have a clear plan for Iraq, according to the Annenberg poll.[86]

May 25, 2004: WASHINGTON—U.N. envoy Lakhdar Brahimi will soon announce the make-up of an Iraqi interim government, and nuclear scientist Hussain Shahristani, who spent a decade in the notorious Abu Ghurayb prison for refusing to participate in Saddam Hussein's nuclear program, is the leading candidate to become prime minister, U.S. officials say.

President Bush's plan for transforming Iraq meets resistance from European leaders and some Iraqis due to questions about how much control the interim government will have over Iraqi and U.S. military forces.[87]

May 25, 2004: WASHINGTON—U.S. officials have obtained new intelligence, deemed highly credible, indicating al Qaeda or other terrorists are in the United

States and preparing to launch a major attack this summer, according to the Associated Press.

Of most concern, the official says, is that terrorists may possess and use a chemical, biological or radiological weapon that could cause much more damage and casualties than a conventional bomb.

The FBI also has already created a special task force whose purpose is to ensure that no valuable bits of information or intelligence fall through the cracks—as happened repeatedly before the Sept. 11 attacks.[88]

Homeland Security Director Tom Ridge didn't even know about this news release until after it appeared on TV. With no new threat information, and Bush falling on his face in Iraq, could this merely be a political distraction?

May 25, 2004: PORTLAND, Ore.—"Some of the top economists will tell you that the global instability created by President Bush's foreign policy—the uncertainty about the Middle East—is costing us a $10 to $12 per barrel premium today," Senator John Kerry says.

"We're less safe in the world today because of what the president has done," he says. "I think we've lost allies, we've lost respect, and we've lost leverage."[89]

May 26, 2004: WASHINGTON—*The New York Times* acknowledges that its coverage of whether Saddam Hussein had weapons of mass destruction "was not as rigorous as it should have been" and "we wish we had been more aggressive in re-examining the claims as new evidence emerged—or failed to emerge."

Accounts of Iraqi defectors were not always weighed against their strong desire to have Saddam Hussein ousted. Articles based on dire claims about Iraq tended to get prominent display, while follow-up articles that called the original ones into question were sometimes buried. In some cases, there was no follow-up at all."

One of the prime sources used by the publication was Ahmed Chalabi, the Iraqi exile whose organization was subsidized by the Pentagon and who "has provided most of the front-page exclusives on WMD to our paper," according to an e-mail she sent to a colleague.[90]

May 26, 2004: WASHINGTON—U.S. Army Maj. Gen. Geoffrey Miller, dispatched by senior Pentagon officials to bolster the collection of intelligence from prisoners in Iraq last fall, inspired and promoted the use of guard dogs to frighten the Iraqis, according to sworn testimony by the top U.S. intelligence officer at the Abu Ghurayb prison.

"He said that they used military working dogs at Guantánamo Bay, Cuba, and that they were effective in setting the atmosphere for which, you know, you could get information" from the prisoners, Col. Thomas Pappas told the Army investigator, Maj. Gen. Antonio M. Taguba, according to a transcript provided to the *Washington Post.*

But Miller, whom the Bush administration appointed as the head of Abu Ghurayb this month denies, through an intermediary, that the conversation took place.[91]

May 26, 2004: WASHINGTON—The Bush administration has "openly eroded human rights" in fighting the war on terror and sparked a backlash that has made the world more dangerous, Amnesty International charges.

"As a strategy, the war on terror is bankrupt of vision and bereft of principle," asserts Amnesty's secretary-general, Irene Khan, in releasing the human rights group's annual report. She condemns terrorists and armed factions, but says governments are "losing their moral compass."

"Sacrificing human rights in the name of security at home, turning a blind eye to abuses abroad and using pre-emptive military force where and when it chooses have neither increased security nor ensured liberty," Kahn says of the United States.

The response by governments to violent groups, many of which kill civilians, has often been troubling and self-defeating, Amnesty officials say. Under cover of fighting "terrorists," many governments kill civilians and use torture and indefinite detention to challenge militants.

Amnesty challenges the Bush administration for using what it termed "indiscriminate and disproportionate means." The United States weakens international norms when it fails to honor the Geneva Convention or guarantee access to lawyers and trials.[92]

May 26, 2004: BAGHDAD, Iraq—The Pentagon leaves open the possibility that some captured fighters could be declared exempt from the Geneva Convention, the Associated Press reports.[93]

May 26, 2004: LONDON (AP)—Far from being crippled by the U.S.-led war on terror, al Qaeda has more than 18,000 potential terrorists scattered around the world and the Iraq war is swelling its ranks, a report says.

Al Qaeda is probably planning major attacks on the United States and Europe, and it may be seeking weapons of mass destruction, the International Institute of Strategic Studies says in its annual survey of world affairs.

Driving the terror network out of Afghanistan in late 2001 appears to have benefited the group, which dispersed to many countries, making it almost invisible and hard to combat, according to the survey.

The U.S. occupation of Iraq brought al Qaeda recruits from across Islamic nations. Up to 1,000 foreign Islamic fighters have infiltrated Iraqi territory, where they are cooperating with Iraqi insurgents, the survey says.

The London-based institute is considered the most important security think tank outside the United States. Its findings on al Qaeda's expanding structure and growing support by allied terrorist networks around the world comport with similar assessments from governments and other experts.[94]

May 27, 2004: The International Institute for Strategic Studies (IISS) cites evidence that Osama bin Laden and his followers hope to use nuclear or other mass destruction weapons against the United States and its close allies.

The vast and poorly guarded Russian nuclear arsenal remains at the top of the worry list. But number two is Pakistan, where a black market in nuclear materials and know-how was run by senior nuclear scientist Abdul Qadeer Khan.

Securing stockpiles of nuclear materials within Russia at the current pace, it would take 13 years to finish the job—quite possibly too late.

Funding for programs to secure nuclear weapons and materials is only about $1 billion a year. When Russian President Vladimir Putin and Bush last met, the issue wasn't even on their agenda.[95]

Funding to stir up a hornet's nest in Iraq is about $5 billion a month, 60 times what is being spent to safeguard nuclear stockpiles. President Bush's report card on the war on terror is in, and the results aren't pretty.

May 27, 2004: According to a poll commissioned in May by the Coalition Provisional Authority, only 2 percent of Iraqis view U.S.-led forces as liberators.[96]

The sequence of events ends here with plenty of evidence for drawing conclusions. The June 30, 2004 transfer of sovereignty looms as a ceremonial procedure with little hope for improved security. Over 800 Americans have died in Iraq from March 2003 through May 2004. There is no reliable count on the thousands of Iraqis, militants and civilians, who have lost their lives.

NOTES TO CHAPTER 10

1 David Crary, "Iraqi inmates were allegedly abused," *The Mercury News*, April 29, 2004, p. 8A.

2 Thom Shanker, "Pentagon: Saddam's agents to blame," *The Mercury News*, April 29, 2004, p. 1A.

3 "Poll: Iraqis Impatient With U.S. Presence," *AP*, April 29, 2004, 1:37 PM ET, http://www.nytimes.com/aponline/international/AP-Iraq-Poll.html.

4 "Major Developments in Iraq," *AP*, April 29, 2004, 12:33 PM ET, http://www.nytimes.com/aponline/international/AP-Iraq-Developments.html.

5 Julia Prodis Sulek, "Left with memories," *The Mercury News*, May 2, 2004, p. 1A.

6 AP, "Powell blames terror error on new system," *USA Today*, June 10, 2004; and Josh Meyer (LAT), "Powell vows to fix errors in '03 global terror report," *The Mercury News*, June 14, 2004, p. 10A.

7 Thom Shanker and Jacques Steinberg, "Bush vows to punish Iraqi abuse," *The Mercury News*, May 1, 2004, p. 14A.

8 Rajiv Chandrasekaran and Scott Wilson, "Saddam-era officers replace Marine units," *The Mercury News*, May 1, 2004, p. 1A.

9 Warren P. Strobel, "Triumphant mood fades amid difficulty of struggle for Iraq," *The Mercury News*, May 1, 2004, p. 1A.

10 "Troops Without Armor in Iraq," *The New York Times*, April 30, 2004, Section A, Page 26.

11 Anthony Ramirez, "National Guard Officer Offers Criticism of Bush's Iraq Plans," *The New York Times*, May 2, 2004, Section 1, Page 16.

12 Hannah Allam, "Iraqi rebels claim victory," *The Mercury News*, May 2, 2004, p. 1A.

13 Sewell Chan and Michael Amon, "Army checking charges of Iraqi prisoner abuse," *The Mercury News*, May 2, 2004, p. 16A.

14 Dexter Filkins, "U.S. hostage flees to safety of patrol," *The Mercury News*, May 3, 2004, p. 1A.

15 Ibid.

16 James Risen, "Prisoner abuse probes widen," *The Mercury News*, May 3, 2004, p. 1A.

17 Dexter Filkins, "New General to lead Iraqi force," *The Mercury News*, May 4, 2004, p. 9A.

18 Thom Shanker and Dexter Filkins, "U.S. reprimands prison supervisors," *The Mercury News*, May 4, 2004, p. 1A.

19 Steven Thomma and Hannah Allam, "U.S. cancels troop cuts," *The Mercury News*, May 5, 2004, p. 9A.

20 Shannon McCaffrey and Sumana Chatterjee, "Pentagon probes inmate deaths," *The Mercury News*, May 5, 2004, p. 1A.

21 Sewell Chan, "Iraqi prison population to be halved," *The Mercury News*, May 5, 2004, p. 10A.

22 Gail Gibson and Scott Shane, "U.S. reliance growing for private workers," *The Mercury News*, May 5, 2004, p. 8A.

23 Jim Rutenberg and Laura M. Holson, "Filmmaker rails at Disney," *The Mercury News*, May 6, 2004, p. 9A.

24 William Douglas and Carol Rosenberg, "On Arab TV, Bush concedes abuse," *The Mercury News*, May 6, 2004, p. 10A.

25 Matthew Schofield, "Iraqi abuse scandal also roiling Britain," *The Mercury News*, May 6, 2004, p. 15A.

26 Don Van Natta Jr., "Harsh tactics more routine in prisons, experts say," *The Mercury News*, May 7, 2004, p. 1AA.

27 Howard Schneider, "Arabs find photos deeply disturbing," *The Mercury News*, May 7, 2004, p. 2AA.

28 Elisabeth Bumiller and Eric Schmitt, "Bush 'sorry' for abuse, vows Rumsfeld will stay," *The Mercury News*, May 7, 2004, p. 1A.

29 James Kuhnhenn, Drew Brown and Sumana Chatterjee, "Far worse to come," *The Mercury News*, May 8, 2004, p. 1A.

30 Jackie Spinner, "MP's job: 'Make it hell so they would talk'," *The Mercury News*, May 8, 2004, p. 1A.

31 Thomas E. Ricks, "Military splits over Iraq; many blame Rumsfeld," *The Mercury News*, May 9, 2004, p. 16A.

32 Mark McDonald, "Heroin trade booms in Afghanistan," *The Mercury News*, May 9, 2004, p. 16A.

33 Dexter Filkins, "U.S. sets first trial for Iraq abuse," *The Mercury News*, May 10, 2004, p. 1A.

34 Jeffrey Smith, "Both parties criticize Pentagon for abuse; new photos surface," *The Mercury News*, May 10, 2004, p. 15A.

35 Patrick E. Tyler, "Blair apologizes for abuse," *The Mercury News*, May 10, 2004, p. 16A.

36 Dexter Filkins, "A Grisly message of revenge," *The Mercury News*, May 12, 2004, p. 1A.

37 Ron Hutcheson and James Kuhnhenn, "Bush says Rumsfeld 'doing a superb job'," *The Mercury News*, May 11, 2004, p. 1A.

38 Bob Drogin, "Red Cross report details abuse, mistaken detentions in Iraq," *The Mercury News*, May 11, 2004, p. 7A.

39 Dexter Filkins, "A Grisly message of revenge,"…

40 Eric Schmitt, "General, Pentagon aide spar over prison report," *The Mercury News*, May 12, 2004, p. 1A.

41 Jim VandeHei, "Kerry: Bush failed in Iraq," *The Mercury News*, May 13, 2004, p. 5A.

42 Sumana Chatterjee, "Tough questions about war," *The Mercury News*, May 13, 2004, p. 6A.

43 Carl Hulse and Sheryl Gay Stolberg, "Lawmakers appalled at new images of abuse," *The Mercury News*, May 13, 2004, p. 1A.

44 Carol Rosenberg, "New evidence of degradation," *The Mercury News*, May 13, 2004, p. 10A.

45 *The New York Times*, "CIA interrogation methods border on abuse," *The Mercury News*, May 13, 2004, p. 7A.

46 Eric Schmitt, "Bush seeks $25 billion more for war," *The Mercury News*, May 14, 2004, p. 5A.

47 Eric Schmitt, "Harsh interrogations banned," *The Mercury News*, May 15, 2004, p. 1A.

48 David Johnston, "Article says Rumsfeld OK'd harsh Iraq prison methods," *The Mercury News*, May 16, 2004, p. 21A.

49 Danny Hakim, "At $2 a Gallon, Gas Is Still Worth Guzzling," *The New York Times*, May 16, 2004, Section 4, Page 14.

50 Bob Drogin, "More inmate deaths emerge," *The Mercury News*, May 16, 2004, p. 1A.

51 Frank Davies, "Courts wary of unchecked power," *The Mercury News*, May 16, 2004, p. 20A.

52 Tom Hamburger, "Senators want top-level probe," *The Mercury News*, May 17, 2004, p. 1A.

53 Ian Fisher (NYT), "Leader of Iraqi council slain," *The Mercury News*, May 18, 2004, p. 1A.

54 William Branigin (WP), "Shell with nerve agent explodes near convoy," *The Mercury News*, May 18, 2004, p. 9A.

55 Esther Schrader and Barbara Demick, "Troops in S. Korea headed to Iraq," *The Mercury News*, May 18, 2004, p. 10A.

56 Eric Schmitt and Douglas Jehl (NYT), "Interrogators reportedly ordered inmates stripped," *The Mercury News*, May 18, 2004, p. 8A.

57 Carl Hulse and Christopher Marquis (NYT), "GOP divided on abuse inquiry," *The Mercury News*, May 19, 2004, p. 8A.

58 Joseph L. Galloway, "Army recalling ex-soldiers to augment Iraq shortage," *The Mercury News*, May 19, 2004, p. 9A.

59 Edward Wong (NYT), "Armies told to leave holy cities," *The Mercury News*, May 19, 2004, p. 10A.

60 Jonathon S. Landay, "Pentagon to stop funding group of Iraqi exiles," *The Mercury News*, May 19, 2004, p. 10A.

61 Scott Wilson and Sewell Chan (WP), "U.S. strikes Iraqi village, killing 40," The *Mercury News*, May 20, 2004, p. 1A.

62 Jackie Spinner (WP), "At sentencing, tearful soldier apologizes for abuse of Iraqis," *The Mercury News*, May 20, 2004, p. 1A.

63 Eric Schmitt (NYT), "Abuse reports delayed in reaching generals," *The Mercury News*, May 20, 2004, p. 18A.

64 Warren P. Strobel and Jonathon S. Landay, "Deaths may fuel perception of attack on Islam," *The Mercury News*, May 20, 2004, p. 15A.

65 Josh White and Scott Higham (WP), "Interrogators directed prison police, officer says," *The Mercury News*, May 20, 2004, p. 17A.

66 "U.S. general orders review of secret prisons," *The Mercury News*, May 20, 2004, p. 12A.

67 Hannah Allam and Robert Moran, "U.S. raids former ally's home in Iraq," *The Mercury News*, May 21, 2004, p. 1A.

68 Elisabeth Bumiller and Carl Hulse, "Bush Rallies GOP lawmakers," *The Mercury News*, May 21, 2004, p. 3A.

69 Scott Higham and Joe Stephens (WP), "Inmates detail abuse, identify U.S. soldiers," *The Mercury News*, May 21, 2004, p. 15A.

70 Warren P. Strobel and John Walcott, "Exile's aide suspected of leaking data to Iran," *The Mercury News*, May 22, 2004, p. 1A.

71 William Douglas and Joseph Galloway, "President to outline strategy for Iraq," *The Mercury News*, May 22, 2004, p. 15A.

72 Robert Moran, "Military defends airstrike in Iraq," *The Mercury News*, May 23, 2004, p. 1A

73 Michael Matza, "22 Arab leaders meet for Tunisia summit," *The Mercury News*, May 23, 2004, p. 19A.

74 Nicole C. Wong, "Nobel laureate urges U.S. to leave Iraq," *The Mercury News*, May 23, 2004, p. 1B.

75 National Center for PTSD, Department of Veterans Affairs, "The Stress of war," *The Mercury News*, May 23, 2004, p. 25A.

76 Hadi Mizban, "U.S., Iraqi forces raid mosque in Al-Kufah for weapons," *The Mercury News*, May 24, 2004, p. 9A.

77 Jonathan S. Landay, "Much is riding on Bush's speech on Iraq tonight," *The Mercury News*, May 24, 2004, p. 8A.

78 Daniel Cooney and Omar Sinan, "Death toll soars in liberated Iraq," *The Mercury News*, May 24, 2004, p. 9A.

79 Jonathan S. Landay, "Much is riding on Bush's speech on Iraq tonight,"…

80 Scheherezade Faramarzi, "Videos suggest party before attack," *The Mercury News*, May 24, 2004, p. 10A.

81 Ron Hutcheson, "Bush outlines transition for Iraq," *The Mercury News*, May 25, 2004, p. 1A.

82 Maria Recio, "Nader wants U.S. out of Iraq by year's end," *The Mercury News*, May 25, 2004, p. 6A.

83 Eric Schmitt and Thom Shanker (NYT), "Four-star general to replace top U.S. commander in Iraq," *The Mercury News*, May 25, 2004, p. 10A.

84 Warren Hoge (NYT), "U.S., Britain present power-transfer plan," *The Mercury News*, May 25, 2004, p. 10A.

85 "Michael Moore's '9/11,' big winner at Cannes, is nearer to U.S. release," *The Mercury News*, May 24, 2004, p. 2A.

86 Jim Puzzanghera, "California's war support falls drastically in poll," *The Mercury News*, May 25, 2004, p. 1A.

87 Ron Hutcheson and Warren P. Strobel, "U.N. Envoy to unveil interim leadership," *The Mercury News*, May 26, 2004, p. 1A.

88 Curt Anderson (AP), "Potential summer attack in U.S.," *The Mercury News*, May 26, 2004, p. 5A.

89 James Kuhnhenn, "Kerry launches new tour to promote U.S. security," *The Mercury News*, May 26, 2004, p. 10A.

90 Howard Kurtz (WP), "N.Y. Times regrets Iraq stories," *The Mercury News*, May 26, 2004, p. 3A.

91 R. Jeffrey Smith (WP), "Officer: General OK'd use of dogs," *The Mercury News*, May 26, 2004, p. 17A.

92 Peter Slevin (WP), "Human rights group blasts Bush's war on terror," *The Mercury News*, May 27, 2004, p. 16A.

93 Jackie Spinner, "Iraqis to take over prison operation," *The Mercury News*, May 27, 2004, p. 14A.

94 "Report: al—Qaeda Ranks Swelling Worldwide," *The Associated Press*, May 26, 2004, 12:47 a.m. ET.

95 Daniel Sneider, "War in Iraq isn't fighting terrorists, it's recruiting them," *The Mercury News*, May 27, 2004, p. 9B.

96 Richard W. Stevenson (NYT), "Panel's findings will dog Bush," *The Mercury News*, June 17, 2004, p. 22A.

PART III

THE IMPLOSION OF THE CHENEY PRESIDENCY

11

September 11—The Golden Opportunities

Both Richard Clarke and Paul O'Neill claimed that the Bush administration unduly focused on Iraq, both before and after Sept. 11, 2001, and the sequence of events supports their claim.

Paul Wolfowitz resented Clarke's focus on bin Laden prior to the attacks (events 4-2001). Counterterrorism officials in the Pentagon told the Sept. 11 commission that Rumsfeld and his aides "were not especially interested" in their agenda (events 7-5-2001).

Condoleezza Rice, the national security advisor to the President, has virtually no public comments about al Qaeda prior to Sept. 11 to point to as evidence that she was as engaged in the terrorism issue as she was in Bush's other foreign-policy agendas. Primarily a Europeanist, she was missing more than a background on counterterrorism, she was also missing interest in it, as her conversation with Gary Hart (events 9-6-2001) revealed.

Senator Dianne Feinstein's request for a meeting with Vice President Cheney demonstrated a similar lack of interest (events 9-10-01).

Right after the Sept. 11 attacks, Secretary of Defense Donald Rumsfeld was more anxious to attack Iraq than get involved with the terrorists responsible (events 9-12-2001). And Bob Woodward exposed the extent to which Vice President Cheney was in a "fever" over attacking Iraq (events 2002-2003).

Condoleezza Rice claimed that there was no "silver bullet" that would have allowed the administration to protect America from the attacks. However, many golden opportunities did show up in the sequence of events, any one of which, with proper follow through, could have either foiled the plot or at least offered a greater level of protection for America.

The FBI received information that unidentified Arabs planned to fly an "explosive-laden plane" from an unnamed country into the World Trade Center (events 8-1998). Along with many similar threats, this was a clue for anyone interested in national security that terrorists might use a plane as a missile and they might strike the WTC.

Dropping the ball—Operations level

1. Two of the hijackers aboard American Airlines Flight 77, which hit the Pentagon, were located in January 2000 in Kuala Lumpur, Malaysia. The CIA says it warned the FBI, but neither agency places either of them on a watch list until August 2001 (events 1-2000).

2. An Iranian in custody in New York City told local police of a plot to attack the World Trade Center (events 5-2001).

3. Someone called the U.S. Embassy in the United Arab Emirates saying that a group of bin Laden supporters was in the U.S. planning attacks with explosives. The CIA and the FBI were still investigating this lead in August 2001 and didn't make any progress or suggest any protective measures before the Sept. 11 attacks occurred, indicating a lax attitude regarding the threat of a terrorist attack (events 5-2001).

4. Four men are convicted in the bombings of U.S. embassies in Kenya and Tanzania. Witnesses testified at the trial that Osama bin Laden was sending al Qaeda agents to the United States for flight-school training and acquiring planes (events 5-29-2001).

5. Pakistanis were taken into custody in the Cayman Islands after they were overheard discussing hijacking attacks in New York City; they were questioned and released, and the information was forwarded to U.S. intelligence (events 6-4-2001).

6. CIA and FBI meet to go over surveillance of the Malaysia meeting. New York-based FBI Cole investigators are not shown a photograph of Khallad, a USS *Cole* bombing suspect. "…June meeting when three but not all of the photographs were disclosed to FBI agents, and the subsequent description of those events—if all of that had worked the way it could have worked…you could have had a completely different result."—Louis J. Freeh, former FBI Director (events 6-2001).

7.   German intelligence alerted the U.S. CIA, Britain's MI-6, and Israel's Mossad that Middle Eastern terrorists were training for hijackings and targeting American and Israeli interests (events 6-2001).

8.   FBI Agent Ken Williams sends a memo to the counterterrorism division at the FBI's Washington headquarters. It outlines a theory that Middle Eastern students at an Arizona flight school could be al Qaeda agents training for hijackings. FBI analysts review the memo but do nothing. The White House, FBI Director Robert Mueller, and Attorney General John Ashcroft are informed about the memo only after the September 11 attacks (events 7-10-2001).

9.   British intelligence shared "general" information that it had learned through surveillance of Khalid al-Fawwaz, a Saudi Arabian dissident who has publicly acknowledged being a bin Laden operative. Fawwaz, suspected of participating in the 1998 U.S. embassy bombing in Kenya, wasn't arrested until after Sept. 11 (events 7,8-2001).

10. "…all it had to do was put this [Moussaoui] on Intelink. All it had to do was is go out on Intelink and the game's over. It ends. And this conspiracy rolls up." Bob Kerrey, Sept. 11 Commission, former senator from Nebraska (events 8-2001).

11. The FBI is not able to find Khalid al-Midhar or Nawaf Alhamzi. "Had I been informed by the FBI that two senior al Qaeda operatives that had been in a planning meeting earlier in Kuala Lumpur were now in the United States…I would like to think that I would have…tried to get their names and pictures on the front page of every paper…and caused a successful nationwide manhunt for these two, two of the 19 hijackers."—Richard A. Clarke, former counterterrorism advisor (events 8-2001).

12. U.S. investigators confirmed in October that a 29-year-old Iranian in custody in Germany's Langenhagen prison last year made phone calls to U.S. police from his deportation cell that an attack on the World Trade Center was imminent in "the days before the attack." The warning was considered the threat of a madman (events Early 9-2001).

Many FBI agents, CIA agents, and police officers were not privy to the hundreds of threat warnings. What if President Bush and Vice President Cheney were as impassioned about the impending terror threat as they were about attacking Iraq? Would the operating levels of government have focused more and followed through more on possible terror threats? Would the Sept. 11 story have ended differently?

Dropping the ball—Higher level

An FBI agent in Minneapolis, Minnesota writes a memo to headquarters suggesting Zacarias Moussaoui is training to learn to fly planes into buildings. The agent "mentioned the possibility of Moussaoui being that type of person that could fly something into the World Trade Center," FBI Director Robert Mueller later tells Congress. The FBI notifies the CIA about Moussaoui, but neither agency tells the White House Counterterrorism Security Group. The Federal Aviation Administration, also told about Moussaoui, decides not to warn airlines about a possible threat, an FAA official says (events Early 9-2001).

Dropping the ball—Commander in Chief

1. Bob Woodward unveiled documents on February 28, 2004 that reveal that President Bush neglected to address CIA Director George Tenet's January 2001 warnings about the menace of Osama bin Laden and the proliferation of Weapons of Mass Destruction (WMD). Nothing was done to reckon with bin Laden's threats. Woodward summarizes, "He dropped the ball" (events 1-2001).

2. President Bush rejected the recommendation for a Department of Homeland Security from the U.S. Commission on National Security report he received in January 2001 (events 1-31-2001). Not until it was too late, after the horrific Sept. 11 attacks, did he change his mind and create the department (events 10-8-2001).

3. In more than 40 briefings, President Bush was told by CIA Director George Tenet of terror threats involving al Qaeda (events 7-5-2001). According to Condoleezza Rice, CIA Director George Tenet took his terror warnings directly to President Bush. Mr. Tenet said in July, "The system was blinking red." Did the President show any interest in protecting America (events 7-2001)?

4. At this time, the U.S. Sky Marshal program was not active for domestic flights. Even though hijacking U.S. planes for attacks against America

was mentioned twice in his August 6, 2001 brief, and in countless previous threats, President Bush was not motivated to even strengthen the sky marshal program, a minimal response to such an ominous brief. With all of the al Qaeda interest and prior threat warnings in hijacking and airports, shouldn't some of the September 26, 2001 security measures have started after this brief instead of waiting until after the attacks (events 8-6-2001)?

5. After reading the 8-6-2001 brief, President Bush was still not motivated to have his first cabinet-level meeting on the terror threat from al Qaeda. He saw no reason to make protecting America a cabinet-level priority (events 8-6-2001).

6. President Bush reviewed the Aug. 6th PDB while vacationing in Crawford, Texas. After receiving the warnings, he continued his 30-day vacation, the longest presidential vacation in U.S. history (events 8-6-2001).

All the Bush administration did was issue low-level FAA warnings without any presidential punch, and after time, warning fatigue diminished the impact of the casual notices. On a scale from 1 (totally inept) to 10 (exceptional brilliant), the administration's performance, and especially the Commander in Chief's performance, yields a negative number. This lame effort is so far off the chart, it can't be explained by incompetence alone. There had to be another factor, a powerful force, that distracted the top echelon of the Bush administration with such a fervor, that there was insufficient energy and focus left to address the persistent stream of dire warnings leading up to the attacks.

And there was.

12

Comparing Iraq to Vietnam

History has a nasty habit of repeating itself.

But which model will the occupation of Iraq follow? The allied occupations of Japan and Germany following World War II, which were successful? Or the quagmire in Vietnam that offered no opportunity for success? If the Persian Gulf War had nothing in common with the U.S. intervention in Vietnam, then why would the second war against Iraq be any different? Does military supremacy always deliver a successful mission?

The best model for predicting how an occupation of Iraq by a Western power in 2003 might turn out would undoubtedly be the occupation of Iraq by the British in 1917 under very similar circumstances—and it doesn't offer much encouragement (events 1917 & 2003).

Answering the above questions becomes clearer when viewing through the lenses of moral authority and legitimacy. Does Pearl Harbor ring a bell? Have we forgotten Germany's march through Europe and the Holocaust? Germany and Japan wreaked worldwide havoc, and after four very painful years, the Allied powers had full legitimacy in splitting up Germany, demilitarizing Japan, and occupying both countries until satisfactory replacement governments took hold.

In the Persian Gulf War, Iraq invaded Kuwait and the Kuwaitis fully supported outside intervention to drive Saddam's army out of their county. Several Arab nations were part of the coalition joining the U.S., and the cost of the operation was spread across many nations. When the invaders were driven out of Kuwait, the foreigners left the country. By not marching into Baghdad to force a regime change, the first President Bush completed a legitimate and successful mission. There was no messy occupation with unwanted foreign troops getting picked off.

Saddam Hussein's ruthlessness provided the only hint of legitimacy for an outside power to invade Iraq and impose a regime change, and the celebration after the fall of Baghdad revealed the joy of his removal that many Iraqis shared.

From all other perspectives, the preemptive invasion of Iraq paints an extremely ugly picture.

Saddam offered to allow 5,000 U.S. troops to march through his country at will in search of weapons of mass destruction, but there was no interest in this offer. Iraq never did threaten the security of the U.S. and removing weapons wasn't the driving force for the invasion. Purging weapons while leaving Saddam in charge wouldn't yield the corporate profits that Cheney was seeking.

The lack of interest in merely removing illicit weapons, the fact that frightening stockpiles of such weapons were never found, the nasty presence of imperialism and cronyism with the contracting, the absence of any connection between Saddam Hussein and the Sept. 11 attacks, and the arrogance and fabricated propaganda that led up to the 2003 invasion all undermined any and all moral authority that the Bush administration might have been seeking. If we learned nothing else about the experience in Vietnam, it is that propaganda is not a valid substitute for legitimacy.

And the prisoner abuse scandal was the final insult that obliterated any hope for legitimacy in the occupation.

The American interventions in Vietnam and the 2003 invasion of Iraq have many similarities and many differences.

Differences—Offering some hope for success

1.   The billions of U.S. dollars going into the *rebuilding* of Iraq dwarf anything spent for such purposes during the Vietnam War. Over a decade of sanctions left Iraq's economy and infrastructure in shambles, and most of what was still working was bombed in the U.S. invasion. Iraqis understood the benefit of the rebuilding projects, which were a very positive force in the effort to win the "hearts and minds" of the Iraqis. However, sabotage from the insurgency continues, and persistent security problems have stopped many of the reconstruction projects in their tracks. The higher priority projects that continue have 25% of their costs going to security—and they hope that is enough. While still a significant positive factor, the billions for rebuilding just weren't enough to overcome the many other negative factors.

2.   In Iraq, a *ruthless dictator* who was despised by two of the three factions was removed providing an initial boost to the effort to win the "hearts and minds" of the Iraqi people that was never present in Vietnam. In

April 2003, American troops were viewed to be liberators by some who despised Saddam Hussein. However, the fall of Baghdad was a humiliating experience for many Iraqis, and the joy of Saddam's removal gave way over time to a strong undercurrent of nationalism—totally unexpected by the Bush administration. And as the factions competed for power, there was less and less focus on Saddam Hussein's absence. It was a done deal. By May 2004, only two percent of the Iraqis viewed the U.S.-led troops as liberators (May 27, 2004). Instead, the foreigners were almost universally perceived as invaders and unwelcome occupiers.

3. One fourth of the soldiers sent to Vietnam were *drafted*, which added to the opposition to the war (events 4-18-2004). The draft also resulted in "fragging," where Americans were killing each other on the battlefield (events 1969-1973). There are no draftees being sent to Iraq—so far.

4. North Vietnam was supplied by and supported by *China and Russia*. While Iraq isn't getting military resources or support from a major power, the insurgents don't appear to have any problem obtaining weapons to disrupt the occupation. China's involvement might have prevented the U.S. from marching soldiers into Hanoi, but conquering Baghdad and capturing Saddam provides a glimpse of what it would have been like for U.S. troops to takeover Hanoi. How much did this action help secure peace in Iraq? Did the guerilla war go away?

5. North Vietnam represented a *unified opposition* that is not present in Iraq after Saddam was quickly removed from power. In North Vietnam, the dictator was respected, where in Iraq, Saddam was feared, and to a great extent despised. It should be noted that Iran is a potential, if not already actual, source of unified opposition to U.S. actions in Iraq. Also, it's not clear that the absence of a centralized opposition would have delivered any meaningful improvement in the Vietnam effort. It has been the nagging decentralized opposition of guerilla warfare that most frustrated U.S. troops in both wars.

6. *Scale*: The Vietnam conflict lasted over 10 years, with escalating troop strength reaching 542,000 in 1969, and more than 47,000 Americans killed in action. In its first 16 months, the troop strength in Iraq has risen to 138,000 and is escalating, and over 800 Americans have been killed in action—so far (through May 2004). Note that both the troop strength and casualties do not include other coalition countries or the

growing number of private contractors. It will take much more time for the numbers in Iraq to challenge the numbers from Vietnam—if U.S. presidents continue the occupation. In order for the killed in action to catch up with Vietnam, it will also take more troops. It is difficult for the insurgents to kill the young Americans that aren't placed in front of them.

Difference—Impact Unclear

In Vietnam, the U.S. replaced the French in a country that was sliced in half, leaving the northern half with a functioning government, a popular leader, and a standing army. The U.S. frequently bombed the northern cities, sprayed tons of chemicals on the South, occupied the South with a half million foreign soldiers, and turned out to be an unwelcome visitor in both halves—except for the puppet government in the South.

In Iraq, the U.S. invaded an entire nation, deposed its unpopular dictator, occupied the entire nation with fewer foreign soldiers, and turned out to be an unwelcome visitor—except for the puppet government and the Kurdish faction in the north, which has and needs minimal occupation.

Similarities of the interventions in Vietnam and Iraq

1. The U.S. invades a foreign country promising freedom, but *lacking political legitimacy.* In Iraq, the illicit weapons aren't found, and the connection to Sept. 11 never existed. In Vietnam, the dubious "domino theory"—inspired by the McCarthyism Era—was more fiction than reality.

2. *International opposition* further weakens legitimacy. In both cases the U.S. is unable to gain support from a majority of the U.N. Security Council and most nations oppose the military action. More countries have assisted with the U.S. intervention in Iraq, but their involvement is minimal and declining. Even most populations of the cooperating countries are decidedly against the U.S. agenda, placing their governments in jeopardy. Primary ally Britain reduces troops from 26,000 to 8,200, while U.S. troop strength is escalating. This absence of international support denies the U.S. the luxury of time to properly complete nation

building, in stark contrast to the nation building in Japan and Germany following World War II.

3.   There is a *puppet government* propped up by a foreign power, becoming tainted and illegitimate due to this outside affiliation, and therefore not accepted by the people. And the will of the indigenous population is the ultimate determinate of success or failure with nation building. A no-win situation develops where a premature withdrawal creates a security vacuum, but a prolonged presence de-legitimizes the local government, and also triggers security problems.

4.   *Nationalism* spurs anger at the foreign occupiers, viewed by many local people as imperialists, and foments opposition. There is always more political will to defend one's own country (Iraqis and Vietnamese won't give up, prefer endless war to defeat) as opposed to intervening in a far-away country's business (foreign occupiers would rather leave than have endless war). The U.S. misunderstood the culture of a foreign country and the damage caused by denying self-determination. The Vietnamese were one culture and didn't want to be "sliced in half." The Iraqis don't want a western superpower telling them how they should be governed. Neither the Vietnamese nor the Iraqis accepted the Americans with open arms.

5.   U.S. *military superiority* is not in doubt. The U.S. would win any battle involving conventional warfare, whether it's against the North Vietnamese army, the Viet Cong, or Iraq's army.

6.   Due to military inferiority, the local opposition shifts strategy and the conflict degenerates into *guerilla warfare*, where U.S. forces are challenged to distinguish between friend and foe. Military superiority becomes irrelevant against "hit and run" tactics, especially when the foreign power is constrained and must win the "hearts and minds" of the local population for nation building.

7.   The frustration of fighting a guerilla war without knowing who is friend or foe yields high *suicide rates*. There was a rate of 15.6/100,000 soldiers in Vietnam, and even worse 17.3/100,000 soldiers in Iraq—where the more conventional First Gulf War lost only 3.6/100,000 soldiers to suicide (events 5-23-2004).

8. Even though the militant opposition represents only a small percentage of the occupied population, U.S. forces suffer casualties almost daily with *little visible progress* on winning the peace, creating an appearance of a hopelessly permanent conflict.

9. When there are ongoing *civilian casualties*, whether due to collateral damage from U.S. military operations or from opposition insurgents, it is difficult for U.S. forces to win the "hearts and minds" of the people, which is a prerequisite for providing security and nation building.

10. There is debate about whether *more troops* would provide better pacification, or lead to more casualties. And then, more troops are added to the conflict.

11. How many times during the Vietnam War were Americans told, "Victory is just around the corner?" With Iraq, we hear the need to *"stay the course"* and that "progress is being made," even when the situation is rapidly deteriorating.

Differences—Quagmire More Likely

1. America's role in the Holy Land conflict in the past five decades created a strong negative image among Arabs and Muslims, even before the first bomb was dropped in Iraq. This *lack of credibility* with the Iraqi people frustrated the nation building effort, which requires a high level of trust. In Vietnam, there was little challenge of this nature.

2. Images of Iraqi civilian casualties on *Arab TV* create a greater challenge than any negative publicity in the Vietnam conflict. The prisoner abuse scandal magnified this negative publicity factor to the point of no foreseeable recovery. This phenomenon constrained U.S. military actions more than China did in the Vietnam conflict.

3. Iraq has three *major incompatible factions*, which makes nation building a greater challenge, even if the U.S. did have credibility with the local population from the beginning. Saddam's unusually long run atop this country might be evidence that only a ruthless dictator could hold these diverse factions together in a manner that had some semblance of political stability.

4. There was less conventional warfare in Iraq where the conflict quickly became entirely guerilla warfare, primarily *urban warfare*, which creates more civilian casualties and is more difficult to prosecute than in Vietnam where some opportunities in major offensives allowed U.S. military superiority to matter.

5. With Iraq, *foreign terrorists* and porous borders provide plenty of reinforcements for the resistance, creating a more vexing challenge than support from other governments that can be confronted by a superpower. The brash invitation by President Bush to "Bring them on!" provided further encouragement for this source of the opposition. The worst-case scenario is still possible. The violence could explode into a full-scale Jihad (Holy War).

6. The natural resources in Vietnam are of comparatively minimal value. The presence of *vast oil reserves* in Iraq, fervent U.S. protection of all oil facilities, American control of all funds resulting from oil sales, and vast sums of money made by politically well-connected American contractors due to the war all make it extremely difficult to convince the local population that the American involvement in Iraq has nothing to do with imperialism. As the troops from countries without an imperialist agenda withdraw while U.S. troops escalate, the sting of resentment gets even stronger.

7. The prospects for success in Iraq are substantially inferior to Vietnam due to the *ineptness* of the neocons making the battle decisions in the Bush administration. This problem could be expected to disappear if Bush is voted out of office, but until then, the two dozen blunders documented in Chapter 14 cannot be ignored.

8. The net impact of the Vietnam exit—albeit somewhat messy and embarrassing—was that Vietnam regained sovereignty from foreign occupiers, obtained security and peace, and was politically stabilized. No public figure has since suggested that it would be a good idea to slice Vietnam in half once again, and prop up another puppet government in the southern half.

The *exit chaos* from Iraq would dwarf that of Vietnam, with sectarian civil war likely as the factions joust for power, possibly destabilizing neighboring countries in a region already overloaded with tension, and very likely endangering the flow of oil for years. The collapse of Iraq would threaten the world economy. What will happen in the next 5, 10, 20 years that will suddenly make this exit chaos not a problem?

Due to the extent of this exit chaos, few public figures have the courage to declare that we should get out of Iraq immediately. The dismal scenario that a withdrawal creates is the clincher. The prisoner abuse scandal is huge, but even putting it aside, the Iraq war is worse than Vietnam because this time—there is no damage-free exit.

A Look at the Criteria for Military Intervention

The Vietnam War, the Persian Gulf War, and the Iraq war are put to President Clinton's criteria for military intervention, which yields more clues on how the second conflict with Iraq might pan out.

1. Clear mission objectives:

   The first Gulf War had a clear mission—drive Iraq's army out of Kuwait.

   The Vietnam War and the second war with Iraq both involved the messy process of occupying a local population in the hopes of forcing them to accept a government propped up by foreigners.

2. Palpable danger to international peace:

   In the first Gulf War, Iraq had invaded Kuwait, abusing both its sovereignty and its citizens.

   With Vietnam it was the dubious "domino theory," a throwback to the McCarthyism Era, which had no connection to reality and never materialized.

   With the second war with Iraq, it was suspicious claims of weapons that never were found and links to Sept. 11 that didn't exist, both based on fabricated intelligence and neocon propaganda.

3. Clear exit strategy:

   The first Gulf War had a clear exit option when Iraq's army was expelled from Kuwait—and there was no attempt to march troops into Baghdad to overthrow Saddam's government.

The Vietnam War and the second war with Iraq both had exit strategies based solely on wishful thinking with an exit from the second war with Iraq offering the most dangerous consequences of all.

4.   Calculable costs:

In the first Gulf War, driving Iraq's army out of Kuwait had calculable costs, and they were shared by other countries, including Arab countries.

With the Vietnam War and the second war with Iraq, no one knew how many troops would be sufficient or how long the mission would take. There would be no way to compute even a rough estimate of the costs—either financially or in terms of casualties.

Regime change—whether in Vietnam or Iraq—requires winning the war and winning the peace. For a superpower intervening in a third world country, the first part—the only part the Bush administration focused on—is easy, but the latter objective can prove to be out of reach—bogging down into guerilla warfare that just won't quit. It might be a misunderstanding of a different culture. It might be intentions that lack nobility. It might be a country with such contentious factions that it could only be secured by ruthless leadership. It might be all three.

The only defendable position on Iraq in 2003 was to work with the U.N.—the bane of the neocons—and definitely not to invade Iraq alone or with a coalition that was merely window dressing. But President Bush obliterated that alternative. Now, there are very few remaining palatable options for Iraq.

The U.S. policy makers should have known better. Bush had the advantage of the Vietnam experience—a superpower imposing a puppet government on a smaller country can easily lead to a quagmire—as a warning. He also had Colin Powell's "Pottery Barn rule" as a warning, but just like the avalanche of the Sept. 11 terror warnings, he ignored any and all danger signs.

Would a Different Approach Offer Some Hope?

Could it be that the fractious combination of various ethnic groups, influential clerics, and the multitude of tribes in Iraq could only be held together by a ruthless regime? Even entering Iraq with legitimacy wouldn't create an easy nation building experience if this entire country were to be swallowed in one gulp. And expecting democracy to flourish where autocratic rule has been a cultural reality for centuries might not be realistic. A different approach could be considered.

One alternative would be to partition Iraq into three countries in order to split up the three major factions.

Carve out the northern portion of Iraq and establish Kurdistan, which is what the Kurds have wanted for many years. Their army, the *pesh merga*, has provided excellent security in northern Iraq. They have essentially been autonomous since 1991 and they had already created a free, democratic mini-state within Saddam's Iraq. Their desire for autonomy within Iraq is an irritant to the other factions so let them have their own state.

The Kurdish population has their own language and a strong sense of nationalism. They are fully supportive of the mission of statehood and are more culturally prepared for a secular democratic state than the Sunnis or the Shiites, yielding a higher probability for success. There would be fewer security problems and fewer troops would be required for pacification because they already have a militia.

While easier than trying to pacify Iraq in its entirety, this move would still have many challenges. The city of Kirkuk has a population of one million including Kurds, Arabs, Turkmen, and Assyrian Christians. Over the years, Saddam Hussein's ethnic cleansing had disrupted this mixture by driving out thousands of Kurds and replacing them with Arabs. The return of the displaced Kurds has generated some friction, and politically, each faction has little trust for the others. The Sunnis and Shiites might send in militias to challenge Kurdistan, especially if it means the Kurds will gain control of the oil fields in the north. Most of the 25 million Kurds in the Middle East aren't even in Iraq. Turkey, Syria, Iran, and Azerbaijan have significant Kurdish populations. These countries, along with a Kurdish-free Iraq, could be expected to be hostile to a new land-locked Kurdistan. And with so many Kurds currently settled in surrounding countries, population shifts, reverse ethnic cleansing, and boundary-line issues could complicate relations for years.

Nevertheless, it is extremely unlikely that there will be anything resembling political stability in the region until the 25 million Kurds finally achieve the self-determination they have craved for decades.

Carving off the southern portion of Iraq for a Shiite nation would be the next step. The Shiites feel very strongly about creating an Islamic state, but possibly a stable and peaceful one. Self-determination is crucial to success, so a compromise might be a necessary factor with this move.

The Sunni triangle would be saved for last since Saddam's former stronghold is the most contentious. During the Iraq war, it was apparent the Sunnis didn't want the table turned on them with the Shiites—60% of the total Iraqi population—controlling a democracy. But with Saddam, the Shiites and the Kurds out of the picture, the Sunnis would have much less to fear. If U.S. troops vacated the other two new nations formed from Iraq, the Sunnis might trust that the foreign occupation for them also wouldn't be permanent. One obstacle that would need to be resolved is the fact that the Sunni triangle is also land-locked. Another potential challenge is that the Sunni nation may end up with the least oil reserves of the three new countries.

Ideally, the above three steps would be taken one at a time. However, since the 2003 invasion opened the entire can of worms, the three moves would have to be handled simultaneously.

Attempts at nation building would need to avoid any suspicion of imperialism and the other blunders such as harsh treatment of detainees, closing newspapers or significant civilian casualties. A complete U.S. corporate withdrawal would be mandatory to gain the trust of the local population, which is essential.

However, even this alternative has the above-mentioned hurdles. Achieving political stability in the Middle East is an extremely challenging goal, and the U.S. has precious little of the needed credibility to sponsor a major change. The only way to make this approach look good is to compare it to the approach that President Bush has been pursuing.

Presidential candidate John Kerry promoted internationalizing the effort, getting the U.N. to be in charge and NATO forces providing security. This would be a good direction to pursue because the U.N. has greater legitimacy than the U.S. in Iraq as well as in the entire Middle East. Unfortunately, while this option might have been available to the Bush administration early on, the situation has degenerated to the point that few other nations are willing to increase their involvement.

The Bush administration has lobbied for the assistance of more nations and made concessions to achieve an appearance of broad international support. But for any possibility of success in internationalizing the Iraq war, full decision-making power would have to be shared only between the U.N. and the Iraqis, with the U.S. relinquishing its military command. This is not an option in the Bush administration.

The U.S. would also have to execute a complete corporate withdrawal. Under no circumstances would the Iraqis accept that U.S. intentions are altruistic if

Bechtel and Halliburton are still in their country reaping billions. This is also not an option in the Bush administration. Dick Cheney wouldn't permit it.

For a meaningful chance at success, the war in Iraq would have to be fully internationalized, there would have to be a complete U.S. corporate withdrawal, and Iraq would need to be partitioned.

The Exit after Trying to Build a New Iraq in "One Gulp"

Trying to hold all of Iraq together and hoping for peace is an exercise in futility. If the competing factions ever settle down with the U.S. troops still inside Iraq, they would only be waiting for the foreigners to leave. Then the real war would begin—a civil war over political power and oil revenue. And the Jihadists aren't likely to allow the violence to subside while U.S. troops and corporations are still occupying an Arab country.

The exit from Iraq following the Bush plan will very likely be a disaster leading to a civil war inside Iraq, the destabilization of neighboring countries, the interruption of the flow of oil, and the disruption of the world economy. And there is no indication that an exit will become any less severe at any date in the future. But how long will Americans permit the continuation of useless violence and the steady stream of coffins coming home? So at some point, an American president will have to essentially admit failure by withdrawing the U.S. troops.

This will not happen as long as George W. Bush is president. He will never confirm that his invasion of Iraq was a mistake of this magnitude. He refuses to admit to any of his many mistakes.

As long as the U.S. has troops and corporations in an Arab country with incompatible factions, the other nations of the world will just sit back and let America wallow in its own quagmire.

Let's face it. This time we're really stuck!

13

Reviewing the Justifications

There never was any intention to launch a surprise attack. If the justifications for invading Iraq were valid, why was the planning for war (events 11-21-2001 and 12-2001) so secretive? President Bush claimed that he didn't want to appear anxious for war, and he didn't want to stir up international angst when "war is my absolute last option..." However, the secrecy and the sequence of events raise concerns about the motivation for war.

As soon as President Bush took office, and even more so after the Sept. 11 attacks, Bush, Defense Secretary Rumsfeld, Paul Wolfowitz, Richard Armitage, many more neocons, and especially Vice President Cheney all appeared to be obsessed with attacking Iraq. These dominant players were determined to let no alternative evidence rise to the surface, except for allegations that would justify going to war.

A review of the 14 possible motivations for war should help explain the obsession in the Bush administration for launching an expensive and life-threatening attack on Iraq:

[1] <u>The concern about the proliferation of weapons of mass destruction</u>

America supported Saddam Hussein until August 1990, when U.S. foreign policy towards Iraq changed 180 degrees—and for the first time, advocated regime change in Iraq.

However, the prolonged use of chemical weapons against Iran (events 1980's) and the considerable brutal repression and the use of chemicals on the Kurds (events 3-16-1988) in his own country were insufficient to turn U.S. foreign policy against Saddam Hussein during those years. It is important to note that the Republican neoconservative ideology was dominant both then and now. President Reagan (hero of the neocons), the first President Bush, Donald Rumsfeld, Dick Cheney, Richard Armitage, Paul Wolfowitz, Douglas Feith and George

Shultz were all in some high-level position of power during the 1980's when the U.S. supported Saddam and his buildup of weapons of mass destruction (WMD). The second Bush presidency also contained Dick Cheney, Donald Rumsfeld, Richard Armitage, Paul Wolfowitz, and Douglas Feith and had George Shultz waiting in the wings for Bechtel contracts.

The atrocities cited during the march to the Iraq war were historical in nature, and if a response to them were justified, does it make sense that it happens 15 years later—especially when many of the current principals were in high government positions during the actual time frame of the offending events?

U.S. intelligence agencies had few if any independent sources of information in Iraq. Without its own sources of information, the United States came to rely increasingly on Iraqi exiles and Kurds living in areas of Iraq that had been under U.S. protection. However, intelligence professionals at the CIA, the Defense Intelligence Agency and the State Department regarded many of the exiles, particularly Ahmed Chalabi and his Iraqi National Congress, with disdain. Much of their information has been found to be marginal at best, and frequently exaggerated or fabricated. CIA Director George Tenet has acknowledged that official government assessments of Iraq included information from known fabricators and has promised an investigation (events 2-5-2003).

Iraq's weapons programs had been more than marginalized by the First Gulf War. They had been completely destroyed. And the West had no hard evidence to the contrary. The report from David Kay confirmed that Saddam had no illicit weapons (events 1-23-2004), and the U.N. inspectors, assisted by U.S. intelligence assets, were on the way to prove it in March 2003 when they were kicked out due to the impending invasion.

When an attack was imminent, Saddam offered to let 5,000 U.S. troops enter Iraq and look for themselves (events February 2003), but the Bush administration reacted to these events with an increased sense of urgency to launch the attack on Iraq before this important WMD justification for war completely slipped away.

The reason?

It didn't matter what weapons Iraq did or did not have. The Bush administration was determined to invade Iraq and depose Saddam Hussein. There was no level of cooperation that could substitute for the regime change that was considered mandatory.

Weapons of mass destruction have been forbidden in the Middle East for many years. If non-proliferation is the concern, what about the other countries? Israel has had nuclear, biological and chemical weapons for decades. Pakistan has had nuclear weapons for decades, and we knew it was selling this technology to other rogue nations. Iran and North Korea had nuclear programs that were well ahead of Iraq's non-existent program.

How did Iraq jump to the top of the list?

The deal with the guilty scientist Kahn in Pakistan (events 2-4-2004) and the U.S. reward for Pakistan (events 3-18-2004) further undercut the WMD factor as a justification. By supporting Pakistan after its multi-decade nuclear weapons proliferation programs supplying Iran, Libya, and North Korea were uncovered, and rewarding this behavior with loans and new weapons; the Bush administration demonstrates a low priority with respect to the proliferation of weapons of mass destruction. The higher priority went to finding bin Laden in order to improve Bush's reelection chances.

It was convenient for the Bush administration that Saddam Hussein had waged chemical warfare in the past, and due to failed intelligence some believed that Iraq still had some illicit weapons. However, Dick Cheney's meddling with the CIA on this issue, and his role in supporting the fabricated INC intelligence that was funneled to the media are telling indications of deception. There is no doubt that the hawks wanted to use the WMD issue in order to sell the war to the public.

If WMD were found, Bush would have been lucky and probably gotten away with a plausible justification for war that really didn't matter that much to the hawks who pressed for regime change. And as much as the neocons would like to reverse course this time around and claim the high moral ground on illicit weapons, the presence or absence of WMD was clearly not the motivation for this administration's march to war.

We will need to look further.

[2] <u>The link between Iraq, al Qaeda, and the September 11, 2001 attacks</u>

We have learned that the Bush administration was focused on attacking Iraq from the very beginning, but there were no concrete actions prior to the Sept. 11 attacks. What a perfect fit it would be if the attacks could be the pretext for regime change in Iraq that was wanted all along. Not surprisingly, the justification for invading Iraq that President Bush wanted above all others was that Saddam Hussein was somehow involved with the Sept. 11 attacks. His pressing Richard Clarke for this connection on the very next day (events 9-12-2001) was anything but subtle.

Few initiatives in the White House received as much energy as the drive to find a link between Iraq and al Qaeda. It was an all-agency effort, and anything that could be construed as a link was pounced upon and served up to the media. Whenever Bush was selling war with Iraq, he would frequently mention the Sept. 11 attacks implying—if not insisting—that a clear connection was there.

A connection was never found.

Unlike with the WMD issue, weak intelligence was not a significant factor with this incorrect justification. It was the politicizing of intelligence that played the prominent role—and it hit an historical peak. For counterterrorism experts, the notion of a link between the secular dictator and an Islamist terrorist was so unlikely that it didn't even warrant a search. In addition, evidence supporting the absence of a link was found on Saddam Hussein when he was arrested (events 1-14-2004). But the administration got what it wanted even though the connection never existed.

A *New York Times*/CBS poll (events 3-14-2003) showed that 45 percent of Americans believed Saddam Hussein was "personally involved" in the Sept. 11 attacks. The administration didn't need to find a link to the dictator. The campaign to sell the link was a huge success even without any accurate intelligence to back it up. The massive propaganda campaign with fabricated evidence of connections between Saddam and the terrorists, much of it taxpayer financed, achieved what the hawks wanted.

While Dick Cheney may still be obsessed with promoting this connection, President Bush conceded after the war was already underway—what his administration knew before the war started—that there was no link between Saddam Hussein and the terrorists behind the Sept. 11 attacks.

There may have appeared to be some confusion, but this was not in any way a motivation for the war.

[3] <u>Saddam was a ruthless dictator.</u>

When the first two justifications evaporated, President Bush needed to fill the vacuum. No problem. Saddam Hussein had other available sins to offer. He was a ruthless dictator that routinely tortured political prisoners. He had used poison gas—even on Iraqi citizens—the rebelling Kurds. His behavior and the war on terror gradually became the primary reasons offered by the Bush administration for the war, and few people stepped forward to proclaim that Saddam was really a nice guy who should remain in power.

One of the problems with this backup option is that the world has many ruthless dictators. Just before the invasion in 2003, *Parade* magazine listed the 10 worst dictators and Saddam Hussein came in third. Bush decided to skip number one, Kim Jong II of North Korea, and two, Crown Prince Abdullah of Saudi Arabia, when Saddam was selected for removal. And no one else on the list seemed to be of interest (events 2-2003).

How does Saddam Hussein get selected for removal?

The most curious discrepancy is Bush's complete acceptance of Crown Prince Abdullah versus his demand that Saddam Hussein must be removed. Could this have anything to do with the fact that American oil companies had many lucrative business arrangements with Saudi Arabia in 2003, but none with Iraq?

The bloodshed in the Congo was the largest human catastrophe during the 2003 invasion of Iraq with 3.5 million dead so far, but the Bush administration shows no interest in this issue (events 1999-2003). How does Bush's "humanitarian concern" bring Iraq to the top of the list?

The "Saddam is a bad guy" approach just wouldn't have the punch needed to sell the public on starting a war with Iraq. However, with the war already started, it could be combined with other reasons in an attempt to stave off public criticism for taking the country to war with the two main justifications collapsing.

While the ruthless dictator pitch appears to have at least some merit, it fails to reveal anything about the real motivations for war because it suffers from the same problem as the fear of WMD. The same neoconservatives who were in a fever pitch to attack Iraq in 2003, were staunch supporters of Saddam Hussein and Iraq during the 1980's when the dictator was actually showing how ruthless he could be. President Reagan, Donald Rumsfeld, George Shultz, Paul Wolfowitz, Richard Armitage, President George H.W. Bush, and Dick Cheney were aggressively arming Saddam with WMD in the eighties. Clearly Saddam's ruthless behavior wasn't a matter of great concern to this group.

More recently, the dictator has been de-fanged due to the beating his army took in the first Gulf War—it has never recovered—and the many years of U.N. sanctions that limited the resources available to him. With the whole world breathing down his neck, he knew he couldn't use chemical weapons and get away with it.

For other players, the ruthless dictator justification might provide some motivation to go to war, but Saddam's behavior was clearly no problem for the neocons in the eighties, and just as clearly not the driving force that was pressing for Iraqi regime change in 2003.

[4] <u>To provide freedom and democracy for Iraq—later throughout the Middle East</u>

President Bush's position on promoting freedom and democracy for Iraq—and eventually the entire Middle East—was remarkably consistent. Both before and after the start of the war, he would repeat this vision. It should be noted that this alone doesn't come close to a proper justification for a preemptive invasion, but it is possible that Bush actually believed that U.S. military power could force a Western-style democracy onto Iraq. And that other Arab nations would eagerly convert to democracy soon thereafter.

Unfortunately, most of the Bush administration's Middle East policies have revolved more around wishful thinking than constructive action. The "road map" in the Holy Land left both the details and the enforcement up to the Israelis and the Palestinians, and rapidly became road kill with little hope for peace. And the "liberation" of Iraq has gradually evolved into a nasty occupation.

Whoever is calling the shots for the Bush administration in the Middle East has demonstrated an alarming lack of understanding of the region. What a shame. While insufficient on its own, this could have been at least a small part of the motivation—for the President, but not necessarily all of the neocons—for going to war.

[5] <u>To support the War on Terror</u>

President Bush and Condoleezza Rice consistently promoted the war on Iraq as part of the war on terror—both before and after the invasion. Although few of the other hawks promoting the war were focusing on this aspect.

The war in Afghanistan, which also was supposed to be part of the war on terror, may have the net effect of increasing terrorism. Opium production there has gone up from 185 tons annually in the Taliban days to 3,600 tons annually (events 2-10-2004) since the U.S. invasion, and drug money is a major source of funding for terrorism.

Saddam Hussein's support for Palestinian terrorism explains why Israel was eager to see the regime change in Iraq. It also enabled Bush to claim a connection between Iraq and terrorism, but most experts on counterterrorism considered an invasion of Iraq to be an inflammatory event that would undermine the war on terror—which it did. Without any terrorism to speak of prior to the 2003 invasion, Iraq became a haven for terrorism and a rallying cry for their cause. It is difficult to imagine what would assist terror groups more with their recruitment efforts than an unprovoked invasion of an Arab country with vast oil reserves by a superpower with two former energy executives in the top positions of power. And making matters worse, this invasion is eclipsed with a prisoner abuse scandal yielding sexually humiliating images for everyone to view on TV.

Both the invasion of Iraq and the prisoner abuse scandal have become valuable recruiting tools for the terror networks, creating a bounty to al Qaeda and their affiliates. Both the decision to attack Iraq and the decision to recklessly abandon the Geneva Convention have aided and abetted the enemy in the war on terror.

What was left of American prestige after the preemptive war on Iraq when no weapons were found became further bruised by the graphic images of abuse coming out of Iraq—and there won't be a recovery anytime soon. Now, prisoners released from Abu Ghurayb prison in Iraq will have much greater credibility than ever before when they chronicle their abuse—and many more Iraqis will switch over to the other side and take up arms against coalition occupiers.

Instead of invading Iraq and spending $60 billion annually for that war, the Bush administration should have increased the $1 billion annually spent on securing nuclear weapons and fuel in Russia and in the former Soviet Union countries to speed up the completion of that project. Keeping these weapons out of the hands of terrorists would be a far better use of taxpayer money than the huge sum used to increase terrorism in Iraq.

Nevertheless, the war on terror may well have been part of Bush's personal motivation for invading Iraq—it wouldn't be the first time he shot himself in the foot. But we will have to keep looking for the driving force behind the neocon fever pitch to go to war.

[6] Due to Iraqi U.N. resolution violations

From November 1990 to December 1999, Saddam Hussein repeatedly violated 16 U.N. Security Council Resolutions regarding international peace and security, but if this is the criteria, should Iraq be the first to be dealt with?

Former Congressman Paul Findley notes in his book, *Deliberate Deceptions: Facing the Facts About US-Israeli Relationship*, that Israel was in violation of 68 U.N. Resolutions from 1955 to 1992 (events 1995).

An additional 40 U.N. resolutions critical of Israel were deflected by U.S. vetoes in the last 30 years (events 3-8-2003).

It should also be noted that Saddam was not cited for any U.N. violations during the 2½ years of the Bush administration prior to the invasion. While the Iraqi violations offer some justification for action, this issue didn't appear to be high on the neocons list of motivations for war, they were primarily historical, and were probably thrown in for good measure during the march to war.

[7] <u>The U.S. strategic interest in maintaining the flow of oil</u>

The strategic importance of oil in Middle Eastern foreign policy has been no secret. President Eisenhower publicly acknowledged the contribution of Middle Eastern oil to the Western economy years ago (events 1956).

It may seem odd to many Americans that the U.S. would become a strong supporter of Saddam Hussein throughout the 1980's, especially knowing that he was a brutal dictator and was already using chemical weapons, which the U.S. strongly opposed publicly.

However, in managing the balance of power in the Indian Ocean and Persian Gulf, U.S. foreign policy-makers have toppled progressive governments, supported cruel dictators, and even abandoned their closest allies due to the dependence of the Western world on Middle Eastern oil (events 1950's–1980's).

More recently, Paul Wolfowitz noted that a transformed Iraq would help secure oil supplies (events 12-3-2002). But the most telling indication of priorities were the U.S. troops rigorously guarding the oil ministry facility during the fall of Baghdad while the unguarded museums were looted of historical treasures dating back to the beginning of civilization (events 4-10-2003). This priority on oil could have been to support the strategic flow of oil, or it could have been a clue regarding the economic value of the vast Iraqi oil reserves.

In the first Gulf War, the first President Bush drove the Iraqi army out of Kuwait, and then declared the mission accomplished and withdrew the American troops. Maintaining the strategic flow of oil was an obvious justification for this war, and the American exit without toppling Saddam Hussein clearly eliminated any motivation for oil profits.

Maintaining the flow of oil was also a top concern for the second President Bush as he noted after the major fighting that he was pleased that the oil facilities weren't harmed more than they were. It is also very likely that the Bush administration wanted to increase Iraq's oil production to satisfy the U.S. and world appetite for this resource. Dick Cheney's energy policy shunned conservation and favored increasing oil production, even in environmentally sensitive areas.

The support for this justification is fairly broad, including more than just the neocons, because the disruption of oil could significantly impact the U.S. and world economies. However, there was minimal emphasis on oil in the pre-war march so as not to imply an imperial quest for oil profits. Just how important was the oil factor in the march to war in Iraq?

[8] U.S. allies in the region

President Bush mentioned his concern for the many U.S. allies in the region, several of which are oil-producing nations. Saddam had invaded Kuwait in late 1990, and he could possibly have been a threat to the smaller countries adjacent to Iraq, although his military and weapons programs were marginalized more than most realized due to the many years of U.N. sanctions.

But of all the Middle East countries, the special relationship that the U.S. has with Israel is second to none. Paul Wolfowitz visualized that a transformed Iraq would reduce the threat to Israel (events 12-3-2002)—without mentioning the many other U.S. allies in the region. Also to be noted is the tremendous push to install Ahmed Chalabi as the head of a new Iraq government (events 11-22-2002). He was unique in his promised support for Israel.

The prime minister of Israel, Ariel Sharon, indicated that he was hoping for positive changes in the Middle East after a regime change in Iraq (events 2-27-2003). Finally, American public figures who strongly supported Israel, also strongly supported the Iraq war with few exceptions.

Most commonly, a client state will fight a war on behalf of an allied super-power. To the extent that the motivation for regime change in Iraq was to protect the security interests of Israel, it is the reverse of the norm, and a historically unique situation.

In any event, there is no doubt that protecting U.S. allies in the region, especially the previously targeted Israel, was undoubtedly an important motivation for pursuing a regime change in Iraq.

[9] U.S. national security

During the march to war, President Bush suggested that regime change in Iraq was necessary for U.S. national security. Even before Iraq's decline in the nineties, Saddam never had any weapons with a range to threaten the North American continent. However, Bush's argument is that Saddam Hussein could provide terrorists with weapons of mass destruction, which could then be deployed against U.S. interests, possibly even on American soil.

This claim was made while the Bush administration was still implying, if not proclaiming, a link between al Qaeda and Saddam Hussein. Many terror cells operate in a local region, but al Qaeda had demonstrated a global reach. It turns out that the Islamist fundamentalist al Qaeda and the secular dictator Saddam had little in common to form a union. In fact, al Qaeda considered Saddam an enemy because of his treatment of the Shiites in Iraq.

While the threat proposed by Bush is theoretically possible, it was unlikely, and very few others expressed a concern of this nature. It gave the President additional punch to suggest that U.S. national security was threatened, but there is no evidence that this was a significant motivation for regime change in Iraq.

[10] To avenge the assassination attempt on the first President Bush

The Kuwaitis uncovered an assassination attempt by Saddam on the first President Bush and notified U.S. authorities (events 4-1993). Since he was no longer in office, the 41st President was unable to do anything about it himself. President Clinton responded by firing a missile into the intelligence headquarters in Baghdad (events 6-27-1993). After that, the issue received little public attention.

Did the son have a grudge against Saddam Hussein due to the attempt on his father's life?

If the desire to depose Saddam Hussein didn't occur at the front end of the 43rd President's term, the possibility of a revenge motive could be quickly discarded. Unfortunately, we learn that the quest for regime change in Iraq was in fact an immediate priority of the Bush administration, which indicates that the revenge factor is still a possibility.

However, it is unlikely this factor was a major driver for the march to war. The fever to get rid of Saddam Hussein on the part of Vice President Cheney, Defense Secretary Rumsfeld, Paul Wolfowitz, Richard Perle and the other neocons—which is not likely to be related to the personal revenge factor—was the main push for the war. We need to keep looking to find what, in addition to maintaining the strategic flow of oil and the security interests of U.S. allies, are the remaining drivers for the preemptive invasion.

[11] Gain a better military foothold in the Middle East

American geostrategic planning for the Middle East was couched in terms of denying the Soviets oil resources and potential bases from which to launch an assault upon the Persian Gulf (events 1956).

There is a need to rely less on military bases in Saudi Arabia where the U.S. is very unpopular. Also, Turkey wouldn't provide the use of military bases that was desired for the second war with Iraq. Would cooperation from Qatar and Kuwait be sufficient in order to provide the desired bases for future U.S. endeavors in the Persian Gulf?

The U.S. is reducing the size of foreign military bases and plans to construct a network of smaller bases closer to potential trouble spots such as the Middle East (events 3-25-2004).

Are there plans for permanent military bases in Iraq? Are sites already picked? A regime change in Iraq could well create an opportunity for new Middle East bases—an option that was not available with Saddam Hussein in power.

Ahmed Chalabi promised that American bases could be placed inside Iraq if he becomes the next leader (events 2-22-2004). Could that be one of the reasons the neocons were promoting Chalabi so vigorously?

The constant turbulence in the Middle East, the difficult scramble for bases in the war started in 2003, and the desire for more military bases combined to create a reasonable level of motivation for regime change. This was not an advertised benefit of war with Iraq, but it definitely was a factor in the decision matrix, especially on the part of the military and the neocons, who shun diplomacy in favor of war.

[12] For political gain—the 2002 and 2004 elections

The first President Bush pushed his approval rating well over 80% in the first Persian Gulf War, and the second President Bush maintained his elevated Sept. 11 approval rating throughout the Afghanistan war. Was the White House interested in chumming his approval rating prior to the 2002 and 2004 elections enough to promote a war for this purpose?

Among the motives for the Iraq war, Richard Clarke argues, were the politics of the 2002 midterm election. "The crisis was manufactured, and Bush political advisor Karl Rove was telling Republicans to 'run on the war,'" Clarke writes (events 1-2002). Precisely the same claim is reported by ABC News, as noted in the sequence of events (events 1-18-2002).

Bush denies any ambitions for political gain from the Sept. 11 attacks (events 1-24-2002). However, the war president theme was ubiquitous in the Bush 2004 campaign ads and his speeches (events 2-13-2004); and the first Bush campaign ads featured the President next to the charred remains of the attacks (events 3-3-2004).

In order to be a war president, you need a war. If Saddam Hussein agrees to disarm and allow U.S. troops to inspect his country to accomplish same, that wouldn't be expected to create the desired bounce in the approval rating provided by a full-fledged attack.

When Karl Rove noted George W. Bush's approval rating zooming after the Sept. 11 attacks and the invasion of Afghanistan, and remembered the bounce George H. W. Bush received in the first Gulf War, he must have gladly embraced the neocons obsession with regime change in Iraq. A war could easily be expected to raise Bush's chance for reelection.

The political gain was a strong motivating factor to go to war with Iraq, which could explain the frantic rush to war when it appeared that Saddam was cooperating and there might be no illicit weapons after all. This motivation may not have materialized until after the Sept. 11 attacks. For the neocons, however, the fever to attack Iraq started years before the second President Bush even started his term. Were there other factors behind their push to war?

[13] Control of oil and corporate profits in Iraq and Middle East

What Eisenhower didn't say when he discussed the importance of oil in U.S. Middle Eastern foreign policy, was that in 1954 his administration was instrumental in obtaining, at Britain's expense, a major share of the Anglo-Iranian Oil Company's (AIOC) concession in Iran. There was no disguising the fact that American economic interests were the primary beneficiaries of U.S. policy and yielded enormous profits from oil operations (events 1956).

Richard Armitage admitted in 1990 that the Reagan and Bush administrations were well aware of Saddam's brutality, but still, the U.S. was more interested in maintaining a healthy relationship with Iraq because the country's vast oil reserves were beneficial to U.S. interests (events 1990). In promoting regime change, Paul Wolfowitz notes that France and Russia, and not the U.S., have the lucrative oil contracts in Iraq (events 9-17-1998). These statements are more than an interest in maintaining the flow of oil. There was a well-understood desire amongst the neocons to recapture lucrative oil contracts from Iraq, which was no longer possible after the American involvement in the 1991 Gulf War.

The scene with U.S. troops guarding the oil ministry facility during the fall of Baghdad while the museums were looted (events 4-10-2003) can have more than one interpretation. The priority could be merely the desire to maintain the strategic flow of oil with no lust for oil profits involved. On the other hand, with U.S. companies denied any lucrative oil contracts since the first Gulf War and with no prospects of receiving any contracts while Saddam Hussein was still in power, the neocons had a clear motivation to reestablish American companies with a foothold in the country with the second highest oil reserves in the world. In fact, the corporate interests at stake are even broader.

The 'military-industrial complex' has a far bigger hand in shaping and directing U.S. foreign policy today than when departing President Dwight Eisenhower delivered his warning. The operatives who have taken charge at the Pentagon, as well as conservative think tanks and institutes to which they are linked, are generously supported by the gun, missile and bomb makers—and now even other corporate interests linked to military action.

The invasion of Iraq is coupled to lucrative contracts for reconstruction after the bombing, and the development of oil due to Iraq's large reserves, so weapons manufacturers wouldn't be the only corporations to benefit from an invasion.

The plot thickens when luminaries such as Dick Cheney and George Shultz pass back and forth between high-level government and corporate positions like revolving doors—keeping their government connections to further their private interests. The huge amount of dollars at stake, and the no-bid awards to Halliburton (Cheney) and Bechtel (Shultz) have a particularly foul stench to them.

The worst situation is the Halliburton contracting that has already passed the $6 billion point. Cheney received a $30 million golden parachute from Halliburton just before becoming Vice President. Was this a down payment in order to get the company major contracts?

Cheney didn't have to worry about Halliburton getting selected for reconstruction contracts in Iraq. He knew that he could convince President Bush to order a no-bid situation with only six well-connected American companies invited, leaving Halliburton with the most experience in the type of engineering services needed. All viable competitors to Halliburton for the major work would then be out of the picture. With this arrangement, Cheney didn't even have to meddle with the procurement process, Halliburton was a given, but there was one additional part of the bargain that Cheney did need to fulfill.

He needed to make sure that there was something to rebuild.

If Saddam is merely disarmed, and there is no regime change, then there is nothing to rebuild—and no ensuing profits. Now the importance of regime change, as opposed to disarmament or containment, is sufficiently compelling to explain Cheney's fever. He constantly bullied the U.N. weapons inspectors, spent hours with the CIA to cherry pick the most ominous intelligence data, and promoted the INC propaganda machine that pumped fabricated evidence into the media. There was only one option:

The U.S. must go to war with Iraq!

The revolving door has worked well for Dick Cheney and the others in the good ole boys network who have passed through it. He was given the CEO position of a huge corporation without any prior business experience, and he received a generous golden handshake when he left to reenter government.

The numbers also work out well for Halliburton. Their net profit from Iraq will undoubtedly exceed a billion dollars, after making a paltry $30 million thank you to Cheney. The well-connected Shultz has secured smaller contracts for Bechtel, but the company will certainly earn far more than the amount of their campaign contributions to the appropriate coffers.

Sadly, the math doesn't work out so well for taxpayers. Over $200 billion has been spent or budgeted on Iraq already and up to $100 billion annually from now on will be needed for the conflict that will be getting more troops. When the tragic loss of life is added to the tally, it's an extremely heavy price to pay to get rid of a cruel dictator in a third world country, especially when the promise of a peaceful democracy in Iraq appears to be so elusive.

The corporate profit potential for reconstruction, security, oil field, and munitions contractors dealing in Iraq is enormous. So far it has all gone to well-connected American companies, and it was undoubtedly the most significant driver in the march to war led by Dick Cheney.

[14] Place the United States on permanent war footing

Because the president has declared that we are in a war against terror, not just against Iraq and Afghanistan, that it will be a long war, and that no time frame for a return to peace has been provided, a question emerges: Has the country been placed into a permanent war?

The influence of the neoconservatives on the Bush administration in general and the push to war in particular, is undeniable. This motivation folds neatly into their agenda which includes significant increases in defense spending, followed by exerting U.S. military supremacy in order to achieve global leadership and to shape a new century favorable to American principles and economic interests. This would certainly include using military power to gain control of valuable natural resources such as Iraq's oil, which could substantially benefit American corporate interests such as Halliburton, Bechtel, and various oil companies.

At this point, there is the somewhat undefined general war on terror, the war in Afghanistan which has mostly dropped from news coverage, but is far from over, and the Iraq war for which an exit strategy appears to be totally unavailable. What is next?

In the run up to the Iraq war, there was friction with Syria and some of the neocons hinted that action might be needed there next. If the Iraq War had gone as smoothly as Cheney and Chalabi had promised, U.S. troops would probably be in Syria before the end of 2004. However, with the Pentagon budget and the troops spread so thin, several parties have questioned why we invaded Iraq before Afghanistan was put away.

Much to the chagrin of the neocons, there is a limit to how many wars the Pentagon can handle at the same time, and it doesn't help to start ill-defined wars with no exit strategies. Therefore, future invasions will probably be put off for a while.

But as long as the neocons remain in control of the White House, the invasions, which are followed by security operations that require many troops in hazardous conditions for long periods, will continue for a period of time so long that the country will essentially be in a state of permanent war from now on. The President, whoever it is at the time, whether it be year 2005 or 2015, will be advising the public that rooting out terrorism is hard work that takes a lot of time and that it is important to "stay the course."

This state of permanent war might appear to be a result of events as opposed to a motivation or justification for war. However, a close reading of the Project for a New Century Statement of Principles (www.newamericancentury.org/statementofprinciples.htm) can easily lead to a different conclusion. Was Sept. 11 the pretext for the neocons to finally release the militant push for a new world order that they have always wanted?

No wonder the push for war

Weapons of mass destruction, the supposed link to al Qaida, and the presence of a ruthless dictator had very little to do with the real justifications for invading Iraq. But there were plenty of motivators that received less public attention that can explain the fever.

The primary drivers for invading Iraq in 2003 were to maintain and increase the flow of oil from the Middle East, to protect U.S. allies in the region, to build new American military bases in Iraq, to achieve political gain for Bush as a war President, to generate billions in revenues for favored American corporations, and to fulfill the neoconservatives' dream of plunging the nation into a permanent war—where military supremacy can provide the leverage to further U.S. economic interests around the globe.

14

A Flood of Blunders in Iraq

Leaving America vulnerable while sleeping through Sept. 11 threats was an act of omission, but invading Iraq was an act of commission. For President Bush, the stakes in Iraq are higher. This one is definitely his baby and the mistakes are numerous, enormous, and have created grave dangers for American troops, the vast majority of which are performing their duties professionally and with great courage:

1. The pre-war claims that weapons of mass destruction were in Iraq (events 1-29-2002, 1-30-2003). No stockpiles of WMD were found, and American prestige suffers greatly.

2. A pre-war claim that Iraq had ties to al Qaeda and Sept. 11 (events 3-14-2003). No valid supporting evidence ever surfaces.

3. A pre-war claim that Iraqis would welcome us with open arms (events 12-3-2002 & 2002-2003). Many American soldiers were killed by insurgents—even after Saddam was captured.

4. A pre-war intensive State Department-led planning effort called "The Future of Iraq Project" was completely ignored by Pentagon planners, leaving security in Iraq dangerously uncovered and adding to the loss of American and Iraqi lives (events 4-30-2004).

5. Ignoring international resistance, invading Iraq, and attempting regime change in a complex country with three major competing factions, when lacking credibility in the region. Colin Powell's Pottery Barn rule, "You break it, you own it!" lands on deaf ears (events 3-19-2003). There is no recovery for the first five blunders.

6. In an attempt to kill high-value targets, 50 air strikes were ordered in a one-month period. They all failed: resulting in dozens of civilian casualties (events 3-19-2003). No recovery available.

7. The failure to exploit American influence immediately after the fall of Saddam in order to broaden the international role and stakes in Iraq (events 4-9-03). Later efforts are too little, too late.

8. Protecting the oil facilities and the oil ministry but failing to control the looting during the fall of Baghdad (events 4-10-03). No recovery available. The message has been sent.

9. The disbanding of the Iraqi army and firing of all Iraqi military officers (events 5-2003). Policy reversed (events 4-21-2004).

10. The firing of Iraq's ruling Baath Party, including teachers and doctors, (events 5-2003). Policy reversed (events 4-21-2004).

11. The cronyism and corruption in contracting, especially Halliburton and Bechtel, led to an Iraqi impression—most likely true—that the U.S. appointed council members and selected corporations are primarily motivated to enrich themselves (events 4-17-2003, 5-2003). No attempt to recover.

12. The "Mission Accomplished" banner (events 5-1-2003). Karl Rove acknowledged regret (events 4-16-2004). No recovery available.

13. Canceling local elections in An-Najaf when democracy was promised (events 6-22-2003). No attempt to recover.

14. President Bush's "Bring them on!" comment inviting terrorists to enter Iraq and join the fight, further endangering U.S. troops (events 7-2-2003). No recovery available.

15. Placing Chalabi and other exiles with no connection to the current citizens of Iraq in the puppet government that the U.S. tried to impose on the Iraqis (events 7-13-2003). Partial reversal giving some interim government decision to the U.N. (events 4-6-2004). Complete reversal with raid on Chalabi's home and office (events 5-20-2004).

16. In September 2003, President Bush appealed to other nations at the U.N. to contribute money and troops for the effort in Iraq. The tardiness in making the appeal, his 'I-told-you-so' tone and the refusal to give any decision-making control to the U.N. set the stage for the disappointing response. It was an embarrassing diplomatic failure (events 9-23-2003).

17. The reluctance to move closer to influential Cleric Sistani on the issue of Iraqi elections (events 12-13-2003, 1-21-2004). The election timing decision is given to the U.N. (events 4-6-2004).

18. The hasty closure of al-Sadr's newspaper after U.S. promised the Iraqis freedom of speech. The paper had not promoted violence (events 3-28-2004). This inflammatory action fueled an insurrection that led to many American deaths and several hundred Iraqi deaths, a high percentage of which were civilians. No recovery available.

19. In AL-Fallujah, the parties responsible for killing and mutilating four Americans were to be surrendered or U.S. Marines would wage an overwhelming response "at the time and place of our choosing" (events 4-1-2004). After a month's standoff, U.S. marines reversed policy and withdrew from AL-Fallujah, trying to convince everyone it was "not a retreat" (events 5-1-2004). Iraqis declared victory in AL-Fallujah (events 5-1-2004).

20. Suspected of murdering another cleric as well as stirring up violence with his army, the militant cleric Muqtada al-Sadr, who was holed up in An-Najaf, was to be taken "killed or captured" by the U.S. Marines (events 4-13-2004). After a month's standoff, U.S. Marines still hadn't made any offensive in An-Najaf (events 4-30-2004), and later yet, still more threats (events 5-18-2004).

21. Giving in to Ariel Sharon on keeping West Bank settlements, which inflamed Arabs and endangered U.S. troops in Iraq (events 4-14-2004). No attempt to recover.

22. Setting a firm June 30, 2004 transfer of full sovereignty, then waffling to offer only strictly-limited sovereignty to the Iraqis (events 4-22-2004). No recovery—U.S. retains final say on its military moves.

23. A costly miscalculation at the Pentagon has left American soldiers in Iraq in thin-skinned Humvees, nearly defenseless against the insurgent fire they face daily (events 4-30-2004). There are not enough vehicles, not enough ammunition, not enough medical supplies, and not enough water. The troops are still waiting for more body armor (events 5-1-2004). Many American soldiers lost their lives due to this mismanagement of the war.

24. The prisoner abuse scandal, including stripping, beating, sexually abusing, sexually humiliating, and a host of other tactics was far and away
the biggest blunder of the war (many early May events). Rejecting the
Geneva Convention following Sept. 11 set the stage for this debacle (1-
2002). And the release of the humiliating photos unleashed a firestorm
of international criticism, significantly boosting the recruitment of
insurgents and terrorists, and therefore, aiding and abetting U.S. enemies both in Iraq and in terrorist networks.

The U.S. publicly stated that the Iraqi prisoners would be treated according to
the Geneva Convention (highlights extracted from *The Mercury News*, May 9,
2004, p. 17A, citing "The Laws of War: A Comprehensive Collection of Primary
Documents on International Laws Governing Armed Conflict"), but almost all
of them were violated. Below are some of the conventions with the revealed
abuses bolded and the offenses in parentheses:

- Article 13: Prisoners must be **humanely treated** (events 4-28-2004:
  naked pyramid); not subjected to physical mutilation, medical experi-
  ments; **protected against acts of violence** (events 5-4-2004: beatings;
  5,6-2003: kicked in head, back, groin; 5-12-2004: POWs ordered to
  fight; 5-14-2004: beating; 5-16-2004: froze to death), **intimidation**
  (events 5-8-2004: wires on fingers, toes, penis, electrocution), **insults**
  (events 5-7-2004: naked on leash, mocking naked POW), public curios-
  ity.

- Article 14: **Entitled to respect for their persons and their honor** (events
  5-4-2004: sodomized; 5-7-2004: masturbate in front of others).

- Article 17: Only required to give name, rank, serial number when questioned; prisoners who refuse to answer may not be **threatened** (events 5-
  9-2004: vicious dogs with naked POW; 5-13-2004: drowning threat),
  insulted (events 5-12-2004: simulate oral sex) or **exposed to unpleasant
  treatment of any kind** (events 5-4-2004: drenched in phosphoric liquid;
  5-6-2004: shackled in awkward positions, manipulating the levels of pain
  medication; 5-10-2004: raped POW; 10-2003: extensive burns).

- Article 22: Interned only in premises affording **hygiene and healthful-
  ness** (events: 5,6-2003: POW urinated on; 5-21-2004: retrieving food
  from toilets); interned in camps, **not prisons** (events 4-28-2004: Abu
  Ghurayb prison).

- Article 27: **clothing** (events 5-7-2004: clothing denied), underwear, foot-
  wear shall be supplied.

- <u>Article 29</u>: Prisoners shall have for their use, day and night, conveniences which conform to rules of **hygiene** (events 5-7-2004: sleep, food, clothes, mattress denied).

- <u>Article 70</u>: **Be able to write to family or prisoner-of-war agency, send and receive mail** (events 5-11-2004: families in dark, no communication for months).

The vision for ignoring the Geneva Convention came from the highest levels starting in January 2002 due to a post-Sept. 11 lust for intelligence from detainees. In Iraq, the Bush administration was anxious to find weapons of mass destruction right away, and by August 2003, it was very anxious to obtain intelligence on the insurgency that was spinning out of control. As a result, the prisoner abuses spanned many prisons, ignored repeated attempts for over a year by the International Red Cross to draw attention to the mistreatment, and culminated in the 1,800 repulsive photos that sabotaged any moral authority that the U.S. had with the Iraqi people and the international community.

It is a cruel irony that Abu Ghurayb prison—the scene of many of Saddam's torture sessions—was the location for some of the worst abuses. For this monumental blunder to be merely listed as one of two dozen blunders belies its order of magnitude. This egregious foul-up alone was sufficient to destroy any hope for success in the ill-fated intervention, even if every other move by the military was flawless.

<u>The impact of the blunders:</u>

Prior to the release of certain photos, the most damaging blunders in the prosecution of the war were the pair of "no-win" situations in AL-Fallujah and An-Najaf. In both cases, some parties, including the die-hard neocons, argued that egregious acts of violence must be met with overwhelming force to demonstrate that no violent activity will be tolerated. Otherwise, the resistance would be emboldened and far more difficult to put down.

Other parties were quick to point out that the use of overwhelming force will cause too many civilian casualties that will be broadcast on Arab TV and destroy any chance of winning the "hearts and minds" of the Iraqis, which is a prerequisite in order to pacify the nation. And any assault on the holy city of An-Najaf would inflame the Muslim population beyond repair.

In both cities, the Bush administration chose a third alternative—make bold threats of force, and then back down and retreat with a whimper, resulting in a distressing double-barreled demonstration of military weakness that no one rec-ommended or could possibly embrace. The two thrills of victory handed to the insurgents on a silver platter produced a boost for their cause that went beyond their wildest dreams.

With almost every move he makes as Commander in Chief, Bush is either handing the opposition a victory, inflaming the Arabs that he is trying to win over, and/or providing the insurgents and terrorists with excellent recruitment material to swell their ranks. In both the war on terror and the Iraq war, he has managed to aid and abet the enemy more than any previous president in any pre-vious conflict in the history of our nation.

The coalition was merely window dressing and the whole world knew it. The war in Iraq was a unilateral action by the American neocons, led by Vice Presi-dent Dick Cheney, who were in firm control of U.S. foreign policy. America has little credibility with Arabs in the Middle East, who suspected cronyism and imperialism from the beginning. The incredibly numerous blunders by the Com-mander in Chief merely added to the futility of this conflict.

Any action against Saddam had to have been performed with the U.N. in charge—not the Western superpower—and with the support and participation of Arab nations as with the first Gulf War, if there was any interest in success.

But the neocons would have no part of the U.N.

Instead, the U.S. pays the full price for the war in blood and dollars and vastly diminished international prestige, with hopes for success merely wishful think-ing.

The celebration after the fall of Baghdad was brief and misleading. What took four presidents and almost two decades in Vietnam, George W. Bush was able to accomplish in a matter of months—take the world's greatest superpower stum-bling into battle looking confused and impotent.

15

Look Who's Waffling

President Bush finished his April 13, 2004 news conference with, "One thing is for certain, though, about me, and the world has learned this: When I say something, I mean it. And the credibility of the United States is incredibly important for keeping world peace and freedom."

Bush says this after two years of firmly committing himself against positions for investigations and appearances only to waffle and reverse himself weeks or months later. He follows this statement the next day by going back on his word (and five decades of U.S. foreign policy) on a major issue in the Israeli-Palestinian conflict.

Sept. 11 Flip Flops

1. The Bush administration strongly opposes the creation of an independent commission to investigate the intelligence failures leading to the Sept. 11 attacks (events late 2001 & 5-20-2002). Bush reverses position and agrees to the independent commission (events 11-14-2002).

2. "I have no ambition whatsoever to use this as a political issue," President Bush, in reference to the Sept. 11 attacks (events 1-24-2002). President Bush's re-election team unveiled his first campaign advertisements and they use the events of Sept. 11, 2001, to focus on his "steady leadership" during turbulent times (events 3-3-2004). Shortly thereafter, public testimony in front of the Sept. 11 commission uncovered his dismal stewardship ignoring threat warnings leading up to the attacks, and the Sept. 11 ads disappeared.

3. The Bush administration opposes the release of the August 6, 2001 Presidential Daily Brief to Congress (events 5-20-2002), later releases it to Congress, then releases it to the independent commission, then even-

tually declassifies it for the public (events 4-10-2004). The same run-around and stonewalling occurs with thousands of other classified documents that eventually are released to the independent commission (events 4-2-2004).

4. Bush administration opposes the extension of the Sept. 11 independent commission (events 11-27-2003). Reverses position and agrees to the extension (events 2-4-2004).

5. In negotiations with the Sept. 11 independent commission, President Bush would only appear together with Vice President Cheney, in front of only two commission members, and for only one hour (events 2-26-2004 & 3-9-2004). Later he changes his position and will appear in front of the entire commission for more than one hour (events 3-30-2004). However, he was never willing to testify under oath, and never willing to appear without Dick Cheney at his side.

6. The Bush White House blocked the transfer to the Sept. 11 commission of three-quarters of the nearly 11,000 pages of material from the Clinton administration, which was gathered over a two-year period (events 4-1-2004). When pressed, it reversed course and released the national-security documents to the panel (events 4-2-2004).

Flip Flops in Iraq

President Bush was also given an opportunity to demonstrate his "steady leadership" in the Iraq war:

1. Bush decides not to expand the international role and stakes in Iraq (events 4-9-03). A policy reversal in 2004 for more international involvement appears to be too late.

2. The Iraqi army is disbanded and all Iraqi military officers are fired (events 5-2003). The policy is reversed (events 4-21-2004).

3. Thousands of teachers and doctors of Iraq's ruling Baath Party are fired (events 5-2003). The policy is reversed (events 4-21-2004).

4. Bush opposes the creation of an independent commission to investigate the intelligence failures regarding the Iraq weapons of mass destruction

that were never found (events 1-30-2004). He reverses position and agrees to the Iraqi intelligence commission (events 2-2-2004).

5. In AL-Fallujah, the parties responsible for killing and mutilating four Americans were to be surrendered or U.S. Marines would wage an overwhelming response (events 4-1-2004). After a month's standoff, U.S. Marines reversed policy and withdrew from AL-Fallujah (events 5-1-2004).

6. The militant cleric Muqtada al-Sadr, who was holed up in An-Najaf, was to be taken "killed or captured" by the U.S. Marines (events 4-13-2004). Second thoughts abort the offensive, so over a month later it is merely more threats (events 5-18-2004).

7. By giving in to Ariel Sharon on keeping West Bank settlements, Bush reversed himself and five decades of U.S. foreign policy (events 4-14-2004).

8. Bush sets a firm June 30, 2004 transfer of sovereignty, then waffles to offer only strictly-limited sovereignty (events 4-22-2004).

9. Iraqi General Saleh who had been selected to lead a new Iraqi security force in AL-Fallujah does not take charge after all. His selection to secure the city was condemned by the Shiite majority due to past atrocities. The reversal indicated the level of confusion vexing the U.S. military (events 5-2-2004).

10. The neocons enthusiastically supported Ahmed Chalabi, to the tune of $33 million, looking beyond his prior conviction for embezzling, hoping that he would be the next leader in Iraq. Chalabi and other exiles with no connection to the current citizens of Iraq are placed into the puppet government that the U.S. imposed on the Iraqis (events 7-13-2003). The policy is partially reversed and the U.N. is given some of the interim government decision (events 4-6-2004). And in May 2004, completely reversed, as the U.S. instructed the Iraqi police to raid his home and take all of his hard copy and computer files, suspecting him of supplying Iran with sensitive information among several other complaints (5-20-2004).

In political ads, Bush is hoping to gain votes by painting John Kerry as someone who waffles and flip-flops too much.

16

The Cast of Clowns

Richard Clarke's claim that President Bush didn't consider the terror threat urgent was so upsetting to Bush's supporters, that Clarke was the recipient of many ferocious personal attacks. While it was pointed out that he placed a more positive spin on the administration's terror effort while still employed than afterwards, this author, and presumably everyone else, was unable to identify any statement in his testimony to the Sept. 11 commission that was in conflict with known facts. Similarly, there were no revelations of factual errors from Paul O'Neill who was also the target of personal attacks from Bush supporters.

The assessment isn't quite so rosy for several members of the Bush administration.

Richard Armitage contradicted Condoleezza Rice's claim regarding a pre-Sept. 11 White House military strategy regarding al Qaeda. The CIA contradicted Rice's assertion that Bush had ordered the Aug. 6 briefing. And Rice's claim that Bush put "Iraq to the side" on Sept. 16, 2001, was contradicted by an order signed by Bush on Sept. 17 directing the Pentagon to begin planning military options for an invasion of Iraq (events 3-26-2004).

Rice, in turn, has contradicted Vice President Dick Cheney's assertion that Clarke was "out of the loop" on counterterrorism and his intimation that Clarke had been demoted. Rice has also contradicted herself—criticizing Clarke for being the architect of failed Clinton administration policies, but retaining Clarke so the Bush administration could continue Clinton's terrorism policies (events 3-26-2004).

The title and 10 references inside the August 6, 2001 Presidential Daily Brief indicate planning for an attack on U.S. soil, pointing out Washington and New York (twice), which were the eventual Sept. 11 attack locations. However, after the Sept. 11 attacks, Condoleezza Rice insisted for many months—and reiterated on March 24, 2004—that intelligence during the summer pointed exclusively to an attack on foreign soil (events 8-6-2001).

326

Testifying before the Sept. 11 Commission on April 8, 2004 under oath, Dr. Rice claimed that the August 6, 2001 brief was merely historical information on eight occasions—even though two recent events suggested planning was in progress and the FBI was conducting many related investigations at the time (events 8-6-2001).

Dr. Rice also testified before the Sept. 11 panel on April 8, 2004 under oath that "there was nothing in the August 6, 2001 brief that suggested an attack was coming on New York or Washington, D.C..." when those very same locations were specifically mentioned as targets in the brief.

Did the pressure preceding her April 8, 2004 testimony result in the White House putting Dr. Rice out on a limb, while denying the true impact of the August 6, 2001 brief in order to protect the President? Did no one in the Bush administration predict the outcry over her mischaracterization of the brief that led to its declassification, and the damage to her credibility that followed?

Secretary of State Colin Powell was both isolated and frustrated in his battle with Vice President Cheney, President Bush, Donald Rumsfeld, and Paul Wolfowitz. He saw the complex reality of Middle East intervention and the blinders worn by the neocons in control, but he was powerless to keep the regime change train from roaring down the tracks.

He had four choices.

He could stay on and accept the flawed decision to invade Iraq. He could stay on and vigorously promote the decision. He could resign and be silent on his opposition, stating only personal reasons. Or he could resign and publicly criticize the decision, as did Cyrus Vance (events 4-28-1980). Unfortunately, the loyalty ingrained from several decades of military service trumped good judgment, and Powell remained on as Secretary of State, seized the mission desired by his boss, compromised his own credibility, and enthusiastically propelled the disastrous plan to reality.

Defense Undersecretary Paul Wolfowitz was the primary architect of the Iraq war, but he had no idea there would be any resistance to worry about. How could someone with his background fail to understand the most basic realities of the Middle East—and claim that the Iraqis would welcome U.S. troops as liberators (events 12-3-2002)? Colin Powell and Richard Clarke knew that a preemptive invasion of Iraq would be a huge mistake, but the Oval Office only had ears for the neocons. Dr. Wolfowitz, the neoconservative's intellectual, was the only real hope to save the Bush administration from shooting itself in the foot with a preemptive invasion of Iraq, which would leave a trail of debt, destruction, and human tragedy in its wake. Instead, he did a gigantic belly flop into the sea of

Arab anger and nationalism that should have been more than obvious to even a casual observer.

To his credit, CIA Director George Tenet did brief President Bush about the terrorist threats 40 times prior to the Sept. 11 attacks. However, his claim that Iraq's possession of weapons of mass destruction was a "slam dunk," (events 12-21-2002) and his sitting behind Colin Powell in February 2003 while fabricated evidence was placed in front of all of the nations of the world were disgusting failures (events 2-5-2003).

While Attorney General John Ashcroft's request not to be bothered with discussions of terror threats from Acting FBI Director Thomas Pickard prior to the Sept. 11 attacks certainly deserves a nomination for the worst performance in Bush's cabinet, that award belongs to someone else (events summer 2001).

Special envoy Donald Rumsfeld made friends with Saddam Hussein in 1983 and greased the wheels so that President Reagan could facilitate providing more weapons of mass destruction (WMD) to the Iraqi leader. This, at a time when Saddam was using chemical weapons in Iran and against his own Kurdish population (events 12-20-1983 & 3-1984). The same Defense Secretary Donald Rumsfeld insisted in 2003 that Iraq should be invaded because Saddam had WMD, and in fact Rumsfeld knew where they were (events 3-30-2003), when none were found.

Defense Secretary Donald Rumsfeld, who scuttled the Tiger Force investigation in late 1975 (events 12-1975), is the same Defense Secretary Donald Rumsfeld who was responsible for the military in 2003 during the scandalous Iraqi prisoner abuse when the Red Cross complaints of abuse were ignored for over a year (events 5-7-2004). And minimal attention was given to the abuse issue until the infamous pictures were released. He was obviously more concerned about the release of the photos than the abuse itself.

Special envoy Donald Rumsfeld, who pitched the Aqaba pipeline deal for Bechtel in late 1983 (events 12-20-1983), is the same Defense Secretary Donald Rumsfeld who was vigorously promoting regime change in Iraq in 2003, which set up lucrative contracts for Bechtel, Halliburton, and other well-connected firms.

Donald Rumsfeld, who was one of two people most vocal about refusing to go along with the U.N. investigation of Iraqi human rights abuses in 1989 shortly after the abuses occurred (events 1989), is the same Defense Secretary Donald Rumsfeld who was lobbying for a U.N. resolution authorizing an invasion of Iraq in 2003 for the very same behavior.

Rumsfeld adds to his legacy with a poor performance in the Iraq war. He insisted on a low troop count, rebuking General Eric Shinseki in the process (events 4-30-2004), which turned out to be inadequate and left troops poorly supplied with complaints ranging from a lack of water to thin-skinned Humvees that sorely needed armor. For someone so eager to promote the invasion, he was clueless on how to plan for or secure the operation, but he did secure a "You are doing a superb job" from his boss (5-10-2004).

When President Ronald Reagan wanted assistance with his "moral clarity"—which included arming Saddam with weapons of mass destruction—special envoy Rumsfeld was there to help out. And when Reagan left office, Secretary of Defense Dick Cheney was there to extend the nasty job of arming and empowering Saddam.

Vice President Dick Cheney's special relationship with Halliburton generated handsome returns for both of them as Cheney flipped back and forth between powerful government positions and the giant corporation (events 1995-2001). Any attempt on his part to pretend that the march to war and corporate profit are unrelated is belied by his own behavior. Little else could explain the fever—an incapacitating obsession—to attack Iraq that he possessed and transmitted to others in the Bush administration creating an atmosphere where the most dire threats were completely ignored by top officials, leaving the country at the mercy of terrorists on September 11, 2001.

All too often for the neoconservatives, the truth is the enemy, propaganda is the weapon of choice, and no one does it better than Dick Cheney. "Backseat" used his frequent visits to the CIA and his close relationship with the Iraqi National Congress (INC) to coordinate their massive media campaign resulting in 108 articles based upon fabricated or exaggerated evidence to encourage the invasion of Iraq (events 2002).

Cheney bullied weapons inspectors and screened out any CIA intelligence that wasn't consistent with his agenda. He vigorously promoted the fabricated link between Saddam Hussein and al Qaeda like a running spigot. And when Joseph Wilson questioned the Niger uranium claim that turned out to be based upon forged documents, it was Cheney's staff, including his chief of staff, who retaliated and called six reporters leaking that Wilson's wife was a CIA agent (2-5-2004).

In spite of Wesley Clark's being pressured by the White House to blame Iraq (events 9-11-2001), Richard Clarke's meeting with the President insisting that a link to Saddam be found (events 9-12-2001), Cheney's promotion of fabricated evidence through the INC to insist that a link to Iraq exists (events 2002), President Bush's State of the Union speech claiming that Iraq sought uranium from Niger (events 1-28-2003), and with all the fever about the administration's concerted effort to pin the Sept. 11 attacks on Iraq, the media attention on the propaganda to support the march to the Iraq war still focused mostly on inaccurate intelligence, rather than deliberate deception.

Cheney's role in the Bush administration demonstrated such unprecedented power that he has been dubbed "co-President" and "President of foreign policy" by various parties. It is well known that Cheney had an iron grip on U.S. foreign policy where Bush had no experience, but his domestic influence was hardly lacking. When it was time to let Paul O'Neill go, it was Cheney who told him he was fired (events 1-19-2004). It was also Cheney who drove through the second round of tax cuts for the affluent backers of the administration.

Dick Cheney, sometimes referred to as Bush's ventriloquist, had an arm-lock on the presidency that was so tight it only allowed the most minor of decisions to slither out of the Oval Office without his blessing. It could easily be argued that the word "Vice" should have been dropped from his title, and that the country has a titular head of state that is merely a puppet, floundering from a relentless assault of disastrous and corrupt advice.

In the march to war, Cheney represented the worst combination of imperialism, cronyism, and deception that had ever seized the Oval Office. His lust for revolving-door corporate payback was so strong he had no qualms about heaving hundreds of dedicated American soldiers into coffins to achieve his precious regime change, far exceeding the minimum threshold of "high crimes and misdemeanors" for impeachment proceedings, and yet an overly timid Congress never even censored him.

Is he really going to get away with it?

President Bush was so blinded by ideology and inebriated with arrogance while pressing his campaign for regime change in Iraq, he completely wiped out the global outpouring of goodwill and sympathy for America that followed the Sept. 11 attacks. Without taking advantage of any pre-war planning or paying any attention to the warnings of the disaster that would be created, George W. Bush—propelled by a monumental dearth of wisdom—used a pre-emptive strike against Iraq to disarm weapons of mass destruction that were never found, to avenge a link to the Sept. 11 attacks that didn't exist, and to support a war on terror that was severely exacerbated by the invasion and occupation that he ordered.

And he leaves U.S. troops stuck in Iraq with no exit in sight.

Bush set the stage for prisoner abuse when he quickly dismissed the rules of the Geneva Convention for the detainees at Guantánamo Bay, Cuba and kept the handling of detainees under a shroud of secrecy. The pressure to gain intelligence was immense, and he sent a clear message that America doesn't have to follow the rules with these captives. The plummeting U.S. image caused by the brash decision to invade Iraq eroded even further after the prisoner abuse scandal, and resulted in a massive international credibility problem for the United States that will take at least a generation to repair.

President Bush hoped that the threat warnings regarding Osama bin Laden and his group of terrorists were merely false alarms because he wanted to stay focused on Saddam Hussein and Iraq. He also hoped that the use of an independent commission to investigate the Sept. 11 attacks, a common U.S. approach to national calamities, could be avoided. Bush further hoped that the Iraqis would accept U.S. occupation forces with open arms when a majority of Iraqis want the occupiers to leave (events 4-29-2004). This continuous cycle of rosy predictions and wishful thinking, the cornerstone of the Bush administration, left his term awash in secrecy and damage control that will be the legacy of the Bush presidency—not the historic remaking of the Middle East into a region blessed with freedom, peace, and democracy.

With a second term, Bush could add to his legacy with the reinstitution of the military draft to support a couple of wars that he started, which don't offer any hope of allowing U.S. troops to come home.

President Bush entered office with a lack of combat experience, and a publicly admitted lack of foreign policy experience. He adds to his credentials as Commander in Chief with a complete lack of action amidst the Sept. 11 terror threats and the incredible number of blunders and flip-flops in his Iraq war that he should never have started. Even the neocons who promoted the invasion of Iraq have skewered Bush for his many blunders in the conflict (events 4-30-2004).

When this research began, the primary interest was determining the motivation for the preemptive invasion of Iraq and the prospects of U.S. intervention in an Arab country as opposed to an assessment of the Commander in Chief. In addition, the lack of an itemized listing of blunders by all past presidents presents somewhat of a challenge when comparisons are desired. But there is no documentation on blunders during a previous administration that comes close to equaling the incompetence revealed by the sequence of events in the Bush administration.

George W. Bush's incredibly poor performance, sleeping through the Sept. 11 terror threats, with a war on terror that invigorates the recruitment of more terrorists, with countless incredible battlefield blunders in Iraq, and the unprecedented demolishment of American prestige when alliances are desperately needed leads to the inescapable and frightening conclusion that in these troubled times, the worst Commander in Chief in the history of our nation, and the greatest threat to our national security, is sitting in the Oval Office in 2004.

And given how far he has lowered the bar, could any future president possibly fit below it?

Epilogue

Due to the sequence of events documented above, history will not be kind to George W. Bush. His embattled years will undoubtedly be regarded as a low point in American history—even below the Nixon years, which at least had the one high point of thawing relations with China.

The Bush presidency was a continuous stream of bungled decisions, damage control maneuvers, and cover-ups that unraveled including ignoring the Sept. 11 threats and the horrendous mistakes of initiating and mishandling the war in Iraq culminating in the prisoner abuse scandal.

The scale of the damage caused by the neoconservatives is devastating and unprecedented. Their illusions and wishful thinking have severely undermined U.S. interests, trapped the country in a losing war, and their names are on all of the coffins flying back into Dover Air Force Base. Incompetence on this scale has deadly consequences that cannot be tolerated.

The November 2004 election is a referendum on the neocons and George W. Bush's request for another four years is an opportunity for the American public to exercise their right and perform some damage control of their own. But that can't be the end of it.

The neoconservatives were put out of business during the Clinton years, but they came back with a vengeance. They will be lusting for the White House in 2008, 2012, and beyond, fully prepared to wreak even more havoc with their ideological extremism. Correcting this disaster will involve more than merely voting Bush out of office in 2004. In order to motivate the Republican Party to reform by purging the neocons from their top tiers of influence, it will require a prolonged vigilance on the part of citizens to vote the trigger-happy hawks out of office. The message must be strong and it must be repeated over and over again.

Otherwise, there may be another alarmingly inept performance by a similar cast of clowns looming in America's future.

Index

0-595-32390-1

Printed in the United States
21028LVS00005B/1-42